ACS SYMPOSIUM SERIES **338**

# Solving Hazardous Waste Problems

## Learning from Dioxins

**Jurgen H. Exner,** EDITOR

*International Technology Corporation*

Developed from a symposium sponsored
by the Division of Environmental Chemistry
at the 191st Meeting
of the American Chemical Society,
New York, New York,
April 13–18, 1986

American Chemical Society, Washington, DC 1987

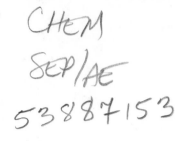

**Library of Congress Cataloging-in-Publication Data**

Solving hazardous waste problems.
  (ACS symposium series, ISSN 0097-6156; 338)

  "Developed from a symposium sponsored by the
Division of Environmental Chemistry at the 191st
Meeting of the American Chemical Society, New York,
New York, April 13-18, 1986."

  Includes bibliographies and indexes.

  1. Dioxins—Environmental aspects—Congresses.
2. Hazardous waste sites—Environmental aspects—
Congresses. 3. Environmental chemistry—Congresses.

  I. Exner, Jurgen H. II. American Chemical Society.
Division of Environmental Chemistry. III. American
Chemical Society. Meeting (191st: 1986: New York,
N.Y.) IV. Series.

TD196.C5S64    1987    363.7'384    87-1389
ISBN 0-8412-1025-X

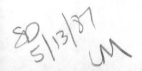

# ACS Symposium Series

## M. Joan Comstock, *Series Editor*

# Foreword

The ACS SYMPOSIUM SERIES was founded in 1974 to provide a medium for publishing symposia quickly in book form. The format of the Series parallels that of the continuing ADVANCES IN CHEMISTRY SERIES except that, in order to save time, the papers are not typeset but are reproduced as they are submitted by the authors in camera-ready form. Papers are reviewed under the supervision of the Editors with the assistance of the Series Advisory Board and are selected to maintain the integrity of the symposia; however, verbatim reproductions of previously published papers are not accepted. Both reviews and reports of research are acceptable, because symposia may embrace both types of presentation.

# Contents

# Preface

SOCIETY'S CONCERN ABOUT POLLUTANTS IN THE ENVIRONMENT requires pollution control and cleanup of hazardous waste sites. The 1986 Congressional reauthorization of the Comprehensive Environmental Response Compensation and Liability Act (CERCLA, or Superfund), similar initiatives in the Departments of Defense and Energy, and industry efforts may lead to expenditures on waste cleanup of $10-20 billion over the next five years. The problems are great, and the solutions are complex and expensive. Solutions require the cooperative effort of the public, government, industry, and the technical community. Yet, the methodology for achieving these solutions remains poorly understood, and advances in solving hazardous waste problems are rarely reported or are scattered in diverse literature sources.

The symposium on which this book is based was intended to publicize recent advances in the methodology of cleanup of sites contaminated with polychlorinated dibenzodioxins (PCDDs). PCDDs, and especially 2,3,7,8-tetrachlorodibenzo-$p$-dioxin (TCDD), are well-studied classes of chemicals that can serve as a model of approach to other hazardous chemical waste issues. Paul des Rosiers and I called on experts from many disciplines to define the potential problem, assess the risk, and describe the management of that risk. The multidisciplinary perspective covered the detection of the contaminant in the environment, its toxicology to living organisms, risk assessment through exposure routes, and elements in management of the risks. Because of the emotional nature of the dioxin issue, we strove to include speakers from many points of view. I have tried to maintain this balance in the book. I sincerely thank Paul des Rosiers for helping organize the symposium and all contributors.

It is my hope that this book can define a very complex problem and describe solutions. The examples of dioxin cleanup issues and procedures are offered to provide engineers, health scientists, regulators, lawyers, business people, and other concerned individuals with a methodology applicable to other hazardous chemicals. I believe that science can detect pollutants in the environment and estimate their potential health risk. Society as a whole, scientist and nonscientist, determines acceptable risk. Society also plays a major role in managing risk because we face many problems and have limited resources to deal with them all.

I hope that we can address these important problems with sound information and a spirit of cooperation among the diverse interests, and I hope that we remember the fundamental intent: to solve hazardous waste problems.

Jurgen H. Exner
International Technology Corporation
Martinez, CA 94553

December 1, 1986

# Chapter 1

# Perspective on Hazardous Waste Problems Related to Dioxins

Jurgen H. Exner

International Technology Corporation, 4585 Pacheco Boulevard, Martinez, CA 94553

Polychlorinated dibenzo-p-dioxins (PCDD) represent a highly
visible, well-studied class of pollutants that are acutely
toxic to animals. Information about these chemicals and
experience with many environmental contamination episodes
serve as a guide for solving hazardous waste problems
caused by other pollutants. Solutions require the recognition
of a problem, such as the widespread distribution of a
pollutant in the environment, releases of pollutants from
chemical processes, or their presence at hazardous waste
sites. After concern about the presence of pollutants in
the environment arises, the risk posed by chemicals such
as dioxins must be assessed. Such risk assessment requires
an understanding of the acute and chronic toxicity of the
pollutant and knowledge of pathways by which humans and
animals can be exposed to the chemical. Subsequent risk
management involves social, political, legal, and economic
factors that interact with potential technical options.
The major issues relating to cleanup of dioxins in the
environment are described from experiences at sites in the
United States and Europe.

Hazardous waste problems permeate our society. Potential
threats to human health from pollutants in the environment arouse
great social and scientific controversy. Social concern has led
to numerous environmental laws and regulations such as the
Resource Conservation and Recovery Act of 1976 and amendments of
1984 (RCRA) and the Comprehensive Environmental Response,
Compensation, and Liability Act of 1980 and its 1986 amendments
(CERCLA). RCRA addresses current waste by requiring stringent
record keeping of all waste production, collection, treatment,
storage, and disposal activities. CERCLA, or Superfund, addresses
the cleanup of hazardous waste sites in the U.S.A. Out of about
25,000 sites that may exist in this country, about 25% have been
examined, and about 1000 sites have now been placed on a priority
list. During the last six years, studies on cleanup have begun at
about 450 sites, but remedial action under Superfund has begun at
only a few. In addition, cleanups by private industry have begun
also. Progress has been impeded by a lack of understanding of the
cleanup process and appropriate technologies, by uncertainties
about risks and how to estimate and manage them, by political
indecision, and by public fears. During this period, however, a
methodology for addressing pollution problems has developed which

0097-6156/87/0338-0001$06.00/0

continues to be refined. No other pollutant, with the possible
exception of polychlorinated biphenyls (PCB), has contributed more
to our understanding of waste issues than the polychlorinated
dibenzo-p-dioxins (PCDD).

## Dioxin as a Model in Waste Cleanup

PCDD represent a class of 75 compounds containing one to eight
chlorine atoms on the dibenzo-p-dioxin moiety. These various
dioxin isomers show remarkable differences in toxicity. At
present, our concern focuses primarily on the compounds containing
four, five, and six chlorine atoms at the 2,3,7,8- positions.
This variability in toxicity contributes to the complexity of
obtaining adequate scientific information.

Investigations of PCDD, and especially 2,3,7,8- tetrachlorodibenzo-p-dioxin (2,3,7,8- TCDD), has led to major advances in
environmental sampling and analysis, in toxicology, risk assessment, risk management, and waste treatment. Techniques used for
dealing with dioxin contamination represent the most advanced
procedures for hazardous waste cleanup. These advanced techniques
were developed because of:

(1) Great public concern over well-publicized environmental
contamination episodes such as the Agent Orange
controversy, the Seveso release, and the Missouri
episode,

(2) Very high acute animal toxicity and carcinogenicity,
which has led to cleanup to unprecedented low residual
concentrations, and

(3) Unwillingness by commercial waste disposers to accept
dioxin-contaminated waste, a decision which led to
testing of many novel dioxin treatment schemes.

Despite the attention paid to dioxin, these pollutants do not
pose as acute a hazard as a large spill of a lethal gas (such as
the Bhopal tragedy), or a burning disposal site. Rather, concern
about dioxin focuses on long-term effects such as potential cancer
formation or bioaccumulation in the food chain. Unlike many
pollutants, PCDD are very insoluble in water and are not as likely
to leach into groundwater as, for example, halogenated solvents.
In contrast to air pollutants such as volatile hydrocarbons, PCDD
have very low vapor pressure so that the vapor phase does not
represent a major exposure route for dioxin. Finally, unlike
pollution problems caused by chemicals produced for useful
purposes, dioxin is a minute, unwanted byproduct of chlorophenol
production and of combustion processes.

## Problem Definition

Concern about dioxin's effect on human health can be traced to
a number of industrial exposures, its recognition as a byproduct
in the production of large-scale quantities of chlorophenols such
as 2,4,5- trichlorophenol (TCP) and pentachlorophenol (PCP), the
finding of birth defects in animals exposed to 2,3,7,8- TCDD, and
the recognition in the 1970's of a more general environmental
contamination due to emissions from combustion sources.

**Dioxin and Chlorophenols.** In 1954, workers in a chemical plant in

Hamburg, Germany, suffered skin eruptions similar to acne. This affliction can be caused by exposure to chlorinated organic chemicals. In this case, the exposure was traced to 2,3,7,8- TCDD, a byproduct formed in ppm concentration during the production of 2,4,5- TCP. TCP is an intermediate in the production of 2,4,5- trichlorophenoxyacetic acid (2,4,5- T), an herbicide with widespread past use. The presence of 2,4,5- T in Herbicide Orange, a defoliant used in the Vietnam War, introduced 0.1 - 50 ppm of 2,3,7,8- TCDD to the formulation known as Herbicide Orange (1). The finding that this contaminant led to birth defects in animals caused large political controversy and the cancellation of Herbicide Orange use. Ever since, the political emotions of the Vietnam War, the uncertainties about health effects on soldiers and civilians exposed to the spraying, and further contamination episodes have maintained the public's and news media's attention on dioxin. Similarly, great scientific effort has been expended on providing information to deal with health concerns and legal issues.

Seveso. In 1976, a chemical plant producing 2,4,5- TCP, an intermediate in the production of hexachlorophene, a bacteriocide, had an emergency pressure release (2). About 2 kg of TCDD plus additional amounts of TCP, ethylene glycol, and sodium hydroxide were released over a populated area of 1810 ha. Evacuation of hundreds of inhabitants and extensive remediation efforts maintained public attention over the next ten years (3).

Missouri. In 1971, a used oil transporter sprayed oil contaminated with TCDD on riding arenas and roads in Missouri for dust control. The death of about 60 horses and illnesses in children led to an investigation by the Centers for Disease Control (CDC). Health effects were attributed to TCDD in the oil in 1974 (4). However, governmental agencies responsible for action were under the mistaken impression that TCDD had a half-life in the environment of one year and, therefore, carried out only minimal cleanup. In 1982, this problem resurfaced when Times Beach, a community near St. Louis, was evacuated after TCDD concentrations above 1,000 ppb were detected in soil samples. Decisions on this evacuation were carried out under an atmosphere of scientific uncertainty, public emotion, and political pressures within U.S. EPA. At present, there are 43 contaminated sites in Missouri, some of which are being excavated and restored.

Hamburg, Germany. The Seveso experience focused renewed public attention on the Boehringer plant, the same chemical plant at which TCDD first was detected as a byproduct of 2,4,5- TCP. The presence of TCDD in 2,4,5- T led to a halt in production of the herbicide. Two years later, the remaining facility was closed because a range of PCDD and PCDF congeners was detected in a sophisticated recycle process involving thermal decomposition of lindane to trichlorobenzene. Cleanup of this $50 million facility involves building and equipment decontamination, soil and groundwater cleanup, and destruction of production residues.

New Jersey. Diamond Shamrock owned a 2,4,5- T production facility in Newark, New Jersey from 1951-1971. The facility was owned by

several different companies until 1983, when TCDD was detected at
the plant site, in the surrounding neighborhood, and the adjoining
river. Diamond Shamrock repurchased the property, cleaned up the
neighborhood by excavating contaminated areas, and will begin
remediation of the site after approval of plans by the State of
New Jersey Department of Environmental Protection.

Pentachlorophenol (PCP) Users. PCP has been used as a wood
preservative for many years. PCP contains octa-, hepta-, hexa-,
and pentachlorinated dioxins. Since PCP was applied generally in
an oil solution, spills and discharges from this operation have
led to widespread migration of PCP and its impurities. The
magnitude of these environmental discharges and possible remedial
measures are being examined by U.S. EPA and responsible parties.

Sources From Combustion Processes. In 1977, PCDD and PCDF were
detected in particulate emissions from municipal incinerators
(5). Similar data were soon reported from around the world. In
1980, workers at Dow Chemical Company, using the most sensitive
and specific analytical techniques of that time, detected a range
of PCDD in residues from many combustion processes (6). These
workers postulated that all combustion processes that contain
chlorine sources produce PCDD. Although this postulate is not
supported in all situations, dioxin emissions from combustion
sources are major contributors to PCDD in the environment (7).
    At present, municipal incinerators, hazardous waste
incinerators, and metal smelters discharge from 1-100 ng/Nm$^3$ of
PCDD, about 1-100 g/year per facility. The possibility of PCDD in
exhaust emissions from cars has been raised recently, and the U.S.
Environmental Protection Agency (EPA) has examined a range of
other possible dioxin sources.

Dioxin in the Environment. 2,4,5- T manufacturing sites or areas
where dioxin has been spilled contain from 1 ppb to 50 ppm of
PCDD. Environmental soil background is in the ppt range.
Buildings involved in chemical manufacture of 2,4,5- T contain
about 1-50,000 ng/m$^2$. Buildings contaminated by PCB fires contain
about 1-1,000 ng/m$^2$ of 2,3,7,8- TCDD equivalents. PCDD
concentrations in ambient air are below the detection levels of
several pg/m$^3$. However, continued increases in the sensitivity of
analytical procedures are allowing detection of 0.2 pg/m$^3$ in some
urban air samples.
    Fish in the Great Lakes and Baltic contain 1-100 ppt of PCDD
and the fat of snapping turtles accumulates about 400 ppt. In
general, fat accumulates about 20 times the amount of dioxin
present in the food source (8).
    The fat of humans contains 1-20 ppt of TCDD. Other dioxin
isomers are also present, including up to 900 ppt of octachloro-
dibenzodioxin (OCDD). A low level background of 1-10 ppt of
2,3,7,8- TCDD in the fat of mother's milk appears to be common in
some parts of the industrialized world (8).
    In considering environmental analysis for PCDD, great care
must be taken that validated sampling and analytical methods are
used. Also, appropriate numbers of samples must be included
before conclusions about the importance of the findings can become
firm.

Clearly, then, PCDD occur in the environment, often at hot spots resulting from discharges from manufacture or spills, and PCDD accumulate in the food chain. Clearly, there is a potential exposure to PCDD in the environment. Since risk is a combination of exposure and of the inherent toxicity of the chemical, the toxicity of dioxins becomes the second criterion in defining whether these pollutants pose concern.

Toxicity. Experimental animals are exceedingly sensitive to TCDD. The LD50, the dose that kills half of a test group, for 2,3,7,8- TCDD is 0.6 μg/kg of body weight for male guinea pigs. Table I shows the acute toxicity of TCDD and the considerable species-dependence of TCDD (9). Reasons for these large differences may be different biochemical elimination or degradation pathways for different animals.

Human beings exhibit acute symptoms such as chloracne, effects on enzyme and nervous systems, and muscle and joint pains. Generally, these effects decrease after exposure is eliminated.

Lifetime daily dosages of 10-100 ng/kg of body weight of 2,3,7,8- TCDD administered to rats led to toxicity and carcinogenicity. At 1 ng/kg body weight per day, no effects were observed over two years (9).

Table I. Acute Toxicity of 2,3,7,8- TCDD During Oral Administration

| Animal | LD50, μg/kg body weight |
|---|---|
| Guinea pig | 0.6 - 2 |
| Rabbit, male | 115 |
| Rat | 22 - 45 |
| Dog | 300 - 3,000 |
| Hamster | 1,157 - 5,051 |

The second part of the problem definition phase shows clearly that PCDD should be a potential concern to humans and animals in the environment. The degree of concern that we as a society should have can be estimated by a formalized risk assessment process.

Risk Assessment
The presence of PCDD in the environment and the acute and chronic toxicity of 2,3,7,8- TCDD and similarly substituted congeners in animals raise concern. How serious should this concern be and what actions are warranted to relieve this concern? These questions are addressed by a risk assessment

procedure which attempts to formalize and make consistent a
general intuitive process of assessing risk. The outcome of such
an assessment often presents the image of a rigorously scientific
determination of the size and certainty of risk. Before accepting
these conclusions, it is imperative that the assumptions and
uncertainties of such risk assessment are understood thoroughly.
For example, it is common practice to use worst-case assumptions
and upper-bound estimates and to combine these repeatedly. The
final risk estimate, then, tends to amplify the real risk by
several orders of magnitude. Presumably, this overestimation
protects against currently unknown health effects such as adverse
synergistic effects of pollutants. Despite these large uncertainties, regulatory agencies need a formalized, consistent, and site-
specific process of risk assessment to define potential remedial
actions. For each problem, we evaluate how humans can be exposed
to a pollutant and what this exposure can do to their health.

Exposure Routes. Dioxin can enter a person through:

- Dermal contact, absorption through skin,
- Inhalation, breathing of contaminated air, and
- Ingestion, eating contaminated materials such as soil,
  food, or drinking water contaminated by dioxin.

In assessing these three routes, the physical and chemical
properties of PCDD in the environment are important. TCDD is not
significantly degraded by microorganisms although certain fungi
may be able to decompose the chemical over long periods of time.
There are no demonstrated biological degradations of other PCDD.
Under environmental conditions, PCDD are not hydrolyzed nor do
they undergo reactions with environmental chemicals under environmental conditions. PCDD in solutions are photolyzed by sunlight. PCDD exhibit a very low vapor pressure but appear to
photodegrade in the gas phase. PCDD adsorb readily on particulate
matter, log $K_{oc}$ = 6.4 for TCDD. This class of chemicals is very
water insoluble, 10 - 20 ng/ℓ for TCDD, and partitions readily
into organic matter, log $K_{ow}$ = 6.6 for TCDD.

In most cases of environmental contamination by dioxin,
migration of dioxin occurs on suspended particles. Thus, dioxin
in soil can migrate via erosion processes, through air as wind-
blown dust, or in the aqueous phase to rivers or groundwater.
Dioxin in the vapor phase does not appear as a significant
exposure source except at the point source of some combustion
processes.

Leaching of pollutants to ground or surface waters is a major
pathway of environmental contamination. Leaching of TCDD from
soil containing 8-26,300 ng/g yielded aqueous leachates of
0.1 - 55.5 ng/ℓ (10) . These data suggest that TCDD movement in
soil is slow. However, TCDD in Missouri has been detected at
greater than 6 ft, in New Jersey at greater than 13 ft, and at
even lower depths at Hamburg and Hyde Park. Examination of this
information suggests that this downward migration is due to
chromatographic desorption of TCDD by other organic pollutants
such as chlorinated and aromatic solvents.

The major route by which humans are exposed to PCDD is
ingestion of soil and food. Children in contaminated areas can

ingest contaminated soil. The magnitude of this potential
exposure is the major factor in the 1 ppb action criterion set for
contaminated sites in Missouri (11). Grazing cattle ingest soil
and accumulate PCDD in fat. Fish and other aquatic animals
accumulate dioxin from water, sediment, or food sources.
Vegetables may contain small amounts of dioxin at the surface,
possibly as dust particles trapped in the outer membranes (12).
Accumulation of PCDD through the root system of plants appears to
be very low, presumably because of the low water solubility of
these compounds.

Additional exposure variables include duration of exposure,
the absorbed fraction, the bioavailability, climatic conditions,
and body weight. However, the major question in risk assessment,
other than the exposure dose, addresses the effect of the
pollutant on humans.

Human Health Effects. Examination of exposure routes estimates
the potential dose and length of exposure to people. The crucial
question for any risk assessment, then, involves the effect that
the exposure to the toxicant has on the human being. Several
groups of workers and populations have been exposed to dioxin.
Studies of workers exposed to industrial accidents, such as the
1949 Monsanto accident in Nitro, West Virginia, herbicide
applicators in Scandinavia, U.S. military personnel who sprayed
Agent Orange in Vietnam, and the population near Seveso showed
chloracne to be the major common symptom of exposure to dioxin. A
recent study of Quail Run, Missouri, residents suggests a lowering
of the immune response system by exposed residents. Other
concerns that have surfaced are possible increases of soft-tissue
sarcomas and birth defects. However, since all of these studies
involve epidemiologic investigations of groups of exposed people,
these studies' conclusions are subject to scientific argument
because of:

- group size, which affects the statistical validity of the
  results,
- the accuracy of the exposure dose and its duration, and
- appropriate controls, which incorporate uncertainty about
  lifestyle variables, smoking for example, which may affect
  the results.

Inconclusive or conflicting results from such studies are very
disturbing to the public but reflect scientific uncertainty.
Recent advances in PCDD analysis of human adipose and blood
analyses which can detect and possibly differentiate between
background and exposure offer an opportunity to resolve some of
the concerns about exposure levels in such epidemiologic studies.

In the absence of human testing data, toxicity evaluations
rely on extrapolating animal test data to humans. One major
concern in this extrapolation is how similar animals such as rats
are to humans. This question is especially critical for the case
of dioxins, which show considerable toxicity variation between
different species. The second major uncertainty in the extrapolation is the model that relates animal data to potential
effects on humans. Of the several models that have been proposed,
the linearized - multistage model is being used by U.S. EPA. This

model gives the highest plausible upper limit of risk and leads to
lifetime acceptable daily intake of 0.0064-0.0572 pg/kg B.W.
Dutch, Swiss, and Ontario workers, on the other hand, used
threshold-based extrapolations to calculate acceptable lifetime
daily dosages of 1-10 pg/kg B.W. of TCDD, because these agencies
assume TCDD to be a cancer promoter rather than an initiator (9).
    Nevertheless, PCDD, and especially 2,3,7,8- TCDD, exhibit high
acute toxicity and many chronic effects in animals.  It is
prudent, therefore, to estimate acceptable exposure limits.  In
considering cleanup, it is imperative to establish acceptable
levels of cleanliness.  The risk assessment process tries to
address this number, which has been the subject of much debate.
How clean is clean indeed?  In this author's opinion, we must
address different criteria based on practical concerns.  Thus,
new emissions should be regulated to the most rigorous health-
protective standards.  For cleaning of old sites, a reasonable
risk of one excess cancer in 100,000 - 1,000,000 may be a prudent
compromise between resources needed to carry out the cleanup and
potential risk.
    This question of whether it is scientifically valid to derive
the lifetime control limit by using threshold or non-threshold
models defines what cleanup levels are proposed for a site.  The
action level proposed by CDC for residential soil in Missouri is 1
ppb, based on a series of exposure assumptions and on virtually
safe doses for $10^{-6}$ cancer risk of 0.0276 pg/kg/day (11).  If one
assumes a different threshold - based model, as did Dutch, Swiss,
German, and Canadian workers (9), one obtains maximum allowable
daily intake of 1-10 pg/kg/day.  If one uses the same exposure
calculations as CDC, one could then accept 4-40 ppb in residential
soil according to these allowable daily intakes.  CDC and EPA have
allowed 7 ppb as acceptable residual concentrations at an industrial site in New Jersey (13).  At Seveso, cleanup levels were set
at 45 ppt for nonagricultural soil and 7 ppt for agricultural soil
(3).  Office buildings in the United States have been cleaned to
3-25 ng/m$^2$ of 2,3,7,8-TCDD equivalents on surfaces and to less
than 10 pg/m$^3$ in the office air (14).  Appropriate cleanup levels
continue to arouse great controversy, and one can achieve varying
levels depending on the method one chooses for assessing the
risk.  In each case, the final cleanup level often represents an
excruciating compromise between scientific, social, legal, and
economic factors.
    Table II illustrates an important concept in PCDD toxicity,
the concept of toxicity equivalent factors.  In situations where
exposure to many different dioxin congeners can occur, for
example, in buildings after PCB fires or in PCP contaminated wood
treatment sites, acute and chronic animal toxicity data do not
exist for the complex mixtures.  By comparing a number of standard
tests, regulatory agencies have developed toxicity equivalency for
many dioxin and furan isomers (15).  Although there continues
scientific debate on the validity of this concept, and although
the numbers may change with time, such an assessment seems a
pragmatic approach to a difficult, time-consuming, and costly
toxicological research program.

Table II.  PCDD Toxicity Equivalents

| Compound | Relative Potency |
| --- | --- |
| 2,3,7,8- TCDD | 1 |
| Other TCDD | 0.01 |
| 1,2,3,7,8- PeCDD | 0.5 |
| 1,2,3,6,7,8- HxCDD | 0.04 |
| 1,2,3,7,8,9- HxCDD | 0.04 |
| 1,2,3,4,7,8- HxCDD | 0.04 |
| Other HxCDD | 0.0004 |
| OCDD | 0 |

Risk Management
    Management of the risk posed by an environmental contaminant
presents the final challenge in the process of solving hazardous
waste problems.  Once a concern has been identified and a potential risk has been estimated, reduction or removal of that risk
must be addressed.  The cleanup represents a fascinating political
process that incorporates the public's perception of the risk,
divergent social values and philosophies, legal constraints,
economic considerations, and technical alternatives.
    The public has heard about dioxin's high acute toxicity, its
potent carcinogenicity, and its reproductive effects on animals.
Dioxin has been intertwined with an unpopular war and claimed to
cause malformed babies and health abnormalities.  Dioxin led to
the temporary evacuation of the residents of Seveso and the
permanent relocation of about 2,000 residents in Times Beach,
Missouri.  In general, the public fears the presence of dioxin and
follows complex scientific discussions of risk assessment with
great difficulty.  The general desire is to remove this unwanted
intrusion and hazard.  What the unfortunate victims of a dioxin
contaminated area soon find out, however, is that emotional
response to dioxin by other communities and environmental regulations prevents the simple solution of removing dioxin wastes to
another site for disposal or treatment.  At this time, no commercial landfills or incinerators accept dioxin-containing wastes.
Rather, dioxin wastes must be stored on site, and thermal destruction processes must be approved by U.S. EPA.  Similarly, destruction processes such as incineration, thermal desorption, photolysis, or chemical destruction require complex permitting
procedures.  The duration of these permit activities and the need

to prepare site-specific applications for mobile technologies are major obstacles in the development of new waste treatment technology for dioxins and other pollutants.

Legal obstacles also affect the course of cleanup actions. In many cases, a responsible party for a waste site is identified. Subsequent negotiations often result in carefully worded consent agreements specifying a rigorous course of action. Often, however, these agreements, which have judicial status, are signed before a site has been investigated completely. The work, then, tends to fulfill the requirements of the consent agreement rather than solving the problem that is uncovered during the investigation. In some cases, private or potential class-action suits prevent action by potentially responsible parties because taking action may be considered an admission of guilt. Other legal factors include regulatory restraints such as disposal restrictions or transport prohibitions.

Economic, technical, and social values are closely related in achieving solutions. Setting the cleanup standard includes social and political factors in addition to the risk assessment methodology. One factor, cost, relates directly to the cleanup standard. For example, excavating contaminated soil at one site in Missouri would cost 30% of envisioned cost if the cleanup standard were set at 10 ppb rather than at 1 ppb. Alternatively, excavation and thermal destruction of dioxin in soil is philosophically more attractive than containment and perpetual monitoring of the site. Yet, two aspects argue against destruction technology. First, the CERCLA guidelines for remediation at Superfund sites have, until very recently, focused on proven technology such as containment. Second, costs of destruction tend to be three to ten times higher than containment. In some cases, potential exposure to people can be eliminated by removing the people from the source of contamination. This solution may be the low cost solution, but it still requires maintenance of a waste site. Perhaps more important, the relocation solution destroys a community and has negative social consequences. Thus, social, economic, and technical considerations remain intertwined.

## Cleanup Actions at Dioxin Contaminated Sites

During the last decade, various remedial actions were carried out on dioxin-contaminated wastes in the United States and Europe. Historically, building rubble from industrial accidents was used as fill or disposed in the ocean. In 1977, about 2.2 million gallons of Agent Orange and similar herbicide formulations was incinerated on the ship Vulcanus in the Pacific (1). This solution was simplified by the ability to transfer the waste to the ship at a remote location in the Pacific and by the large quantity of liquid waste, which made the incineration on ship economically possible. The destruction efficiency of this at-sea-incineration was about 99.9% according to the limits of analytical detection at that time.

Seveso. The release in 1976 at Seveso required cleanup of about 200,000 m$^3$ of contaminated soil material, mostly soil containing 2,3,7,8- TCDD in ppb concentrations, and about 41 drums of reactor residues containing ppm levels of dioxin. Italian authorities examined photochemical, chemical, and thermal processes as poten-

tial destruction or cleanup options (3). Construction of a large
incinerator was prevented by cost and local opposition. The
population feared that Seveso would become the center for
treatment of Italy's waste after the immediate problem was
resolved. Eventually, the contaminated soil was excavated and
placed into two specially constructed landfills of 140,000 and
60,000 m$^3$ at a total cost of about $200 million (3). Two
landfills were constructed because two municipalities were
involved, and neither wanted to accept dioxin waste from the
other. The drums, originally destined for a landfill in East
Germany, eventually were found in a French butcher shop. In 1985,
this waste was incinerated in a Ciba-Geigy incinerator in Basel,
Switzerland, at an estimated cost of $2.5 million.


Verona, MO. During the 1970's, Syntex attempted to dispose of the
tank residue from a hexachlorophene production carried out by a
lessee, Nepacco, which had become defunct. Attempts at incineration in commercial incinerators in Minnesota and Texas were
blocked by legal action. Disposal on the Vulcanus, in conjunction
with the Agent Orange burn, faltered because of low volume, 4,300
gal, which made it economically unattractive to the ship's
operators, and because of transportation difficulties in shipping
the waste from Missouri to the Pacific. Syntex then used a
specially developed process that could be applied on site, safely,
within existing governmental regulations. The photochemical
process reduced the TCDD concentration from 343 ppm to 0.2 ppm,
less than was present in commercial 2,4,5- T, and destroyed over 7
kg of TCDD (16). Residues from this operation were originally
scheduled for incineration in the EPA's mobile incinerator in
1982. At that time, the design of the mobile incinerator and
existing regulatory concepts prevented incineration of dioxin
wastes above 1 ppm. However, redesign and operation of the
incinerator in 1985 proved these concerns invalid (17).


Missouri. In 1981, U.S. EPA Region 7 personnel began a renewed
investigation into the fate of other waste material produced by
Nepacco. Diligent investigatory work led them to over 100 sites
on which dioxin-containing waste oil may have been spread for dust
control. A large amount of preliminary sampling, which often used
composites of relatively large areas, confirmed 43 contaminated
sites, many of which were residential areas. These sites
contained dioxin at concentrations up to 1,600 ppb at depths of up
to several feet.
   We began our evaluation of immediate response options shortly
before the buyout of Times Beach. Table III lists some of the
options that could be implemented in a short time frame and which
would remove people from dioxin exposure at Quail Run Mobile Home
Manor (A), and two other sites (18).

Table III. Options and Relative Costs for Immediate Response at Three Missouri Sites.

| Option | Relative Cost, $ | | |
|---|---|---|---|
| | Site A | B | C |
| Cover and leave | 1.0 | 1.0 | 1.0 |
| Buy out and stabilize | 6.2 | 12.5 | 1.1 |
| Excavate, store on site, restore area | 7.2 | 8.6 | 1.0 |
| Excavate, transport to commercial landfill, restore | 26.0 | - | - |
| Excavate, commercial incinerator, restore | 123 | - | - |

Examination of the relative costs for immediate action showed that excavation, on-site storage, and site restoration achieved the objective of separating the population from dioxin exposure as economically as buy out and relocation of residents.

In addition to immediate response options, we also examined a variety of longer-term options. The two most reasonable options were long-term storage of the contaminated soil in a centralized landfill or incineration in a specially designed, large-scale incinerator, with appropriate economics of scale (19, 20).

Despite much further evaluation of other treatment options by the Missouri Governor's Task Force (21) and other organizations, the concepts of storage or incineration remained the most promising. U.S. EPA and the State of Missouri faced great public opposition to a landfill such as the one at Seveso. Consequently, two paths of action emerged. EPA transported the mobile incinerator to Missouri and carried out a pilot test (17). This demonstration verified the expected capability of destroying dioxin-contaminated soil and sludge to 99.9999 %. Concurrently, a comprehensive excavation and storage plan was developed (22). This document included a safety and health plan, ambient air and industrial hygiene sampling, an excavation procedure for removing soil at 6-inch intervals, and a statistical sampling and analysis plan to validate that a cleaned area meets the required degree of cleanliness of less than 1 ppb dioxin (23). A community relations plan was an integral part of both projects, and it was this concern for public involvement that helped achieve useful action in Missouri. At this time, soil has been excavated from the Cashel, Sullins, and Quail Run sites. The soil has been placed in bags which are stored in buildings erected at each contiguous site. The sites have been restored and are being inhabited.

The actions taken in Missouri can serve as a model for responding to large environmental contamination in populated areas. However, decisions at other sites must consider site-specific factors such as potential groundwater contamination or land use, i.e., is it an industrial area, a residential area, or farm or grazing land. Also, the quantity of pollutant must have a bearing on decisions because long-term effects on the environment can be more serious for large quantities than for minimal amounts. Table IV summarizes some remediations and site-specific factors affecting the decisions.

Table IV. Site-Specific Factors in Remediation

| Site | Dioxin Concentration ppb | Quantity Estimate | Geographic Features |
|------|--------------------------|-------------------|---------------------|
| Jacksonville, AR | 0 - 1,200[a] | 250 g[a] | Plant site adjacent to residential |
|  | 15,000 - 50,000 | 264 lbs | area, fractured bedrock |
| Newark, NJ | 0 - 20,000[a] | 10 - 100 lbs | Plant site in heavily populated area near river |
| Niagara Falls, NY | 0 - 1,000[a] | 100 - 2,000 lbs. | Closed landfills containing large amounts of organic residues, fractured bedrock |
| Missouri sites | 0 - 1,600[a] | 40 - 70 lbs | Mostly residential, fractured limestone under clay |

a. In soil

The Arkansas and New Jersey sites became contaminated because of production of 2,4 - D and 2,4,5 - T. The estimated 264 lbs of dioxin at Jacksonville are contained in drummed TCP residues. The Love Canal and Hyde Park landfills in New York probably contain larger quantities of dioxin than any sites other than the Georgswerder landfill in Germany. Because these landfills also contain large quantities of TCP and chlorinated solvents, leaching from these sites into ground or surface water is probable. All the sites exhibit an underground geology of fractured bedrock which makes leaching of dioxin possible in the presence of solvents. Such subsurface migration into the environment is least likely for those Missouri sites that contain only TCDD.

Remedial action at sites other than Missouri has been affected by site-specific factors and legal factors. Consent agreements at the New York landfills and the Arkansas site allowed temporary control measures such as containment, capping, and monitoring. In New Jersey, the proximity to a river, the high population density, and the magnitude of the problem make it difficult to work out reasonable destruction options such as excavation and incineration. Yet, barrier walls, caps, and groundwater pumping and treating require indefinite monitoring and maintenance, and the land serves no further useful function. So, the decision on which cleanup option to pursue becomes exceedingly complex.

Current Cleanup Options for Dioxin Wastes. Governmental regulations and dioxin's negative image currently prevent off-site disposal or treatment of dioxin-contaminated wastes. In response to a need to destroy dioxin wastes, a number of novel process adaptations have been proposed and tested. These processes include incineration, physical-chemical, and biological processes. In addition, on-site containment, storage, and monitoring remain economic alternatives.

Microbial destruction of dioxin congeners remains an elusive goal. At present, small conversions of 2,3,7,8- TCDD in solution by fungi have been achieved in very small - scale laboratory experiments. Extrapolation of this concept to organic wastes or contaminated soil, on a large scale, faces formidable technical obstacles. This concept, as presently envisioned, appears about five years away from being realized in practical applications.

Over the last five years, U.S. EPA has supported research on a chemical dehalogenation process for destroying PCB and dioxin. Nucleophilic displacement of aromatic halides by alkali-metal polyglycoxides occurs readily at elevated temperatures. This reaction readily dechlorinates PCB in mineral oil at 100° and proceeds similarly with 1,2,3,4- TCDD in organic solvents. The addition of dipolar, aprotic solvents such as dimethyl sulfoxide increases the reaction rate and allows dechlorination reactions in dry systems at ambient conditions. Initial tests of this concept for soil decontamination at Shenandoah Stables, Missouri, failed because of high moisture content of the soil and low temperatures. The process was used successfully in the summer of 1986 to remove penta-, hexa-, hepta-, and octachlorodibenzodioxins from 9,000 gal of fuel oil that also contained 2 % PCP. This operation, however, left about 30 drums (ca. 1,500 gal) of polyglycol/DMSO/water/KCL/KOH waste, the ultimate disposal of which is uncertain. The process is being tested further on PCB - contaminated soil which is excavated and placed into a reactor system. The major questions on this process remain economics, residual solvents in treated oil or soil, and ultimate disposal of the polyglycol residues. The final disposal of chemical treatment residues presents a similar problem as residues from photochemical destruction of dioxin.

Incineration of dioxin wastes is the most versatile destruction process of those presently available. The mobile incinerator treated a combination of soil, sludge, and solvents

successfully. However, costs associated with such a small
research-oriented unit were greater than $2,000 per ton, so that
considerable efforts are under way to improve the mobile
incinerator and to explore other thermal destruction processes.
One such method, the Huber reactor, has been tested at Missouri
and Gulfport, Mississippi. Although these tests destroyed dioxin
in dioxin - contaminated soil, two aspects of the process remain a
concern. First, the soil must be dried to less than 2 % moisture
and reduced in size to about 100 microns. Second, in part because
of these pre-treatment steps, costs for this process are estimated
in the range of $700/ton.

Two very promising alternatives for treating dioxin - contaminated soil are the Shirco process and the thermal desorption
method. The Shirco process places contaminated soil on a moving
grate. The soil is heated by infrared heaters or by burners, and
vapors are destroyed in a secondary combustion chamber. This
process has been demonstrated on a small scale at the Times Beach
test facility and will be tested further under various private and
governmental sponsorships.

The thermal desorption process, sponsored by U.S. Air Force,
has been demonstrated on a small scale, 100 - 200 lbs/hr, at
Gulfport, Mississippi, and Johnston Island. The process consists
of indirect heating of contaminated soil in a rotating cylinder.
The desorbed vapors can be destroyed in a secondary combustion
chamber or collected in a condensing or scrubber system. The
demonstration unit incorporated a scrubber and photolysis system
rather than a combustion unit for the following reasons:

- The desorption part was the operation of interest since
  combustion had been demonstrated by U.S. EPA, and
- a physical-chemical treatment was presumed to be easier to
  permit than an incineration device.

Considerations of regulatory obstacles, then, defined the path of
technology development in this instance.

Future Developments. Cleanup of sites contaminated by pollutants
should accelerate after the recent reauthorization of Superfund.
Methodology for investigating sites must improve, particularly
sampling and analysis procedures that are effective and
efficient. Risk evaluation and risk management continue to evolve
as society gains more experience. Since these risk evaluations
require considerable judgment about public will, legal
constraints, and scientific facts, decisions will vary from
country to country, from state to state, and possibly from
community to community. In developing this experience base, we
must remember to protect the environment and people by placing
stringent restrictions on new or continuing emissions and by
incorporating risk and benefit in assessing the necessary cleanup
level for existing, old sites. In the technical area, immediate
advances can be made in improving the efficiency of incineration
processes by understanding temperature and residence time
relationships in the desorption and secondary combustion
chamber. For example, is the two second and 1,200° C requirement
for secondary combustion necessary for dioxin wastes?
Developments in improving incinerator operations can reduce also

emissions from these thermal processes. Research on in situ treatment of contaminated wastes offers clear public and economic advantages. Carefully designed, understood, and applied biological systems offer promise for achieving in-place treatment of dioxin and other pollutants at low capital costs over the next ten years.

## Literature Cited

1.  Young, A.L.; Calcogni, J.A.; Thalken, C.E.; Tremblay, G.W.; "The Toxicology, Environmental Fate and Human Risk of Herbicide Orange and Its Associated Dioxin," National Technical Information Service AD/A-062143, Springfield, VA, 1978.
2.  Carreri, V. in "Dioxin: Toxicological and Chemical Aspects," Cattabeni, F.; Cavallaro, A.; Galli, G., Eds., Spectrum Publications: Jamaica, NY, 1978, p.1.
3.  Fortunati, G.V., in "Chlorinated Dioxins and Dibenzofurans in Perspective," Rappe, C.; Choudhary, G.; Keith, L.H., Eds., Lewis Publishers Inc.: Chelsea, MI, 1986, p.541.
4.  Carter, C.D.; Kimbrough, R.D.; Liddle, J.A.; Cline, R.F.; Zack, M.M.; Barthel, W.F.; Koehler, R.E.; Philipps, P.E., Science 1975, 188, 738.
5.  Olie, K.; Vermeulen, P.L.; Hutzinger, O., Chemosphere, 1977, 8, 455
6.  Bumb, R.R. et al.; Science 1980, 210, 385.
7.  Crummett, W.B.; Townsend, D.I.; Chemosphere 1984, 13, 777.
8.  Rappe, C. in "Solving Hazardous Waste Problems: Dioxins," Exner, J.H., Ed.; ACS SYMPOSIUM SERIES No.___, American Chemical Society: Washington, D.C., 1987, p___.
9.  Kociba, R.J., in "Solving Hazardous Waste Problems: Dioxins," Exner, J.H., Ed.; ACS SYMPOSIUM SERIES No.___; American Chemical Society: Washington, D.C., 1987; pp___ - ___.
10. Jackson, D.R.; Roulier, M.H.; Grotta, H.M.; Rust, S.W.; Warner, J.S.; in "Chlorinated Dioxins and Dibenzofurans in Perspective," Rappe, C.; Choudhary, G.; Keith, LH., Eds., Lewis Publishers: Chelsea, MI, 1986, p.185.
11. Kimbrough, R.; Falk, H.; Stehr, P.; Fries, G., J. Tox. Environmental Health 1984, 14 , p.47.
12. Facchetti, S.; Balasso, A., Fichtner, C.; Frare, G.; Leoni, A.; Mauri, C.; Vasconi, M.; in "Chlorinated Dioxins and Dibenzofurans in Perspective," Rappe, C.; Choudhary, G.; Keith, L.H.; Eds., Lewis Publishers: Chelsea, MI, 1986, p.225.
13. E. Noble, personal communication, 1985.
14. Gravitz, N.; Fan, A.; Neutra, R.R.; California Department of Health Services, "Interim Guidelines for Acceptable Exposure Levels in Office Settings Contaminated with PCB and PCB Combustion Products," 1983.
15. Bellin, J.S.; Barnes, D.G.; Toxic and Industrial Health, 1985, 1 , 235.
16. Exner, J.H., Johnson, J.D., Ivins, O.D., Wass, M.W., Miller, R.A., in "Detoxication of Hazardous Waste," Exner, J.H., Ed., Butterworth: Stoneham, MA, 1982, p.267.
17. Kleopfer, R.D.; Hazel, R.H.; Freestone, F.; desRosiers, P.E., in "Chlorinated Dioxins and Dibenzofurans in Perspective,"

Rappe, C.; Choudhary, G.; Keith, L.H.; Eds.; Lewis
Publishers: Chelsea, MI, 1986, p.511.
18. Exner, J.H.; Erikson, D.G.; Cibulskis, R.; Keffer, W.D.; in
"1984 Hazardous Material Spills Conference Proceedings,"
Ludwigson, J., Ed., Government Institutes, Inc., Rockville,
MD, 1984, p.245.
19. Exner, J.H.; Erikson, D.; "Quick-Response Engineering
Assessment of Removal Options for Quail Run Mobile Home Park,
MO, Dioxin Contamination," Draft Report to U.S. EPA Region 7,
Kansas City, KS, September 1, 1983.
20. Exner, J.H.; Alperin, E.S.; Groen, A.; Morren, C.E.; Kalcevic,
V.; Cudahy, J.J.; Pitts, D.M.; in "Chlorinated Dioxins and
Dibenzofurans in the Total Environment," Keith, L.H.; Rappe,
C.; Choudhary, G., Eds., Butterworth: Stoneham, MA, 1985,
p.47.
21. Finch, J.A. Jr. et al., "Final Report of the Missouri Dioxin
Task Force," State of MO, October 31, 1983.
22. Keffer, W.U.; Wurtz, S.; Newbore, G.; Howard, D.; Exner, J.H.;
"Quail Run Hazard Mitigation Plan," U.S. EPA Region 7 Report,
Kansas City, KS, 1984.
23. Exner, J.H.; Keffer, W.J.; Gilbert, R.O.; Kinnison, R.R.;
Hazardous Waste and Hazardous Materials, 1985, 2, p.503.

RECEIVED January 14, 1987

# DISTRIBUTION AND TOXICOLOGY

# Chapter 2

# Global Distribution of Polychlorinated Dioxins and Dibenzofurans

**Christoffer Rappe**

**Department of Organic Chemistry, University of Umeå, S-901 87 Umeå, Sweden**

Polychlorinated dioxins and dibenzofurans have been
identified in technical products and pesticides, most
of which are not very widely used today. Other sources
are incinerators of various types like MSW incinerators, but also hazardous waste incinerators and industrial incinerators. PCDDs and PCDFs have also been
identified in exhausts from cars running on leaded
gasoline with halogenated additives. Background levels of PCDDs and PCDFs have been identified in fish
and other aquatic organisms from the Great Lakes and
the Baltic Sea, and also in human adipose tissue
samples from USA, Canada, Sweden, Japan and Vietnam
as well as in samples of breast milk from Sweden,
Denmark, West Germany, the Netherlands, Yugoslavia
and Vietnam. The isomeric pattern in all these biological samples is very similar.

The polychlorinated dibenzodioxins (PCDDs) and dibenzofurans are
two groups of compounds that exhibit similar chemical and physical
properties, the chemical structures are given below:

PCDDs

PCDFs

0097-6156/87/0338-0020$06.00/0
© 1987 American Chemical Society

The number of chlorine atoms in these compounds can vary between one and eight ($x+y = 1-8$) to produce 75 PCDD and 135 PCDF posi-
tional isomers. A few of these have strong toxic effects, specifically 2,3,7,8-tetra-CDD and the other 2,3,7,8-substituted $Cl_4$, $Cl_5$
and $Cl_6$ PCDD and PCDF isomers, in all 12 congeners, see Table I.

Table I.  The Most Toxic PCDD and PCDF Isomers

| PCDDs | PCDFs |
|-------|-------|
| 2,3,7,8-Tetra-CDD | 2,3,7,8-Tetra-CDF |
| 1,2,3,7,8-Penta-CDD | 1,2,3,7,8-Penta-CDF |
| 1,2,3,6,7,8-Hexa-CDD | 2,3,4,7,8-Penta-CDF |
| 1,2,3,7,8,9-Hexa-CDD | 1,2,3,6,7,8-Hexa-CDF |
| 1,2,3,4,7,8-Hexa-CDD | 1,2,3,7,8,9-Hexa-CDF |
| | 1,2,3,4,7,8-Hexa-CDF |
| | 2,3,4,6,7,8-Hexa-CDF |

In the present presentation the primary interest is focused on reports discussing the contamination and distribution of all PCDDs and
PCDFs and not only 2,3,7,8-tetra-CDD in various matrices in the environment and in the general population. This enables the possibility to discuss congener profiles as well as patterns of individual
isomers.

Sources of PCDDs and PCDFs

Commercial and technical products. During the 1960's and 1970's most
of the interest was focused on the PCDD and PCDF contamination in
technical products like 2,4,5-T and other chlorophenoxy acids,
pentachlorophenol and other chlorinated phenols, and PCB. The levels
were found to vary from batch to batch, but the analyses were mostly
non-isomer specific. The major contaminant in 2,4,5-T was 2,3,7,8-
-tetra-CDD, normally in the lower ppm-range or less (1). In general,
technical pentachlorophenols were found to be the most contaminated
products, levels were reported in the range of 1000 ppm, mainly for
octa-CDD, but also a multitude of lower chlorinated congeners (1).
       As a result of the increasing concern over PCDD and PCDF impu-
rities, efforts were made to reduce the levels in the commercial
products. These operations, however, often resulted in an increased
volume of contaminated waste streams. Very, very few analyses were
made or reported on PCDD and PCDF levels in these waste streams, but
numerous outbreaks of chloracne and other skin problems should have
indicated a potential problem. These waste streams are now recognized as the source of numerous environmental problems.

       In many industrialized countries the use of products contami-
nated by PCDDs and PCDFs is nowadays highly reduced. For instance
2,4,5-T, earlier a major herbicide in most countries, is now only
produced and used in New Zealand and PCB is being phased out as dielectric fluid in transformers and capacitors in most countries
during the 1980's.

Municipal incinerators.. In 1977-1978 two European groups reported
that a series of PCDDs and PCDFs could be found in fly ash samples
collected in the electrostatic precipitator of municipal solid
waste (MSW) incinerators (2,3). Buser and Bosshardt (3) studied
fly ash from a MSW incinerator and an industrial heating facility,
both in Switzerland. In the former the total level of PCDDs was reported to be 0.2 ppm and of PCDFs 0.1 ppm. In the industrial incinerator the levels were 0.6 ppm and 0.3 ppm, respectively. Since then
a great number of reports from Europe, U.S.A., Canada, and Asia have
confirmed the original findings. However, for many years the interest was focused on the analysis of fly ash samples and not on the
analysis of the total emissions, which could be explained by sampling problems.

Most of the analyses of samples from incinerators have been
done using non-validated and non-isomer specific sampling and ana-
lytical methods. Recent studies show the presence of a multitude of
PCDD and PCDF congeners, in fact all isomers seem to be present (4).
Moreover, a striking similarity in the isomeric pattern of PCDDs and
PCDFs was found between samples from different incinerators (4,5).

Various models have been used to convert a multitude of levels
of more or less toxic PCDDs and PCDFs into a more simple expression
like "TCDD equivalents" or "toxic equivalents" (6). In Sweden and
in this report the approach discussed by Eadon et al. (7) has been
used.

Emissions from MSW incinerators operating under good conditions
are in the range of 1-100 ng TCDD equivalents /Nm$^3$ (8, 9) resulting
in total annual emissions of 1-100 g of TCDD equivalents from a
normal size MSW incinerator; 50 000 - 200 000 tons/year. The major
chlorine source in the MSW are plastic material like PVC and blea-
ched and unbleached paper (10). New technologies are now available to
reduce the emissions.

Hazardous waste incinerators. Hazardous waste incinerators have also been the object of public concern. However, available data indicate the emissions from such incinerators operating under good conditions are of the same magnitude as emissions from MSW incinerators.
The isomeric patterns of PCDDs and PCDFs are similar to those reported from MSW incinerators (4,5).

Industrial processes. Recent work in our group has identified industrial high-temperature processes like copper smelters and electrical arcing furnaces in steel mills as sources of environmental
contamination of PCDDs and PCDFs (8). The copper smelter used scrap
copper containing PVC-coated wires and cords. In the steel mill a
high portion of the alloys or stainless steel was recycled. This
recycled material was contaminated by PVC or polychlorinated paraf-
fins (8). The emission from these sources seem to be of the same
magnitude as emissions from MSW incinerators. However, due to a
larger number of units, the total emissions from these industrial
processes could exceed the emissions from MSW incinerators. The
emissions from coal fired power plants, wood and peat burners seem
to be very low (per Nm$^3$) but the very large number of units could
make a significant total contribution (8).

Automobiles. Very recently Ballschmiter et al. identified a series
of PCDDs and PCDFs in used motor oil from automobiles (11). These
authors also reported on a striking similarity in the isomeric pattern of the PCDFs found in this matrix and in samples from MSW incinerators (11). Ballschmiter et al. suggest chlorinated additives
in the motor oil or in the gasoline as possible sources for the PCDDs
and PCDFs, but no quantitative data is given (amount per km). Also
very recently Marklund et al. reported on a study where real car
exhausts were analyzed for PCDDs and PCDFs (12). The test cars were
collected in two groups

1.    Cars equipped with a catalytic converter using unleaded gaso-
      line with no halogenated scavengers.
2.    Cars with no catalytic converter using leaded gasoline (0.15
      g/l) and a dichloroethane scavenger (0.1 g/l).

Before the test runs the motor oil was exchanged in all cars.

    No PCDDs and PCDFs could be identified in the cars using the
unleaded gasoline, while the emission average from the cars running
on leaded gasoline was found to be 30-540 pg/km of TCDD equivalents
(Eadon). It was assumed that the chlorinated scavenger (dichloroethane) was the precursor to the PCDDs and PCDFs formed. It was estimated that the total amount of PCDDs and PCDFs from cars in Sweden using leaded gasoline with halogenated scavengers is in the
range of 10-100 g TCDD equivalents/year (12).
    An extreme good similarity was reported for the isomeric pat-
tern of the tetra- and penta-CDFs found in automobile exhausts and
in emissions from MSW incinerators (12) and steel mills, see Figure
1.

## Levels of PCDDs and PCDFs in Environmental Samples

Soil and sediments. A great number of analyses have been performed
on soil and sediment samples, preferentially from "hot spots" where
levels of PCDDs and PCDFs, mainly 2,3,7,8-tetra-CDD, as high as ppm
have been reported, e.g. Seveso, Times Beach and Love Canal. In a
few studies background levels of PCDDs and PCDFs in soil and sediment samples are reported. However, in most of these studies non-
-validated and non-isomer specific analytical methods are used.
These studies indicate background levels in the low ppt range, but
in general no specific isomers are reported.
    Olie (13) reported on the analysis of 14 soil samples collec-
ted from 11 locations in previously sprayed habitats of southern
Viet Nam during the period 1980-81. 2,3,7,8-Tetra-CDD was identified in four of these samples in levels of 16-31 ppt.
    Recent data (5) using validated ($^{13}$C) and isomer specific
analytical methods indicate that new sediments from the archipelago
of Stockholm, Sweden, contain ppt or sub-ppt levels of a variety of
PCDD and PCDF isomers. The isomeric profiles found in these sediments are very similar to those found in samples from MSW and industrial incinerators and car exhausts.

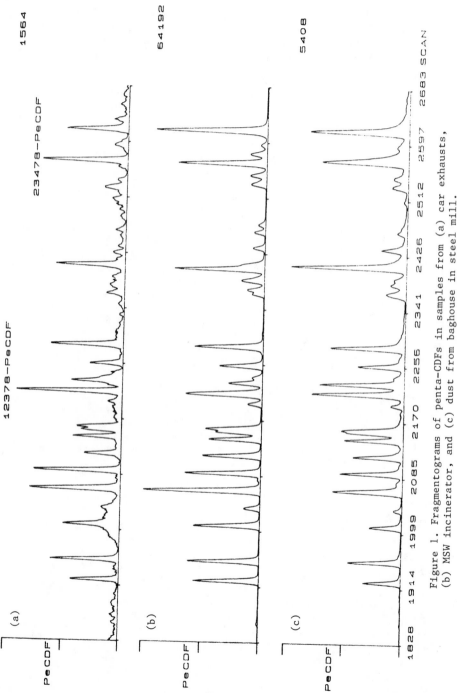

Figure 1. Fragmentograms of penta-CDFs in samples from (a) car exhausts, (b) MSW incinerator, and (c) dust from baghouse in steel mill.

Air and particulate. Due to sampling and analytical problems very
few data are available on the levels of PCDDs and PCDFs in normal
urban air. Samples of air particulates from Washington, D.C., and
St. Louis, MO, USA have been analyzed by Crummett et al. (14) and
Czuczwa and Hites (15). Crummett et al. (14) report on isomer specific analyses for tetra-CDDs and hexa-CDDs while Czuczwa and Hites
(15) only report a congener profile and do not discuss any specific
isomers. In both studies octa-CDD was found to be a major constitu-
ent, reported in levels of 150-200 ppb. The level of 2,3,7,8-tetra-
-CDD was 5-50 ppt and of 2,3,7,8-tetra-CDF was 100-380 ppt (14).
    Recent studies using pre-spiked ($^{13}$C) air samples and iso-
mer specific analytical methods (5) indicate that sub pg/m$^3$ levels
of a variety of PCDDs and PCDFs can be found in air sampled in an
industrialized area. The isomeric patterns found in these samples
were very similar to those found in samples from MSW and industrial
incinerators, car exhausts and also in new sediments (5).
    Also very recently Oehme et al. (16) reported on a study where
urban air was investigated by high-volume sampling of 1000 m$^3$ of air
using a glass fiber filter and polyurethane foam as collection media.
Measurable amounts of a large number of PCDDs and PCDFs were found
in cities and industrialized regions, while the levels in remote
areas were lower. The highest levels were in the order of 5-10 pg/m$^3$
for the sum of all PCDDs and PCDFs. In suburban areas the levels
were lower by a factor of 5-10 (16).

Aquatic organisms. In the late 1970s and early 1980s analytical
methods were developed to analyze for 2,3,7,8-tetra-CDD as well as
other PCDDs and PCDFs (Table 1) in biological samples. Due to the
high toxicity of these compounds the detection levels should be in
the order of pg/g (ppt) or lower. Such analyses are complicated and
expensive and up to now only a limited number of analyses are reported, mainly from U.S.A., Canada and Sweden.
    Mitchum et al. (17) reported on levels up to 400 ppt of
2,3,7,8-tetra-CDD in a waterway associated with the production of
2,4,5-T. Levels ranging from 4-695 ppt of 2,3,7,8-tetra-CDD were
found for the edible portion of various fishes from Saginaw Bay,
U.S.A., the highest concentrations were detected in bottom-feeding
catfish and carp. In all 36 samples were analyzed and 26 of these
were reported to have detectable amounts: > 5-10 ppt of 2,3,7,8-
-tetra-CDD. Ten samples contained concentrations greater than 40 ppt
(18).
    Rappe et al. identified a series of tetra to octa-CDFs in fat
samples of a snapping turtle from Hudson River and gray seal from
Baltic Sea. The total levels of PCDFs in these samples were 3 ng/g
and 40 pg/g, respectively. In both samples the major PCDFs consisted of the most toxic isomers: 2,3,7,8-tetra-, 2,3,4,7,8-penta-
and 1,2,3,4,7,8- and 1,2,3,6,7,8- hexa-CDF (19).
    Fish and other aquatic animals from the Great Lakes have been
analyzed and the data indicate low background levels (1-300 ppt) of
a series of PCDDs and PCDFs. Norstrom et al. have analyzed pooled
samples of herring gull eggs collected in 1982 from various parts
of the Great Lakes. In all samples 2,3,7,8-tetra-CDD was found in
levels ranging from 9 to 90 pg/g (20). In another study Stalling
et al. (21) were not able to identify measurable levels of tetra-CDDs

and other PCDDs in fish samples from Lake Superior (the detection level was 2-5 pg/g). The difference in these two studies could be explained by the migration of the herring gulls during the winter. On the contrary a series of PCDFs could be identified in the Lake Superior fish samples (15-40 ppt), indicating a more widespread background levels for the PCDFs than for the PCDDs. Stalling et al. also reported on the analysis of fish samples from Lakes Michigan, Huron and Ontario. Total levels of PCDFs were found to be 12-290 ppt (21). The toxic 2,3,7,8-substituted PCDDs and PCDFs were present in all samples, the highest levels being found in samples from Lake Huron, Lake Ontario and Tittabawasee River. The residue pattern found in the fish and locally high levels suggest a strong influence by point source discharges (21). The Baltic Sea is another system studied which could be of interest because this is a system without any known point sources. Some relevant data from the Baltic Sea are collected in Table II (22).

Table II.   Levels of PCDDs and PCDFs Found in Samples from the Baltic Sea (22)

|  |  | Seal pg/g | Salmon pg/g | Guillemot pg/g | Herring pg/g |
|---|---|---|---|---|---|
| 2,3,7,8- | TCDD | 28 | 6 | 17 | 0.6 |
| 1,2,3,7,8- | PeCDD | 60 | 22 | 26 | ND |
| 1,2,3,4,7,8- | HxCDD | 2.9 | 0.8 | 0.9 | ND |
| 1,2,3,6,7,8- | HxCDD | 69 | 6.6 | 18 | ND |
| 1,2,3,7,8,9- | HxCDD | 3.6 | 0.2 | 1.6 | ND |
| 1,2,3,4,6,7,9-HpCDD | | 0.4 | 0.5 | ND | ND |
| 1,2,3,4,6,7,8-HpCDD | | 1.2 | 0.9 | 0.6 | ND |
| | OCDD | 2.5 | 4.3 | 0.2 | ND |
| 2,3,7,8- | TCDF | 12 | 62 | 0.2 | 3.9 |
| 1,2,3,7,8- | PeCDF | 3.7 | 24 | 1.8 | 1.2 |
| 2,3,4,7,8- | PeCDF | 125 | 82 | 97 | 5.6 |
| 1,2,3,4,7,8- | HxCDF | 1.1 | 9.1 | 4.7 | 0.6 |
| 1,2,3,6,7,8- | HxCDF | 2.4 | 6.3 | 10 | 0.4 |
| 2,3,4,6,7,8- | HxCDF | 1.5 | 5.1 | 4.5 | 0.7 |
| 1,2,3,4,6,7,8-HpCDF | | 0.2 | 41 | 0.5 | 0.5 |
| 1,2,3,4,6,7,9-HpCDF | | ND | 0.6 | ND | ND |
| 1,2,3,4,6,8,9-HpCDF | | ND | 2.2 | ND | 0.2 |
| 1,2,3,4,7,8,9-HpCDF | | ND | 0.9 | T | ND |
| | OCDF | 1.8 | 61 | T | ND |

ND = not detected  < 0.1 pg/g
T  = trace

An interesting observation is that in the majority of the aquatic samples only the toxic 2,3,7,8-substituted congeners are found, compare Tables I and II. Crustaceans seem to be an exception from this general behaviour; Norstrom et al. (23) reported in 1985 that hepatopancreas from crabs from the Canadian Pacific coast

contain other congeners, e.g. 1,2,4,7,8-penta-CDD and 1,2,3,6,7,9-/
/1,2,3,6,8,9-hexa-CDD. Recent analyses of hepatopancreas and meat
from crabs and lobsters collected at the U.S. Atlantic Coast and
the Swedish West Coast confirm this observation (5). The levels
in the hepatopancreas were found to be 10-100 times higher than
the levels found in the meat. Consequently crustaceans are good
signal organisms to study sources of environmental pollution of
PCDDs and PCDFs, the highest levels of pollutants are found in the
hepatopancreas.

Terrestrial animals. At the time of the accident in Seveso, Italy
in 1976 more than 81 000 animals were  inhabiting  the contaminated
zones. The main part were rabbits (25 000 ) and poultry and other
small animals (55 500), but also 349 cattle, 233 pigs, 49 horses,
31 sheeps and 49 goats were in the zones. Many of these animals
died, others were killed. A large number of these animals were
analyzed for  2,3,7,8-TCDD by a method with a detection level at
250 pg/g (24). The results are collected in Table III.

Table III.  TCDD analyses on liver of farm animals from contaminated
           zones and surrounding areas (1976-1979) (24)

| Animal | Number of samples | TCDD-containing samples (>250 pg/g) | TCDD maximum level ng/g |
|--------|-------------------|-------------------------------------|--------------------------|
| Rabbits | 698 | 433 | 633 |
| Poultry | 83 | 35 | 24 |
| Cattle | 43 | 21 | 94 |
| Horses | 12 | 2 | 88 |
| Pigs | 13 | 0 | – |
| Goats | 25 | 17 | 1 |

Nygren et al. (22) analyzed bovine samples: fat, liver and
milk and identified the same 2,3,7,8-substituted PCDDs and PCDFs
as were found in the aquatic samples. However, the levels were lower
and normally close to the detection limit, see Table IV. This indicates that the background levels are higher in the aquatic environment than in the terrestrial environment, which is in agreement with
earlier experience for substances such as DDT and PCB.

Levels of PCDDs and PCDFs in Human Samples

Adipose tissue.  In April 1984 Rappe et al. (25) reported on a series of the toxic 2,3,7,8-substituted PCDDs and PCDFs in samples of
human adipose tissue from Northern Sweden. A series of reports presented at the dioxin conferences in Ottawa, Canada in October 1984,
Miami, Fl, U.S.A. in April 1985 and in Bayreuth, West Germany in
September 1985 confirmed these observations, and it is clearly
shown that there is a background of PCDDs and PCDF in the general
population in the industrialized part of the world. In Table V are

Table IV. Levels of PCDDs and PCDFs found in bovine fat, bovine liver, bovine milk and cream samples (22)

| | Cow fat Sweden pg/g | Cow liver Sweden pg/g | Cow fat Scotland pg/g | Milk Denmark pg/g fat | Milk Scotland pg/g fat | Cream Sweden pg/g fat |
|---|---|---|---|---|---|---|
| 2,3,7,8- TCDD | ND | ND | NA | NA | NA | NA |
| 1,2,3,7,8- PeCDD | ND | ND | 2 | T | 5 | ND |
| 1,2,3,4,7,8- HxCDD | ND | ND | 1 | ND | 3 | ND |
| 1,2,3,6,7,8- HxCDD | ND | ND | 2 | 6 | 6 | 18 |
| 1,2,3,7,8,9- HxCDD | ND | ND | ND | 6 | 2 | ND |
| 1,2,3,4,6,7,8- HpCDD | 3 | 4 | 3 | 9 | 2 | 42 |
| OCDD | 9 | 10 | 3 | < 86 | 3 | 16 |
| 2,3,7,8- TCDF | ND | ND | ND | ND | ND | 2 |
| 2,3,4,7,8- PeCDF | ND | ND | 5 | 3 | 8 | 4 |
| 1,2,3,4,7,8- HxCDF | ND | ND | 1 | ND | 3 | 3 |
| 1,2,3,6,7,8- HxCDF | ND | ND | 1 | 8 | 2 | T |
| 2,3,4,6,7,8- HxCDF | ND | ND | 1 | 4 | 2 | 3 |
| 1,2,3,4,6,7,8- HpCDF | ND | ND | 2 | < 7 | 3 | 6 |
| OCDF | ND | ND | ND | < 7 | < 15 | < 20 |

ND = not detected  (< 1.0 pg/g)
NA = not analyzed
T = trace

Table V.  Levels of PCDDs and PCDFs in Human Adipose Tissue (ppt on wet weight)

| Isomer | | Sweden n=31 (22) | USA/NY n=8 (26) | Canada n=46 (26) | Japan n=13 (27) | N Viet Nam n=9 (26) | S Viet Nam n=15 (26) |
|---|---|---|---|---|---|---|---|
| 2,3,7,8- | TCDD | 3 | 7.2 | 6.4 | 9 | < 2 | 18 |
| 1,2,3,7,8- | PeCDD | 10 | 11.1 | 10 | 15 | < 2 | 9.1 |
| 1,2,3,6,7,8- | HxCDD | 15 | 95.6 | 81 | 70 | 5.6 | 57 |
| 1,2,3,7,8,9- | HxCDD | 4 | NA | NA | 12 | NA | NA |
| 1,2,3,4,6,7,8- | HpCDD | 97 | 164 | 135 | 77 | 17 | 121 |
| | OCDD | 414 | 707 | 850 | 230 | 52 | 900 |
| 2,3,7,8- | TCDF | 3.9 | NA | NA | 9 | NA | NA |
| 2,3,4,7,8- | PeCDF | 54 | 14.3 | 15 | 25 | 7.2 | 12 |
| 1,2,3,4,7,8- | HxCDF | 6 | NA | NA | 15 | NA | NA |
| 1,2,3,6,7,8- | HxCDF | 5 | 31.3 | 16 | 14 | 7.7 | 33 |
| 2,3,4,6,7,8- | HxCDF | 2 | NA | NA | 8 | NA | NA |
| 1,2,3,4,6,7,8- | HpCDF | 11 | 16.5 | 30 | NA | 4.2 | 17 |
| | OCDF | 4 | NA | NA | NA | NA | NA |

ND = not detected (< 1.0 pg/g)
NA = not analyzed

collected some relevant data from U.S.A., Canada, Sweden and Japan.
For comparison, data from North and South Viet Nam are also included
in this table (22, 26, 27). Data from other countries seem not to be
available.

It is interesting to note the similarity in isomers, levels,
and isomeric pattern in these samples collected from the industrialized countries on three continents. The PCDD profile shows increasing
levels with increasing number of chlorine atoms, the level of OCDD
is 400-900 ppt while the PCDF profile has a maximum for 2,3,4,7,8-
-penta-CDF or 1,2,3,6,7,8-hexa-CDF. The difference in levels found
between samples from North and South Viet Nam can be explained by
the difference in industrial activities between the two parts of the
country.

Breast milk. In April 1984 Rappe et al. also reported on the analyses of five samples of breast milk from West Germany (25). In January 1985 Rappe reported on the analyses of four samples of breast
milk from the Umeå region in northern Sweden (28), and in May Nygren
et al. reported on additional single samples from Denmark and Viet
Nam. In September 1985 Fuerst et al. reported on the analyses of 53
samples of breast milk from West Germany (29). The data from these
investigations are collected in Table VI together with data from
pooled samples of breast milk from the Netherlands and Yugoslavia
(5). Low levels of PCDDs and PCDFs were found in all samples from
all these countries. Discussing the specific isomers and levels we
find great similarities between adipose and breast milk samples as
shown in Tables V and VI (4,5,9).

## Conclusions

Available data, although from very few countries, indicate a general
low background for 2,3,7,8-substituted PCDDs and PCDFs in the environment, especially for aquatic organisms and also in the general
population.

In most biological samples only the most toxic PCDD and PCDF
isomers were found, see Tables I-VI. In addition, two $Cl_7$ and two
$Cl_8$ congeners were also found. An exception from this general behaviour is the crustaceans, where a multitude of isomers could be
identified.

A poor correlation was observed between the isomeric distribution found in environmental and human samples on one side and the
potential sources on the other. This indicates a combination of sources e.g. incineration and technical products in addition to environmental and biological degradation. Of special interest here is the
observation of 1,2,3,7,8-penta-CDD in all biological samples. This
isomer is found in all samples from incinerators and also in low
levels in a few technical pentachlorophenol formulations (5).

It is of great importance that ultratrace analyses of PCDDs and
PCDFs are generated by representative sampling and validated analytical methods. Greater efforts should be devoted to interlaboratory
studies, e.g. Albro et al. (30). Several of the analytical methods
used in this study generated data of high quality. However, other
methods were not so safe, a large portion of the reported data were
false positives or false negatives.

Table VI. Levels of PCDDs and PCDFs Found in Breast Milk (ppt on fat weight)

| | | Sweden n=4 (28) | W. Germany n=5 (25) | W. Germany n=53 (29) | Viet Nam n=1x (22) | Denmark n=1 (22) | Netherlands n=3 (5) | Yugoslavia n=2 (5) |
|---|---|---|---|---|---|---|---|---|
| 2,3,7,8- | TCDD | 0.6 | 1.9 | ND | < 0.5 | NA | 9.7 | < 1.0 |
| 1,2,3,7,8- | PeCDD | 6.5 | 12.9 | 11.0 | 7.0 | 31 | 44 | 5.5 |
| 1,2,3,4,7,8- | HxCDD | 2.5 | NI[a] | 8.6 | ND | 13 | 25 | 3.5 |
| 1,2,3,6,7,8- | HxCDD | 19 | NI[a] | 32.9 | 50 | 97 | 251 | 15 |
| 1,2,3,7,8,9- | HxCDD | 6.3 | NI[a] | 6.4 | 24 | 32 | 23 | ND |
| 1,2,3,4,6,7,8-HpCDD | | 59.5 | 72.8 | 48.8 | 150 | 174 | 130 | 28 |
| OCDD | | 302 | 434 | 143 | 754 | 328 | 744 | 106 |
| 2,3,7,8- | TCDF | 4.2 | 5.4 | 1.7 | 9.4 | 4.0 | 2.8 | < 1.0 |
| 1,2,3,7,8- | PeCDF | < 1 | < 1 | 2.0 | < 1 | 4.5 | ND | ND |
| 2,3,4,7,8- | PeCDF | 21.3 | 36.4 | 21.1 | 21 | 31 | 79 | 25 |
| 1,2,3,4,7,8- | HxCDF | 4.7 | NI[b] | 8.3 | 15.0 | 13 | 8.9 | 3.7 |
| 1,2,3,6,7,8- | HxCDF | 3.4 | NI[b] | 6.9 | 11.0 | 52 | 10.3 | 3.6 |
| 2,3,4,6,7,8- | HxCDF | 1.4 | NI[b] | 3.2 | 4.2 | 11 | 6.4 | 1.3 |
| 1,2,3,4,6,7,8-HpCDF | | 7.4 | 9.2 | 7.4 | 23.0 | 46 | 39 | ND |
| OCDF | | 3.2 | 2.4 | 27.0 | 46.0 | ND | ND | ND |

NI = not isomer specific
ND = not detected
NA = not analyzed

a) Total level of hexa-CDDs = 23.4 ppt
b) Total level of hexa-CDFs = 26.0 ppt

Literature Cited

1. Rappe, C. Env. Sci. Technol. 1984, 16, 78 A  90 A.
2. Olie, K.; Vermeulen, P.L.; Hutzinger, O. Chemosphere 1977,
   8, 455-459.
3. Buser, H.R.; Bosshardt, H.-P. Mitt. Geb. Lebensm. Hyg. 1978,
   69, 191-199.
4. Rappe, C.; Marklund, S.; Kjeller, L.O.; Bergqvist, P.-A. and
   Hansson, M. In "Chlorinated Dioxins and Dibenzofurans in the
   Total Environment". Keith, L.H.; Rappe, C.; Choudhary, G.,
   Eds.; Butterworth: Stoneham, MA, 1984; Vol. II p. 401.
5. Unpublished data: University of Umeå, Sweden.
6. Bellin, J.S.; Barnes, D.G. Toxicology and Idustrial Health 1985,
   1, 235-248.
7. Eadon, G.; Aldous, K.; Hilker, P.; O'Keefe, P.; Smith, R. "Chemical data on air samples from the Binghamton State Office
   Building", 1983. Memo from Center for Lab Research, New York
   State Department of Health, Albany, NY 12201, 7/7/83.
8. Marklund, S.; Kjeller, L.-O.; Hansson, M.; Tysklind, M.;
   Rappe, C.; Ryan, C.; Collazo, H.; Dougherty, R. In "Chlorinated Dioxins and Dibenzofurans in the Total Environment".
   Rappe, C.; Choudhary, G.; Keith, L., Eds.; Lewis Publishers,
   1986, Vol. III p. 79.
9. "PCDD and PCDF Emissions from Incinerators for Municipal Sewage Sludge and Solid Waste-Evaluation of Human Exposure".
   WHO Regional Office for Europe, Copenhagen, Denmark, IPC/CEH
   003/m 06 1986.
10. Churney, K.L.;  Ledford, A.E.; Bruce, S.S.;  Domalski, E.S. U.S.
    Department of Commerce Report NBSIR 85-3213, 1985.
11. Ballschmiter, K.; Buchert, H.; Niemczyk, R.; Munder, A.;
    Swerev, M. Chemosphere. In press.
12. Marklund, S.; Rappe, C.; Tysklind, M.; Egebäck, K.-E.
    Chemosphere. In press.
13. Olie, K. In "Herbicides in War. The Long-term Ecological and
    Human Consequences". Westing, A.H.; Ed. SIPRI, Stockholm,
    Sweden, 1984, p. 173.
14. Crummett, W.B.; Nestrick, T.J.; Lamparski, L.L. In "Dioxins in
    the Environment". Kamrin, M.A.; Rodgers, P.W. Eds. Hemisphere
    Publishing, New York, N.Y. 1985, 75-76.
15. Czuczwa, J.M.; Hites, R.A. Env. Sci. Technol. 1986, 20,
    195-200.
16. Oehme, M.; Manø, S.; Mikalsen, A.; Kirschmer, P. Chemosphere,
    1986, 15, 607-617.
17. Mitchum, R.K.; Moler, G.F.; Korfmacher, W.A. Anal. Chem. 1980,
    52, 2278-2282.
18. Harless, R.L.; Lewis, R.G. In "Chlorinated Dioxins and Related
    Compounds. Impact on the Environment". Hutzinger, O.; Frei, R.
    W.; Merian, E.; Pocchiari, F.; Eds., Pergamon Press, Oxford,
    1982, p. 25.
19. Rappe, C.; Buser, H.R.; Stalling, D.L.; Smith, L.M.;
    Dougherty, R.C. Nature, 1981, 292, 524-526.

20. Norstrom, R.J.; Hallett, D.J.; Simon, M.; Mulvihill, M.J.
    In "Chlorinated Dioxins and Related Compounds. Impact on the
    Environment". Hutzinger, O.; Frei, R.W.; Merian, E.; Pocchiari,
    F.; Eds., Pergamon Press, Oxford, 1982, p. 173.
21. Stalling, D.L.; Smith, L.M.; Petty, J.D.; Hogan, J.W.;
    Johnsson, J.L.; Rappe, C.; Buser, H.R. In "Human and Environ-
    mental Risks of Chlorinated Dioxins and Related Compounds".
    Tucker, R.E.; Young, A.L.; Gray, A.P., Eds., Plenum Press, New
    York and London, 1983, p. 221.
22. Nygren, M.; Rappe, C.; Lindström, G.; Hansson, M.; Bergqvist,
    P.-A.; Marklund, S.; Domellöf, L.; Hardell, L.; Olsson, M.
    In "Chlorinated Dioxins and Dibenzofurans in the Total Envi-
    ronment". Rappe, C.; Choudhary, G.; Keith, L.; Eds., Lewis
    Publishers, 1986, Vol. III. p. 79.
23. Norstrom, R.J.; Simon, M.; Rappe, C.; Bergqvist, P.-A.
    Chemosphere. In Press.
24. Pocchiari, F.; Di Domenico, A.; Silano, V.; Zapponi, G.
    In "Accidental Exposure to Dioxins. Human Health Aspects".
    Coulston, F.; Pocchiari, F., Eds., Academic Press, New York
    and London, 1983, p. 5.
25. Rappe, C.; Bergqvist, P.-A.; Hansson, M.; Kjeller, L.-O.;
    Lindström, G.; Marklund, S.; Nygren, M. Banbury Report 18:
    Biological Mechanisms of Dioxin Action. Cold Spring Harbor
    Laboratory, NY, U.S.A. 1984, p 17-25.
26. Schecter, A.; Gasiewicz, T.; Ryan, J.J.; Gross, M.; Weera-
    singhe, W.C.A.; Constable, J. Presentation at this conference.
27. Ono, M.; Wakimoto, T.; Tatsukawa, R.; Masuda, Y. Chemosphere.
    In Press.
28. Rappe, C. In "Organo Halogen Compounds in Human Milk and
    Related Hazards" Report on a WHO Consultation. WHO Regional
    Office for Europe, Copenhagen, Denmark, IPC/CEH 501/m 05.
    August 1985.
29. Fuerst, P.; Meemken, H.-A.; Groebel, W. Chemosphere. In Press.
30. Albro, P.W.; Crummett, W.B.; Dupuy, A.E.; Gross, M.L.;
    Hansson, M.; Harless, R.L.; Hileman, F.D.; Hilker, D.;
    Jason, C.; Johnson, J.L.; Lamparski, L.L.; Lau, B. P.-Y.;
    McDaniel, D.D.; Meehan, J.L.; Nestrick, T.J.; Nygren, M.;
    O'Keefe, P.; Peters, T.L.; Rappe, C.; Ryan, J.J.; Smith, L.M.;
    Stalling, D.L.; Weerasinge, N.C.A.; Wendling, J.M. Anal. Chem.
    1985, 27, 2717-2725.

RECEIVED November 25, 1986

# Chapter 3

# National Dioxin Study

Paul E. des Rosiers

U.S. Environmental Protection Agency (RD-681), Washington, DC 20460

This report presents the results of EPA's investigation of potential 2,3,7,8-TCDD (dioxin) contamination. The study represents a two-year, nationwide, multi-media evaluation initiated at the request of the U.S. Congress in 1983. The majority of dioxin contamination at Tier 1, 1a, 2 and 2a sites remained on-site. At sites where concentrated 2,4,5-TCP production wastes were stored or disposed, 2,3,7,8-TCDD concentrations were as high as 356 ppm. At most sites, however, 2,3,7,8-TCDD levels in soil were usually in the ppb range. In fish samples from nearby lakes and streams, 2,3,7,8-TCDD was measured in terms of ppt. Only two Tier 3 sites were extensively contaminated and comprised large facilities handling 2,4,5-T, 2,4,5-TP and 2,4,5-TCP with extent of contamination limited to one or two soil samples above 1 ppb. CDDs and CDFs were present in stack emissions from all sources tested in Tier 4 and most, but not all, of the combustion source categories reported in the literature. CDD and CDF emissions from some sources have estimated risks to the most exposed individual of $10^{-5}$ or more; these sources include a secondary copper smelting facility, a sewage sludge incinerator, and some municipal incinerators. At Tier 5 pastureland, rice field, and sugarcane sites, 2,3,7,8-TCDD levels in contaminated soils ranged from 0.6-564 ppt, with 67 percent below 5 ppt; levels in fish filets were between 8 and 23 ppt. At the three Tier 6 regionally selected sites, none was extensively contaminated. At one site, however, groundwater contamination was found at the 0.07-0.10 ppt level in three samples. The Tier 7 investigation established the prevalence of 2,3,7,8-TCDD in the environment: 2,3,7,8-TCDD was detected infrequently and at very low levels in background soil samples with the highest level being 11.2 ppt.

This chapter not subject to U.S. copyright.
Published 1987, American Chemical Society

## Basis of Concern

Numerous incidents of dioxin contamination have resulted in a high level of public awareness and concern. This concern carries over into present efforts to implement cleanup actions and conduct disposal operations.

Among the best known incidents was exposure of U.S. forces to Agent Orange in Viet Nam. A defoliant, Agent Orange, was contaminated with 2,3,7,8-TCDD. A large number of suits was filed against the manufacturers of these chemicals. These cases have now been settled out-of-court, thus the issue of cause and effect was not addressed.

In Seveso, Italy, an industrial accident involving 2,4,5-trichlorophenol (2,4,5-TCP)/hexachlorophene (HCP) manufacture resulted in widespread, low-level 2,3,7,8-TCDD contamination. Effects included evacuation of segments of the community, animal deaths, extensive cleanup efforts, and treatment of over 100 cases of chloracne alleged to be associated with the accident.

In Times Beach, Missouri, waste oil from 2,4,5-TCP/HCP manufacture, contaminated with 2,3,7,8-TCDD, was used to control dust on roads. The result was the well-known government 'buy-out' of the town. Use of waste oil at several Missouri horse arenas resulted in acute human health effects and the death of sixty-five horses and several small animals. Subsequent use of the horse arena materials as fill at building construction sites resulted in further cleanup problems.

2,3,7,8-TCDD and other chemical contamination of adjacent land and water as a result of industrial waste disposal at the Love Canal, 102nd Street, and Hyde Park sites in Niagara Falls, New York, posed health risks. 2,3,7,8-TCDD contamination was also found to be extensive at the Vertac facility in Jacksonville, Arkansas, both on- and offsite.

In 1979, investigations at a municipal incinerator in Hempstead, New York, led to the discovery that dioxins (CDDs) and furans (CDFs) were being emitted during the combustion process.

In 1980, a PCB transformer fire in the basement of the State Office Building in Binghamton, New York, resulted in distribution of soot containing high levels of CDDs and CDFs, including the 2,3,7,8-isomers, throughout the building. Cleanup costs to date exceed the original construction cost of the building.

In 1981, reports from Canada demonstrated the presence of 2,3,7,8-TCDD in Great Lakes' fish. These reports coincided with reports of contamination of fish in several U.S. rivers, notably the Titabawassee River in Michigan.

## The National Dioxin Strategy

At the time of the Congressional request for a study, the Environmental Protection Agency (EPA) was in the midst of responding to contamination in Missouri and other locations. EPA also had rulemaking proceedings underway to address various aspects of the dioxin problem.

EPA's National Dioxin Study had three objectives:
° To study the extent of dioxin contamination and the associated risks to humans and the environment;
° To implement or compel necessary cleanup action at contaminated sites; and
° To evaluate further both disposal alternatives to alleviate current problems and regulatory alternatives to prevent future contamination.

On December 15, 1983, EPA issued a "national dioxin strategy" for investigating, identifying, and cleaning up sites contaminated by dioxin (1). Within the framework of this strategy was a plan that called for research to be conducted on the technical feasibility and economics of alternative methods for disposal and destruction of wastes and soils contaminated by dioxin.

To implement this strategy, EPA established seven categories (tiers) of investigation and study ranging from the most probable contamination to the least. These are:

Tier 1.   2,4,5-TCP production sites and associated waste disposal sites.

Tier 2.   Sites and associated waste disposal sites where 2,4,5-TCP was used as feedstock for pesticidal products.

Tier 3.   Sites and associated waste disposal sites where 2,4,5-TCP and its derivatives were formulated into herbicidal products.

Tier 4.   Combustion sources such as municipal and hazardous waste incinerators, PCB transformer/capacitor fires, reactivation furnaces for spent granular activated carbon, boilers burning PCBs or pentachlorophenol (PCP)-treated wood, etc.

Tier 5.   Sites where herbicides derived from 2,4,5-TCP have been and are being used on a commercial basis such as rights-of-way, rice fields, forests, certain aquatic areas, and pastureland.

Tier 6.   Organic chemical and pesticide manufacturing facilities where improper quality control of certain production processes would have resulted in the formation of 2,3,7,8-TCDD.

Tier 7.   Control sites where contamination of 2,3,7,8-TCDD is not suspected. These are to be compared with known contaminated sites to form a background level for the strategy studies.

## Toxicity Equivalence

While the primary focus of this study was on contamination associated with 2,3,7,8-TCDD, EPA was also concerned with human exposure from other isomers of chlorinated dibenzo-p-dioxin and dibenzofuran.

EPA (2) and others have developed a number of weighting schemes to compare the toxicities of various chlorinated dioxin and furan isomers to that of 2,3,7,8-TCDD, the most studied, and generally considered to be the most toxic isomer. Toxicity

Equivalence Factor (TEF) approaches express the toxicity of CDD/CDF mixtures in terms of "2,3,7,8-TCDD equivalents." This allows comparison of the toxicity of mixtures for purposes of risk assessment and remedial action planning.  EPA's TEFs for isomers and homologs of CDD/CDF are shown in Table 1.

With the exception of 2,3,7,8-TCDD, the 2,3,7,8-substituted HxCDDs and 2,3,7,8-TCDF, these TEFs are not based on the results of major animal (reproductive, carcinogenic) studies.  Generally, TEFs are based on estimates of the relative toxicity from in vitro tests whose relationship to the chronic effects of concern is largely presumptive.  Nevertheless, studies on systemic effects continue to reinforce the view that the short-term assays provide important fundamental information on the toxicity of the CDDs/CDFs.

## Tiers 1 and 2/1a and 2a, Production and Disposal Sites

Tier 1 comprises 2,4,5-TCP production sites and associated waste disposal sites (Tier 1a); whereas Tier 2 represents sites where 2,4,5-TCP was employed as a precursor in the manufacture of pesticides such as 2,4,5-T, 2,4,5-TP (Silvex), or hexachlorophene, and associated waste disposal sites (Tier 2a).

EPA used a three-phased approach.  First, information was collected to identify these sites.  EPA then used its enforcement authorities to verify production facilities and associated waste disposal sites.  As needed, EPA collected additional data from site visits and employee interviews.

Next, EPA screened the sites through field testing to determine actual 2,3,7,8-TCDD contamination.  EPA employed a biased sampling approach.  Instead of taking samples randomly, EPA sampled in the locations most likely to be contaminated with dioxin (i.e., loading, storage, or production areas).  If offsite migration of contaminated material was suspected, EPA sampled outside the facility boundary.  Quality assurance/quality control protocols, following Superfund-authorized procedures, were developed to ensure that all data generated would be of known quality.

Finally, if a level of 2,3,7,8-TCDD contamination requiring a cleanup response (i.e., >1 ppb) was identified, potentially responsible parties (PRPs) were encouraged to take appropriate response action.  If necessary, response activities were performed under Superfund.

All activities were coordinated with state and local authorities as well as other federal agencies such as the Centers for Disease Control (CDC), the National Institute for Occupational Safety and Health (NIOSH), the Food and Drug Administration (FDA), and the Federal Emergency Management Agency (FEMA). Community relations played an important role in all activities conducted during the identification, screening, and cleanup of dioxin-contaminated sites.

Table 1.  Relative Potency Factors Used in Estimating
2,3,7,8-TCDD Equivalents

| Compound(s) | Relative Potency Factor or TEF[a] |
|---|---|
| 2,3,7,8-TCDD | 1.0 |
| Other TCDDs[b] | 0.01 |
| Penta-CDDs | 0.5 |
| Hexa-CDDs | 0.04 |
| Hepta-CDDs | 0.001 |
| Octa-CDD | 0.000 |
| 2,3,7,8-TCDD | 0.1 |
| Other TCDFs[b] | 0.001 |
| Penta CDFs | 0.1 |
| Hexa-CDF | 0.01 |
| Hepta-CDFs | 0.001 |
| Octa-CDF | 0.000 |

[a] Relative potency factor for the most toxic 2,3,7,8-
substituted isomer.
TEF = toxic equivalence factor = relative toxicity
assigned.
CDD or CDF concentration x TEF = 2,3,7,8-TCDD equivalents.
[b] In situations where 2,3,7,8-TCDD or -TCDF was not
chemically analyzed in the sample, then TCDDs and TCDFs
will have a relative potency factor of 1.0 and 0.1,
respectively.

Results.  Originally, about 450 Tier 1 and 2 sites (50 production
sites and about 400 associated waste disposal sites) were expected.
After systematic searching, the number of sites has been more
clearly defined.  In total, there were 99 dioxin sites in Tiers 1
and 2.  Table 2 shows a breakdown of sites by tier (3):

Table 2.  Dioxin Sites by Tier

| Tier | Number of Sites |
|---|---|
| 1 | 11 |
| 1a | 53 |
| 2 | 9 |
| 2a | 26 |

Tier 1 and 2 sites are located in six of the ten EPA Regions.
Figure 1 is a graphic representation of dioxin-contaminated site
locations by Region (3).

Seventeen dioxin sites are on the current Superfund National
Priorities List (NPL); four more have been proposed in Updates 2
and 3 to the NPL.  Most of these NPL sites, such as Love Canal

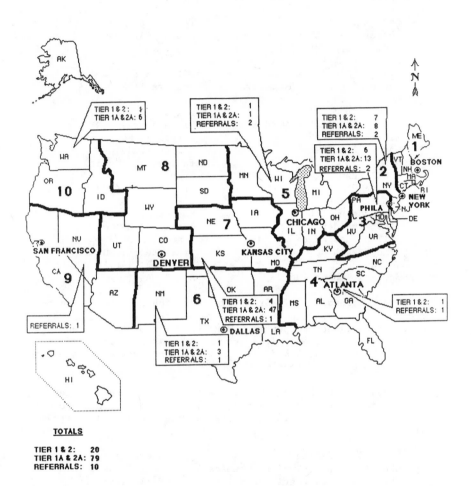

Figure 1. Regional Distribution of Dioxin Tier 1/Tier 2 Sites

in Niagara Falls, New York, are on the NPL for chemical contamination problems in addition to dioxin. The 21 sites on the NPL or proposed NPL (Updates 2 or 3) are (3):

| | |
|---|---|
| Cashel Residence | Fenton, MO |
| Conservation Chemical | Kansas City, MO (Update 3) |
| Diamond Shamrock | Newark, NJ |
| Drake Chemical | Lock Haven, PA |
| Fike Chemicals | Nitro, WV |
| Hooker Chemical (Hyde Park) | Niagara Falls, NY |
| Hooker Chemical (Love Canal) | Niagara Falls, NY |
| Hooker Chemical (S-Area) | Niagara Falls, NY |
| Hooker Chemical (102nd St.) | Niagara Falls, NY |
| Minker Residence | Imperial, MO |
| Moyers Landfill | Collegeville, PA |
| NIES | Furley, KS (Update 2) |
| Quail Run | Gray Summit, MO (Update 2) |
| Rohm & Haas | Bristol, PA (Update 3) |
| Romaine Creek | Imperial, MO |
| Shenandoah Stables | Moscow Mills, MO |
| Stout Residence | Imperial, MO |
| Sullins Residence | Fenton, MO |
| Times Beach | Times Beach, MO |
| Vertac | Jacksonville, AR |
| Western Processing | Kent, WA |

Under the National Dioxin Strategy, sites found to be contaminated in Tiers 3 through 7 are referred to the Office of Solid Waste and Emergency Response (OSWER) for possible Superfund (CERCLA) action. These sites are then considered along with the sites in Tiers 1 and 2 and all other hazardous waste sites managed under the Superfund program.

Additionally, the EPA Regions are responding to several sites, not identified through the National Dioxin Strategy, where dioxin may be present. Following is a list of the ten dioxin referral sites:

| | |
|---|---|
| Bogle Dioxin Site | Alexandria, VA |
| Chem All, Inc. (Sonford Chemical) | Port Neches, TX |
| Chemspray Inc. (Agrisystems) | Belleglade, FL |
| E.T.M. Enterprises | Grand Ledge, MI |
| (Parsons Chemical Works, Inc.) | |
| Farmingdale Garden Labs | Farmingdale, NY |
| Riverdale Chemical Co. | Chicago Heights, IL |
| Smith-Douglas | Norfolk, VA |
| Stauffer Chemical (Montrose Chemical) | Henderson, NV |
| Union Carbide Agricultural Products | St. Joseph, MO |
| W.A. Cleary | Somerset, NJ |

Of the 99 Tier 1 and 2 production and waste disposal sites, ten are classified as requiring "no further action" under the Strategy based on sampling results indicating very low or undetectable levels of 2,3,7,8-TCDD. These sites are:

| | |
|---|---|
| Calgon Corporation | Pasadena, TX |
| Drake Chemical | Lock Haven, PA |
| Eastman Kodak | Rochester, NY |
| Georges Creek | Poca, WV |
| GROWS | Morrisville, PA |
| Millmaster Onyx | Berkeley Heights, NJ |
| Moyers Landfill | Collegeville, PA |
| Rhone-Poulenc | Portland, OR |
| South Charleston Landfill | South Charleston, WV |
| Union Carbide | South Charleston, WV |

Of those sites where dioxin was detected at levels of concern, the most common materials contaminated were soil and dust. At certain sites, production waste, contaminated equipment, and contaminated building materials were found. As expected, these sites were generally the production facilities of Tiers 1 and 2 and those waste disposal sites where intact waste or scrapped equipment was stored or disposed. The majority of dioxin contamination at Tier 1, 1a, 2 and 2a sites remained on-site. Furthermore, the 2,3,7,8-TCDD was usually confined to areas where waste materials were stored, loaded, processed, or, in the case of 28 Missouri sites, sprayed on roads to control dust. In seven cases, offsite migration at levels of concern has been confirmed. They are:

| | |
|---|---|
| Diamond Shamrock | Newark, NJ |
| Brady Metals | Newark, NJ |
| Love Canal | Niagara Falls, NY |
| 102nd Street | Niagara Falls, NY |
| Hyde Park | Niagara Falls, NY |
| Vertac | Jacksonville, AR |
| Bliss Tank Property | Frontenac, MO |

Levels of Contamination.   Where 2,3,7,8-TCDD was detected, levels generally were highest in the vicinity of actual waste handling operations (e.g., processing, loading, and storage). At sites where concentrated 2,4,5-TCP production wastes were stored or disposed, 2,3,7,8-TCDD concentrations were as high as 356 ppm. At most sites, however, 2,3,7,8-TCDD levels in soil were usually in the ppb range. In fish samples from nearby lakes and streams, 2,3,7,8-TCDD was measured in terms of ppt.

Cleanup Activities.   Cleanup actions have focused on reducing potential exposure through inhalation or ingestion of dioxin-contaminated soils or dust. Many techniques have been developed and/or evaluated by the EPA Office of Research and Development (4) and have been employed by OSWER and others in cleanup activities.

Tier 3, Formulators

Tier 3 consists of facilities and associated waste disposal sites where 2,4,5-TCP and its derivatives were formulated into pesticidal products. Generally, these products are herbicides, insecticides, fungicides, and germicides:

| | |
|---|---|
| 2,4,5-trichlorophenol (2,4,5-TCP) | fungicide, bactericide |
| 2,4,5-trichlorophenoxyacetic acid (2,4,5-T) | plant hormone; herbicide; defoliant |
| silvex (2,4,5-TP) | herbicide; plant growth regulator |
| erbon | herbicide |
| ronnel | insecticide |
| hexachlorophene | topical anti-infective (restricted); germicidal soaps; veterinary medicine |
| isobac 20 | topical anti-infective (restricted); germicidal soaps; veterinary medicine |

Figure 2 depicts sampling locations nationally.

Findings.   EPA estimates that approximately 8 percent of the 312 facilities identified in the FATES database are contaminated above 1 ppb in soil or above detection limits of approximately 10 ppq - 1 ppt in other media. At dioxin-contaminated sites, the extent of contamination was usually limited to one or two soil samples with concentrations of 2,3,7,8-TCDD above 1 ppb. Only two Tier 3 sites were extensively contaminated and comprised large handlers of 2,4,5-T, 2,4,5-TP, or 2,4,5-TCP (5).

## Tier 4, Combustion Sources

This section summarizes the findings of Tier 4, the portion of the study dealing with combustion sources. Tier 4 was designed as a screening study to determine which combustion source categories emit CDDs and at what concentrations. The main focus was on releases to the ambient air; however, other samples, such as ash and scrubber water, were also obtained to determine if these compounds were released to other media. Because some combustion sources were known to emit a wide range of CDDs and CDFs, Tier 4 samples were analyzed for specific groups (homologs) of CDD and CDF compounds, as well as for 2,3,7,8-TCDD, the compound of most concern.

There are millions of combustion sources in the United States. Residential heating units burn oil, gas, coal and wood for heat. Larger commercial, institutional, and utility boilers burn fossil fuels to generate heat and electricity. Many industrial processes involve the combustion of fuels and other raw or waste materials to produce heat and/or recover products of marketable value. Other processes, such as incineration, use combustion to reduce the volume of unwanted waste products and to recover heat and

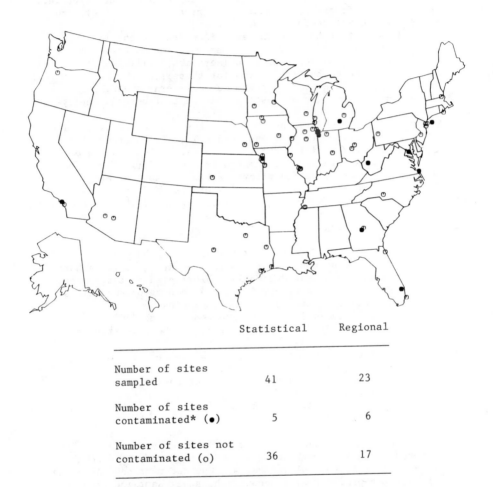

|                                     | Statistical | Regional |
|-------------------------------------|:-----------:|:--------:|
| Number of sites sampled             | 41          | 23       |
| Number of sites contaminated* (●)   | 5           | 6        |
| Number of sites not contaminated (o)| 36          | 17       |

*More than 1 ppb in soil or detectable
 levels in other media.

Figure 2. Locations of Sampled Tier 3 Sites.

other resources from the waste products. Open fires, both accidental (e.g., structural and forest fires) and intentional (i.e.,
those set for forest management and agricultural burning), are
other examples of combustion sources.

Assessment of CDD and CDF emissions from combustion sources
has received limited study. Previous work included studies of
emissions from hazardous waste incinerators, utility boilers, and
municipal waste combustion. Even for those source categories that
had previously been tested, there is considerable variation in
the extent and quality of testing and the test methods employed.

Study Design. The large number of combustion source categories
made it impractical to test each under Tier 4. A study plan was
developed that identified those source categories that were
believed to have the greatest potential for emitting CDDs to the
atmosphere. Selection and prioritization of source categories
for testing were based upon a review of CDD-related studies
reported in the literature and engineering judgment. Information
from this review suggested that the following conditions were
most important for CDD formation:

o  Presence of CDD in the materials being burned;
o  Presence of CDD precursors in the materials being burned
   (e.g., chlorinated phenols, chlorinated benzenes); and
o  Presence of chlorine, fuel, and combustion conditions
   conducive to CDD formation, including:
   °  Relatively low combustion temperature (500-800°C);
   °  Short residence time of fuel in the combustion zone
      (<1-2 seconds);
   °  Lack of adequate oxygen (resulting in incomplete
      combustion);
   °  Lack of adequate processing of fuels (e.g., burning of
      wet garbage); and
   °  Lack of supplemental fuel to promote combustion
      efficiency.

Consistent sample collection procedures were used at each site
selected. Sampling methodologies and procedures are described
in three Tier 4 protocol documents. One document describes the
ash sampling procedures; a second, the stack sampling procedures;
and a third, the quality assurance measures and procedures (6).
The stack testing method used at Tier 4 sampling sites is the
state-of-the-art method, with minor modifications, proposed for
use by a joint American Society of Mechanical Engineers (ASME)
and EPA Work Group for municipal incinerators.

Results. All planned sampling efforts for Tier 4 have been
completed. Approximately 350 CDD and CDF samples (20-25% of which
were for internal quality assurance purposes) were collected.
Thirteen sources were stack tested and 74 sites were tested under
the ash sampling program. Collected samples were sent to the
appropriate analytical laboratory in accordance with established
procedures.

The results from each of the 13 sites stack tested under Tier 4 are presented in Table 3. Data presented in this table represent concentrations of emissions measured in the stack gases and are not representative of ground-level concentrations where people reside. In addition, the specific 2,3,7,8-tetra isomers for both CDD and CDF are presented in the respective tables.

These CDD/CDF stack concentrations have been normalized to a uniform stack oxygen concentration of 3 percent. This method removes the effect of dilution and is a more representative means of comparing what is being produced by the various combustion processes.

Table 4 lists the Tier 4 source in descending order of measured 2,3,7,8-TCDD concentration and provides total CCD and CDF concentrations.

Findings. This investigation included a review of information in the literature, as well as a sampling program designed to collect data for combustion source categories believed to have the greatest potential to emit CDDs and CDFs. Although all of the data have yet to be analyzed and fully interpreted, the following findings can be made:

o   CDDs and CDFs are present in stack emissions from all sources tested in Tier 4 and most, but not all, of the combustion source categories reported in the literature.

o   There is considerable variability in emission rates both among source categories and, in some instances, sources within the same source category. For example, the CDD emissions range from "nondetected" at seven coal-fired power plants tested (detection limit at less than 1 ng/dscm) to approximately 12,000 ng/dscm of total CDDs at a secondary copper smelter facility. Most of the combustion source categories fall within an intermediate range, generally two to three orders of magnitude less than the concentration at the secondary copper smelting facility.

o   There is also considerable variability in the estimated risk to people residing in the vicinity of the sources tested. For most sources, risks to the most exposed individual were relatively low, i.e., in the range of $10^{-6}$ to $10^{-10}$.

o   CDD and CDF emissions from some sources have estimated risks to the most exposed individual of $10^{-5}$ or more. These sources include a secondary copper smelting facility, a sewage sludge incinerator, and some municipal incinerators. These findings are presently being considered by EPA with regard to whether CDD should be listed as a hazardous air pollutant under Section 112 of the Clean Air Act.

Table 3.  Tier 4 CDD/CDF Stack Testing Results (6)  (ng/dscm @ 3% O2)[a]

| Source | 2,3,7,8-TCDD/ 2,3,7,8-TCDF | Chlorinated Dibenzo-p-dioxin/Dibenzofuran Homologs | | | | | | Total[b] Tetra-Octa |
| --- | --- | --- | --- | --- | --- | --- | --- | --- |
| | | Other Tetra- | Penta- | Hexa- | Hepta- | Octa- | | |
| Drum and Barrel Furnace | 0.05/0.90 | 1.2/14 | 0.72/6.2 | 0.79/3.0 | 1.3/2.0 | 0.92/0.55 | | 5.0/27 |
| Industrial Carbon Regenerator | ND[c]/ND[c] | 0.57/1.2 | 0.44/0.37 | 0.98/0.59 | 0.90/0.61 | 0.81/0.54 | | 3.7/3.3 |
| Industrial Waste Incinerator | 4.5/21 | 77/570 | 100/610 | 150/650 | 230/470 | 61/66 | | 630/2400 |
| Kraft Paper Recovery Boilers | | | | | | | | |
| Plant A | ND/0.02 | ND/0.16 | ND/0.06 | 0.06/0.07 | 0.18/0.16 | 0.49/0.13 | | 0.73/0.59 |
| Plant B | ND/0.01 | ND/0.13 | ND/ND | 0.10/0.34 | 0.26/0.17 | 0.83/0.07 | | 1.2 /0.71 |
| Plant C | ND/0.01 | 0.13/0.46 | 0.15/0.46 | 0.39/0.59 | 0.88/0.50 | 1.4 /0.09 | | 2.9 /2.1 |
| Secondary Copper Smelter[d] | 170/ 5,100 | 1,400/ 18,000 | 2,300/ 19,000 | 2,200/ 6,000 | 5,900/ 11,000 | 3,700/ 7,200 | | 16,000/ 65,000 |
| Sewage Sludge Incinerators | | | | | | | | |
| Plant A | 0.05/NR[e] | 11/33 | 0.18/10 | 0.51/0.10 | 2.5 /0.50 | 5.3 /0.10 | | 20/44 |
| Plant B | ND/2.1 | 0.40/19 | ND/4.8 | ND/1.6 | 0.22/ND | 0.98/0.07 | | 1.6/28 |
| Plant C | 0.14/54 | 8.1/150 | 1.1 /110 | 7.0 /32 | 21/60 | 15/45 | | 53/450 |
| Wire Reclamation Incinerator[d] | 0.07/0.40 | 1.2 /29 | 2.2 /22 | 14/65 | 130/230 | 290/230 | | 440/580 |
| Wood-fired Boiler (Salt laden wood) | 0.28/1.8 | 47/37 | 48/33 | 49/13 | 39/6.5 | 11/0.92 | | 220/83 |
| Wood Stoves | NR[e]/NR[e] | NR/NR | NR/NR | NR/NR | NR/NR | NR/NR | | NR/NR |

a = ng/dscm @ 3% O2, nanograms per standard cubic meter of flue gas, normalized to 3-percent oxygen.

b = values across may not add up to totals due to rounding off.

c = ND, not detected, usually at less than 0.1 ng/dscm @3% O2.

d = Estimated values; stack sampling results for this site do not meet analytical quality assurance objectives, but represent lower level estimates.

e = NR, not reported due to organic interference.

Table 4. Tier 4 and Other Sources Listed in Rank Order by
2,3,7,8-TCDD Concentrations (6) (ng/dscm @ 3% $O_2$)[a]

| Source | 2,3,7,8-TCDD | Total CDDs | Total CDFs |
|---|---|---|---|
| *Secondary Copper Smelter[b] | 170 | 16,000 | 65,000 |
| Municipal Waste Incinerator-Plant B | 26 | 6,400 | 11,600 |
| Municipal Waste Incinerator-Plant E | 16 | 4,300 | 5,300 |
| *Industrial Waste Incinerator | 4.5 | 630 | 2,400 |
| Hazardous Waste Incinerator | 1.4 | 77 | 190 |
| Municipal Waste Incinerator-Plant D | 0.8 | 710 | 150 |
| Municipal Waste Incinerator-Plant A | 0.7 | 53 | 260 |
| *Wood-fired Boiler | 0.28 | 200 | 83 |
| *Sewage Sludge Incinerator-Plant C | 0.14 | 53 | 450 |
| *Wire Reclamation Incinerator | 0.07 | 440 | 580 |
| *Sewage Sludge Incinerator-Plant A | 0.05 | 20 | 44 |
| *Drum and Barrel Furnace | 0.05 | 5 | 27 |
| Hospital Incinerator | ND[c] | 330 | 735 |
| Municipal Incinerator-Plant F | NR[d] | 210 | 250 |
| Municipal Incinerator-Plant C | NR | 46 | 120 |
| *Industrial Carbon Regenerator | ND | 3.7 | 3.3 |
| Municipal Carbon Regenerator | ND | 3.3 | 4.8 |
| *Kraft Paper Recovery Boiler-Plant C | ND | 2.9 | 2.1 |
| *Sewage Sludge Incinerator-Plant B | ND | 1.6 | 28 |
| *Kraft Paper Recovery Boiler-Plant B | ND | 1.2 | 0.7 |
| *Kraft Paper Recovery Boiler-Plant A | ND | 0.7 | 0.6 |
| (Co-fired Boiler) | ND | ND | ND |
| Coal-fired Utility Boilers | NR | ND | ND |
| (7 plants) | | | |

[a] ng/dscm @ 3% $O_2$ = nanograms per standard cubic meter of flue gas
normalized to 3 percent oxygen.
[b] Data reported for this site are "estimated minimum." The true
value may be higher.
[c] ND = Not detected, generally at less than 1 ng/dscm @ 3% $O_2$.
[d] NR = Not reported.

o Considering the fact that Tier 4 focused on source categories and individual sources that were generally believed
to have an above-average potential to emit CDD compounds,
the results suggest that routine emissions of CDD and CDF
compounds from many combustion source categories may not
present a significant problem. However, since only a
relatively small number of sources were tested, some
sources that were not tested might also have CDD and CDF
emissions that could result in elevated risks.

Future Work. Although the majority of the planned Tier 4 study
has been completed, there are a number of continuing efforts that
EPA plans to pursue with respect to CDD emissions from combustion
sources. These include the following:

o A detailed technical report describing the Tier 4 program
will be prepared once all of the data (e.g., ash data)
has been analyzed and interpreted. Completion of the
Tier 4 technical report is scheduled for late 1986.

o  EPA is currently considering whether CDDs should be listed
   as a hazardous air pollutant category.  A decision on
   whether to list CDD is expected by spring of 1987.
o  EPA has a project underway to respond to the requirements
   of Section 102 of the Hazardous and Solid Waste Act of 1984
   (HSWA) concerning CDD emissions from municipal incinerators.
   This effort is intended to identify design and operating
   guidelines to minimize CDD emissions.
o  EPA will continue to coordinate with other environmental
   protection agencies (e.g., Environment Canada and the State
   of New York) in order to obtain the CDD/CDF test data that
   are currently being collected.  It is expected that data
   for several municipal incinerator tests will be released by
   New York State later in 1986.
o  EPA plans to continue its efforts to standardize and refine
   stack sampling and analytical procedures that will reflect
   improvements in the state-of-the-art.  The recommended ASTM
   stack test methodologies for municipal incinerators are
   currently under EPA review and evaluation.

## Tier 5, Use Sites

Tier 5 sites comprise areas where 2,4,5-TCP and pesticidal
derivatives (including 2,4,5-T, Silvex, hexachlorophene, Erbon,
Ronnel, and Isobac 20) were or are being used on a commercial
basis.  In this tier, a statistical sample was not possible due
to the variety uses and conditions.

Tier 5 sampling was generally limited to those areas where
the use of 2,4,5-T or Silvex has been documented, since information
from the EPA Office of Pesticide Programs indicated that these two
compounds have been more heavily used in specific areas and thus
have a greater potential for causing significant human exposure to
dioxin.  The other compounds were of lesser interest due to:
(a) low levels of active ingredient pesticide in the end-products;
(b) use on very small areas; or (c) a wide diversity of uses at low
levels of application.  Lack of documentation on use also made it
impractical to focus on these other compounds.

A total of 26 Tier 5 sites was sampled, including six forest
sites, seven rice fields, two canals adjacent to sugarcane fields,
one sugarcane field, three rights-of-way, three rangeland areas,
one multiple use area, and three aquatic sites (used for recreation,
fisheries, or multiple uses).

The environmental media to be sampled were determined by the
EPA regional offices on a site-by-site basis.  They included soils,
stream sediments, fish tissue, vegetation, and animal tissue.  All
analyses were done at detection levels of approximately 1 ppt,
because soil concentrations below 1 ppb can be of concern in certain
types of areas, such as grazing lands.

Results.  2,3,7,8-TCDD has been detected at 15 of the 26 sites
including two rights-of-way, one aquatic use site, two sugarcane
fields, canals adjacent to one sugarcane field, four rice fields,
three forest areas, one rangeland area, and one multiple use area.

Over 40 percent of the soil and sediment samples taken at contaminated sites had 2,3,7,8-TCDD present above the detection limit of approximately 1 ppt (5). Two sites had detectable levels in fish. At one of these, all fish samples were contaminated at levels up to 23 ppt in filets. 2,3,7,8-TCDD levels in soils at contaminated sites were between 0.6 and 564 ppt with 67 percent below 5 ppt; levels in sediments were between 0.7 and 200 ppt with 61 percent below 5 ppt; and levels in fish filets were between 8 and 23 ppt. No 2,3,7,8-TCDD was detected in animal tissue or vegetation samples collected from land used for grazing or raising crops; however, only a limited number of these samples was collected.

Findings. Since the source of 2,3,7,8-TCDD at the one severely contaminated Tier 5 site (Petenwell Flowage, Wisconsin) does not appear to be related to pesticide use, further national investigation of Tier 5 sites does not appear to be warranted. However, as described in greater detail under the Tier 7 discussion, further investigations of pulp and paper mills are being conducted.

## Tier 6, "Other" Chemical Manufacturers

Tier 6 consists of organic chemical and pesticide manufacturing facilities where improper quality control within production processes could cause products or waste streams to become contaminated with 2,3,7,8-TCDD. Facilities producing any of sixty selected compounds were identified. The objective of the sampling for this tier was to determine the percentage of facilities with concentrations of 2,3,7,8-TCDD above 1 ppb in soil or at detectable levels in other environmental media (e.g., fish in nearby streams).

Findings. EPA estimates that 9 percent of the 66 facilities originally identified as Tier 6 sites are contaminated. None of the three sites was extensively contaminated with 2,3,7,8-TCDD (5). Based on these findings, further national investigation of Tier 6 sites for 2,3,7,8-TCDD does not appear to be warranted.

## Tier 7, Background Sites

Tier 7 consists of sites that did not have previously known sources of 2,3,7,8-TCDD contamination. The Tier 7 investigation was intended to establish the prevalence of 2,3,7,8-TCDD in the environment and to provide a basis for comparison with results from the other tiers. The specific objectives of the sampling were to:

o Determine the percentage of sites in the EPA Urban and Rural Soil Networks that have detectable levels of 2,3,7,8-TCDD in soil at a detection limit of approximately 1 ppt.
o Determine the percentage of sites in the combined U.S. Geological Survey's (USGS) National Stream Quality Accounting Network and Benchwork Network that have detectable levels of 2,3,7,8-TCDD in fish tissue at a detection limit of approximately 1 ppt.

Findings. Of the statistically selected soil sites, 142 of 200
rural and 221 of 300 urban sites were sampled. The remaining 58
rural sites and 79 urban sites could not be sampled because of
difficulty in locating the site (130 sites) or because permission
to collect a sample was denied (7 sites). Of the 100 statistically
selected fish sites, 90 were sampled. The remaining ten sites
could not be sampled because of lack of water, fish, or success in
catching fish at the time sampling was attempted.

### Soil

° 2,3,7,8-TCDD was detected infrequently and at very low levels
  in background soil samples. 17 of 221 urban sites and 1 of
  138 rural sites had detectable levels, with the highest level
  found being 11.2 ppt (5).

### Fish

° 2,3,7,8-TCDD was detected more frequently in background fish
  samples. EPA estimates that 21 percent of the USGS national
  national monitoring network sites have detectable levels.
  The frequency of detection is greater (31 percent) at sites
  selected by EPA's regional offices, many of which are near
  industrial and urban areas.

° An even higher proportion (23 of 29) of Great Lakes' fish
  sampling sites had detectable levels, which is consistent
  with previous findings and is not surprising since the type
  and size of fish sampled in the Great Lakes and the long
  water retention times tend to increase the potential for
  bioaccumulation.

° 2,3,7,8-TCDD levels in filet samples could be a cause for
  concern at specific locations under certain consumption
  patterns; local exposure conditions need to be evaluated to
  determine a level of concern for those areas.

° Fish and shellfish from estuarine and coastal waters are
  rarely contaminated; two of the three sites where 2,3,7,8-
  TCDD was detected are in areas heavily influenced by
  industrial discharges.

° Certain types of pulp and paper mill discharges need to
  be further evaluated as possible sources of 2,3,7,8-TCDD.
  Both EPA and the industry are undertaking more detailed
  investigations.

### Summary of Pertinent Regulations

As defined in the RCRA dioxin-listing rule (7), which became
effective on July 15, 1985, the waste streams designated as
acutely hazardous are:

F020 – Wastes (except wastewater and spent carbon from HCl purification) from the production or manufacturing use (as a reactant, chemical intermediate, or component in a formulating process) of tri- or tetrachlorophenol, or of intermediates used to produce their pesticide derivatives. (This listing does not include wastes from the production of hexachlorophene from highly purified 2,4,5-TCP.)

F021 – Wastes (except wastewater and spent carbon from HCl purification) from the production or manufacturing use (as a reactant, chemical intermediate, or component in a formulating process) of pentachlorophenol, or of intermediates used to produce its derivatives.

F022 – Wastes (except wastewater and spent carbon from HCl purification) from the manufacturing use (as a reactant, chemical intermediate, or component in a formulating process) of tetra-, penta-, or hexachlorobenzenes under alkaline conditions.

F023 – Wastes (except wastewater and spent carbon from HCl purification) from the production of materials on equipment previously used for the production or manufacturing use (as a reactant, chemical intermediate, or component in a formulating process) of tri- and tetrachlorophenols. (This listing does not include wastes from equipment used only for the production or use of hexachlorophene from highly purified 2,4,5-TCP.)

F026 – Wastes (except wastewater and spent carbon from HCl purification) from the production of materials on equipment previously used for the manufacturing use (as a reactant, chemical intermediate, or component in a formulating process) of tetra-, penta-, or hexachlorobenzene under alkaline conditions.

F027 – Discarded unused formulations containing tri-, tetra-, or pentachlorophenol or discarded unused formulations containing compounds derived from these chlorophenols. (This listing does not include formulations containing hexachlorophene synthesized from prepurified 2,4,5-TCP as the sole component.)

F028 – Residues resulting from incineration or thermal treatment of soil contaminated with EPA hazardous waste codes F020, F021, F022, F023, F026, and F027.

Moreover, this rule replaced the regulation concerning the disposal of 2,3,7,8-TCDD-contaminated waste under the Toxic Substances Control Act (TSCA)--the so-called Vertac Rule--which was revoked on the same date. Unfortunately, the dioxin-listing rule currently does not cover thermally stressed PCBs, a source of CDDs and CDFs

from transformer and capacitor fires (8) and in abandoned hazardous
waste sites. The rule, however, may be modified to list this
category in the future.

Land disposal of the listed wastes must be conducted pursuant
to additional special standards implemented during the course of
the permit proceeding. Since all of these wastes are specifically
identified as candidates for being banned from land disposal in two
years under the Hazardous and Solid Waste Amendment (HSWA) (see also
RCRA-amended Section 3004 (e) and (h)(4)), EPA proposed an interim
regulatory regime for their land disposal (9). This rule became
final on November 8, 1986, and, as a result, wastes identified by
the hazardous waste codes F020, F021, F022, F023, F026, F027, and
F028 must be treated to a level below 1 ppb in the waste extract
for each of the following specific categories of CDDs and CDFs:

    TCDD--tetrachlorodibenzo-p-dioxins
    TCDF--tetrachlorodibenzofurans
    PeCDD--pentachlorodibenzo-p-dioxins
    PeCDF--pentachlorodibenzofurans
    HxCDD--hexachlorodibenzo-p-dioxins
    HxCDF--hexachlorodibenzofurans

One ppb is the routinely achievable detection limit using method
8280 of SW-846: Test Methods for Evaluating Solid Waste Physical/
Chemical Methods (1982) (7, Appendix X). (In test method 8280,
the proposed quantification level for 2,3,7,8-TCDD in water is
10 ppt. However, due to the interferences inherent in leachate
samples and the variability of waste matrices, EPA considers
that, generally, CDD wastes subject to this rule will have a
detection limit of 1 ppb. It should be noted that because the
treatment standard for CDDs is set at "no detection," it is
important to calibrate to the levels specified in method 8280.
An interlaboratory validation of the method has recently been
conducted and reported (10).)

These listed wastes also must be treated below detection
limits for 2,4,5-trichlorophenol, 2,4,6-trichlorophenol, 2,3,4,6-
tetrachlorophenol, and pentachlorophenol. The detection limits
for these constituents are 50, 50, 100, and 10 ppb, respectively,
in the waste extracts using methods 3510/8270 identified in
SW-846.

EPA also is granting the maximum two-year variance to the
effective date of the land disposal restrictions (9) for dioxin-
containing wastes because of a finding that there is a lack of
capacity to treat and dispose of these wastes. Thus, the
effective date of this final rule is November 8, 1988.

Literature Cited

1.  U.S. Environmental Protection Agency (1983). Dioxin Strategy.
    Washington, DC, November 28.

2.  Bellin, J.S. and Barnes, D.G. (1985). Procedures for
    estimating risks associated with exposures to mixtures
    of chlorinated dibenzodioxins and -dibenzofurans (CDDs

and CDFs). Adopted by the Risk Assessment Forum, U.S. EPA, Washington, DC, November 21.

3. U.S. Environmental Protection Agency (1986). National Dioxin Strategy, Tier 1 and 2 Accomplishments. Draft Technical Support Document. Office of Solid Waste and Emergency Response, Washington, DC, January.

4. des Rosiers, P.E. (1985). Methodologies for materials contaminated with PCDDs and related compounds. Paper presented at the 5th International Symposium on Chlorinated Dioxins and Related Compounds, Bayreuth, Federal Republic of Germany, September 16–19.

5. U.S. Environmental Protection Agency (1986). The National Dioxin Study, Tiers 3, 5, 6, and 7. Draft Final Report. Office of Water Regulations and Standards, Washington, DC, April.

6. U.S. Environmental Protection Agency (1986). National Dioxin Study, Tier 4--Combustion Sources. Draft Project Summary Report. Office of Air Quality Planning and Standards, Research Triangle Park, NC, April.

7. U.S. Federal Register (1985), 50 (9), 1978–2006.

8. des Rosiers, P.E., Westfall, B., Campbell, B. and Lee, A. (1986). PCB fires: preliminary correlation of chlorobenzene and PCB contents of the fluid with PCDF and PCDD contents of soot. In: Proceedings: 1985 EPRI PCB Seminar, EPRI CS/EA/EL-4480, Project 2028, March, 7-26--7-39.

9. U.S. Federal Register (1986), 51 (9), 1602–1766.

10. Ballard, J.M., Vonnahme, T.L., Nunn, N.J., Youngman, D.R. and Billets, Stephen (1986). Performance of RCRA Method 8280 for the analysis of dibenzo-p-dioxins and dibenzofurans in hazardous waste samples. EPA/600/S4-86/021, July.

RECEIVED December 10, 1986

# Chapter 4

# Animal Toxicity Studies
## of 2,3,7,8-Tetrachlorodibenzo-*p*-dioxin
### Derivation of Lifetime Exposure Control Limit Recommendations for Humans

R. J. Kociba

Health and Environmental Sciences, Dow Chemical Company, Midland, MI 48674

Of the multiple toxicity studies performed with TCDD, those deemed most useful as the basis for derivation of human lifetime exposure control limit recommendations are the animal lifetime dose-response (carcinogenicity) studies, and the mechanistic studies wherein TCDD has been categorized as not being a mutagen nor possessing potential to interact directly with DNA. Multiple studies concur in reporting that the carcinogenic response noted in the animal studies with TCDD was reflective of a promoter mechanism rather than an initiator mechanism. While control limit recommendations for TCDD were originally derived by some regulatory agencies on a non-threshold assumption for extrapolation from the animal studies to humans, (assuming cancer initiation potential), more recently other regulatory agencies have utilized the newer data indicating a promoter (rather than initiator) mechanism as the valid basis for a threshold-based method of extrapolation from these animal studies to humans. Overall evaluation of all pertinent data indicates it is scientifically valid to derive the human lifetime control limit recommendations for TCDD through the use of a threshold-based process of extrapolation from the animal lifetime (carcinogenicity) studies.

Over the past fifteen years there have been extensive studies of the toxicologic properties of the 2,3,7,8-tetrachlorodibenzo-p-dioxin isomer (TCDD). Relatively speaking, less data are available for the other chlorinated dibenzo-p-dioxins and furans. These various toxicity studies have been the subject of several previous reviews (1, 2, 3, 4). The purpose of this present paper is to evaluate the basis upon which these animal toxicity studies have been utilized as the basis for extrapolation to man for the purpose of developing lifetime exposure limit control recommendations.

0097-6156/87/0338-0054$06.00/0

## Comparative Toxicity as Measured by Acute Lethality

The comparative data on the acute lethality of the chlorinated
dibenzo-p-dioxins and furans in laboratory animals are included in
Table I. Evaluation of these data indicates that TCDD is the most
toxic of this series. For the guinea pig, the single dose oral LD50
value is reported to be 0.6-2.0 µg/kg B.W., while in the hamster the
single dose oral LD50 value is reported to be 1157-5051 µg/kg B.W.
The biologic factors that account for this large difference (up to
5000 fold) in species susceptibility in acute toxicity have not yet
been defined. The other laboratory animal species (mouse, rat,
monkey, rabbit and dog) in which TCDD has been tested have single
dose oral LD50 values that are found to be somewhere between the most
sensitive species (guinea pig) and the least sensitive species
(hamster).
　　The question of likely sensitivity of man relative to the acute
toxicity of TCDD in various laboratory animals has been addressed
independently by Neal (17) and also by Tschirley (18). Both of these
scientists have concluded from data on inadvertent human exposures
that man appears to be less sensitive to TCDD than certain of the
laboratory animals, such as the guinea pig. It is important to note
that the most extensive animal studies of TCDD chronic
toxicity/carcinogenicity used for extrapolation to man have been
conducted with rats and mice, both of which represent species which
are relatively more sensitive to TCDD toxicity. This fact indicates
that the human exposure control limits derived from these chronic
toxicity/carcinogenicity studies conducted in rats and mice supply an
additional margin of safety inherent in the subsequent extrapolation
process to man. Table I also lists the single dose oral LD50 values
for the other chlorodibenzo-p-dioxins and furans that have been
reported. Those tetra, penta, hexa and hepta isomers with the 2,3,7,
and 8 positions chlorinated represent those isomers with greater
toxicity as compared to the lesser chlorinated or fully chlorinated
isomers that are considerably less toxic. This wide variation in
acute toxicity of one isomer relative to another isomer is typified
by the greater than six orders of magnitude differential between the
LD50 values of 0.6-2 µg/kg for TCDD and the LD50 value of $>15 \times 10^6$
µg/kg for the 1,3,6,8-tetrachlorodibenzo-p-dioxin when tested in the
very same species (guinea pig).

## Comparative Biologic Activity as Measured by In Vitro Tests

Tables II and III are summary compilations of the relative biologic
activities of chlorinated dibenzo-p-dioxins and furans, respectively,
as measured by in vitro tests such as enzyme induction, epithelial
keratinization or the "flat cell" effect in XB/3T3 cell cultures.
For comparative purposes, the biologic activity of each isomer is
expressed as a fraction relative to the biologic activity of TCDD in
each type of test. Inspection of these data indicate that as a
general rule the 2,3,7,8-substituted tetra, penta, hexa and hepta
isomers have typically elicited the higher levels of biologic
activity in these in vitro assays.

Table I. Comparative Single Oral Dose LD50 Values For Chlorodibenzo-p-Dioxin And Chlorodibenzo-p-Furan Isomers

| Chlorodibenzodioxin | Guinea Pig | Mouse | Rat | Oral LD50 Values (µg/kg) | | | | Ref. |
| --- | --- | --- | --- | --- | --- | --- | --- | --- |
| | | | | Monkey | Hamster | Rabbit | Dog | |
| 2,3,7,8-Tetra | 0.6-2 | 114-284 | 22-45 | 70 | 1157-5051 | 115 | >300,<3000 | (5,6,7,8,9) |
| Unsub | | >50,000 | >1,000,000 | | | | | (10,11) |
| 2,3-Di | | | >1,000,000 | | | | | (11) |
| 2,7-Di | | | >1,000,000 | | | | | (11) |
| 2,8-Di | >300,000 | >2,000,000 | >1,000,000 | | | | | (5) |
| 1,3,7-Tri | | 8,470,000 | >5,000,000 | | | | | (6,12) |
| 2,3,7-Tri | | >15,000,000 | >5,000,000 | | | | | (12) |
| 1,2,3,4-Tetra | 29,444 | >3,000 | >1,000,000 | | | | | (6,11) |
| 1,3,6,8-Tetra | >15,000,000 | | >10,000,000 | | | | | (11) |
| 1,2,3,7,8-Penta | 3.1 | >2,987,000 | | | | | | (13) |
| 1,2,4,7,8-Penta | 1,125 | 337.5 | | | | | | (6) |
| 1,2,3,4,7,8-Hexa | 72.5 | >5,000 | | | | | | (6) |
| 1,2,3,6,7,8-Hexa | 70-100 | 825 | | | | | | (6) |
| 1,2,3,7,8,9-Hexa | 60-100 | 1250 | | | | | | (6) |
| 1,2,3,4,6,7,8-Hepta | >600 | >1440 | | | | | | (6) |
| Octa | | >4,000,000 | >1,000,000 | | | | | (5) |
| **Chlorodibenzofuran** | | | | | | | | |
| 2,8-Di | 5-10 | >15,000,000 | >15,000,000 | | | | | (12) |
| 2,4,8-Tri | <10 | >15,000,000 | >5,000,000 | | | | | (12) |
| 2,3,7,8-Tetra | 120 | >6000 | >1000 | 1000 | | | | (14,15) |
| 2,3,4,7,8-Penta | | | | | | | | (16) |
| 2,3,4,6,7,8-Hexa | | | | | | | | (16) |

Table II. Comparative Biologic Activity (In Vitro) Of Chlorodibenzo-p-dioxins Relative To TCDD

| Chlorodibenzo-p-dioxin | AHH Activity in Rat Hepatoma Cells | AHH Activity in Chick Embryo Liver | ALA Synthetase in Chick Embryo Liver | Keratinization of XB/3T3 Cells |
|---|---|---|---|---|
| 2,3,7,8-Tetra | 1/1 | 1/1 | 1/1 | 1/1 |
| Unsub. | Inactive | Inactive | Inactive | Inactive |
| 1-Chloro |  | Inactive | Inactive | Inactive |
| 1,3-Di | Inactive | Inactive | Inactive | Inactive |
| 1,6-Di | Inactive | Inactive | Inactive | Inactive |
| 2,3-Di | Inactive | Inactive | Inactive | Inactive |
| 2,7-Di | Inactive | Inactive | Inactive |  |
| 2,8-Di | Inactive | Inactive | Inactive |  |
| 1,2,4-Tri | 1/920-1/3060 | 1/1666 | Inactive | 1/100 |
| 2,3,7-Tri | 1/57-1/242 | 1/12 | Active | 1/100 |
| 1,3,7,8-Tetra | 1/1666-1/5900 |  |  |  |
| 1,2,3,4-Tetra | Inactive | Equiv. | Inactive | Inactive |
| 1,3,6,8-Tetra | Inactive | Inactive | Inactive | 1/2 |
| 1,2,3,7,8-Penta | 1/5-1/53 | Active | Active |  |
| 1,3,4,7-Penta | 1/21-1/132 |  |  |  |
| 1,2,4,7,8-Penta | Inactive |  |  |  |
| 1,2,3,6,7,9-Hexa | Inactive | Inact./Equiv. | Inact./Equiv. |  |
| 1,2,4,6,7,9-Hexa | 1/10-1/20 | Active | Active |  |
| 1,2,3,4,7,8-Hexa | 1/114-1/523 | 1/5 |  | 1/200 |
| 1,2,3,7,8,9-Hexa | 1/71-1/947 |  |  |  |
| 1,2,3,6,7,8-Hexa | 1/10,200 |  |  |  |
| 1,2,3,4,6,7,9-Hepta | 1/282-1/367 |  |  |  |
| 1,2,3,4,6,7,8-Hepta | 1/1666-1/4594 |  |  |  |
| Octa (99.2%) | 1/53,000 | Inactive | Inactive |  |
| Octa (>99%) |  |  |  |  |
|  | (Ref. 19, 20) | (Ref. 21, 22, 23) |  | (Ref. 24) |

Biologic Activity expressed as fractions relative to TCDD (1/1).

Table III. Comparative Biologic Activity (In Vitro) Of Chlorodibenzofurans Relative To TCDD

| Chlorodioxin/furan | AHH Activity in Rat Hepatoma Cells | AHH Activity in Chick Embryo Liver | Keratinization of XB/3T3 Cells | Flat Cell Effect in XBF/3T3 Cells |
|---|---|---|---|---|
| 2,3,7,8-Tetra Dioxin | 1/1 | 1/1 | 1/1 | 1/1 |
| Chlorodibenzofuran | | | | |
| Unsub. | Inactive | Inactive | | |
| 2,8-Di | Inactive | Inactive | Inactive | |
| 2,4-Di | | Inactive | | <1/743 |
| 2,6-Di | | Inactive | | |
| 2,4,8-Tri | | | Inactive | |
| 2,3,8-Tri | 1/20,714 | | | |
| 2,4,6-Tri | Inactive | | | |
| 1,4,6,8-Tetra | Inactive | | | |
| 1,3,6,7-Tetra | | Inactive | | |
| 2,3,6,8-Tetra | Inactive | | | |
| 2,4,6,8-Tetra | Inactive | | | |
| 2,3,7,8-Tetra | 1/92 | 2/3 | 1/20 | 1/10 |
| 1,2,3,7,8-Penta | 1/1,928 | 1/7 | | |
| 1,3,4,7,8-Penta | | | | |
| 2,3,4,8- | | 7/10 | | |
| 1,2,4,7,8-Penta | 1/31,428 | | | |
| 2,3,4,6,7,8-Hexa | 1/24,286 | | | 1/118 |
| 1,2,3,4,6,8,9-Hepta | | | | |
| Octa | | | | 1/1400 |
| | (Ref. 19) | (Ref. 21) | (Ref. 24) | (Ref. 25) |

Biologic Activity expressed as fractions relative to TCDD (1/1).

## Development and Interim Use of Toxicity Equivalent Factors

It is this type of comparative in vitro data on biologic activity as
summarized in Tables II and III that has been used as the basis for
deriving the concept of Toxicity Equivalent Factors (TEF) that has
been proposed by certain regulatory agencies in lieu of generating
chronic toxicity data on each isomer of concern. Table IV depicts
the TEFs currently being proposed by US EPA for the
chlorodibenzo-p-dioxins and furans (26). Although the concept of
using the TEF (derived from short term or in vitro tests) may seem to
be a readily available and attractive interim procedure, two recent
studies have both reported a lack of correlation between the TEF
predicted toxicity and the actual toxicity observed in subchronic
animal studies. The first of these two studies has been reported by
Doyle and Friess (27) and is summarized in Table V. In these studies
the subchronic animal toxicity actually observed was considerably
less than what had been predicted by the enzyme induction assays.
Suter-Hofman (28) also reported a lack of correlation between the
toxicity predicted by the use of TEF when compared to the actual
toxicity observed in a subchronic toxicity test wherein animals were
given a mixture of dioxin and furan isomers. In this study, a
toluene extract of municipal incineration particulate emissions was
fed to rats. Analysis indicated the extract to contain 2,3,7,8-TCDD
as well as additional chlorinated dioxins and furans at
concentrations that were calculated to be supplying a dose level of
65 ng of 2,3,7,8-TCDD/kg BW/day or a composite dose level
representing all the chlorinated dioxins and furans of 2000 ng of
2,3,7,8-TCDD TEF/kg BW/day. Using previous rat toxicity studies with
2,3,7,8-TCDD as the reference point, the extract caused only a slight
degree of toxicity of the magnitude predicted for a dose level of 65
ng of 2,3,7,8-TCDD/kg BW/day. The severe toxicity and lethality
predicted by the use of the TEF scheme to be associated with a
composite dose level of 2000 ng of 2,3,7,8-TCDD TEF/kg BW/day was not
observed in the rats. Thus, it appears as if the 2,3,7,8-TCDD TEF
scheme (based on in vitro assays) for total chlorinated dioxins and
furans substantially overpredicts the actual toxicity observed when
in vivo studies of combinations of multiple dioxins and furans are
conducted.

## Other Toxicity Data on TCDD and Related Compounds

The extensive toxicologic data available on TCDD and other dioxin and
furan isomers from animal tests for rabbit ear chloracnegenicity,
teratogenicity/fetotoxicity, reproductive toxicity, mutagenicity,
clastogenicity, and carcinogenicity have been compiled and reviewed
in previous publications (1, 2, 3, 4). Because of space limitations
these data cannot be completely reviewed here, and the previous
reviews should be consulted for specific details. Overall, the
concensus is that the qualitative and quantitative aspects of these
various toxicologic endpoints have been adequately defined for TCDD.

Table IV. Toxicity Equivalent Factors (TEF) Proposed By U.S. EPA
For Isomers Of Most Interest

| Isomer | TEF[a] | Isomer | TEF |
|---|---|---|---|
| 2,3,7,8-TCDD | 1 | 2,3,7,8-TCDF | 0.1 |
| 1,2,3,7,8-PeCDD | 0.5 | 1,2,3,7,8-PeCDF | 0.1 |
|  |  | 2,3,4,7,8-PeCDF | 0.1 |
| 1,2,3,4,7,8-HxCDD | 0.04 | 1,2,3,4,7,8-HxCDF | 0.01 |
| 1,2,3,7,8,9-HxCDD | 0.04 | 1,2,3,7,8,9-HxCDF | 0.01 |
| 1,2,3,6,7,8-HxCDD | 0.04 | 1,2,3,6,7,8-HxCDF | 0.01 |
|  |  | 2,3,4,6,7,8-HxCDF | 0.01 |
| 1,2,3,4,6,7,8-HpCDD | 0.001 | 1,2,3,4,6,7,8-HpCDF | 0.001 |
|  |  | 1,2,3,4,7,8,9-HpCDF | 0.001 |

In each homologous group the relative toxicity for the isomers not listed above is 1/100 of the value listed above.

[a]TEF = Toxic Equivalent Factor = relative toxicity assigned.

(Ref. 26)

Table V. Lack Of Predictive Correlation Between AHH Enzyme Induction And 90 Day Feeding Studies In Rats

| Chlorodioxin/Furan | Rat Liver AHH Enzyme Induction Activity Relative to TCDD | Comparative Results of 90-Day Feeding Studies in Rats |
|---|---|---|
| 2,3,7,8-TCDD | 1/1 | 30 ppb-Expected toxic syndrome, with 25-50% mortality, wt. loss, adverse effects on organ wts, blood and serum parameters |
| 2,3,7,8-TCDF | 1/2 | 60 ppb-Only minor effects-Increased relative liver wts in males |
| 2,7-DiCDF | 1/2 | 60 ppb-No significant effects |
| 2,8-DiCDF | 1/5 | 60 ppb-No significant effects |
| OctaCDF | 1/5 | 60 ppb-No significant effects |
| 1,2,4,7,8-PentaCDF | Inactive | 60 ppb-No significant effects |
| 1,2,3,4,6,7,9-HeptaCDF | Inactive | 60 ppb-No significant effects |

Results of 90 day feeding studies indicate these chlorodibenzo furans were considerably less toxic than might be predicted from their AHH enzyme induction activity. (Ref. 27).

## Use of Animal Toxicity Data for Deriving Exposure Control Limit Recommendations For Humans

For purposes of this review the emphasis will be on those toxicity studies upon which long term or chronic lifetime exposure control limit recommendations have been derived. Thus, the animal data on reproductive toxicity (29, 1, 4), chronic toxicity and carcinogenicity (30, 2, 3), mutagenicity (2, 3, 31) and related mechanistic data (2, 3) are the most pertinent to this discussion. TCDD, as well as various other chlorinated dioxins and furans have been studied extensively in various assays designed to detect mutagenic and clastogenic types of activity. The preponderance of these multiple studies indicates that TCDD (and the other dioxins and furans) does not possess any significant mutagenic/clastogenic potential (2, 3, 4, 31). Other studies have reported a lack of covalent binding of TCDD to DNA or RNA, with maximal binding potential 4-6 orders of magnitude less than most genotoxic carcinogens (32). Likewise, TCDD did not stimulate unscheduled DNA synthesis when tested in rat hepatocytes (33) or in a human cell line (34). The various studies with TCDD in regard to tumor initiation, promotion and cocarcinogenesis that have been reviewed previously (2, 3, 4) indicate that TCDD is more correctly categorized as a tumor promoter rather than an initiator. Of the four chronic animal carcinogenesis studies that have been conducted with TCDD, the one that has been used by essentially all regulatory agencies for derivation of lifetime exposure control limit recommendations is the study by Kociba et al. (30). The pertinent results of that study are summarized in Table VI in a manner that correlates dose levels, observed response (carcinogenicity, toxicity, no-adverse effect level) and terminal tissue levels of TCDD. A lifetime daily dose level of 0.1 µg/kg/day of TCDD caused both toxicity and carcinogenicity, whereas a lifetime dose level of 0.01 µg/kg/day of TCDD caused some toxicity but no definitive carcinogenic response. A lifetime dose level of 0.001 µg/kg/day of TCDD caused no toxicity or carcinogenicity and was defined as the no-observed-adverse-effect-level (NOAEL) in this lifetime study in rats. The NOAEL of 0.001 µg/kg/day defined in this lifetime study (30) is the same NOAEL defined in a multigeneration reproduction study in rats (29). Using this lifetime study of TCDD in rats (30) the U.S. Environmental Protection Agency (EPA), U.S. Food and Drug Administration (FDA), U. S. Center for Disease Control (CDC), Ontario Ministry of the Environment (OMOE), Dutch Government, the Federal Republic of Germany and the Swiss Institute of Toxicology have all derived carcinogenicity based lifetime exposure control limit recommendations. Table VII is a compilation of these carcinogenicity-based control limit recommendations issued by these groups. The U.S. agencies have followed their previous policy decisions to regulate all suspect carcinogens on a non-threshold basis, and have utilized a multistage linearized model to calculate the upper limit lifetime cancer risk estimates. Data summarized in Table VII indicates that this modelling procedure projects that a "virtually safe dose" level of exposure (one additional cancer in one million lifetimes) equates with lifetime exposure to 0.0064, 0.0572 or 0.0276 pg/kg BW/day, respectively, depending on the assumptions

Table VI. Correlation Of Dosage, Response And Tissue Levels Of TCDD At Termination Of Two-Year Toxicity Study In Rats Used As Basis For Derivation Of Cancer-Based Lifetime Exposure Control Limit Recommendations

| Dose Levels of TCDD | | Response | | Terminal TCDD Content ppt | |
|---|---|---|---|---|---|
| μg/kg/day | ppt in Diet | Carcinogenicity | Other Toxicity | Fat | Liver |
| 0.1 | 2200 | Yes | Yes | 8100 | 24000 |
| 0.01 | 210 | No* | Yes | 1700 | 5100 |
| 0.001 | 22 | No | No | 540 | 540 |

*Maximal response of hyperplastic nodules of liver in female rats. (Ref. 30)

Table VII.  Procedures In Use For Extrapolation To Man From Chronic Animal Studies With TCDD

| Agency/Group | Source of Dose/Response Data | Mechanistic Basis for Extrapolation to Man | Results of Extrapolation Process |
|---|---|---|---|
| U.S. EPA (Ref. 35) | 2 year rat study Kociba et al. (Ref. 30) | Non Threshold, Linearized, Multi-stage model (dose/surface area) | V.S.D. for upper-limit cancer risk of $10^{-6}$=0.0064 pg/kg/day |
| U.S. FDA (Ref. 36) | Same | Non Threshold, Linearized, Multi-stage model (dose/body weight) | V.S.D. for upper-limit cancer risk of $10^{-6}$=0.0572 pg/kg/day |
| U.S. CDC (Ref. 37) | Same | Non Threshold, Linearized, Multi-stage Model (liver conc.) | V.S.D. for upper-limit cancer risk of $10^{-6}$=0.0276 pg/kg/day |
| Ontario (Ref. 38) | Same | Threshold, safety factor applied to NOEL | Maximal allowable daily intake=10 pg/kg/day |
| W. Germany (Ref. 39) | Same | Threshold, safety factor applied to NOEL | Max. daily intake= 1-10 pg/kg/day |
| Netherlands (Ref. 40) | Same | Threshold, safety factor applied to NOEL | Allowable daily intake= 4 pg/kg/day |
| Swiss Institute of Toxicology (Ref. 41) | Same | Threshold, safety factor applied to NOEL | Tolerable daily intake= 10 pg/kg/day max. |

inherent in each of the extrapolation procedures used by these 3 U.S. agencies.

In contrast to the U.S. agencies cited above, more recent risk assessments conducted by Ontario, West Germany, Dutch and Swiss agencies have used a threshold basis for extrapolation from the same chronic animal study (30). This threshold based extrapolation has been based on use of more recent mechanistic data indicating that TCDD is more correctly categorized as a cancer promoter with a threshold for its promoter activity rather than a cancer initiator. Using this threshold based extrapolation, the four non-U.S. regulatory agencies or groups listed in Table VII have established a lifetime acceptable daily intake (or maximum daily intake or allowable daily intake or tolerable daily intake) for TCDD (or its toxic equivalents) in the range of 1-10 pg/kg BW/day.

Review of all pertinent data indicates that, based on the demonstration that TCDD acts as a promoter rather than an initiator, a threshold-based safety factor approach is considered the most scientifically appropriate to be used with TCDD when setting an adequate margin of safety to protect the long-term health of the general population. In this regard, the threshold-based approach as utilized by the four non-U.S. agencies is considered the most valid basis for the animal to man extrapolation. In the report issued by the Ontario MOE (38) their expert panel concluded that TCDD produces tumors in rodents by an indirect mechanism, with a threshold level of dosage (0.001 µg/kg/day, or 1 ng/kg/day) below which an increased rate of tumor production due to exposure to TCDD would be unlikely. The NOAEL as defined in the chronic animal studies was used as an indication of where this threshold lies. To this NOAEL, application of a safety factor of 1/100 was considered appropriate in calculating the maximum allowable daily intake for lifetime exposure of humans. This 1/100 safety factor applied to the NOAEL incorporates a number of uncertainties in extrapolating from animal data to humans, particularly an allowance for those segments of the human population that may possibly have an increased level of sensitivity. Application of this 1/100 safety factor to the NOAEL (1 ng/kg/day or 1000 pg/kg/day) defined in the lifetime rat study (30) that is considered most definitive by essentially all of the regulatory agencies was the basis for the Ontario MOE expert panel to recommend a Maximum Daily Intake for 2,3,7,8-TCDD (or its toxic equivalent of other chlorinated dioxins and furans) of 10 pg/kg B.W./day for humans (38). This more recent approach used by these four non-U.S. groups demonstrate the manner in which carcinogenicity - based lifetime exposure control limit recommendations for humans can be realistically derived from the data available from the animal cancer bioassays when interpreted in concert with the data available regarding the likely mechanism of action by which the carcinogenic response occurred in the animal bioassays.

Literature Cited

1.   Kociba, R. J.; Schwetz, B. A. *Assoc. Fd. Drug Offic. Qrtrly,*
     *Bull.* 1982, 46, 168-188.

2.   Kociba, R. J.  In "Public Health Risks of the Dioxins";
     Lowrance, W. Ed.; Wm. Kaufmann: Los Altos, 1984, p. 77.
3.   Kociba, R. J.  In "Biological Mechanisms of Dioxin Action",
     Poland, A. and Kimbrough, R. D. Ed.; Banbury Center, Cold Spring
     Harbor Laboratory:  New York, 1984; p. 73.
4.   Kociba, R. J.; Cabey, O.  Chemosphere 1985, 14, 649-660.
5.   Schwetz, B. A.; Norris, J. M.; Sparschu, G. L.; Rowe, V. K.;
     Gehring, P. J.; Emerson, J. L.; Gergib, C. G.  Environ. Hlth.
     Perspect.  1973, 5, 87-99.
6.   McConnell, E. E.; Moore, J. A.; Haseman, J.; Harris, M. W.
     Toxicol. Appl. Pharmacol.  1978, 44, 335-356.
7.   McConnell, E. E.; Moore, J. A.; Dalgard, D. W.  Toxicol. Appl.
     Pharmacol.  1978, 43, 175-187.
8.   Henck, J. W.; New, M. A.; Kociba, R. J.; Rao, K. S.  Toxicol.
     Appl. Pharmacol.  1981, 59, 405-407.
9.   Olson, J. R.; Holscher, M. A.; Neal, R. A.  Toxicol. Appl.
     Pharmacol.  1980, 55, 67-78.
10.  Courtney, K. D.  Bull. Environ. Contam. Toxicol.  1976, 16,
     674-681.
11.  Saint-Ruff, S.  In "Dioxin:  Toxicological and Chemical
     Aspects"; Cattabeni, F., Cavallaro, A., Galli, G., Ed.; Spectrum
     Public:  New York, 1978, Chapter 15, p. 77.
12.  Bernstein, M.  Summary of Toxicity Data, Ciba Geigy Corp., New
     Jersey, 1981.
13.  Kawamura, K.; Sato, R.; Koshima, M.  Oyo Yakuri  1983, 25,
     703-711.
14.  "Toxicity of 2,3,7,8-Tetrachlorodibenzofuran-Preliminary
     Results"  U. S. EPA Report 56016-75-004, 1976.
15.  Moore, J. A.; McConnell, E. E.; Dalgard, D. W.; Harris, M. W.
     Ann. N.Y. Acad. Sci.  1979, 320, 151-163.
16.  McKinney, J.; McConnell, E. E.  In "Chlorinated Dioxins and
     Related Compounds"; Hutzinger, O., Frei, R. W., Merian, E.,
     Pocchiara, F., Ed.: Pergamon Press: New York, 1981; p. 367-381.
17.  Neal, R.  Interim Report of the Missouri Dioxin Task Force,
     1983, p. 40-41.
18.  Tschirley, F. H.  Scientific American  1986, 254, 29-35.
19.  Bradlaw, J.; Casterline, J.  J. Assoc. Off. Analyt. Chem.  1979,
     62, 904-916.
20.  Bradlaw, J.; Garthoff, L.; Hurley, H.; Firestone, D.  Fd.
     Cosmet. Toxicol.  1980, 18, 627-635.
21.  Poland, A.; Glover, E.  Mol. Pharmacol.  1973, 9, 736-747.
22.  Poland, A.; Glover, E.  J. Biol. Chem.  1976, 251, 4936-4946.
23.  Poland, A.; Kende, A.  Fed. Proc.  1976, 35, 2404-2411.
24.  Knutson, J.; Poland, A.  Cell  1980, 22, 27-36.
25.  Gierthy, J. F.; Crane, D.  Fund. Appl. Toxicol.  1985, 5,
     754-759.
26.  "Procedures of Estimating Risks Associated with Exposure to Mix-
     tures of Chlorinated Dibenzodioxins and Dibenzofurans", U.S.
     Environmental Protection Agency, 1985.
27.  Doyle, E. A.; Fries, G. F.  5th Intern. Symp. on Chlorinated
     Dioxins,  1985, Abst. 116.
28.  Suter-Hofman, M.  5th Intern. Symp. on Chlorinated Dioxins,
     1985, Abst. 115.

29. Murray, F. J.; Smith, F. A.; Nitschke, K. D.; Humiston, C. G.; Kociba, R. J.; Schwetz, B. A. Toxicol. Appl. Pharmacol. 1979, 50, 241-251.

30. Kociba, R. J.; Keyes, D. G.; Beyer, J. E.; Carreon, R. M.; Wade, C. E.; Dittenber, D. A.; Kalnins, R.; Frauson, L. F.; Park, C. N.; Barnard, S. D.; Hummel, R.; Humiston, C. G. Toxicol. Appl. Pharmacol. 1978, 46, 279-303.

31. Wasson, J. S.; Huff, J. E.; Loprieno, N. Mut. Res. 1978, 47, 141-160.

32. Poland, A.; Glover, E. Cancer Res. 1979, 39, 3341-3344.

33. Althaus, F. R.; Lawrence, S. D.; Sattler, G. L.; Longfellow, D. G.; Pitot, H. C. Cancer Res. 1982. 42, 3010-3015.

34. Loprieno, L.; Sbrana, I.; Rusclano, D.; Lasciafari; Lari, T. In "Chlorinated Dioxins and Related Compounds"; Hutzinger, O., Ed.: Pergamon Press: New York, 1983, Vol. 5.

35. Hiremath, C. B.; Bayliss, D. L.; Bayard, S. 5th Intern. Symp. on Chlorinated Dioxins, 1985, Abst. 131.

36. "Statement by Sanford A. Miller Before the Congressional Subcommittee on Natural Resources, Agriculture Research and Environment", U.S. Food and Drug Administration, 1983.

37. Kimbrough, R. D.; Falk, H.; Stehr, P.; Fries, G. J. Toxicol. Environ. Hlth. 1984, 14, 47-93.

38. "Scientific Criteria Document for Standard Development No. 4-84-Polychlorinated Dibenzo-p-dioxins (PCDDs) and Polychlorinated Dibenzofurans (PCDFs)", Ontario Ministry of the Environment, 1985.

39. Appel, K. E.; Beck, H.; Hildebrandt, A. G.; Lingk, W. 5th Intern. Symp. on Chlorinated Dioxins, 1985, Abst. 132.

40. Evaluation of the carcinogenicity and mutagenicity of 2,3,7,8-tetrachlorodibenzo-p-dioxin (TCDD); classification and no-effect level" Report DOC/LCM 300/292, Dutch State Institute of National Health, 1982.

41. Schlatter, C.; Poiger, H. Assessment of Contamination with 2,3,7,8-TCDD, Institute for Toxicology, University of Zurich, 1985.

RECEIVED November 25, 1986

# Chapter 5

# Effects of Chlorinated Dibenzodioxins

Renate D. Kimbrough and Vernon N. Houk

Center for Environmental Health, Centers for Disease Control, Public Health Service, U.S. Department of Health and Human Services, Atlanta, GA 30333

This paper is a review of the reported effects of 2,3,7,8-tetra-chlorodibenzodioxin (TCDD) on the health of workers in chemical plants and on the general population. Virtually no information exists on the human health effects of other congeners of polychlori-nated dibenzodioxins (PCDDs). Most exposures associated with acute health effects have been occupational, particularly those occurring when reaction vessels have exploded during the production of 2,4,5-trichloro-phenol. Symptoms of 2,3,7,8-TCDD exposure are chloracne, severe fatigue, nervousness, and decreased libido. In addition, workers may complain of weakness, loss of appetite, sleep disturb-ances, and a sensory neuropathy. In two factories, porphyria cutanea tarda was reported in workers. It is not clear, however, whether this illness was caused by the TCDD and/or by hexachlorobenzene and other chemicals, which were also present in the plants. Follow-up studies of highly exposed workers indicated that chloracne was the most persistent health effect. Upon cessation of exposure, many of the other abnormalities either decreased in severity or subsided completely. In a few isolated incidences, members of the general population have been exposed to significant levels of TCDD. In one such episode in Seveso, Italy, the systemic illness was mild and apparently short-lived. In another episode, a child had a hemor-rhagic cystitis, and a few others had chloracne. Both of these symptoms subsided. No convincing chronic health effects have been reported. In case-control studies, an association has been made between soft-tissue sarcoma and exposure to phenoxy herbicides that contained TCDD. Subsequent studies, however, have cast some doubt on these findings, and further studies are needed. There are 75 isomers of chlorinated dibenzodioxins (PCDDs). They vary greatly in toxic ity. The most toxic isomer is the 2,3,7,8-tetrachlorodibenzodioxin (2,3,7,8-TCDD). Other isomers, in which at least three of the 2,3,7,8 positions are occupied by halogens, are also quite active biologically. Most of what we know about the toxicity of these chemicals was developed from animal studies, and most studies conducted were done with the 2,3,7,8-TCDD. Different species respond quite differently to the toxic effects of 2,3,7,8-TCDD. The hamster, for instance, appears to be 1,000 times less sensitive to the toxic effects of 2,3,7,8 TCDD than is the guinea pig. The sensitivity of humans to 2,3,7,8-TCDD is still unknown. From animal studies we have learned that 2,3,7,8-TCDD causes liver toxicity, affects the skin, depresses the cell-mediated immune response, affects reproduction and cell differentiation, and produces cancers in rats and mice (1). But the target organs in different animal species vary and, except for the skin and, perhaps, the liver, it is not clear what other health effects these chemicals may have in humans. It is also unclear what health effects the other PCDDs might have singly or in combination.

## Sources

PCDDs are accidentally formed during the production of chlorinated phenols and related products (2-5). They may also be formed during the burning process in incinerators and through other forms of combustion, such as motor vehicles. The 2,3,7,8-TCDD is usually a minor component of these combustion products. They have been identified in urban dust, in gasoline motor oil, and in diesel motor oil (Ballschmiter, K.; Buchert, H.; Niemczy, K. R.; Munder, A.; Swerrev, M. Chemosphere in press 1986.) Thus, these chemicals are ubiquitous in our environment in very low concentrations and have been identified in fish, lake sediments, human adipose tissue, and milk (6-10). In addition, waste from the production of chlorinated phenols, if poorly controlled, may lead to heavier contamination in local areas (11).

## Human health effects

Exposure to PCDDs may occur in the occupational as well as the general environment. The general population is usually exposed to lower levels than workers. For this reason, workers are the ones primarily examined for acute and chronic health effects, unless subgroups of the general population for some reason have higher exposures.(12).

For most of the PCDDs no information on human health effects is available except that during the production of pentachlorophenol workers have developed a skin disease, chloracne (13) and complaints such as neuralgic pain in the lower extremities, and symptoms such as persistent bronchitis, and eye irritation (14). The bronchitis seems to be more prevalent in workers exposed to technical pentachlorophenol than in those exposed to the other chlorinated phenols.

Humans with a history of exposure to 2,3,7,8-TCDD have been studied most often. Therefore, I will devote most of the rest of this paper to a review of these studies. Although exposure to other PCDDs may be as prevalent or more prevalent in the general population, we have no information on the human health effects of the other PCDDs.

Workers can be exposed to PCDDs during the manufacture of an industrial product, while mixing ingredients for a commercial product, or when packaging the commercial product. The doses that these different populations receive vary widely. Occasionally, maintenance workers and cleanup crews may receive high exposures to such chemicals, which could be avoided through the use of appropriate gear and the practice of good personal hygiene.

Another hazard is peculiar to 2,3,7,8 TCDD. During the production of 2,4,5-trichlorophenol, an exothermic reaction can occur, causing the reaction vessel to explode. This has happened at several production facilities. In almost all of these incidents workers were heavily exposed to 2,3,7,8 TCDD during the cleanup (15-20). Chloracne has developed in the workers, and, in some instances, acute systemic disease. (Chloracne is a skin disease which consists of small skin-colored cysts with a central opening and of blackheads).

Chloracne is produced either by direct contact with the chemical on the skin or as an expression of a systemic disease. Another group of chemicals, the chlorinated biphenyls and the chlorinated dibenzofurans, also produce chloracne. Two outbreaks of poisoning by these chemicals occurred in the general population in Japan and Taiwan. In both instances, the offending chemicals were ingested and generalized chloracne developed in the patients.

The clinical features of chloracne, regardless of the type of chemical causing it, have been most consistent. The most distinctive cutaneous lesion is a skin-colored cyst that measures from 1 to 10 mm in diameter, with a central opening.

The other dominant lesion is the comedo. Usually these lesions start over the maxillary bone, then involve the entire face and the neck. Lesions may also be present on the back, arms, legs, and other areas of the body. Large pustules may form because of secondary infection.

In areas exposed to sunlight, a photosensitivity-type reaction may occur. Conjunctivitis, with swelling of the eyelids and other facial skin, may precede the chloracne.

Once chloracne has developed, it may be active for many years. Often, secondary infections occur, leaving deep-pitted, permanent scars.

In addition to chloracne, acute or chronic health effects, or both, may occur. Acute effects are noticed soon after heavy exposure to TCDD, as after the explosions (21). In such cases, workers usually become ill within 1 week. If workers are continually exposed to lower levels of TCDD, however, signs of illness may not occur for several months. Under such circumstances, the overriding sign is the chloracne. Although in Nitro, West Virginia exposure and occupational illness occurred as early as 1947, it was not until 1957 that TCDD was identified as the culprit (19).

Dermatologists have conducted most investigations of acute poisoning episodes, and their reports primarily focus on the skin lesions. Whether, occasionally, illness without chloracne may occur in exposed individuals is, at present, a matter of debate. In these outbreaks, some workers had severe chloracne without any systemic effects. On the other hand, ailments involving the skin, the eyes, the liver, the nervous system, and, occasionally, the heart were observed in other workers. The eye-related problems included conjunctivitis (inflammation of the conjunctiva) and blepharitis (inflammation of the eyelids).

In addition to the chloracne, hyperpigmentation and hirsutism (increased hair growth) were also reported.

The liver is most consistently affected in severe acute 2,3,7,8-TCDD poisoning. Goldmann et al. (15) described morphological changes in a liver biopsy from an affected worker as mild subacute hepatitis with focal areas of hyaline. The hepatocytes were enlarged, with moderately sized lipid vacuoles in their cytoplasm. A gray pigment that did not stain positive for iron was noted.

Many patients also had a sensory neuropathy (functional and/or pathological changes in the nervous system). In addition to the neuropathy, neurasthenia (functional nervous debility) has been associated with acute 2,3,7,8-TCDD poisoning. Complaints related to neurasthenia have been sleep disturbances, decreased libido, impotence, lack of drive, and mood changes. Unfortunately, these types of complaints cannot be objectively substantiated. They are often the types of complaints associated with aging or with depression and thus they are difficult to evaluate. In many instances, the skin lesions were quite disfiguring, and this may have caused a depression in some patients.

Paresthesias (abnormal sensations such as burning prickling), headache, muscle pain, and leg weakness have been described in workers acutely exposed to 2,3,7,8-TCDD. Loss of appetite and diarrhea were occasionally observed. Most of the other organs did not seem to be affected. In contrast, May (16), reported a poisoning outbreak in which workers suffered severe chloracne but had no other obvious systemic illnesses.

In the only poisoning outbreak in which humans (three chemists) were exposed solely to 2,3,7,8-TCDD, chloracne developed in two patients (22), and they had hyperpigmentation, increasing fatigue, and a tendency to have headaches. One patient complained that his skin was excessively oily. One of these patients lost about 6.5 kg of weight and reported excessive fatigue and loss of vigor. He also had excessive hair growth (hirsutism). About 1 year later, serum cholesterol levels for all three were raised, but clinical laboratory tests showed no other abnormalities. These chemists had been synthesizing 2,3,7,8-TCDD, an activity that poses the greatest hazard of exposure for chemists.

Patients who showed an increase in total serum lipids have also been described by Jirasek et al. (23) and Pazderova-Vejlupkova et al. (24). Many of these patients had abnormal results for glucose tolerance tests, hepatic lesions, increased alpha-1 and gamma globulin in plasma, and decreased plasma albumin. Hypercholesteremia and polyneuropathy were quite prevalent.

In two factories, in addition to chloracne, porphria cutanea tarda (a disturbance of porphyrin metabolism characterized by chronic skin lesions ranging from slight skin fragility to severe chronic scarring, by enlarged livers and by excessive urinary excretion of uroporphyrin and coproporphyrins. Uroporphyrin and coproporphyrin are iron-free cyclic tetrapyrrole derivatives) developed in the workers, (23,25). The possibility of simultaneous exposure to hexachlorobenzene, however, cannot be excluded. Hexachlorobenzene may be a contaminant in the production of

pentachlorophenol. In the episode described by Jirasek et al. (23),
pentachlorophenol was also produced, and four patients with severe
porphyria cutanea tarda also had hirsutism but did not have
chloracne, this was similar to the reaction of patients who had been
poisoned by hexachlorobenzene (26,27). In many of these factories,
follow-up studies were conducted (15,17,24,28-31).

Pazderova-Vejlupkova et al. (24) studied 55 exposed
workers 10 years after their illnesses began. Most workers' health
had improved. Their serum lipid levels did not significantly differ
from those of the controls. Their serum alpha and gamma globulins
had normalized, but elevated mean values of total blood protein were
still present. Increased concentrations of porphryins were no longer
present in urine, skin mainfestations normally seen with porphyria
cutanea tarda were rare, and results of liver function tests had
improved. In the liver biopsies, even for the most severe forms of
poisoning, only mild steatosis or periportal fibrosis were noted.

In 1947 at a Nitro, West Virginia, plant an explosion
occurred during the manufacture of 2,4,5-trichlorophenol. The
accident was reevaluated in 1984 (30). Chloracne still persisted in
55.7% of the workers. Other investigators have also noted this
extreme persistence of chloracne (24,28). Regarding systemic health
effects, not much was found. Hypertension, angina, coronary artery
disease, skin cancer, and cancers of all sites were not significantly
associated with exposure. Among those who had been exposed, 59.1%
had actinic elastosis (degeneration of elastic tissue in the skin
caused by those rays of light beyond the violet end of the spectrum
that produce chemical effects), in contrast to 30.1% among the
controls. The laboratory findings were essentially within the normal
range. After adjustment for age and smoking, the results of
nerve-conduction tests for the controls and the exposed groups did
not differ. The pulmonary function values among those who were
exposed and who currently smoked, however, were lower than values for
those who were not exposed and who did not smoke.

Moses et al. (32) studied a portion of the same cohort
that had been reexamined by Suskind and Hertzberg (30). In 1979, 226
workers were examined and chloracne was still present in 52%. The
chloracne in many of these workers had persisted for 26 years; in 29
workers, it had persisted for 30 years. These workers also showed
elevated gamma glutamyl transpeptidase. The mean gamma glutamyl
transpeptidase was higher in workers with chloracne than in those
without. This survey revealed no other findings of note. The
difference in the results between the follow-up by Moses et al. and
the one by Suskind and Hertzberg can be explained, in part, by the
difference in the composition of the cohorts.

May (29), conducted a similar study 10 years after an
explosion in a factory in which chloracne developed in 79 workers,
and found that only half of the affected workers still had
chloracne. No other adverse health effects were noted that could be
related to the previous exposure.

The mortality data for these different groups did not
indicate any obvious trends. However, Thiess et al. (18) reexamined
74 persons whom Goldmann (15) had previously studied. These workers

had been exposed to TCDD during an uncontrolled reaction at a trichlorophenol facility several decades earlier.

The overall mortality rate of 21 deaths did not differ in this group from the rate expected in three external reference populations or from that observed in two international comparison groups. Of the 21 deceased persons, 7 had cancer, compared with an expected 4.1 rate. Three of these deaths were due to stomach cancer, compared with an expected rate of 0.6. This expected rate was obtained from regional mortality data. One stomach cancer occurred among 148 individuals in the two comparison cohorts. If this particular study by Thiess et al. is carefully reviewed, a number of problems become obvious. One is the choice of the comparison groups. An additional problem is the fact that the number of deaths (19) is so small. We need additional studies with more participants and more carefully selected comparison groups to clarify the observations made by Thiess et al. Several such studies are in progress.

On the other hand, Hardell and Sandstrom (33) and Eriksson et al. (34) conducted two case-control studies in Sweden and reported an increased risk of soft-tissue sarcomas (cancers of soft-tissue) in men who were exposed to trichlorophenol or to phenoxy herbicides. In a third case-control study, investigators suggested that phenoxy herbicides and chlorophenols may also predispose to Hodgkin's lymphoma. Other sources however, provide little support for this theory (35).

Recently, Coggon and Acheson summarized the Swedish studies (36). They concluded: "Further research is urgently needed to confirm or refute these associations, to define the extent of the risk (if any) and to identify the carcinogen(s)." The Swedish studies could not be substantiated by Milham (37). Preliminary results from a case-control study in New Zealand have not indicated an excess risk of soft tissue sarcoma (38). We must kept in mind, however, that the mortality rate for soft-tissue sarcoma for U.S. males between the ages of 40 and 64 is extremely low and ranges from about 5 to 20 per million. This low incidence severely limits the power in some reported studies to detect such rare tumors.

The results of work by Honchar and Halperin (39) and Cook (40) of the United States supported the Swedish studies. Honchar and Halperin (39) noted that in four merged cohorts of exposed workers there were 105 deaths, 3 (2.9%) of which were due to soft-tissue sarcoma. On the basis of national death rates for men age 20 to 80, only 0.07% of the deaths due to soft tissue sarcoma would have been expected. After this was noted, however, another person in one of the four cohorts was found to have a soft-tissue sarcoma (40-42), which made a total of four soft-tissue sarcomas.

A review of tissue sections from these four tumors and from tumors of three additional cases gave some interesting results. Only two of the four cases with documented evidence of exposure and three additional cases, which did not have documented evidence of exposure, were confirmed to be soft tissue sarcomas (43). Thus, upon review by experts, not all of the tumors originally diagnosed as soft tissue sarcomas were found to be soft tissue sarcomas.

Further studies will have to be conducted to determine
whether exposure to these types of chemicals are associated with a
higher incidence of soft tissue sarcomas.

All of these studies, in which associations between
exposure to TCDD and an increased incidence of soft tissue sarcoma
were reported, involved workers who had either manufactured these
compounds or had applied the herbicide 2,4,5-T. In all of these
instances, however, the workers were exposed not only to TCDD but
also to either chlorinated phenols or to phenoxy herbicides.

## General Population

Two poisoning outbreaks have occurred in the general population. One
was in 1976 in Seveso, Italy, when a reaction vessel in a factory
exploded (44,45). The chemicals in the vessel escaped into the air
and descended as a cloud on the surrounding neighborhood. The
chemicals were trichlorophenol, sodium trichlorophenate, ethylene
glycol, sodium hyrdroxide, and TCDD. The population living adjacent
to the plant was exposed to the cloud and later to contaminated
vegetation. Two weeks after the incident, the people living in the
contaminated area were evacuated. In this situation, the exposure
levels in the cloud were probably quite high. A few vegetation
samples collected within the first 2 weeks after the incident
contained up to 15 ppm (mg/kg) of TCDD. Thus, significant exposures
probably occurred during the first few weeks after the explosion.
Within these first few weeks, 22 people (7 adults and 15 children
aged 3 to 13) were hospitalized or admitted to outpatient clinics. A
dermatitis that resembled first-and second-degree burns, with
blisters and, later, crusts developed in these patients. In
addition, lacrimation and the sensation of grit in the the eyes were
reported, but conjunctivitis was not observed. These skin lesions
healed within 2 to 3 months. Between 2 and 8 weeks after exposure, a
number of patients developed blackheads and cysts of different sizes
typical of chloracne. These lesions started to appear as the other
skin lesions were fading.

In the first few days, gastrointestinal disturbances were
also noted. A number of patients had slightly enlarged livers. In
these cases, no evidence was detected of a peripherial neuropathy or
of an effect on the central nervous system. The immune response in
this population was within the normal range.

Since then, a number of health studies have been conducted
in this population (46). A small percentage of the children in the
area had chloracne. The number of cases ranged from 167-196,
depending on whether very mild cases (which were not unequivocal
chloracne) were included in the count and at what time these counts
were made. None of these cases were as disfiguring as cases observed
in some of the workers discussed earlier. Although liver problems,
enlarged livers, and some abnormal results for liver function tests
were reported, when the overall results of these studies were
evaluated, no severe systemic health effects were noted (47,48).

Another episode in which a few people received substantial
exposure to TCDD occurred in Missouri. In 1971, waste from the
production of hexachlorophene at a manufacturing facility in

southwestern Missouri was mixed with salvage oil and sprayed on
various sites throughout the State for dust control (11,49). This
waste had high concentrations of TCDD. The source of the TCDD waste
was a plant where 2,4,5-trichloro-phenol was made for the production
of hexachlorophene. The poisoning episode was first discovered when
a 6-year-old girl from Lincoln County, Missouri, was admitted to St.
Louis Children's Hospital with an acute hemorrhagic cystitis
(inflammation of the urinary bladder with bleeding). The child had
played in the soil of a riding arena. Her first symptoms were
headache, epistaxis (nose bleeds), diarrhea, and lethargy. She then
had a hemorrhagic cystitis. Three other persons who had used the
same riding arena complained of recurrent headaches, skin lesions,
and polyarthralgia (pain in more than one joint). The concentration
of TCDD in the soil of this arena was 30 ppm, or 30 mg/kg. The
child's acute symptoms subsided after a time (50). Chloracne
developed in two little boys, who had played in another contaminated
riding arena, and adults associated with the arena complained of
headaches.

A pilot study was conducted in a small group of people
from another, more recently discovered, contaminated area in Missouri
(51). This group's exposures were much lower. The soil
contamination in most areas was generally less than 1 ppm of TCDD
(mg/kg). The group consisted of 68 people who were possibly exposed
and 35 people who were presumably not exposed. There were no
statistically significant differences in the test results between the
two groups.

Results of an additional study were reported recently
(52). In this study 154 exposed and 155 unexposed persons were
examined. The exposed persons had been living in a mobile home park
in which 2,3,7,8-TCDD contaminated waste oil was sprayed for dust
control. The TCDD contamination dated back to 1971 when
TCDD-contaminated sludge wastes were taken from a hexachlorophene
production facility (11,53). Levels of 2,3,7,8-TCDD up to 2.2 ppm
(mg/kg) were still present more than ten years later. No increased
clinical illness was noted in the group who had lived in the
contaminated mobile
home park. Some differences were noted, however, in the
immunological responses between the two groups. All persons were
given a skin test to measure delayed-type hypersensitivity. Half of
the results in both groups could not be used because two of the four
persons reading the skin tests apparently did not interpret the skin
responses properly. Of the remaining participants, however, 11.8% in
the exposed group and 1.1% in the control group were anergic
(transient reduction or complete lack of reactivity to antigens or
allergens). The relative anergy was noted in 35.3% of the exposed
group versus 11.8% of the control group. The exposed group had a
nonstatistical increased frequency of abnormal T-cell subset test
results. Many parameters can affect the results of these tests, such
as age, psychological stress, alcohol consumption, malnutrition, and
infectious agents (54). It is not clear, in the absence of clinical
disease, what these results mean. Further studies are needed to
confirm these findings. Ratios of subsets of lymphocytes may be

affected by the total lymphocyte count. Apparently the exposed group
had an elevated white blood cell count which was statistically
significant.

The concentration of 2,3,7,8-TCDD has now been measured in
the adipose tissue of 39 persons from Missouri with a history of
residential (19), recreational (5), or occupational (15) exposure,
and 57 persons in a control group. All participants had detectable
levels of 2,3,7,8-TCDD, but the exposed group had significantly
higher levels (p < 0.001). Levels in the controls ranged from
1.4-20.2 ppt (ng/kg), in the recreational group from 5.0-577 ppt
(ng/kg), in the residential group from 2.8-59.1 ppt (ng/kg), and in
the occupationally exposed group from 3.5-750 ppt (ng/kg). The
geometric means for the different groups were: controls 6.4 ppt
(ng/kg), recreational 38.9 ppt (ng/kg), residential 14.6 ppt (ng/kg),
occupational 29.8 ppt (ng/kg). Residential exposure was defined as
either living in close proximity to areas with 2,3,7,8 TCDD
contaminated soil, or having evidence of contamination inside the
home. Recreational exposure was defined of at least one time per
week riding or caring for horses in 2,3,7,8-TCDD contaminated stable
arenas. Occupational exposure was defined as working in a
hexachlorophene production facility or at truck terminals where the
grounds had been sprayed with 2,3,7,8 TCDD contaminated waste
oil.(Patterson, D. G., Jr. Ph.D., Hoffman, R. E., Needham, L. L.,
Roberts, D.W., Bagby, J. R., Pirkle, J. L., Falk, H., Sampson, E. J.,
Houk, V. N. JAMA in press.) The preliminary findings suggest that
people living in 2,3,7,8-TCDD contaminated areas may have slightly
higher body burdens than the general populations. It is possible
that this is unique to Missouri since 2,3,7,8-TCDD was mixed in an
oil when applied to soil and riding arenas and has a greater
bioavailability (55) than when mixed with soil from other areas
(56). In the future these determinations will help in the assessment
of exposure.

In addition, a morbidity study was recently completed
(Ranch Hand study) on pilots who flew spraying missions in Vietnam
and on other Air Force personnel. These members of the military were
exposed to Agent Orange, a mixture of the herbicides 2,4-D and 2,
4,5-T. The 2,4,5-T was contaminated with 2,3,7,8-TCDD, (57). None
of the findings were alarming. Findings differed only in the
occurrence of skin cancers (mostly basal cell carcinomas), which were
significantly higher in the Ranch Hand group when measured against
the comparison group (p = 0.03). Thirty-one basal cell carcinomas
occurred among the Ranch Hand group and 21 among the comparison
group. These results, however, have not been corrected for
geographic area, ethnic backgrounds, and excessive exposure to
sunlight. Preliminary analysis of fertility and reproduction
suggests a clustering of birth anomalies of the skin in Ranch
Handers' children. In addition, the neonatal death rate (p = 0.02)
was significantly increased for the Ranch Hand group. Before their
exposure in Southeast Asia, the Ranch Hand group had 20 newborn
offspring who died, and the comparison group had 17. After their
service in Southeast Asia, however, the Ranch Hand group had 14
neonatal deaths and the comparison group had only 3. The Ranch

Handers also had significant deficits in two specific peripheral leg pulses and in all leg pulses, as a group. Ranch Handers, in addition, had elevated liver enzyme levels and lower cholesterol levels. More Ranch Handers were found to have hepatomegaly (enlarged liver) and verified histories of prior hepatic disease than their counterparts. Additional data analysis and follow-up of the Ranch Handers may clarify some of the preliminary findings made in this cross-sectional study. None of these findings, however, could be related to herbicide exposure because no specific "dose-response effect" could be shown.

The retrospective assessment of exposure in situations like Ranch Hand is extremely difficult, even if the environment is well defined and the exposure levels of a certain chemical are known. In an occupational situation, for instance, two people in the same environment can, for a variety of reasons, receive different doses. The reasons include variations in personal hygiene and in the ability to metabolize and excrete chemicals. For example, some investigators have found that workers who smoke have higher levels of chemicals in their body fluids than their nonsmoking counterparts.

In a retrospective study such as this, when the last exposure to Agent Orange was at least 12 years ago, it is difficult to assess what effect other, later insults may have had on the subjects' health. Furthermore, for purely statistical reasons, some differences will be found if many endpoints are examined. None of the findings in the Ranch Hand study have been confirmed in other studies.

The Centers for Disease Control recently completed a case-control study to determine if men who served in the U.S. military in Vietnam have been at an increased risk of fathering babies with serious congenital malformations. (58). Again, no striking findings were made, and it is not really clear whether this study should be more appropriately classified as a Vietnam experience study because of the great difficulties in appropriately determining exposure to 2,3,7,8-TCDD in Agent Orange.

The same can be said for other anecdotal reports that have linked exposure to the herbicide 2,4,5-T to a variety of undesirable health effects. Some of this information is summarized by Reggiani (44). Since most of the reports are anecdotal, and on reexamination could not be verified, they will not be reviewed here.

In conclusion, the most prevalent lesion in humans after acute exposure to 2,3,7,8-TCDD is a skin lesion referred to as chloracne. This skin disease may be accompanied by hirsutism and hyperpigmentation. After acute exposure to toxic levels, liver function may be impaired and a sensory neuropathy may be present. There may be complaints of weakness, weight loss, severe fatigue, and a general malaise. Many of these acute symptoms and signs revert to normal when exposure ceases. The chloracne is probably the most persistent lesion. No convincing chronic human health effects, other than chloracne, have been reported, nor is the dose of 2,3,7,8-TCDD known that would cause systemic illness or death in humans. Virtually no information is available on other PCDD congeners.

## Literature Cited

1.  Kimbrough, R. D.; Falk, H.; Stehr, P.  J. Toxicol. Environ.
    Health 1984, 14, 47-93.
2.  Buser, H. R.; Bosshardt, H. P.  J. Chromatogr. 1974, 90, 71-77.
3.  Buser, H. R.; Bosshardt, H. P.  J. Assoc. Off. Anal. Chem. 1976,
    59, 562-69.
4.  Buser, H. R.; Bosshardt, H. P.  Mitt. Geb. Lecbensmittelunters
    1978, 69, 191-99.
5.  Kimbrough, R. D.  Pathologist 1983, 37(9).
6.  Czuczwa, J. M.; McVeety, B. D.; Hites, R. A.  Chemosphere 1985a,
    14, 623-26.
7.  Czuczwa, J. M.; Niessen, F.; Hites, R. A.  Chemosphere, 1985b,
    14, 1175-79.
8.  Schecter, A.; Ryan, J. J.; Lizotte, R.; Sun, W. F.; Miller, L.;
    Gitlitz, G.; Bogdasarian, M.  Chemosphere 1985, 14, 933-37.
9.  Ryan, J. J.; Lizotte, R.; Lau, B. P. Y.  Chemosphere 1985a, 14,
    697-706.
10. Ryan, J. J.; Schecter, A.; Lizotte, R.; Sun, W. F.; Miller, L.
    Chemosphere 1985b, 14, 929-32.
11. Carter, C. D.; Kimbrough, R. D.; Liddle, J. A.; Cline, R. F.;
    Zack, M. M.; Barthel, W. F.; Koehler, R. E.; Phillips, P. E.
    Science 1975, 188, 738-40.
12. Hoffmann, R.; Baader, E. W.; Bauer, H. J.  Ind. Med. Surg. 1986
    20, 286-90.
13. Baader, E. W.; Bauer, H. J.  Ind. Med. Surg. 1951, 20, 286-90.
14. Behrbohm, P.  Dtsch. Gesundheitswes. 14, 614-19.
15. Goldmann, P. J.  Schwerste akute Chlorakne durch Trichlorophenol
    Zersetzungsprodukte.  Arbeitsmed Sozialmed Arbeitshyg 1972, 7,
    12-18.
16. May,  G.  Br J Ind Med 1973, 30, 276-283.
17. Zack, J.A.; Suskind, R.R.  J. Occup. Med. 1980, 22, 11-14.
18. Thiess, A. M.; Frentzel-Beyme R.; Link, R.  Am J Ind Med 1982,
    3, 179-189.
19. Kimming, J.; Schulz, K. H.  Dermatologica 1957, 115, 540-46.
20. Dugois, P.; Colomb, L.  Lyon Med 1956, 88, 446-47.
21. Hofmann, H.  Arch Exp Pathol Pharmakol 1957, 232, 228-30.
22. Oliver, R. M.  Br J Ind Med 1975, 32, 49-53.
23. Jirasek, L.; Kalensky, J.; Kubec, K.; Pazderova, J.; Lukas, E.;
    Hautarzt 1976, 27, 328-333.
24. Pazderova-Vejlupkova, J.; Lukas, E.; Nemcova, M.; Pickova, J.;
    Jirasek, L.  Arch Environ Health 1981, 36, 5-11.
25. Bleiberg, J.; Wallen, M.; Brodkin, R.; Applebaum, I.L.  Arch
    Dermatol 1964, 89, 793-97.
26. Cam, S.  Ann Derm Syph 1960, 87, 393-97.
27. Peters, H.A.; Gocmen, A.; Cripps, D.J.; Bryan, G.T.; Dogramaci,
    M. D.  Arch Neurol 1982, 39, 744-49.
28. Poland, A.P.; Smith, D.; Metter, G.; Possick, P.  Arch Environ
    Health 1971, 22, 316-27.
29. May, G.  Br J Ind Med 1982, 39, 128-135.
30. Suskind, R. R.; Hertzberg, V. S.  JAMA 1984, 251, 2372-80.

31.  Frentzel-Beyme, R.  Am J Epidemiol 1981, 114, 425.
32.  Moses, M.; Lilis, R.; Crow, K. D.; Thornton, J.; Fischbein, A.;
     Anderson, H. A.; Selikoff, I. J.  Am J Ind Med 1984, 5, 161-182.
33.  Hardell, L., Sandstrom, A.  Br J Cancer 1979, 39, 711-17.
34.  Eriksson, M. H.; Hardell, O. L.; Axelson, O.; Berg, N. O.;
     Moeller, T.  Br. J. Ind. Med. 1981, 38(1), 27-33.
35.  Hardell, L.; Eriksson, M.; Lenner, P.; Lundgren, E.  Br J Cancer
     1981, 43, 169-176.
36.  Coggon, D.; Acheson, E. D.  Lancet.  1982, 1, 1057-59.
37.  Milham S.  Lancet 1982, 1, 1464-65.
38.  Smith, A. H.; Fisher, D. O.; Giles, H. J.; Pearce, N.
     Chemosphere 1983, 12, 565-71.
39.  Honchar, P. A.; Halperin, W. E.  Lancet 1981, 1, 268-69.
40.  Cook, R. R.  Lancet 1981, 618, 3-14.
41.  Cook, R. R.; Townsend, J. C.; Ott, M. G.; Silverstein, L. G.;
     JOM 1980, 22, 530-32.
42.  Ott, M. G.; Holder, B. B.; Olson, R. D.  J Occup Med 1980, 22,
     47-50.
43.  Fingerhut, M.A.; Halperin, W.E.; Honchar, P.A.; Smith, A.B.;
     Groth, D.H.; and Russell, W.O.  Banbury Report.  1984, 18,
     461-70.
44.  Reggiani, G.  J Toxicol Environ Health 1980, 6, 27-43.
45.  Pocchiani, F.; Silano, V.; Zampieri, A.  Ann NY Acad Sci 1979,
     320, 311-20.
46.  Tognoni, G.; Bonaccorsi, A.  Drug Metab Rev 1982, 13, 447-469.
47.  Reggiani, G.  Arch Toxicol 1978, 40, 161-88.
48.  Reggiani G.  Pergamon Ser Environ Sci 1982, 5, 463-493.
49.  Kimbrough, R. D.; Carter, C. D.; Liddle, J. A.; Cline, R. E.;
     Phillips, P. E.  Arch Environ Health 1977, 32, 77-85.
50.  Beale, M. G.; Shearer, W. T.; Karl, M. M.; Robson, A. M.  Lancet
     1977, 1, 748.
51.  Centers for Disease Control.  MMWR 1984, 33, 54-61.
52.  Hoffmann, R. E.; Stehr-Green, P. A.; Webb, K. B.; Evans, R. G.;
     Kmetson, A. P.; Schramm, W. F.; Staake, J. L.; Gibson, B. B.;
     Steinberg, K. K.  JAMA 1986, 255, 2031-38.
53.  Stehr, P. A.; Forney, D.; Stein, G.; Donnell, H. D.; Falk, H.;
     Hotchkiss, R.; Spratlin, W. A.; Sampson, E.; Smith, S. J.
     Public Health Rep. 1985, 100, 289-293.
54.  Vos, J. G.  Immune suppression as related to toxicology.  CRC,
     Crit. Rev. Toxicol., 1977, 67-101.
55.  McConnell, E. E.; Lucier, G. W.; Rumbaugh, R. C.; Albro, P. W.;
     Harvan, D. J.; Hass, J. R.; Harris, M. W.  Science, 1984, 223,
     1077.
56.  Umbreit, T. H.; Hesse, E. J.; Gallo, M. A.  Science, 1986, 232;
     497-499.
57.  Lathrop, G. D.; Wolfe, W. H.; Albanese, R. A.; Moynahan, P. M.
     Brooks Air Force Base, Texas:  USAF School of Aerospace
     Medicine, Aerospace Medical Division, 1984.
58.  Erickson, J. D.; Mulinare, J.; McClain, P. W.; Fitch, T. G.;
     Levy, M. J.; McClearn, A. B.; Adams, M. J.  JAMA 1984, 252,
     903-12.

RECEIVED January 2, 1987

# RISK ASSESSMENT: EXPOSURE

# Chapter 6

# 2,3,7,8-Tetrachlorodibenzo-*p*-dioxin: Environmental Chemistry

Glenn C. Miller[1] and Richard G. Zepp[2]

[1]Department of Biochemistry, University of Nevada—Reno, Reno, NV 89557
[2]Environmental Research Laboratory, U.S. Environmental Protection Agency, Athens, GA 30613

For molecules of its size and molecular weight, 2,3,7,8-tetrachlorodibenzo-p-dioxin (2,3,7,8-TCDD) is one of the most toxic, least water soluble, least volatile, and most resistant to thermal and biological transformations. The combination of these properties has presented a challenging problem in assessing human hazards ascribable to TCDD because, although exposure concentrations are often low, the time frame for transport and most degradative processes in the environment is generally long. Under normal environmental conditions the only transformation process that is fairly rapid for dioxins is photolysis.

This introductory chapter is designed to provide a general background on the environmental transformation and transport of TCDD, with emphasis on its environmental chemistry. It is not a complete review of the substantial amount of literature available on the topic, but is meant to set the stage for the following papers that discuss certain aspects of this subject in greater detail.

2,3,7,8-TCDD is a symmetrical molecule, generally synthesized by the condensation of two molecules of 2,4,5-trichlorophenol in the presence of base at high temperatures (1).

2,4,5-trichlorophenol                    2,3,7,8-TCDD

An abbreviated list of its physicochemical properties is given in Table I. A more complete list of other properties is presented by

0097-6156/87/0338-0082$06.00/0
© 1987 American Chemical Society

Schroy and co-workers (2). Because of the extreme character of many
of these properties, refinement of these values is an ongoing process. Reports on improved measurements of water solubility and
vapor pressure were recently published (3,5).

Table I. Selected Chemical and Physical Properties of 2,3,7,8-TCDD

| Property | | Reference |
|---|---|---|
| Molecular weight | 321.974 | |
| Vapor pressure | | |
| (25° C) | $7.4 + 0.4 \times 10^{-10}$ torr | (3) |
| (30° C) | $3.46 \times 10^{-9}$ | (2) |
| (54.6° C) | $1.37 \times 10^{-7}$ | (2) |
| (71° C) | $1.19 \times 10^{-6}$ | (2) |
| Melting point | 305.0° C | (4) |
| Solubility in: | | |
| (all at 25° C) | | |
| water | 19.3 nanograms/liter | (5) |
| benzene | 570 milligrams/liter | (6) |
| methanol | 10 milligrams/liter | (6) |
| acetone | 110 milligrams/liter | (6) |
| Partition coefficient | $1.4 \times 10^6$, $3.0 \times 10^8$ | (7,8) |
| (octanol/water) | $(4.24 \pm 2.73) \times 10^6$ | (5) |
| Molecular diffusivity: | | |
| in air (calculated) | $4.7 \times 10^2 cm^2/s$ | (3) |
| in water (calculated) | $5.1 \times 10^{-6} cm^2/s$ | (3) |
| Photolysis quantum yields | | |
| (313 nm) | | |
| water-acetonitrile | | |
| (90:10) | 0.0022 | (9) |
| hexane | 0.049 | (9) |

## Sources and Distribution

2,3,7,8-TCDD and related dioxins and dibenzofurans have come from
two primary sources: (a) impurities in 2,4,5-trichlorophenol and
related chemicals and (b) combustion processes. The products that
have been manufactured from 2,4,5-trichlorophenol include herbicides
such as 2-(2,4,5-trichlorophenoxy)propionic acid (silvex), 2,3,5-
trichlorophenoxyacetic acid (2,4,5-T), and the disinfectant hexachlorophene (10). As discussed above, 2,3,7,8-TCDD is produced as a
byproduct when 2,4,5-trichlorophenol is synthesized, and is found in
significant concentrations in the synthesis residue (still bottoms).
Chemical wastes containing 2,3,7,8-TCDD have been released directly
into the environment. In some cases it has migrated from chemical
waste dumps. For example, sediment samples taken near the Love

Canal site in New York contained 0.9-312 ppb 2,3,7,8-TCDD, which
presumably originated at a chemical waste dump (11). 2,3,7,8-TCDD
was also spread over wide areas in Missouri when 2,4,5-trichloro-
phenol waste was incorporated into waste oil and used to control
dust on roads, parking lots and horse arenas. The estimated volume
of contaminated Missouri soil ranged from 150,000 to 400,000 cubic
meters (12).

Agricultural and wartime use of trichlorophenol-based herbicides such as 2,4,5-T and silvex also has resulted in release of
2,3,7,8-TCDD at low concentrations in many countries.

2,4,5-T                                 silvex

These herbicides have been used extensively in silviculture for control of deciduous trees in conifer forests (13). As a military defoliant, 2,4,5-T was mixed with 2,4-dichlorophenoxy acetic acid
(2,4-D), and an estimated 10 million gallons of this mixture was
applied in South Vietnam under the name of Agent Orange. Subsequent
analysis of human samples from South Vietnam has found 2,3,7,8-TCDD
at elevated levels compared to samples from North Vietnam where
Agent Orange was not used (14).

More recently, environmental contamination by chlorinated
dioxins and furans released during combustion processes has been
recognized. These substances are formed not only during incineration of chlorinated phenols, but also during combustion of materials
in home fireplaces and municipal incinerators (10). Chlorinated
dioxins and dibenzofurans also are formed during fires involving
polychlorinated biphenyls (15).

Another potential source for the more toxic dioxin congeners is
the photoreduction of the higher chlorinated dioxins, i.e. the octa-
chloro and heptacholoro congeners, to the lower chlorinated isomers.
There are conflicting results concerning which positions are photoreduced on the dioxin aromatic rings. If the 1,4,6,9-positions are
most rapidly reduced, toxic tetra, penta and hexachloro isomers (2,
3,7,8-substituted) may result. If, however, the lateral (2,3,7,8)
positions are photoreduced, the resulting products are substantially
less toxic. The available information on this question is mixed.
Buser (16) observed that UV irradiation of solutions of octachlorodibenzo-p-dioxin (OCDD) resulted in preferential formation of 1,2,3,
4,6,7,9-hepta-CDD, which indicates primary initial loss of the
lateral (2,3,7,8) chlorines. This preferential loss of lateral
chlorines was also observed by Dobbs and Grant (17). Alternatively,
Lamparski and co-workers (18) report preferential loss of chlorine
atoms from the 1,4,6,9-positions as the initial photoreduction of
OCDD when irradiated on a wood surface. Cull and Dobbs (19) observed no preferential loss from either position. Both heptachloro

isomers were formed in similar yields. The reason for these differences remains unknown.

Because of their low water solubility and low volatility, 2,3,7,8-TCDD and related dioxins are predominantly sorbed on particles, particularly soils and sediments. Assessing exposure to these compounds requires the ability to predict their time-varying concentrations in those important environmental compartments. Both biological and non-biological transformation and transport processes must be considered, including hydrolysis, oxidation, reduction and phototransformation. For 2,3,7,8-TCDD, attempts have been made to model each process in several environmental systems, with varying degrees of success. Because of the toxicity of 2,3,7,8-TCDD, various model compounds have been utilized, particularly other chlorinated dioxins. Caution must be taken when extending these results to 2,3,7,8-TCDD, however, because this isomer is in many ways toxicologically and chemically unique. There is often only limited rationale for estimating the properties of 2,3,7,8-TCDD based on the behavior of other isomers, i.e. 1,4,6,9-TCDD.

## Biological Transformations

In contrast to the profound effect that 2,3,7,8-TCDD can have on biological systems, most biological systems have little impact on 2,3,7,8-TCDD. Early studies by Matsumura and Benezet (20) demonstrated that microbial metabolism was very slow if it occurred at all. Further work confirmed that although 2,3,7,8-TCDD is indeed relatively stable to microbial metabolism, two isolated microorganisms that gave water soluble metabolites were identified. In both aquatic sediment and terrestrial soil systems, metabolism of 2,3,7,8-TCDD was demonstrated. Addition of nutrients such as glucose, mannitol, and bactopeptone stimulated the transformation (21).

Substantial microbial degradation of 2,3,7,8-TCDD in oxic environments has not been demonstrated in field studies. Biodegradation was sufficiently slow that essentially all of the originally applied 2,3,7,8-TCDD in an experimental plot at Eglin Air Force Base in Florida in 1972 was still there in 1985 (22). Kimbrough and co-workers (23), estimated that the half-life for polychlorinated dibenzodioxins in soils was 10 years. Over a short (20 day) period, Pocchiari (24) did not observe increased rates of microbial degradation of 2,3,7,8-TCDD in organic-nutrient-amended soils from Seveso, Italy.

In a model ecosystem using aquatic sediment and lake water, metabolism played only a minor role in the loss of 2,3,7,8-TCDD (25). Volatilization was suggested to be the major mode of disappearance in samples incubated 39 days or more. The half-life under the conditions of the experiment in this model ecosystem was on the order of 600 days. Microbial metabolism appeared to be enhanced when microbial growth was stimulated; under such conditions metabolites were observed. One organism which can degrade 2,3,7,8-TCDD at an appreciable rate is the white rot fungus, Phanerochaete chrysosporium (26). The ability of this fungus to metabolize 2,3,7,8-TCDD was suggested to be dependent on an extracellular ligin-degrading enzyme system.

The lack of appreciable metabolism of 2,3,7,8-TCDD in aerobic environments can in part be explained by the high oxidation state of

the molecule. The six electron withdrawing atoms on 2,3,7,8-TCDD
reduce the ease of oxidative metabolism. Although the available
information is not substantial, reduction may be as important as
oxidation. Evidence exists that 2,3,7,8-TCDD may be slowly degraded
by anaerobic microorganisms in an organic matrix used for secondary
treatment of chlorophenolic wastewaters (27).

Further support that reduction may be important for 2,3,7,8-
TCDD is provided by the observation that it undergoes reduction to
the lower chlorinated isomers in electron impact mass spectrometry
when hydrogen is used as the gas chromatographic carrier gas (28).
In addition, degradation of 2,3,7,8-TCDD in basic solutions of
polyethyleneglycol and oxidants actually appears to occur by reductive processes, since the products are the lower chlorinated dioxins
(29).

## Abiotic Transformation

### Oxidation, Hydrolysis and Reduction.

2,3,7,8-TCDD is not suscept-
ible to hydrolysis at environmental temperatures (3) and is highly
stable to chemical oxidation. TCDD exhibits thermal stability at
environmental temperatures. Indeed, the thermal stability of TCDD
is such that temperatures of 1400°F to 2400°F are used for efficient
(>99.9999%) degradation of 2,3,7,8-TCDD from contaminated soils
(30). Reaction rates with hydroxyl radicals have not been measured,
although Podoll and co-workers (3) estimated the vapor phase rate
constant to be on the order of $3 \times 10^8$ $M^{-1}s^{-1}$. Using average OH
radical concentrations to be $3 \times 10^{-15}$ M, a half life of 200 hours
was estimated for oxidation of TCDD in the atmosphere.

### Photodegradation.

Of all the possible natural degradation mechan-
isms, photodegradation has been suggested to be the most significant (3,9,10,27). 2,3,7,8-TCDD undergoes rapid degradation when
exposed to ultra-violet light in the presence of a hydrogen (reducing) source. The photochemistry of dioxins has been reviewed by
Choudhry and Hutzinger (31) and Esposito and coworkers (27).

Dulin and coworkers (32) have measured the quantum yield for
photolysis of 2,3,7,8-TCDD in an acetonitrile/water mixture and in
hexane (Table I). The more than 20-fold difference in quantum yield
confirms either the need for a hydrogen source for efficient photolysis, or that the reaction pathway is substantially altered on going to a largely water solvent. The absorption spectra of 2,3,7,8-
TCDD in acetonitrile shows a strong band centered at 309 nm with an
extinction coefficient of 7020 $M^{-1}cm^{-1}$, whereas in hexane the band
is centered at 304 nm with extinction coefficient of 5640 $M^{-1}cm^{-1}$.
For sunlight photolysis, the higher quantum yield in hexane may be
partially offset by reduced spectral overlap of 2,3,7,8-TCDD with
the solar spectrum. In hexane, under identical conditions, the
quantum yield for photolysis of 2,3,7-trichlorodibenzo-p-dioxin was
0.20, which was over four times higher than for 2,3,7,8-TCDD. Using
the photolysis quantum yield, Podoll and coworkers (3) determined
that the photolysis half-lives in surface waters varied from 21
hours in summer to 118 hours in winter.

Choudhry and Webster (33) also found low quantum yields for
photolysis of 1,2,3,4,7-pentachorodibenzo-p-dioxin and 1,2,3,4,7,8-
hexachlorodibenzo-p-dioxin of $9.8 \times 10^{-5}$ and $1.1 \times 10^{-4}$, respec-

tively in water:acetonitrile (4:6) solutions. Both of these solvents are poor hydrogen donors, evidenced by the low quantum yields.
Assuming that the quantum yields are the same in pure water, half
lives of both compounds are 15 and 6 days, respectively, for the
compounds in summer sun at 40° N. Botre' and coworkers (39) found
that 2,3,7,8-TCDD was most rapidly lost in micelles of 1-hexadecyl-
pyridinium chloride ($t_{1/2}$ 4 hrs) compared to micelles of sodium
dodecyl sulfate ($t_{1/2}$ 8 hrs) and methanol ($t_{1/2}$ 18 hrs). Unfiltered
mercury lamps were used in these studies.

Nestrick and coworkers (34) observed a striking difference in
the photolysis rates of a series of tetrachlorinated dibenzo-p-
dioxins. 2,3,7,8-TCDD underwent the most rapid photolysis in hexa-
decane. The rate of photolysis was 148 times more rapid than that
of the 1,4,6,9-TCDD isomer when exposed to light from an RS sunlamp.
Other TCDD isomers had relative photolysis rates varying between 2.7
times slower (1,3,7,8-TCDD) to 24 times slower (1,3,6,9-TCDD). The
problem with relating these results to outdoor conditions is that
the overlap of the absorption spectra of each of the isomers with
the emission spectra of the RS sunlamp was not considered (35).
2,3,7,8-TCDD has an absorption band at 310 nm (extinction coefficient of 5590) in chloroform (36). This wavelength is also near the
most intense emission band (314-316 nm) of the RS sunlamp between
290 nm and 320 nm (34). Other tetrachlorinated isomers have absorption maxima at wavelengths different than 2,3,7,8-TCDD. Even with
this consideration, the data support evidence by others that photolysis of TCDD isomers is most rapid for those substituted on the
lateral (2,3,7,8) positions.

Alternatively, Nestrick and co-workers (34) showed that 2,3,7,
8-TCDD was the most stable of the 22 TCDD isomers examined on glass.
1,4,6,9-TCDD was the second most stable TCDD isomer, with a relative
half-life that was 0.099 times that of 2,3,7,8-TCDD. The isomer
most photoreactive on the glass surface, 1,2,3,9-TCDD, exhibited a
half-life that was 0.014 times that of 2,3,7,8-TCDD. RS sunlamps
also were used in this study, and no correction was provided for
different absorption spectra of the various isomers. Although quantum yields would be more interpretable, it is nonetheless surprising
that 2,3,7,8-TCDD photodecomposed the most rapidly in solution, but
most slowly when exposed to light on a glass surface.

Molecular orbital calculations of 2,3,7,8-TCDD and dibenzo-p-
dioxin indicate that excitation of either molecule results in promotion of an electron into an anti-bonding orbital with electron
density primarily located on the 2,3,7,8 positions, with only a
small percentage on the 1,4,6,9 positions (37). The primary photoproducts of 2,3,7,8-TCDD in organic solvent has been suggested to be
the 2,3,7-trichloro isomer and the dichloro isomers (38). These
photoproducts also appear to photodegrade faster than 2,3,7,8-TCDD.
No other photoproducts have been identified from the photolysis of
2,3,7,8-TCDD, except for a "yellow, non-volatile gum" that was formed after extended exposure of methanolic solutions to fluorescent
lamps (38).

Alternatively, a recent study by Dulin and coworkers (9) found
no photoproducts for 2,3,7,8-TCDD in either water or hexane, despite
a careful analysis of the reaction solution for 2,3,7-trichlorodi-
benzo-p-dioxin. They suggested that cleavage of one Ar-O bond is an
alternative photochemical pathway which may predominate during 2,3,

7,8-TCDD photolysis. This mechanism would not result in chlorine replacement by hydrogen and would account for their finding that lower chlorinated dioxins were not produced in detectable quantities.

All of the studies to date have consistently demonstrated that the photolysis rate of 2,3,7,8-TCDD is dependent on the chemical environment in which it resides. Organic solvents dramatically accelerate the photolysis rate. Crosby and coworkers (38) found that, although the half-life of 2,3,7,8-TCDD in methanol under fluorescent lamp irradiation was approximately 3 hours, irradiation on either a Norfolk sandy soil for 96 hours, or as a thin dry film on glass for 14 days showed no loss of 2,3,7,8-TCDD. Wipf and coworkers (39) state that the photolysis rate of 2,3,7,8-TCDD on vegetation is increased by a factor of 25 when olive oil or arachis oil is used as a hydrogen source.

Photolysis of 2,3,7,8-TCDD on soil surfaces has been most studied to date by Liberti and coworkers (40). Their goal was to find methods to accelerate the loss of 2,3,7,8-TCDD from contaminated soil in Seveso, Italy. Unfiltered, high pressure mercury lamps were used in these studies. An important finding in this work is that a temperature dependence on the photolysis rate of 2,3,7,8-TCDD on glass plates was observed. At 23° C the half-life was approximately 50 hours; at 30° C the half-life was approximately 9 hours. Increased volatilization may have accounted for part of the greater loss at the higher temperature. Most significantly, under controlled conditions at 1 cm depth in soils, nearly 100% of the 2,3,7,8-TCDD was lost after nine days of exposure to summer sunlight, with an added hydrogen donor of 1:1 v/v solution of xylene and ethyl oleate. In addition, 40-60% was lost in the "lower" layers, presumably 2-3 cm depth. The surprisingly high loss in the lower layers was suggested to be due to either diffusion of 2,3,7,8-TCDD in the oleate layer or to a "photolytic reaction occuring through radicals."

Crosby and Wong (41) examined the sunlight photolysis of 2,3,7,8-TCDD on glass surfaces using various 2,4,5-T formulations, including Agent Orange, the herbicide Esteron and Esteron formulation without 2,4,5-T. In sunlight, photolysis of 2,3,7,8-TCDD in Agent Orange resulted in nearly 60% loss of 2,3,7,8-TCDD in 6 hours. In the presence of the herbicide, Esteron, 70% was lost in 6 hours, and nearly 90% was lost in 2 hours of sunlight exposure in Esteron formulation without 2,4,5-T. 2,3,7,8-TCDD photolysis loss in Agent Orange also was examined on soil and rubber plant leaf surfaces. Loss was again rapid on the plant surface with 70 to 90% loss in 6 hours. On soils, photolysis was substantially slower and more than 80% of 2,3,7,8-TCDD remained after 6 hours of exposure. Rapid initial loss from the soil was followed by a pronounced decrease in the photolysis rate constant. On 2,3,7,8-TCDD contaminated soils treated with olive oil, photodecomposition also was observed in experiments at Seveso, Italy, although substantial data scatter was apparent (42).

Gebefugi and coworkers (43) irradiated 2,3,7,8-TCDD sorbed on silica gel with pyrex filtered high pressure mercury arc radiation and found that only 8% remained following 18 days of exposure. They concluded that photochemical decomposition of 2,3,7,8-TCDD in sunlight is likely in soils, even without an added organic solvent.

Plimmer (44) also found that 63% of 2,3,7,8-TCDD degraded on silica gel exposed to 20 hours of sunlight and produced a polar product. Only 68% of the original radioactivity was recovered after the 20-hour exposure, suggesting that volatility may be a factor in the loss. On soils, no difference was observed between exposed and non-exposed areas, suggesting that soil exerts a protective effect against the photolysis of 2,3,7,8-TCDD.

Exner and coworkers (45) have recently described a process of in-place detoxication of dioxin-contaminated soil using an unfiltered 450 watt mercury arc lamp. The goal of this work was to determine whether dioxin contaminated soils could be treated by exposure to intense ultraviolet light. As in other studies, an organic solvent greatly accelerated the process. Using Times Beach, Missouri soils, which were heavily contaminated, they demonstrated substantial reduction in the amount of 2,3,7,8-TCDD on the soils when various soil amendments were used. The soil depth in these experiments ranged from 4 to 8 mm and contained: (a) ethyl oleate/o-xylene sprayed at 0.35 L/m$^2$ (27 hour exposure gave 81% removal); (b) ethyl oleate/water surfactant (75-hour exposure gave 68% removal); and (c) aqueous surfactants at 2% w/w of the soils (7 hour exposure gave 63% removal). In the last experiment (3), irradiation of dry soils for 7 hours gave no detectable loss of 2,3,7,8-TCDD, and soils sprayed only with water and irradiated for 7 hours showed only 6% loss of 2,3,7,8-TCDD. Mixing and rewetting the soils with the organic solvent at 30-minute intervals during irradiation resulted in greater loss of 2,3,7,8-TCDD. In each of the experiments using aqueous surfactants, the soils were rewetted during the irradiation. The primary conclusion of this research was that in-place destruction of 2,3,7,8-TCDD occurs readily in the presence of 0.3-3% w/w levels of common agricultural surfactants. It also implied that solubilization and transport to the air/soil surface may be a necessary step for degradation of 2,3,7,8-TCDD by light.

Measurement of the vapor phase photolysis of 2,3,7,8-TCDD is experimentally a major challenge due to the low volatility. Podoll and coworkers (3), however, have estimated the half life of 2,3,7,8-TCDD in the vapor phase to be 55 minutes. This estimate assumed that the quantum yield is the same as in hexane and is invariant with wavelength, that the spectral properties are the same as in solution, and that the mechanisms for transformation are the same. This photolysis half-life is approximately 200 times smaller than that expected for reaction with hydroxyl radical. However, both vapor phase photolysis and reactions with OH radicals would be unimportant if TCDD is predominantly sorbed on particles in the atmosphere. Experimental verification of these estimates is needed, because atmospheric transformation may be an important fate of 2,3,7,8-TCDD and other dioxins which enter the atmosphere from combustion or from wind erosion of contaminated surface soils.

In summary, published investigations to date indicate that:

1. 2,3,7,8-TCDD undergoes relatively rapid photolysis in sunlight when dissolved in solution.
2. The rate of photolysis is dependent on the chemical microenvironment; organic solvents greatly accelerate the photolysis.

3. Photolysis of 2,3,7,8-TCDD in soils is slow, and was not observed in several studies: addition of an organic solvent to the soils promotes the photolysis.
4. Information on how soil properties affect the photo-lysis is lacking. Also, the depth dependence of photolysis is not well understood.
5. Successful modeling of 2,3,7,8-TCDD photolysis in soils requires additional basic information on the significance of photolysis in relation to other fate and transport processes.

## Transport Processes

2,3,7,8-TCDD and related compounds are transported while sorbed on particles, while dissolved in water or other solvents, or while dispersed in the vapor state. If photolysis is the primary pathway for detoxication of TCDD, transport to sunlight exposed areas may be the limiting factor for degradation, especially in soils where ver-tical transport of 2,3,7,8-TCDD is exceedingly slow. Its extremely low water solubility and vapor pressure combine to give a rate of movement expressed in cm/year in soils (22), although added organic solvents can greatly increase the mobility of TCDD. Consequently, estimating the rate of movement of 2,3,7,8-TCDD in soils requires detailed data on the soil characteristics and the presence of sol-vents or oils.

The reported log octanol-water partition coefficient ($K_{ow}$) for 2,3,7,8-TCDD varies from 6.15 to 8.48 (3,7,8). The magnitude of this value, in addition to the low water solubility, suggests that it will be primarily associated with particles in sediment and soil, with a vanishingly small fraction in the non-sorbed phase. This was demonstrated by Jackson and coworkers (46) who examined the solu-bility of 2,3,7,8-TCDD in ten soils. They observed that the soil partition coefficient for ten soils ranged from 0.4 x $10^5$ to 45.8 x $10^5$. Although 2,3,7,8-TCDD would move only very slowly in these soils, if oils or other solvents were present, sorption coefficients may be much lower and thus movement significant.

Volatilization of 2,3,7,8-TCDD from soils is expected to be very slow, due to the low vapor pressure and high octanol-water partition coefficient. Mill (47) estimates that the half-life for vaporization of 2,3,7,8-TCDD from soils will range from many months to years, in the absence of intervening transformation processes. Due to this rather substantial period, and the observed relatively rapid photolysis on soils, vaporization from soils may not be a significant source of 2,3,7,8-TCDD in the atmosphere. The main source of cholorinated dibenzodioxins in the atmosphere is probably municipal and industrial incineration (10). Because of large parti-tion coefficients, dioxins in the atmosphere are likely associated predominantly with particles. Further information is needed, how-ever, to firmly resolve the physical state of dioxins in the atmosphere.

In the top several centimeters of soil, photolysis, volatiliza-tion, mass transport in water either dissolved, sorbed on particles, or complexed with other molecules, and bioturbation are potential processes that affect chemical behavior. Freeman and Schroy (22) have developed a model for movement of 2,3,7,8-TCDD in soils based on volatilization as the predominant transport process. To simulate the effect of temperature on the transport of 2,3,7,8-TCDD in soil a time dependent energy balance model was constructed. Using this model they calculated the expected movement of 2,3,7,8 TCDD at a site at Eglin Air Force Base that had been intentionally contaminated 12 years previously at a depth of 11 cm. Careful analysis of the various depths of the soil indicated that 2,3,7,8-TCDD had dispersed approximately 10 cm during the 12-year period. Agreement was found between the model results and the observed depth profile.

Podoll and coworkers (3) have redetermined the vapor pressure of 2,3,7,8-TCDD. Using this information together with the aqueous solubility, octanol/ water partition coefficient and photolysis quantum yields, investigators have estimated the half-lives for movement and transformation of 2,3,7,8-TCDD in water and air. Even though the vapor pressure (P) of 2,3,7,8-TCDD is low, the water solubility (S) is also very low and the Henry's law constant is therefore significant, and allows vaporization from water.

$$H = P/S = 7.4 \times 10^{-10} \text{ torr}/6 \times 10^{-11} \text{ M}$$

$$= 12 \text{ torr M}^{-1}$$

Using a two film model, the volatilization half-lives for 2,3,7,8-TCDD were estimated to be 32 and 16 days, respectively, in 200 cm deep ponds and rivers.

## Concluding Comments

2,3,7,8-TCDD is the most toxic of the dioxins and remains a primary concern for exposure to humans. Although combustion sources of this compound are now readily accepted, waste contaminated soils and waste dumps remain a costly problem.

The extensive amount of research on this compound has indicated that 2,3,7,8-TCDD is both remarkably stable and is almost exclusively associated with particulate material. Because of the low water solubility and high sorption on soils, it moves only very slowly in natural soils. Human exposure to 2,3,7,8-TCDD in soils is thus a function of movement and degradation (primarily photochemical) on soil particles. Enhanced movement of 2,3,7,8-TCDD in soils also contaminated with oils and/or solvents potentially can increase concentrations near the surface, and this process, along with photolysis on particles, requires further investigation.

## Literature Cited

1. Nestrick, T. J.; Lamparski, L. L.; Stehl, R. H. Anal. Chem. 1979, 51, 2273-2281.
2. Schroy, F. M.; Hileman, F. D.; Cheng, S. C. Chemosphere 1985, 14, 877-880.
3. Podoll, R. T.; Jaber, H. M.; Mill, T. Environ. Sci. Technol. 1986, 20, 490-492.
4. Boer, F. P.; van Remoortere, F. P.; Muelder, W. W. J. Am. Chem. Soc. 1972, 94, 1006-1007.
5. Marple, L.; Runck, R.; Throop, L. Environ. Sci. Technol. 1986, 20, 180-182.

6.  Esposito, M. P.; Teirnan, T. O.; Dryden, F. E.  "Dioxins", U.S.
    EPA, Office of Research and Development, Cincinnati, Ohio,
    EPA-600/2-80-197, 1980.
7.  Kenaga, E. E.  Environ. Sci. Technol. 1980, 14, 553-556.
8.  Surna, L. P.; Hodge, P. E.; Webster, G. R. B.  Chemosphere
    1984, 13, 975.
9.  Dulin, D.; Drossman, H.; Mill, T.  Environ. Sci. Technol. 1986,
    20, 72-77.
10. Hutzinger, O.; Blumich, M. J.; Berg, M. V. D.; Olie, K.  Chemo-
    sphere 1985, 14, 581-600.
11. Smith, R. M.; O'Keefe, P. W.; Aldous, K. M.; Hilker, D. R.;
    O'Brien, J. E.  Environ. Sci. Technol. 1983, 17, 6-10.
12. Yanders, A. F.; Kapila, S.; Schreiber, R. J.  In "Chlorinated
    Dioxins and Dibenzofurans in Perspective"; Rappe, C.;
    Choudhary, G.; Keith, L. H., Eds., Lewis Publishers, Chelsea,
    Mihigan, 1986; pp. 237-239.
13. Ingelog, I.  In "Chlorinated Phenoxy Acids and Their Dioxins";
    Ramel, C., Ed.; Swedish Natural Science Research Council: Lund,
    Sweden, 1978; pp. 240-254.
14. Schecter, A. J.; Ryan, J. J.; Gross, M.; Weerasinhe, N. C. A.;
    Constable, J. D.  In "Chlorinated Dioxins and Dibenzofurans in
    Perspective"; Rappe, C.; Choudhary, G.; Keith, L. H., Eds.;
    Lewis Publishers: Chelsea, Michigan, 1986; pp. 35-50.
15. The Trace Chemistries of Fire--A Source of and Routes for the
    Entry of Chlorinated Dioxins into the Environment, The Chlori-
    nated Dioxin Task Force, The Michigan Division of Dow
    Chemicals, U.S.A.; 1978.
16. Buser, H. R.  J. Chromatography 1976, 129, 303-307.
17. Dobbs, A. J.; Grant, C.  Nature 1979, 278, 163-165.
18. Lamparski, L. L.; Stehl, R. H.; Johnson, R. L.  Environ. Sci.
    Technol. 1980, 14, 196-200.
19. Cull, M-R.; Dobbs, A. J.  Chemosphere 1984, 13, 1984.
20. Matsumura, F.; Benezet, H. J.  Environ. Health Perspect. 1973,
    5, 253-258.
21. Matsumura, F.; Quenson, J.; Tsushimoto, G.  In "Human and
    Environmental Risks of Chlorinated Dioxin and Related
    Compounds"; Tucker, R. E.; Young, A. L.; Gray, A. P., Eds.;
    Plenum Press:  New York, 1983, pp. 191-221.
22. Freeman, R. A.; Schroy, J. M.  Chemosphere 1985, 14, 873-876.
23. Kimbrough, R. D.; Falk, H.; Stehr, P.; Porter, C.; Fries, G.
    Health Implications of 2,3,7,8-TCDD Contamination of Residen-
    tial Soil Center for Disease Control, Atlanta, 1983.
24. Pocchiari, F.  In "Chlorinated Phenoxy Acids and Their
    Dioxins"; Ramel, C., Ed.; Ecol. Bull. Stockholm 1978, 27,
    67-70.
25. Ward, C. T.; Matsumara, F.  Arch. Environ. Cont. Toxicol. 1978,
    7, 349-357.
26. Bumpus, J. A.; Tien, M.; Wright, D.; Aust, S. D.  Science 1985,
    228, 1434.
27. Esposito, M. P.; Tiernan, T. O.; Dryden, F. E.  "Dioxins",
    EPA-600/2-80-197, U.S. Environmental Protection Agency,
    Cincinnati, Ohio; 1980.
28. Lau, B. P.-Y.; Sun, W.-P.; Ryan, J. J.  Chemosphere 1985, 14,
    799-802.

29. Tundo, P.; Facchetti, S.; Tumiatti, W.; Fortunati, U. G. Chemosphere 1985, 14, 403–410.
30. Kleopfer, R. D.; Haxel, R. H.; Freestone, F. J.; des Rosiers, P. E. In "Chlorinated Dioxins and Dibenzofurans in Perspective"; Lewis Publishers; Chelsea, MI 1986; pp. 511–530.
31. Choudhry, G. G.; Hutzinger, O. Residue Rev. 1982, 84, 113.
32. Dulin, D.; Drossman, H.; Mill, T. Environ. Sci. Technol. 1986, 20, 72.
33. Choudhry, G. G.; Webster, G. R. B. Chemosphere 1985, 14, 9.
34. Nestrick, T. J.; Lamparski, L. L.; Townsend, D. I.; Anal. Chem. 1980, 52, 1865.
35. Zepp, R. G. In: "Handbook of Environmental Chemistry", Vol. 2, Part B; Hutzinger, O., Ed.' Springer-Verlag: Berlin; 1980, pp. 19–41.
36. Pohland, A. E.; Yang, G. C. J. Agr. Food Chem. 1972, 20, 1093.
37. Miller, G. C.; Sontum, S.; Crosby, D. G. Bull. Environ. Contam. Toxicol. 1977, 18, 611.
38. Crosby, D. G.; Wong, A. S.; Plimmer, J. R.; Woolson, E. A. Science 1971, 173, 748.
39. Wipf, H. K.; Homberger, E.; Neuner, N. Schlemlker In "Dioxin: Toxicological and Chemical Aspects"; Cattabeni, F.; Cavallaro, A.; Galli, G. Eds.; S. P. Medical and Sci. Books, 1978, p. 201.
40. Botre, C.; Memoli, A.; Alhaique, F. Environ. Sci. Technol. 1978, 12, 335.
41. Liberti, A.; Brocco, D.; Allegrini, I.; Cecinato, A.; Possanzini, M. Sci. Total Environ. 1978, 10, 97.
42. Crosby, D. G.; Wong, A. S. Science 1977, 198, 1337.
43. Crosby, D. G. In "Disposal and Decomtamination of Pesticides"; Kennedy, M. V., Ed.; American Chemical Society Symposim Series, No. 73. 1978, p. 1.
44. Gebefugi, I.; Baumann, R.; Korte, F. Naturwissenschaften 1977, 64, 486.
45. Plimmer, J. Bull. Environ. Contam. Toxicol. 1977, 20, 87.
46. Exner, J. H.; Alperin, E. S.; Groen, A., Jr.; Morren, C. E. Hazardous Waste 1984, 1, 217.
47. Jackson, D. R.; Roulier, M. H.; Grotta, H. M.; Rust, S. W.; Warner, J. S. In "Chlorinated Dioxin and Dibenzofurans in Perspective", Rappe, C.; Choudhary, G.; Keith, L. H., Eds.; Lewis, Publishers: Chelsea, MI, 1986, pp. 185–200.
48. Mill, T. In "Dioxins in the Environment", Damrin, M.; Rodgers, P. W., Eds.; Hemisphere Publishing Co., 1985, pp. 173–193.

RECEIVED January 16, 1987

# Chapter 7

# Persistent Toxic Organic Waste: Is Destruction Necessary?

Douglas J. Hallett

ELI—Eco Logic Inc., Rural Route 2, Acton, Ontario L7J 2L8, Canada

Persistent toxic chemicals are now ubiquitous throughout the global biosphere. Environmental processes such as long-range transport through the atmosphere play a major role in creating this global dispersion. They are also the major exposure route to the human species through the terrestrial food web. Hazard and risk assessment associated with persistent contaminants must focus on dynamics throughout the whole ecosystem and total human exposure. Best available or best practicable treatment processes for wastes that contain persistent contaminants must be evaluated in terms of ecosystem exposure rather than providing diversions. Examples include the diversion of contaminants from an aquatic effluent into sewage sludge that is then either incinerated at low temperature or land farmed; both of these methods allow volatilization into atmosphere. The adoption of loading limits versus acceptable concentrations derived by dilution of persistent toxic substances is necessary. This paper considers the chemical dynamics of persistent organochlorine contaminants in the Great Lakes ecosystem, the major sources, present waste treatment, and the total ecosystem exposure to the human species.

0097-6156/87/0338-0094$06.00/0
© 1987 American Chemical Society

Risk is a function of two variables: toxicity and exposure. This paper concerns not only environmental exposure but ecosystem cycling and ecosystem or true multi-media exposure for persistent organic toxic substances such as chlorinated dibenzo-p-dioxins (PCDD), chlorinated dibenzofurans (PCDF), PCBs, and other chlorinated structures. Although bioaccumulation due to the lipophilicity of organochlorines is important, it is not the sole factor to consider in assessing exposure. If one considers the chemical properties of these molecules to persist, and that these chemicals cycle between water and sediment, water and the atmosphere, and between soil, air and water, one can then begin to understand the multi-media exposure and risk that occurs today. Only then can the total risk for one compound (from any source such as a disposal process be mathematically estimated based on non-occupational ecosystem exposure. This risk estimation is key to understanding and prioritizing dioxin types and sources in the environment and deciding on remedial strategies.

## The Great Lakes Sources And Pathways

The Great Lakes ecosystem is extremely sensitive as well as being relatively polluted with persistent toxic substances. Why? In 1977 our limited understanding led us to believe that the high levels of PCBs in the Great Lakes system were due to the vast number of sources of pollution coming from the eight industrial Great Lakes States and the Province of Ontario in Canada. However, experience with phosphate management in the Great Lakes and a growing knowledge of the physical limnology of these large, deep lakes, which exhibit high surface to volume ratios and extremely long retention times, has revealed that these properties allow the lakes to reach such high levels of persistent contaminants. The high surface to volume ratio allows the lakes to capture large quantities of persistent substances from long range atmospheric transport which brings contaminated rain. Examples include polychlorinated dibenzofurans and dioxins, which along with PCB and toxaphene are found in the sediments and fish of Siskiwit Lake, a remote lake found on Isle Royale, in north central L. Superior. This island has neither industry, agriculture, nor logging (1,2). The deposition rate of chlorinated dioxins and dibenzofurans on this island matches the deposition rate in L. Superior. The common source of these contaminants for both lakes is the atmosphere, which accounts for up to 85 % of the PCB and 100 % of the toxaphene entering L. Superior (3).

It is now obvious that atmospheric transport of persistent toxic organic substances is the major pathway between ecosystems. For dioxin, volatilization of residues from contaminated soils was first noted as a concern at Seveso, Italy (4). The National Research Council of Canada reported that atmospheric emissions were the major source of chlorinated dioxins in the Canadian environment (5). A recent Ontario report estimates that from 8 - 10 kg of 2,3,7,8 -TCDD equivalents enter the Ontario environment annually from combustion of municipal refuse and sewage sludge and that all other combustion sources contribute from 20 - 50 kg annually (6). The only other major source considered was from the use and disposal of chlorinated phenols.

In the Great Lakes we have observed some dramatic trends in persistent residues, particularly in L. Ontario. Spatial trends in sediment have indicated that industrial centres in the lower Great Lakes such as L. Erie and L. Ontario have contributed vast quantities of PCBs and lead into the water.

Temporal trends through time show us a confusing situation. On first glance one can see a dramatic improvement in L. Ontario residues of PCBs, mirex, and dioxin in wildlife and fish between 1970 and 1980 (7). However, from 1980 to 1984 the downward trend stopped for all of these residues. On examining the sediment record at the source of L. Ontario, the Niagara River, we find a deposition rate for PCBs and mirex from 1950 to 1960 at approximately the present day rate. However, at about 1960 a tremendous pulse of PCBs, mirex, chlorobenzenes, and hexachlorobutadiene is shown in the sediment record. The deposition rate tapers off to 1970 when it plateaus at about the 1950's rate (8). The water in the Niagara R. still contains PCB, mirex, chlorinated dioxins, and dibenzofurans. The sources are most likely leachate from the series of landfills in the area containing over 250 million tons of chlorinated waste (9). The phenomenon of rapid declines in industrial areas is quite common in the Great Lakes basin and likely reflects either controlled effluents or lower production of the key persistent contaminants.

If we look at L. Superior, which is far less industrialized than L. Ontario, we find that there has been a slow decline in PCB residues found in fish and wildlife. More importantly, residue levels are now similar to those found in the industrialized Great Lakes. This phenomenon is more characteristic of the global trends (10),(11).

In the Great Lakes region we have begun to follow PCB with mass balance or input-output models. Eisenreich et al, (3) has shown such a model for L.Superior. (Table I).

There is a flux occurring both downwards from the atmosphere and upwards again from the surface-water interaction. Mackay and Paterson (12,13) have considered this phenomenon with fugacity models. Molecules with lower vapour pressure tend to be more strongly sorbed to aerosols and so are more susceptible to washout in precipitation. PCBs such as represented in the mixture Aroclor 1254 have a vapour pressure of 7 x $10^{-5}$ mm Hg (14,15). These will be more readily washed out of the atmosphere than lesser chlorinated biphenyls such as those represented in the mixture Aroclor 1241 with a vapour pressure of 4 x $10^{-4}$ mm Hg. This same property allows for the volatilization of chlorinated biphenyls particularly with 3 and 4 chlorines per molecule during precipitation free periods. (13). Since the vapour pressure varies with temperature, winter seasons with lower temperatures and greater precipitation may encourage an increased downward flux wheras summer seasons would encourage a more upward flux.

Table I. Model of PCBs in Lake Superior

| INPUT | Kg·yr$^{-1}$ | OUTPUT | |
|---|---|---|---|
| ATMOSPHERE | 6,600-8,300 | St. Mary's River | 140 |
| TRIBUTARY | < 1,311 | SEDIMENTATION | 1,000-1,600 |
| MUNICIPAL | 66 | DEGRADATION | ? |
| INDUSTRIAL | 2 | WATER-AIR TRANSFER | ? |
| TOTAL | 8,000-9,700 | TOTAL | 1,140-1,740 |

The vapour pressure of these molecules is then a critical property in terms of movement in the ecosystem, particularly at the air/water interface and at the soil/water interface. We have yet to determine the transfer coefficients and fluxes at these interfaces in the gaseous phase, particularly the upward volatilization from soil and water. Verification will require the use of gas phase samplers.

For chlorinated dioxins and furans we know much less. Estimates place their vapour pressure in a range similar to that of PCB (16). They are expected to move in a relatively similar fashion (17). PCB in L. Huron biota show a slowly declining trend similar to L. Superior. Levels are sharply increased in Saginaw Bay

near Midland, Michigan and the outflows of the
Tittibawassi and Saginaw Rivers. Increasing deposi-
tional rates were shown for total PCDD and PCDF in L.
Huron. These increases correspond temporally with the
production of chloro-aromatics and correspond spatially
similar to PCBs with the proximity to Saginaw Bay and
the Saginaw River system(1). The pattern of chlorinated dioxins and furans corresponded closely to that
of combustion of chloro-aromatics and not fossil fuels
such as coal. Sediment samples from the Great Lakes
show this type of pattern save for L. Ontario where
the pattern more closely fits that of pentachlorophenol. Distinct pattern changes for PCDD and PCDF
were also evident in urban dust from various cities.
Patterns of dust from Chicago are distinctly different
from Midland, Michigan, which are different from
Detroit.

Limited samples of soils near industrial
incinerators at Midland, Michigan show elevated levels
of PCDD ranging from ng/g to ug/g quantities, whereas
rural areas show non-detectable levels. Urban areas
near municipal incinerators in Chicago show detectable
levels of PCDD but at levels ranging from pg/g to ng/g
(18). Similar results were found in Hamilton,
Ontario near a municipal waste incinerator (6).

The most recent and striking example of current
discharge of waste contaminated with PCDD and PCDF is
in the St. Clair River at Sarnia, Ontario, upstream of
the drinking water supplies of the cities of Detroit,
Michigan, and Windsor, Ontario (19). In this case a
large, heavier than water mat of chemicals was found on
the bottom of the Canadian side of the river in both
1984 and 1985. This material contained percentage
levels of perchloroethylene, part per thousand levels
of chlorobenzenes, hexachlorobutadiene, chloropropenes,
octachlorostyrene, and PCBs and parts per billion
levels of PCDD and PCDF. Although the octa- and hepta-
chlorocongeners of PCDD and PCDF predominated, tetra-
chlorodioxins characteristic of 2, 4 -D were found and
mass spectral confirmation of 2, 4 -D was also obtained
in the 1984 sample. It is important to realize that
the presence of dioxin in the waste was the major
public concern whereas it was the presence of water
soluble compounds such as chloropropenes, chlorobenzenes, and perchloroethylene at extremely high
concentrations which posed the greatest immediate
threat to drinking water supplies. However, the less
water soluble chlorinated dioxin/dibenzofuran molecules
pose the greatest long-term threat in that they persist
in sediment at ug/kg levels along approximately a 3 km
stretch of the river bottom both upstream and
downstream of the tarry mat of chemicals. Candidate
sources of this discharge of chemicals, which are no
longer manufactured by local industry, include an

industrial landfill, old sewer lines, and groundwater
contaminated by previous deep well injection of similar
wastes.

## Humans In The Ecosystem

Herring Gulls and the coho salmon living in L.
Ontario have a common food source, alewives and smelt
which are the next step lower on the food chain.
Alewives and smelt are the common source of PCB, DDE
mirex, photomirex, and chlorobenzenes to the gulls and
salmon (Table II)(20). The same relationship for
2,3,7,8-TCDD can be shown.(5)

Table II.  Residues in Gulls and Fish in Ontario

| | Alewives and Smelt (mg/kg) | Coho Salmon (mg/kg) | Herring Gull eggs (mg/kg) |
|---|---|---|---|
| PCB | 2.21 | 5.7 | 138 |
| DDE | .47 | .97 | 17.4 |
| Mirex | .09 | .23 | 4.4 |
| Photomirex | .03 | .11 | 1.6 |
| HCB | .024 | .097 | 0.52 |
| BHCH | .002 | .012 | .078 |
| TCDD (5) | $14 \times 10^{-6}$ | $30 \times 10^{-6}$ | $55 \times 10^{-6}$ |
| Heptachlor epoxide | .003 | .015 | .007 |
| Dieldrin | .029 | .087 | .060 |
| | n=12 | n=10        n=47 | n=125 |

When one examines residues in the human population
in Ontario (Table III), one finds exactly the same
residues that are found in Herring Gulls and fish.
Human body fat contains approximately the same
concentrations as those found in alewives and smelt
taken from L. Ontario.

Since Herring Gulls and coho salmon accumulate
these residues from their common food supply, it seemed
logical to consider the human exposure routes
thoroughly, particularly the food supply. An early
study by Bennet (23) followed total non-occupational
environmental exposure of PCB to humans. This study
showed that for PCB the atmospheric pathway contam-
inates plants directly, livestock indirectly, and
ultimately contributes the major human environmental
dosage of PCB. Exposure from drinking water and the
atmosphere directly are inconsequential relative to
food exposure. A more recent modelling effort (17) for
2,3,7,8-TCDD again shows food as the major route of

Table III.  Residues in Humans in Ontario

| | Adipose Tissue(21) (mg/kg) | | Breast Milk(22) -fat basis (mg/kg) |
|---|---|---|---|
| | Kingston | Ottawa | Ontario | Ontario |
| PCB | 3.0 | 2.0 | 2.1 | 0.756 |
| DDT | 3.429 | 2.694 | 4.069 | 0.983 |
| Mirex | 0.027 | 0.011 | 0.02 | – |
| Photomirex | 0.009 | 0.006 | – | – |
| HCB | 0.106 | 0.078 | 0.013 | 0.0184 |
| BHCH | 0.136 | 0.065 | – | – |
| TCDD | $12 \times 10^{-6}$ | $8.6 \times 10^{-6}$ | – | – |
| Heptachlor epoxide | 0.035 | 0.037 | 0.07 | 0.012 |
| Dieldrin | 0.036 | 0.043 | 0.10 | 0.194 |

exposure being transmitted from air to soil and then to plants and livestock.  Based on these two studies a search of the literature was begun for residue values for PCDD and PCDF in food.  No literature was available on general levels of dioxins in foods save for anomalous cases such as near chlorophenol production facilities and accidents.

In order to obtain exposure information on PCDD and PCDF as well as more realistic information on PCB and other persistent residues, a direct food composite survey was taken from supermarkets throughout the city of Toronto in the summer of 1985 (24).  Only food grown in Ontario was sampled.  Food was divided into five categories: leafy vegetables, fruit, root vegetables, milk, and meat and eggs.  Chlorobenzenes were detected in all composites, with the most common congeners being the trichloroisomers.  Lindane was detected in all composites except cows' milk.  Other hexachlorocyclo- hexane isomers were also prevalent.  DDT and its metabolites were still found in all composites.  PCB were detected in fruit, milk and meat/eggs composites with the highest concentration found in fruit.  Concentration of all the above residues, when detected, range from 0.1 to 1 ug/kg on a fresh weight basis.

Residues of PCDD and PCDF were detected in highest concentration in the fruit composite with the predominent residues being Penta-CDF, (0.28 ug/kg), Hex-CDF (2.0 ug/kg), Hex-CDD (0.45 ug/kg), Hep-CDF (6.6 ug/kg), Hep-CDD (1.2 ug/kg) Octa-CDF (1.2 ug/kg) and Octa-CDD (1.2 ug/kg).  Residues in milk were the second highest with the predominant congeners being Tetra-CDF, Tetra-CDD, Pe-CDF, Hep-CDF, Hep-CDD, Octa-CDF, and Octa-CDD all found between 0.01 and 0.1 ug/kg.  Root vegetables and the meat/eggs composite were contam- inated at lower concentrations.

These residue concentrations fit well with the fugacity III model prediction of Mackay et al (17) and begin to confirm that our food is the major exposure route for PCDD and PCDF.

## Discussion

PCDD and PCDF are found widespread in the human population in a similar fashion to PCB, DDT and its metabolites, chlorobenzenes, and other common persistent organochlorines. Since food is influenced by environmental residue trends, human residue levels and exposure levels will likely follow environmental trends closely. In the Great Lakes basin area overall trends are not declining for either PCB or PCDD and PCDF except in localized areas.

Based on these findings several immediate recommendations are evident:

a) Risk estimates must consider the total multi media exposure routes for PCB, PCDD and PCDF. They must also consider that any additional risk posed by a potential increase in the exposure to these compounds must be considered from the point of view that exposure, and therefore risk, is already present.

b) Epidemiological studies must consider that populations with potential increased exposure are being compared with populations already exposed. Ambient exposure must be thoroughly documented and understood at current levels if we are to understand incremental risk.

c) Environmental records show that residue levels of these compounds increased during the period from 1940 to 1960 and no major downward shift has occurred on a widespread basis to match this increased deposition rate. Human residues for these compounds will not decline until measures are taken to either permanently contain or destroy the major sources of these compounds.

## Sources

The major sources of PCDD and PCDF in the Great Lakes basin are low temperature municipal waste and sewage sludge incinerators, and leachate from past disposal practices, some of which were designed to contain wastes (6). All of these current source types are the result of engineering treatment designed to reduce the concentration of these compounds in discharges to water bodies.

In the case of sewage sludge incineration, chemical wastes have been preconcentrated in the sludge to reduce the aqueous effluents. Current low

temperature incineration practices lead to traces of
PCDD and PCDF. Sludge absorption does little to reduce
the net flow of persistent contaminants to the
ecosystem but merely diverts them from the water to the
atmosphere where they will either be transported or
condensed out, ultimately entering the water. It is
these municipal and sludge incineration sources that
likely provide the greatest impact on human exposure
through food. In the case of landfill leachate and
areas where liquid wastes are available for cost-
effective recovery, destruction would certainly seem
the most desirable option over attempts to re-contain
the waste.

The most cost-effective solution to both problems
would be the on-site destruction of any available
liquid waste containing persistent residues such as
PCBs, PCDD and PCDF. This option would eliminate the
transportation cost as well as risk in addition to
removing any future risk, liabilty and cost. Remedial
measures must not simply divert residue movement from
the water into the air, such as in landfill remediation
where temporary storage lagoons for leachate can allow
rapid volatilization of PCBs, PCDD and PCDF.

Future Directions

1.       Liability for possession and production of
persistent toxic chemicals, particularly PCDD and PCDF
is going to increase. In Ontario the recent
promulgation of the "Spills Bill" has placed the
liability for immediate cleanup and damages for a spill
of toxic chemicals directly on the transporter and
producer. This bill will eventually increase the cost
of transportation of waste and promote on-site
destruction devices.
2.       The long-term liability for possession of
persistent toxic chemicals, particularly PCDD and PCDF
is also going to increase. Multi-media hazard,
exposure and risk assessments are now becoming more
common in the U.S.A. and Canada and will place a higher
emphasis on direct and indirect toxic chemical exposure
from the atmosphere. Storage, transfer, waste reduction and destruction facilities, and even some
recycling facilities will come under severe pressure to
meet new atmospheric standards. These standards will
include provision for contemporary local air transport
models which are key to the assessment of exposure and
risk posed by highly toxic chemicals. Effective
destruction will remove this liability.
3.       Over the next decade aquatic effluents as
well as atmospheric emissions in the Great Lakes basin
will likely be considered in terms of loading

requirements rather than current concentration guidelines. This approach is already being used by the six states in co-operation with the USEPA who are grappling with a loading reduction strategy for PCB into Lake Michigan. This same approach is called for by the Canadian and U.S. technical committees on the Niagara River and a new IJC Loadings Task force is beginning work on L. Ontario. If loadings in these areas are to be reduced by 50 %, destruction of in situ sources of chlorinated persistent compounds such as PCB, PCDD and PCDF will most likely be required.

4.        Finally, PCDD and PCDF are becoming recognized as one of the most prevalent toxic chemical groups in industrialized areas. They are prevalent in human tissues. Preliminary evidence verifies exposure models showing food as the major vector. Dioxins may be one of the most prevalent residues in certain food types such as milk and fruit. Since emissions to the air are the most likely pathway to food, our priority must lie with reducing the creation of these compounds through improper combustion of organochlorine precursors and reducing the overall cycling of these compounds by destruction of existing major sources to the air, water and soil of our ecosystem.

## Literature Cited

1    Czuczwa, J.M. and Hites, R.A. 1986. Environ. Sci. Technol. 1986. 20 No. 2 195-200.
2    Swain, W.R. Abstracts 25th Conf. International Association for Great Lakes Research. 1982.
3    Eisenreich, S.J., B.B. Looney, and J.D. Thornton. Environ. Sci. Technol. 1981. 15: 30-38.
4    Hallett, D.J., Hutter, M.P. In "Environmental Fate of Chlorinated Dioxins and Related Compounds"; O. Hutzinger, Pergamon Press, 1982.
5    National Research Council of Canada, Ottawa, Canada. 1982. NRCC Publication No. 18574, p.251.
6    Ontario Ministry of the Environment. Scientific Criteria Document No. 4-84. 1985. Toronto, Canada.
7    Hallett, D.J. In "Persistent Toxic Substances and the Health of Aquatic Communities." John Wiley and Sons In press.
8    Durham, R.W. and Oliver, B.G. J. Great Lakes Res., 1983. 9:160-168.
9    Hallett, D.J., and Brooksbank, M.G. Chemosphere 1986. (in press).
10   Organization for Economic Co-operation and Development. Proc. PCB Seminar the Netherlands. 1983. p. 410.
11   Rappe, C. In "Solving Hazardous Waste Problems: Remedial Action at Sites Contaminated by

Polychlorinated Dioxins"   191st ACS National
Meeting.  New York, N.Y.  1986.  p.86.

12    Mackay, D. and Paterson, S.  Environ. Sci.
Technol.  1982.  16 6554A.

13    Mackay, D. and Paterson, S.  In "Environmental
Exposure from Chemicals"  Neely, B Ed. CRC Press
(in press).

14    Bidleman, T.F. and Christensen, E.J.  J. Geophys.
Res.  1979  84 No. C12 7857-7862.

15    Murphy, T.J. and Rzeszutko, C.P.  J. Great Lakes
Res.  1977  3, 305-312.

16    Rordorf, B.F.  Chemosphere, 1985, 14, No6/7 885-892

17    Mackay, D. Paterson, S. and Cheung, B.
Chemosphere, 1985, 14 No 6/7 859-864.

18    Dow Chemical.  "The trace chemistries of fire."
1978.  46pp.

19    "St. Clair River Pollution Investigation."
Ontario Ministry of the Environment.  1985.

20    Norstrom, R.J., Hallett, D.J., and Sonstegard,
R.A.  J. Fish. Res. Board. Can.  1978.  35 1401-
1409.

21    Williams, D.T., LeBel, G.L., and Junkins, E.  J.
Toxicol. and Environ. Health.  1984, 13:19-29

22    Frank, R., Ontario Ministry of Agriculture and
Food, (personal communication).

23    Bennet, B.G., Sci. Total Environ., 1983.  29:101-
111.

24    Davies, D.  1986.  Proc. World Conf. on Large
Lakes., Mackinac Mich.

RECEIVED January 14, 1987

# Chapter 8

# Experimental and Calculated Physical Constants for 2,3,7,8-Tetrachlorodibenzo-*p*-dioxin

Leland Marple, Robert Brunck, Bernard Berridge, and Lewis Throop

Syntex Analytical and Environmental Research, Syntex (USA), Inc.,
3401 Hillview Avenue, Palo Alto, CA 94303

The measurement of water solubility, water–octanol and
water–soil partition coefficients presented several
unique challenges. Novel experimental methods and data
are reported for these physical constants. In some
cases, experimental data is at odds with earlier
published values. Comprehensive comparison of all
available estimated, calculated, and experimental data
are presented. The new values impact the calculation
of the mobility of dioxin in soil, as well as other
distribution properties.

In spite of many studies on the physical properties of dioxin,
we were unable to find any definitive work that measured the water
solubility, octanol–water partition, or soil–water partition
constants or coefficients for 2,3,7,8-tetrachlorodibenzo-p-dioxin
(dioxin). The importance of these values in predicting the
migration of dioxin in an environmental setting led us to undertake
a program to measure these physical constants.

WATER SOLUBILITY

Water solubility values in current use that ranged from 0.2 to 2 ppb
were at odds with our observation that in the absence of suspended
matter, the amount of dioxin in environmental water samples analyzed
in this laboratory was rarely more than 2-3 parts per trillion
(ppt). We anticipated that our main difficulties in measuring
dioxin solubility would be separation of solid, adsorbed, and
dissolved dioxin, and the measurement of soluble dioxin in the
equilibrated solutions. During the last two years, we developed
three techniques for measuring the water solubility of dioxin. The
merits and results of each of the methods and comparison with
solubility values from the literature are given below.

Our first method began by subliming 14C-radiolabeled dioxin onto
the cold finger of a small sublimation flask. The sublimate was

0097-6156/87/0338-0105$06.00/0
© 1987 American Chemical Society

then transferred to a second flask that had been silanized and
filled with distilled water.  After equilibration, the major portion
of the water was removed, the dioxin was extracted with hexane, the
hexane extract was evaporated to near dryness, and the residue was
taken up in Oxifluor scintillation fluid for counting.

Measurement of the specific activity of the 14-C dioxin by GC/EC
allowed calculation of the amount of dioxin that was dissolved.
Since the amount of dioxin that dissolved was so small compared to
the amount on the cold finger, the same sublimate could be used for
all equilibrations.  The results for the solubility of 14-C dioxin
are given in Table I.

Table I.  Solubility of 14-C Dioxin in Water from a Sublimed Film

| Equil. time days | Conc. TCDD ppt | Solubility moles/liter |
|---|---|---|
| 1 | 6.8 | $2.0 \times 10^{-11}$ |
| 3 | 12.7 | $3.9 \times 10^{-11}$ |
| 5 | 12.3 | $3.85 \times 10^{-11}$ |

These values were much lower than the 200 ppt value reported by
Crummett and Stehl (1).

To avoid concerns about the radiochemical purity of the labeled
dioxin, the solubility of unlabeled, 98% pure (Cambridge Isotope
Labs) dioxin was determined by a scaled up version of the method
just described.  In this experiment, the entire contents of the
flask was transferred to a separatory funnel, 13-C dioxin was added
as an internal standard, and the combined dioxins were extracted
with hexane.  A capillary GC/MS method was used for quantitation
(5).  A summary of results is given in Table II.

Table II.  Solubility of Unlabeled Dioxin in Water From a Sublimed
            Film

| Equil. time days | Conc. TCDD ppt | Solubility moles/liter |
|---|---|---|
| 1 | 18.6 | $5.8 \times 10^{-11}$ |
| 3 | 15.4 | $4.8 \times 10^{-11}$ |
| 5 | 25.1 | $7.8 \times 10^{-11}$ |
| 5 | 20.7 | $6.4 \times 10^{-11}$ |
| 5 | 16.9 | $5.2 \times 10^{-11}$ |

The high surface to volume ratio of dioxin film afforded by the sublimation flask allows equilibrium to be reached in a short time, and allows easy, complete separation of the solid dioxin from the equilibrated solution. The values obtained were consistent with those obtained with radiolabeled dioxin.

The third method involved equilibration of dioxin present in a compact film on a glass slide, (formed by evaporation of dioxin dissolved in hexane), with water in a 2 liter volumetric flask. A glass stirrer was used for mixing the contents. To avoid problems with the formation of an interfacial film, the flask was rigorously cleaned with boiling concentrated nitric acid, and the cleaned flask was filled to the neck with water for equilibration. A capillary GC/MS method was used for dioxin analysis. Solubility results using this method are given in Table III.

Table III.  Solubility of Unlabeled Dioxin in Water from a Compact Film

| Equil. Time days | conc. TCDD ppt | Solubility moles/liter |
|---|---|---|
| 3 | 10.0 | $3.1 \times 10^{-11}$ |
| 3 | 9.1 | $2.8 \times 10^{-11}$ |
| 3 | 12.2 | $3.8 \times 10^{-11}$ |

A summary of all experimental values (mean values), and earlier reported values is given in Table IV.

Table IV.  Summary of Values for the Water Solubility of Dioxin

| Solubility, ppt | Method | Source |
|---|---|---|
| 2000 | ? | Plimmer, et al (2) |
| 600 | ? | Kearney, et al (3) |
| 200 | ? | Crummet, Stehl (1) |
| 12.5 | 14-C film | Marple, et al (4) |
| 19.3 | thin film | Marple, et al (4) |
| 10.4 | compact film | This work |
| 8.0 | ? | Overcash (5) |

The fact that our three methods give very nearly the same solubility value is taken as evidence that we are measuring the water solubility free of artifacts arising from adsorption, particle suspension, and other phenomena.

OCTANOL/WATER PARTITION

The partition between octanol and water is another useful physical property for which we could find no experimental data in the literature. While we anticipated several experimental problems in the measurement, we soon realized that the primary problem was the physical separation of equilibrated phases. An equilibration cell was designed, Figure 1, in which diffusion was the main mechanism of mass transfer of dioxin from the octanol to the water phase. A slight mechanical movement of the water phase hastened the distribution of dioxin within that phase. Although the volume of the side arm was small in comparison to the volume sampled, the liquid in the standpipe was periodically flushed back into the equilibrating chamber by application of a slight positive pressure to the top of the standpipe.

Equilibrations were started using both mutually unsaturated and mutually saturated phases. The results (Table V) show that equilibrium is achieved quickly starting from mutually saturated phases.

Table V.   Variation of Octanol-Water Partition Coefficients
           for Dioxin with Equilibration Time

| Equil. Time days | Log K ow Phases Unsaturated | Phases Saturated |
|---|---|---|
| 5 | 4.80 | |
| 5 | | 6.53 |
| 12 | 5.70 | |
| 15 | | 6.95 |
| 20 | 6.52 | |
| 31 | 6.22 | 6.59 |

The increase in Kow for unsaturated phases reflects a decreasing dioxin content with time in the water phase. This is thought to be due to the transfer of octanol solvated dioxin into the water phase at the start of the equilibration while the two phases are in the process of reaching mutual saturation. The octanol solvate would be unstable in the aqueous phase, however, preferring to dissociate into octanol and water solvated dioxin. A mean value of the partition coefficient was calculated from measurements in which the systems were thought to be at equilibrium. Table VI compares our mean experimental value with other values found in the literature.

Figure 1.  Equilibration cell used for Octanol-water
partition.

Table VI.  Summary of log Kow Values for Dioxin

| Log Kow | Calc from water | |
| --- | --- | --- |
| 6.9 | calc. | Johnson (6) |
| 7.14 | calc. | Perkaw, et al (7) |
| 8.93 | calc. | Webster, et al (8) |
| 6.15 | ? | Kenaga (9) |
| 6.64 | slow diffusion | Marple, et al (13) |
| 6.40-6.59 | calc from water solubility | Tables I-III |

It should be noted that the octanol-water partition coefficient calculated from the Law of Distribution Between Phases and the experimental water solubility agrees well with our experimetally determined partition coefficient.  This result is expected since the molar solubility of dioxin in both octanol and water is sufficiently low at saturation that there is no significant impact on the activity coefficient of dioxin in either phase.  Further, solubilities of octanol in water, and water in octanol are so slight that there is no significant difference between dioxin solubilities for the pure solvents compared to mutually saturated solvents.

SOIL/WATER PARTITION

The partition of dioxin between soil and water was expected to be largely dependent upon the organic carbon content of the soil.  Experimentally measured partition coefficients are normalized for organic carbon by dividing by the organic carbon content.  Although there are a number of methods for the measurement of organic carbon, the Walkley-Black method (11) is most frequently used.  Using our experimental solubility values and the Koc-solubility relation published by Chiou, Peters, and Freed (12) shown in Table VII, we estimated that log Koc would be in the vicinity of 6.39 - 6.54.

Table VII.  Koc-Solubility Regression Equations
Chiou, Peters, Freed (11)

Log Koc = 4.040 (+0.038) - 0.557 (+0.012) Log S

S = solubility in micromoles/liter, n = 15

Kenaga, Goring (12)

Log Koc = 3.64 - 0.55 Log S

S = solubility in parts per million

If instead the empirical relation developed by Kenaga and Goring was used (13), the log Koc estimate ranged from 6.24 to 6.49.

The main experimental problem was unexplained loss of dioxin to the equilibrating system. In many of our preliminary experiments, small amounts of dioxin equilibrating with water and soil simply disappeared. Uncontrolled adsorption on the surface of the equilibrating vessel, most likely as a scum, was thought to be responsible for the loss. When the surface of all glass in contact with the water phase was cleaned with hot, concentrated nitric acid, the loss was small enough to permit measurement of the dioxin levels in both soil and water phases.

Two representative Missouri soils were selected for investigation: a red clay with a 0.3% organic carbon content, and an alluvial stream soil with a 1.3% organic carbon content. The soils were air dried and screened to remove rocks and gravel before use. Dioxin was added to the system in two ways: a solution of dioxin in toluene was evenly deposited on the soil, and the soil dried before use; or, dioxin was deposited as a visible film on a glass plate which was put into the equilibrating system. A two liter borosilicate flask and a mechanical glass stirrer sealed at the neck were used for equilibration. The apparatus was protected from the light to avoid photodecomposition. Upon completion of the equilibration, the suspension was allowed to settle overnight. A sample of the clear supernatant was drawn off with pipette, then the bulk of the water phase was drawn off to allow collection of the soil. After adding 13-C dioxin to each sample as an internal standard, the dioxins were isolated from each sample by solvent extraction and adsorption chromatography. A capillary GC/MS method was used for the analysis of dioxins in both phases.

Results of our soil partition measurements are collected in Table VIII.

Table VIII. Summary of Organic Carbon Soil-Water Partition coefficients for Selected Missouri Soils

| Soil Type | Equilibration Time | Log Koc |
|-----------|--------------------|---------|
| Red Clay | 25 | 6.45 |
| | 112 | 6.54 |
| | 72 | 6.22 |
| | 25 | 6.39 |
| Stream Alluvial | 29 | 5.96 |
| | 20 | 6.09 |

The first two entries for clay soils are the result of starting with dioxin adsorbed on soil, and the following two are the result of suspending dioxin in the equilibrating system. Although the conversion to logarithms appears to reduce the variation of the measurements, the range of values is quite narrow considering the potential variability of the soil specimens.

The reproducibility of the experiment was briefly examined in two equilibrations where we measured the amount of dioxin transfered to the water phase in contact with a constant amount of dioxin-soil

mixture over a period of several days. Although we expected the
dioxin level in solution to increase with time, there was an equal
and parallel decrease in the dioxin content after the first sampling
period. When both soil and water phases were analyzed at the end of
the experiment, it was clear that about 40% of the dioxin had
migrated to a fixed interface within the equilibrating system.

In addition to the Koc–Solubility relations already mentioned,
we estimated Koc from the Koc–Kow relation developed by Karickhoff
et. al., Log Koc = 1.00 log Kow – 0.21 ($\underline{15}$). Our estimate and
earlier reported values using this relation are compared in Table IX.

Table IX.  Organic Carbon Soil–Water Partition Coefficients
           for 2,3,7,8–TCDD Calculated from Karickhoffs Regression
           Equation and Octanol–Water Partition Coefficients

| Log Koc | Source |
|---------|--------|
| 6.90 | Marple ($\underline{15}$) |
| 6.51 | Mabey, et. al ($\underline{16}$) |
| 6.43 | Marple (this work) |

Experimental values of Koc appear to be in excellent agreement
with Koc estimated from experimental Kow value.  Recalling that log
Koc estimates from solubility relations were 6.39 – 5.64 and 6.24 –
6.49, it is clear that our experimenatl values for the water
solubility, octanol–water partition coefficient, and soil organic
carbon–water partition coefficient are internally consistent.  We
attribute this to having taken steps to minimize losses to unknown
parts of the equilibrating system, and to correct for losses by the
analysis of dioxin in each of the phases involed in the partition
system.

Literature Cited

(<u>1</u>)  Crummett, W.B. and Stehl, R.H., <u>Environmental Health Perspect.</u>
     1973, 5, 15.

(<u>2</u>)  Plimmer, J., Klingbiel V., Crosby, D., Wong, A., "Chlorodioxins
     – Origin and Fate", Adv. Chem. Series 120, E.H. Blair, Ed. p.
     46.

(<u>3</u>)  Kearney, P., Isensee, A., Helling, C., Woolson, E. Plimmer, J.
     loc cit. p. 106.

(<u>4</u>)  Marple, L.W., Brunck, R., Throop, L., <u>Environ. Sci. Technol.,</u>
     (accepted for publication.).

(<u>5</u>)  Overcash, M.R., Private Communication, N. Carolina State Univ.,
     Raleigh, No. Carolina.

(6) Johnson, H., "Aquatic Fate Process Data For Organic Priority Pollutants", W.R. Mabey, ed. EPA Final Report, Contract 68-01-3867.

(7) Perkaw, J., Eschenroeder, A., Goyer, M., Stevens, J., and Wechsler, A., "An Exposure and Risk Assessment for 2,3,7,8-Tetrachlorodibenzo-p-dioxin", Office of Water Regulations and Standards, US EPA, Wash. D.C. (1980).

(8) Webster, Sarna, L. Muir, D. Publication pre-print, "Kow of 1,3,6,8-TCDD and OCDD by Reverse Phase HPLC", Univ. of Manitoba, Winnipeg, Manitoba, Canada R3T 2N2.

(9) Kenaga, E., Environ. Sci. Technol. 1980, 14, 553.

(10) Walkley, A., Black, I.A., Soil Sci, 1934, 37, 29-38.

(11) Chiou, C.T., Peters, L.J., Freed, U.H., Science, 1979, 206, 831-832.

(12) Kenaga, E.E., Goring, C.A.I., "Relationship Between Water Solubility Soil-sorption, Octanol-water Partitioning and Bioconcentration of Chemicals in Biota, ASTM Third Aquatic Toxicology Symposium, Oct. 17-18, New Orleans, LA.

(13) Marple, L.W., Berridge, B., and Throop, L. "Measurement of the Water-Octanol Partition Coefficient of 2,3,7,8-tetrachlordibenzo-p-dioxin", Environ, Sci. Technol. 1986, 20, 397-399.

(14) Karickhoff, S.W. Brown, D.S. Scott, J.A., Water Research 1979, 13, 241.

(15) Mill, T., "Prediction of the Environmental Fate of Tetrachlorodibenzo-p-dioxin", presented at the Conference on Dioxins in the Environment, Mich. State Univ., Mich. December, 1983.

(16) Mabey, W.R., Smith, J.H., Podoll, R.T., Johnson, H.L., Mill, T., Chou, T.W., Gates, J., Partridge, I.W., Jaber, H., Vanderberg, G., "Aquatic Fate Process Data by Organic Priority Pollutants: 1982 Final Report, US EPA, Wash. D.C. 20460.

RECEIVED December 2, 1986

# Chapter 9

# Experiments on the Mobility of 2,3,7,8-Tetrachlorodibenzo-*p*-dioxin at Times Beach, Missouri

Raymond A. Freeman, Frederick D. Hileman, Roy W. Noble, and Jerry M. Schroy

Monsanto Company, St. Louis, MO 63166

The Times Beach Dioxin Research Station was constructed
in 1984 under the direction of the University of Missouri
and the Missouri Department of Natural Resources. The
station offers investigators the opportunity to conduct
experiments under field conditions on a well characterized soil. During the Summer of 1984, a series of six
experiments were established by Monsanto at the station
to study the environmental transport of 2,3,7,8-tetra-
chlorodibenzo-p-dioxin (TCDD) under field conditions.
The plots initially contained uniformly sized soil that
was thoroughly mixed to provide a consistent TCDD level.
The experiments were designed to study the movement of
TCDD in soil. The experiments found that:

1. Vaporization and/or photodegradation at the surface of a contaminated soil is a loss mechanism
   for TCDD.
2. The presence of water and/or sunlight is an important environmental parameter for the mobility
   of TCDD. Water appears to weaken the binding of
   TCDD to the soil matrix.
3. TCDD accumulation by plants has a minimal impact
   on the soil concentration of TCDD.

The environmental behavior of chemicals with a very low volatility,
such as 2,3,7,8-tetrachlorodibenzo-p-dioxin (TCDD), has been the subject of several studies over the last few years. The focus of these
studies has varied from the development of physical property data
(1,2) to lab and field tests of the mobility and/or fate of TCDD.
The mobility and fate studies have involved research on the leaching
of dioxin from the soil (3), vaporization of the organic contaminants
into and out of the soil (4), the biodegradation or chemical decomposition of the organics in the soil column (5), and the photodegradation of the organics in the soil (6,7). These studies usually have
involved laboratory investigations or computer simulation of tests
started many years ago.

0097-6156/87/0338-0114$06.00/0
© 1987 American Chemical Society

When the State of Missouri established the Times Beach Dioxin Research Station in 1984 (8) it provided, for the first time, a facility where researchers could run relatively large field tests using aged TCDD contaminated soil. Previous studies (4) suggested that the mobility of TCDD in the soil was very slow and depends strongly on the ambient meteorological conditions. The Times Beach Dioxin Research Station offered the type of tight security needed for the long term testing required to establish the mobility characteristics of TCDD. The test station also offered a site where the initial soil contaminant level could be analyzed directly at the start of the experiments.

During the Summer of 1984, a series of six experiments were established by Monsanto at the station to determine the rate of environmental transport of (TCDD) under field conditions. The plots initially contained uniformly sized soil that was thoroughly mixed to provide a consistent TCDD level. The experiments were designed to study the movement of TCDD in a soil:

1.  saturated with water (all pores filled with water),
2.  maintained in a "damp" but unsaturated condition,
3.  under natural field conditions,
4.  covered with approximately a 5 cm layer of TCDD free soil,
5.  maintained in a dry environment and protected from the wind, and
6.  maintained in a dry environment, isolated from the sun with an impermeable metallic insulation cover, and protected from the wind.

At various times, soil core samples were taken, carefully sectioned, and analyzed for TCDD.

Experimental Design

The overall goal of this research was to study the mobility of TCDD under actual field conditions to determine the influence of such natural phenomena as: rain, floods, sunlight, and heat. The Missouri Department of Natural Resources established a Dioxin Research Station at the Times Beach Site during the late Spring and early Summer of 1984. Two blocks of Laurel Road were used to establish the Research Station. The TCDD contaminated soil was removed from the road and stainless steel bins (183 cm wide, 244 cm long, 61 cm deep) were buried in the roadbed. The contaminated soil, previously removed from the road, was homogenized by mixing, screened to remove large rocks, and placed into the stainless steel bins. The soil composition has been reported as 11.4 percent sand, 55.2 percent silt, 33.4 percent clay, and 2.0 percent organic matter (9). The process of preparing each bin was monitored to insure uniform mixing and TCDD levels. After preparation, each bin was sampled and covered with an impermeable metallic insulation cover. For more details on the construction procedures used see Yanders (8).

Monsanto rented four bins at the Times Beach Dioxin Research Station (TBDRS) during the summer of 1984. Six complementary experiments were installed in the four bins as:

1.  PLOT A - TBDRS Bin 4B
    A timer controlled watering system was installed to keep the bin
    saturated with water (all pores filled with water).
2.  PLOT B - TBDRS Bin 4C
    A timer controlled watering system was installed to keep the bin
    damp but unsaturated with water.
3.  PLOT C CONTROL - TBDRS Bin 5A
    The bin was partitioned into two equal areas (east and west)
    using an aluminum divider.  The east side of the bin was main-
    tained under natural field conditions as a field control.  The
    west side of the bin was used as described in point 4 below.  See
    Figure 1 for a plan of bin 5A.
4.  PLOT C NURSERY - TBDRS Bin 5A
    The bin was partitioned into two equal areas (east and west)
    using an aluminum divider.  A total of 9,988 g of 3 mm glass
    beads was evenly applied to the west side (area = 2,297 cm2) of
    the bin to serve as a marker layer.  The west side was then
    covered with approximately a 5 cm layer of TCDD free nursery soil
    (<1 ppt of TCDD).  This clean soil over dirty soil experiment was
    designed to detect any upward TCDD movement.  The east side of
    the bin was used as described in point 3 above.
5.  PLOT D UNSHADED - TBDRS Bin 5B
    The bin was covered with a plastic sheet, permeable to ultravio-
    let radiation, to keep out rain and maintain a dry environment
    and protect it from the wind.  The east side of the bin was al-
    lowed to remain in this state and the west side of the bin was
    used as described in point 6 below.  See Figure 2 for a plan of
    bin 5B.
6.  PLOT D SHADED - TBDRS Bin 5B
    One-half of the soil contained in the bin, discussed in point 5
    above, was covered with an impermeable metallic insulation cover
    (west side of bin was covered).  This serves as the basic control
    for the field study.  The soil in this half of Bin 5B was protec-
    ted from rain, wind, and direct sunlight.  The soil concentration
    profile of TCDD, in this half of the bin, was not expected to
    change with time.  The east side of the bin was used as described
    in point 5 above.

## Soil Sample Preparation

Soil and clay samples were dried, weighed and spiked with 24.0 ng of
$^{13}$C labeled 2,3,7,8-TCDD.  Ten g of washed anhydrous sodium sulfate
were added and the samples were stirred, allowed to stand for 12
hours and stirred again.  Samples were mixed again immediately before
the addition of extraction solvents.  The extraction process involved
the addition of 15 mL of methanol (all solvents are Burdick and Jackson "distilled in glass" grade), stirring, and the subsequent addition of 150 mL of hexane.  The samples were shaken for three hr on a
wrist action shaker and the extraction solvent was decanted from the
soil.  The solvent was then successively extracted with 50 mL of
water, concentrated sulfuric acid (until clear), water, and 20 percent potassium hydroxide and water.  The hexane was dried with 10 g
of anhydrous sodium sulfate and passed through a mixed phase column.
The column was prepared from a 25 mL disposable pipet containing (top
to bottom) 2 g of silica gel, 4 g of silica gel plus 40 percent sul-

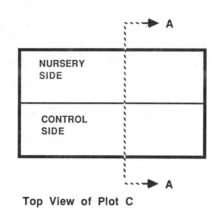

**Top View of Plot C**

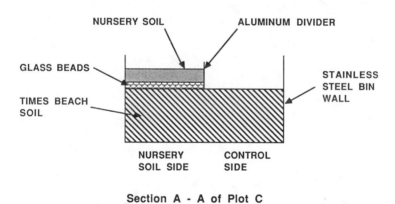

**Section A - A of Plot C**

Figure 1. Diagrammatic Plan for Plot C

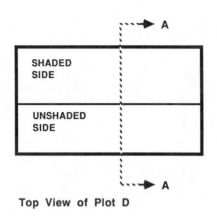

Top View of Plot D

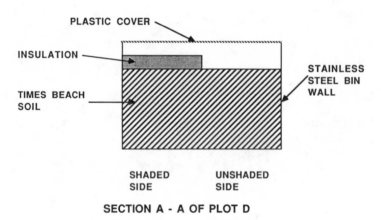

SECTION A - A OF PLOT D

Figure 2.   Diagrammatic Plan for Plot D

furic acid, 1 g of silica gel, 2 g of silica gel plus 36 percent potassium hydroxide, and 1 g of silica gel. The column was eluted with an additional 50 mL of hexane. All the eluant from the mixed phase column was passed directly onto a column prepared from a 10 mL disposable pipet containing 2.5 g of Woelm basic alumina. The alumina column was first eluted with 10 mL of 2 percent methylene chloride/hexane (v/v) and this fraction was discarded. An additional elution was made with 15 mL of a 50 percent methylene chloride/hexane (v/v) solution to elute the TCDD off the column. To this fraction was added a dodecane keeper. The sample was then concentrated to either 30 uL or 50 uL under a gentle stream of nitrogen and submitted for GC/MS analysis.

Plant Sample Preparation

Five-g samples of plant matter (grass and/or plants) were weighed into glass bottles. When weeds were encountered, large stems were avoided. The plants in each bottle were spiked with 100 uL of 100 pg/uL $^{37}$Cl-TCDD in iso-octane by sprinkling the solution over the plant matter and allowing the solvent to evaporate. The plants were then washed three times by shaking with 50 mL portions of hexane for 15 min. The hexane rinses were pooled for each sample and spiked with 20 uL of 240 pg/uL $^{13}$C-TCDD. Blank grass samples were run in the same manner. The hexane rinse samples were then taken through the cleanup procedure described below.

After the plant matter was rinsed with hexane as described above, the plants were spiked with 20 uL of 240 pg/uL $^{13}$C-TCDD. Each sample was digested in 50 mL of 50 percent (v/v) $H_2SO_4$ and shaken for 15 min. The resulting solution was extracted three times with 50 mL portions of hexane. The hexane was removed from the $H_2SO_4$ sample solution by centrifuging at 3000 RPM for 30 to 60 minutes after each hexane extraction. The hexane extractions were then pooled and taken through the cleanup procedure described below.

The hexane solutions described above were subjected to the same cleanup procedure used for the soil samples. The samples were then concentrated to 10 uL under a gentle stream of nitrogen and submitted for GC/MS analysis.

Sample Analysis

The GC/MS analyses were conducted on a Hewlett Packard 5987 GC/MS instrument. The gas chromatographic separations used either a 60 m SP-2330 capillary column or a 30 m DB-5 capillary column. The mass spectrometer was operated in the selected ion monitoring mode analyzing for ions characteristic of the native (unlabeled) 2,3,7,8-TCDD (m/z 320, 322), carbon-13 labeled 2,3,7,8-TCDD (m/z 332, 334). Quantification was achieved by ratioing the area of the native 2,3,7,8-TCDD to the area of the carbon-13 labeled 2,3,7,8-TCDD. The ratio was compared to that obtained for a set of analytical standards and the amount of 2,3,7,8-TCDD determined. The levels present in the original soil or plant sample were determined by dividing the weight of the sample into the measured weight of 2,3,7,8-TCDD present.

For the plant samples an additional analysis was carried out for the distribution of the $^{37}$Cl-TCDD between the rinse and the digested sample. Since the $^{37}$Cl-TCDD was originally spiked onto the outer

surface of the plants, this analysis allowed for the determination of
the effectiveness of the rinsing procedure. For all plant samples,
less than 2 percent of the spiked $^{37}$Cl-TCDD remained on the plants
after the rinse procedure was completed.

## Chronology of Field Samples Taken

On August 7, 1984 the experiments in plots A, B, and D were established. Two soil core samples were taken from plots A, B, C, and D
on August 8, 1984. On August 24, 1984 the experiments in plot C were
established. The nursery dirt used in this experiment was purchased
from a local nursery and contained no TCDD at a detection limit of 1
ppt by weight. On October 9, 1984 a soil core was taken from Plot C
- Nursery side. The cores taken on August 8, 1984 were segmented
into approximately 2.5 cm (1 inch) segments and were placed into
glass bottles. The bottles containing the 2.5 cm segments were
stored in darkness until analysis during the first quarter of 1986.
The core taken on October 9, 1984 was refrigerated in darkness until
being segmented into 1 cm increments for analysis during the first
quarter of 1986.

On July 9, 1985, one soil core was taken from plots A, B, C -
control, C - Nursery, D - shaded, and D - unshaded. In addition,
plants were growing on plots A, B, C - control, and C - nursery. The
plants were cut using garden shears at the soil surface. Care was
taken not to disturb the soil. Any plant matter falling on soil surface was assumed to be contaminated and was not used in the grab
samples taken for TCDD analysis. The total weight of plant matter
cut was measured in the onsite soil laboratory. Samples of the plant
matter were taken and placed into standard glass sample jars. These
samples were returned to the Monsanto Laboratory for refrigerated
storage awaiting analysis. The six soil cores taken on July 9, 1985
were refrigerated in darkness until being segmented into 1 cm increments for analysis during the first quarter of 1986. To reduce the
amount of plants growing on the experimental plots, a total of 1.004
g of the herbicide Oust was applied to plots A, B, C - control, and C
- Nursery. A sample of Oust was found to be free of TCDD at a detection limit of 20 ppt by weight.

On November 4, 1985, one soil core was taken from plots A, B, C
- control, C - Nursery, D - shaded, and D - unshaded. These cores
were returned to the Monsanto Laboratory for refrigerated storage
while awaiting analysis. The soil cores were segmented into 1 cm
increments and were analyzed for TCDD during the first quarter of
1986. In addition, soil surface samples were obtained by scraping
the surface of Plots A, C - Control, and D -Shaded with disposable
stainless steel spatulas. The depth of the soil surface collected in
this manner was approximately 3 mm. These surface samples were returned to the Monsanto Laboratory for storage and later analysis. A
small number of plants was found to be growing on plots A, B, C -
control, and C - Nursery. The plants were cut at the surface using
garden shears and placed into plastic sample bags. All of the plant
matter which did not fall onto the soil surface was returned to the
Monsanto Laboratory for refrigerated storage while awaiting analysis.
It is estimated that at least one-half of the weight of growing
plants were collected in this manner. After the application of the
herbicide Oust, very few plants grew on the plots.

Soil Study Results

All soil cores were segmented into either 2.54 cm (1 inch) or 1 cm
increments and analyzed for TCDD. The TCDD concentration data are
plotted in Figures 3 thru 7 for Plots A, B, C - Control, D - Shaded,
and D - Unshaded. Since the experiment in Plot C - Nursery was designed to yield only a yes or no answer on the mobility of TCDD, it
is discussed separately below. Each concentration point is plotted
at the midpoint of the corresponding soil increment depth. For example, the measured concentration for the 8 cm to 9 cm increment
would be plotted at a depth of 8.5 cm. These experiments were designed to detect the loss of TCDD from the surface soil layers. Thus,
the line shown as the mean in each figure is the average of all measured TCDD concentrations, excluding the surface layer of 0 to 1 cm or
0 cm to 2.54 cm. The dashed lines above and below the mean represent
the 2 standard deviation limits about the mean. Any point falling
outside the upper and lower limits are suspected to be statistically
different from those inside the limits. As can be seen from Figures
3 thru 7, the data are very consistent.

In Figure 3, there is a suspect point plotted at 6.35 cm, taken
in August 9, 1984, with a concentration of 8.2 ppb. There were two
cores taken in August of 1984 for Plot A. The corresponding concentration in the second core was found to be 98 ppb. All TCDD analyses
for the August 1984 cores yield concentrations between 86 and 115
ppb. We conclude that sample is an outlier probably due to human
error in the analysis.

Not plotted on Figure 6 is a suspect point of 326 ppb in the 4
cm to 5 cm soil increment for Plot D - Shaded taken on November 4,
1985. The concentration in the 3 cm to 4 cm soil increment is 175
ppb. The concentration in the 5 cm to 6 cm soil increment is 174
ppb. The 4 cm to 5 cm soil increment was found to contain 134 ppb
when sampled in July of 1985. In addition, the 4 cm to 5 cm soil
increment for the other side of Plot D (Unshaded side) was found to
be 186 ppb in the November 1985 core. There is no known mechanism
for this kind of movement of TCDD in a protected dry environment.
Thus, we conclude that the sample is an outlier probably due to human
error during analysis.

The two outlier samples were not used during later data analysis. All other points except the soil surface samples are consistent
with normal statistical scatter in measured data.

If vaporization and/or photodegradation of TCDD at the soil surface occurs, the soil near the surface should have lower TCDD concentrations than the soil layers below the surface. Previous calculations by the authors indicated that the the lowering would only be
detectable in the top 1 cm of soil after a normal hot Missouri Summer.

Surface soil scrapings were taken from Plots A, C - Control, and
D - Shaded on November 4, 1985. The results of TCDD analyses of
these surface samples were 33 ppb, 66 ppb, and 121 ppb for Plots A, C
- Control, and D - Shaded respectively. These surface TCDD concentrations are compared to the concentrations in the subsurface soil
layers in Figures 3, 5, and 6. Since it is impossible to take a
sample of zero thickness, the surface scraping data are plotted at a
depth of 0.15 cm.

For plots exposed to water and sunlight (Plots A and C - Control) the surface scrapping TCDD concentrations are significantly

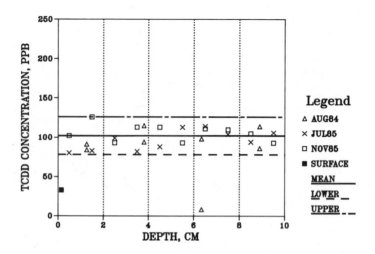

Figure 3.    TCDD Concentration Profile for Saturated Conditions - Plot A

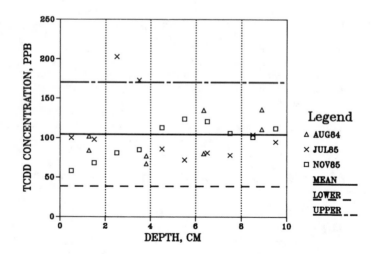

Figure 4.    TCDD Concentration Profile for Damp Conditions - Plot B

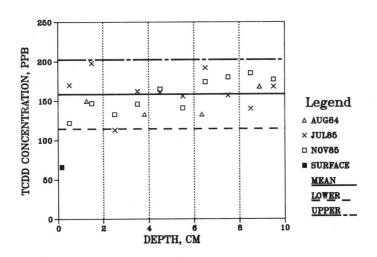

Figure 5. TCDD Concentration Profile for Control Side - Plot C

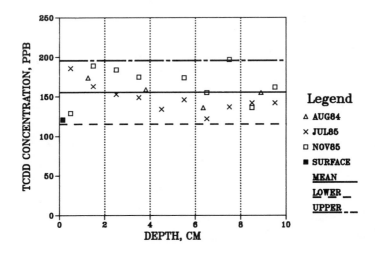

Figure 6. TCDD Concentration Profile for Shaded Side - Plot D

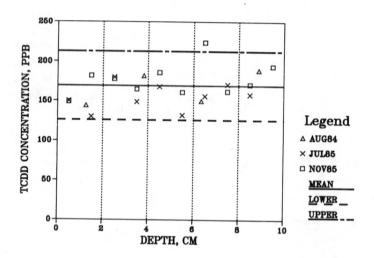

Figure 7.   TCDD Concentration Profile for Unshaded Side - Plot D

lower than the average TCDD concentration of the soil layers below
the 0 cm to 1 cm increment. The lower dashed line of Figures 3 thru
7 represents the lower 2 standard deviation limit from the mean of
the plot TCDD concentration. Thus, the surface scraping TCDD concentrations are statistically lower than TCDD concentrations in the soil
layers below. This result supports the TCDD vaporization and/or photodegradation hypothesis.

For the dry and shaded control experiment (Plot D - Shaded) the
surface scraping sample concentration falls within the 2 standard
deviation limits about the mean. This implies that no statistically
significant loss of TCDD occurred in the dry shaded plot. Therefore,
the presence of water and/or sunlight are important environmental
parameters affecting the mobility of TCDD in soils.

The clean soil over dirty soil experiment (Plot C - Nursery) was
designed to detect the movement of TCDD at very low rates. A 5 cm
layer of TCDD free soil ( < 1 ppt) was applied to the surface of the
plot. The layer of clean soil was separated from the dirty soil by a
layer of new laboratory glass beads. TCDD was detected in all increments of the initially clean soil (Table I). Surface contamination
by blowing dust could account for the surface concentrations of TCDD.
Mixing of the dirty dirt below the glass beads with the clean layers
above during sampling and sectioning would account for TCDD found
above the glass bead layer. However, the simultaneous mixing of the
glass beads would also be expected in the clean layers. This upward
mixing of the clean glass beads did not occur. Downward sifting of
the glass beads into the lower loose soil layers did occur. This
downward mixing could have occurred during the initial application of
the glass beads to the plots or during sampling. Some downward mixing of clean soil with dirty soil may be assumed to have occurred
resulting in dilution of the lower soil increments TCDD concentrations. From this experiment, it may be concluded that TCDD is mobile.

Previous work by Freeman and Schroy (4) indicated that over 67
percent of the 2,3,7,8-TCDD contained in the top 1 cm of soil should
volatilize during the first summer after application. The TCDD concentration in the top 1 cm of soil taken from experimental plots A
and C-Control was found to have decreased by 20 percent and 18 percent respectively over the 15 months of elapsed time. The apparent
rate of loss of TCDD from plots A and C-Control is lower than previously estimated by Freeman and Schroy (4). The TCDD concentration
of the top 1 cm of soil taken from plot D-Shaded was found to have
decreased 7 percent over the same 15 months. A loss of 7 percent is
not statistically significant and it was concluded that plot D-Shaded
remained unchanged over the course of the experiment.

## Plant Study Results

All plant samples taken were analyzed for TCDD using the procedure
presented above. Both the hexane surface rinses and the digested
plant matter were found to contain TCDD (Table II). The surface
rinses represent the TCDD 1) contained in dust adhering to the
plants, 2) bound to the organic surface of the plants, and 3) contained in the outer cell layers of the plant. Many of the surface
rinses had a green color indicating the presence of chlorophyll and
the breaking of plant surface cells. Analysis of the plants taken
from the Nursery side gave TCDD levels comparable to those found on

Table I.   TCDD Concentration as a Function of Depth For
Plot C - Nursery

| Soil Increment cm to cm | | TCDD ppb | Frac. Rock | Frac. Glass | Sample Date Day Mon Yr |
|---|---|---|---|---|---|
| 0.00 | 2.54 | 138.0 | 0.189 | 0.000 | 8 Aug 84 (1) |
| 2.54 | 5.08 | 161.0 | 0.172 | 0.000 | 8 Aug 84 (1) |
| 5.08 | 7.62 | 170.0 | 0.148 | 0.000 | 8 Aug 84 (1) |
| 7.62 | 10.16 | 138.0 | 0.238 | 0.000 | 8 Aug 84 (1) |
| 0.00 | 1.00 | 1.5 | 0.001 | 0.000 | 9 Oct 84 |
| 1.00 | 2.00 | 1.5 | 0.001 | 0.000 | 9 Oct 84 |
| 2.00 | 3.00 | 2.0 | 0.001 | 0.000 | 9 Oct 84 |
| 3.00 | 4.00 | 3.1 | 0.006 | 0.000 | 9 Oct 84 |
| 4.00 | 5.00 | 10.9 | 0.006 | 0.112 | 9 Oct 84 |
| 5.00 | 6.00 | 99.0 | 0.069 | 0.209 | 9 Oct 84 |
| 6.00 | 7.00 | 153.0 | 0.097 | 0.047 | 9 Oct 84 |
| 7.00 | 8.00 | 185.0 | 0.247 | 0.005 | 9 Oct 84 |
| 8.00 | 9.00 | 176.0 | 0.222 | 0.002 | 9 Oct 84 |
| 9.00 | 10.00 | 200.0 | 0.145 | 0.000 | 9 Oct 84 |
| 0.00 | 1.00 | 1.9 | 0.000 | 0.000 | 9 Jul 85 |
| 1.00 | 2.00 | 1.4 | 0.000 | 0.000 | 9 Jul 85 |
| 2.00 | 3.00 | 3.0 | 0.000 | 0.000 | 9 Jul 85 |
| 3.00 | 4.00 | 2.1 | 0.001 | 0.005 | 9 Jul 85 |
| 4.00 | 5.00 | 30.0 | 0.041 | 0.364 | 9 Jul 85 |
| 5.00 | 6.00 | 113.0 | 0.043 | 0.118 | 9 Jul 85 |
| 6.00 | 7.00 | 163.0 | 0.126 | 0.048 | 9 Jul 85 |
| 7.00 | 8.00 | 169.0 | 0.142 | 0.015 | 9 Jul 85 |
| 8.00 | 9.00 | 151.0 | 0.137 | 0.002 | 9 Jul 85 |
| 9.00 | 10.00 | 211.0 | 0.283 | 0.002 | 9 Jul 85 |
| 0.00 | 1.00 | 3.9 | 0.000 | 0.000 | 4 Nov 85 |
| 0.00 | 1.00 | 3.8 (2) | 0.000 | 0.000 | 4 Nov 85 |
| 1.00 | 2.00 | 2.4 | 0.000 | 0.000 | 4 Nov 85 |
| 1.00 | 2.00 | 2.3 (2) | 0.000 | 0.000 | 4 Nov 85 |
| 2.00 | 3.00 | 1.2 | 0.000 | 0.000 | 4 Nov 85 |
| 2.00 | 3.00 | 0.7 (2) | 0.000 | 0.000 | 4 Nov 85 |
| 3.00 | 4.00 | 1.3 | 0.000 | 0.000 | 4 Nov 85 |
| 3.00 | 4.00 | 1.2 (2) | 0.000 | 0.000 | 4 Nov 85 |
| 4.00 | 5.00 | 48.0 | 0.063 | 0.310 | 4 Nov 85 |
| 4.00 | 5.00 | 47.0 (2) | 0.063 | 0.310 | 4 Nov 85 |
| 5.00 | 6.00 | 125.0 | 0.242 | 0.089 | 4 Nov 85 |
| 5.00 | 6.00 | 130.0 (2) | 0.242 | 0.089 | 4 Nov 85 |
| 6.00 | 7.00 | 163.0 | 0.125 | 0.021 | 4 Nov 85 |
| 7.00 | 8.00 | 177.0 | 0.137 | 0.000 | 4 Nov 85 |
| 8.00 | 9.00 | 202.0 | 0.138 | 0.000 | 4 Nov 85 |
| 9.00 | 10.00 | 182.0 | 0.200 | 0.000 | 4 Nov 85 |

Notes:   1.   These samples were taken before the 5 cm of
nursery dirt was applied to the top of the
plot on August 24, 1984.   Thus, 5 cm should
be added to the depths to correspond to the
samples taken later.

2.   Replicate Analysis

Table II.    TCDD Content of Plant Matter Collected From
Plots A, B, and C

| Plot | Plant Wt. g | Plant TCDD ppb | Rinse TCDD (1) ppb | Total Plant ppb | Sample Date Day Mon Yr |
|------|------|------|------|------|------|
| A | 739.0 | 0.378 | 0.139 | 0.517 | 9 Jul 85 |
| A | -- (2) | 0.940 | 0.138 | 1.078 | 9 Jul 85 |
| A | 7.05 | 1.228 | 0.749 | 1.977 | 4 Nov 85 |
| B | 1677.8 | 0.507 | 0.263 | 0.770 | 9 Jul 85 |
| B | -- (3) | 0.106 | 0.033 | 0.139 | 9 Jul 85 |
| B | 6.87 | 2.019 | 1.860 | 3.879 | 4 Nov 85 |
| C - Control | 1529.26 | 0.345 | 0.391 | 0.736 | 9 Jul 85 |
| C - Control | 6.4 | 1.111 | 0.851 | 1.962 | 4 Nov 85 |
| C - Nursery | 1188.6 | 0.158 | 0.029 | 0.187 | 9 Jul 85 |
| C - Nursery | -- (4) | 0.091 | 0.013 | 0.104 | 9 Jul 85 |
| C - Nursery | 2.61 | 1.243 | 0.839 | 2.082 | 4 Nov 85 |

Notes:  1.  Rinse TCDD content reported as g TCDD x 10 9  per
g plant matter (ppb by wt TCDD).

2.  A total of 739 g of plant matter was collected from
Plot A on July 9, 1985.  This is a replicate workup
and analysis for the TCDD concentration.

3.  A total of 1677.8 g of plant matter was collected from
Plot B on July 9, 1985.  This is a replicate workup
and analysis for the TCDD concentration.

4.  A total of 1186.6 g of plant matter was collected from
Plot C - Nursery on July 9, 1985.  This is a replicate
workup and analysis for the TCDD concentration.

Control side of Plot C. The TCDD concentrations in the nursery dirt (1 to 4 ppb) were approximately 30 times lower than the concentrations in the control side of Plot C. Thus, the TCDD was apparently drawn up through the plant roots and stored in the plant cells.

A TCDD material balance was done to determine the impact of the plant uptake of TCDD on the loss from the soil. It was assumed that all of the TCDD found in the plants came from a single 1 cm soil increment of density 1.5 g/cm3. Table III presents the results of this material balance calculation. The TCDD accumulation by the plants would change the soil concentration by less than 0.1 ppb over the time period of the field study. This is small change is well within the analytical and sampling error of this study and can be ignored as a significant TCDD loss mechanism. However, the possible movement of TCDD through the plants and the subsequent evaporation of the TCDD from the plant leaves can not be ruled out as a TCDD loss mechanism by this study.

Assuming no TCDD loss mechanisms in the plants (biodegradation, photodegradation, or vaporization from the leaves), allows the computation of a concentration factor (C.F.). The concentration factor was defined as the average plant concentration (total of plant and rinse data of Table II) divided by the average soil concentration of TCDD. The results of these calculations are given in Table IV. The concentration factor was found to vary widely with a minimum of 0.004 and a maximum of 0.038. These results are consistent with those of Facchetti (10) who found concentration factors of 0.0008 to 4 for maize and beans in field and greenhouse environments. Thus, in an area contaminated with TCDD (> 100 ppb) the concentration in plants and grasses may be assumed to be less than 4 percent of the soil concentration.

Conclusions

1. TCDD is mobile in soils in the field environment represented by typical Times Beach, Missouri soil.
2. Vaporization and/or photodegradation at the surface of a contaminated soil is a loss mechanism for TCDD.
3. The presence of water and/or sunlight is an important environmental parameter for the mobility of TCDD. Water appears to weaken the binding of TCDD to the soil matrix.
4. TCDD accumulation by the plants has a minimal impact on the soil concentration of TCDD. However, the possible movement of TCDD through the plants and the subsequent evaporation of the TCDD from the plant leaves can not be ruled out as a TCDD loss mechanism by this study.
5. Since this experiment was not explicitly designed to study the uptake of TCDD in plants, the mechanism for movement of TCDD through plants should be determined by a properly designed plant uptake experiment.

Table III. Effect of Plant Matter TCDD Takeup on Soil TCDD Concentrations

| Plot | Change in Soil TCDD Concentration ppb | Sample Date Day Mon Yr |
|------|------|------|
| A | 0.0088 | 9 Jul 85 |
| B | 0.0114 | 9 Jul 85 |
| C - Control | 0.0336 | 9 Jul 85 |
| C - Nursery | 0.0052 | 9 Jul 85 |
| A | 0.0002 | 4 Nov 85 |
| B | 0.0004 | 4 Nov 85 |
| C - Control | 0.0004 | 4 Nov 85 |
| C - Nursery | 0.0002 | 4 Nov 85 |

Table IV. Bioconcentration of TCDD in Plant Matter

| Plot | Plant TCDD Concentration ppb (1) | Soil TCDD Concentration ppb (2) | Concentration Factor (3) | Sample Date Day Mon Yr |
|------|------|------|------|------|
| A | 0.80 | 100.15 | 0.008 | 9 Jul 85 |
| B | 0.45 | 101.82 | 0.004 | 9 Jul 85 |
| C - Control | 0.74 | 157.13 | 0.005 | 9 Jul 85 |
| C - Nursery | 0.19 | -- (4) | --- | 9 Jul 85 |
| A | 1.98 | 100.15 | 0.020 | 4 Nov 85 |
| B | 3.88 | 101.82 | 0.038 | 4 Nov 85 |
| C - Control | 1.96 | 157.13 | 0.012 | 4 Nov 85 |
| C - Nursery | 1.09 | -- (4) | --- | 4 Nov 85 |

[1]Average measured total plant matter concentration of TCDD from Table II.

[2]Average of all soil concentrations measured for plot in question.

[3]Concentration factor is defined as
C.F. = plant matter concentration/soil concentration

[4]Plot C - Nursery was initially covered with approximately a 5-cm clean nursery soil layer. The TCDD concentration below the nursery soil layer was found to be much higher than in the nursery soil layer. An average soil concentration will probably not describe the results and therefore was not reported.

130

## Acknowledgment

The authors wish to thank the Missouri Department of Natural Resources for their assistance at the Times Beach Dioxin Research Station. The authors also thank Sam Gibson, Robert Orth, Sally Walker, Jay Wendling, and Gary Thomas for their dedicated work in the analysis of the samples taken during this field study.

## Literature Cited

1.  Schroy, J.M.; Hileman, F.D.; Cheng, S.C. Aquatic Toxicology and Hazard Assessment: Eighth Symposium, ASTM STP 891, R.C. Bahner and D.J. Hansen, Eds., American Society for Testing and Materials, Philadelphia, 1985, p. 409-421.
2.  Palausky, J.; Harwood, T.E.; Clevenger, S.; Kapila, S.; Yanders, A.F., Chlorinated Dioxins and Dibenzofurans in Perspective, C. Rappe, G. Choudhary, and L.H. Keith Eds., Lewis Publishers, Chelsea, Michigan, 1986, p. 211-224.
3.  Jackson, D.R.; Roulier, M.H.; Grotta, H.M.; Rust, S.W.; Warner, J.S. Chlorinated Dioxins and Dibenzofurans in Perspective, C. Rappe, G. Choudhary, and L.H. Keith Eds., Lewis Publishers, Chelsea, Michigan, 1986, p. 185-200.
4.  Freeman, R.A.; Schroy, J.M. Aquatic Toxicology and Hazard Assessment: Eighth Symposium, ASTM STP 891, R.C. Bahner and D.J. Hansen, Eds., American Society for Testing and Materials, Philadelphia, 1985, p. 422-439.
5.  Young, A.L.; Thalken, C.E.; Arnold, E.L.; Cupello, J.E.; Cockerham, L.G. "Fate of 2,3,7,8-tetrachlorodibenzo-p-dioxin (TCDD) in the Environment", USAFA-TR-76-18, U.S. Air Force Academy, Colorado, NTIS, Rep, AD-A033491, 1976.
6.  Liberti, A.; Brocco, D.; Allegrini, I.; Bertoni, G. in Dioxin: Toxicological and Chemical Aspects, Cattabeni, F., Cavallaro, A. and Galli, G., Eds. Medical and Scientific Books, New York, New York, 1978, p. 195-200.
7.  Mill, T., "Prediction of the Environmental Fate of Tetrachlorodibenzodioxin," Paper presented at the Conference on Dioxins in the Environment, Michigan State University, December 6-7, 1983.
8.  Yanders, A.F.; Kapila, S.; Schreiber, R.J. Chlorinated Dioxins and Dibenzofurans in Perspective, C. Rappe, G. Choudhary, and L.H. Keith Eds., Lewis Publishers, Chelsea, Michigan, 1986, p. 237-239.
9.  Palausky, J.; Harwood, J.J.; Clevenger, T.E.; Kapila, S.; Yanders, A.F. Chlorinated Dioxins and Dibenzofurans in Perspective, C. Rappe, G. Choudhary, and L.H. Keith Eds., Lewis Publishers, Chelsea, Michigan, 1986, p. 211-223.
10. Facchetti, S.; Balasso, A.; Fichiner, C.; Frare, G.; Leoni, A.; Mauri, C.; Vasconi, M. Chlorinated Dioxins and Dibenzofurans in Perspective, C. Rappe, G. Choudhary, and L.H. Keith Eds., Lewis Publishers, Chelsea, Michigan, 1986, p. 225-235.

RECEIVED December 29, 1986

# Chapter 10

# Differential Bioavailability of 2,3,7,8-Tetrachlorodibenzo-*p*-dioxin from Contaminated Soils

Thomas H. Umbreit, Elizabeth J. Hesse, and Michael A. Gallo

Department of Environmental and Community Medicine, University of Medicine and Dentistry of New Jersey, Robert Wood Johnson Medical School, Piscataway, NJ 08854

The bioavailability of TCDD from soils contaminated in the environment is an important determinant for risk assessment at TCDD contaminated sites. Literature reports indicate significant variation in bioavailability of TCDD from different sites. Soils from two of the major TCDD contaminated sites are compared for toxicity in guinea pigs and induction of aryl hydrocarbon hydroxylase (AHH) in rats. Times Beach, Missouri, soil is toxic and TCDD is highly bioavailable from this soil whereas Newark, New Jersey, soil is relatively non-toxic and has low bioavailability of TCDD. However, AHH induction in rats was approximately identical. These results confirm previous studies on bioavailability from these soils, and suggest that AHH induction may be an unreliable indicator of bioavailability.

The highly toxic compound 2,3,7,8-tetrachlorodibenzo-p-dioxin (TCDD) is one of a series of related chlorinated dioxins and furans. TCDD and 2,3,7,8-tetra-chlorodibenzofuran (TCDF) are the most highly toxic members of the series. Brominated analogues appear to have similar toxicities to the chlorinated dioxins and furans. Structure activity studies have indicated that the 2,3,7,8 arrangement of halogens is required for maximum toxicity and receptor binding (1). TCDD is formed as a contaminant in the manufacture of the pesticide 2,4,5-T (2,4,5,-trichlorophenoxyacetic acid), which was a component of the herbicide Agent Orange in Vietnam. TCDD has entered the environment via use of contaminated herbicides (Vietnam, various locations in the United States), manufacturing procedures and accidents (Newark, New Jersey; Seveso, Italy; and others), and improper waste disposal (Times Beach and other locations in Missouri).

The major rationale for the cleanup of sites contaminated with TCDD is that the contamination by this highly toxic compound presents a major risk to human health. Risk is made up of the inherent hazard of the compound and the extent of exposure to the compound. Operationally, it has been assumed that most of the TCDD that can be detected by chemical analysis is available to cause toxicity. There has been little evidence until recently regarding the validity of this assumption. Several studies (discussed below) have suggested that the entire amount of TCDD that can be detected in a soil sample may not be completely bioavailable. Rather, some portion of the TCDD may be too tightly sorbed to the matrix to be released in biological systems. Further, the presence of other chemicals in the matrix may interfere with gastric uptake of TCDD or with the receptor mediated toxicity of TCDD.

Examination of the literature regarding bioavailability of TCDD from environmental materials (Table I) reveals several important points. (1). Bioavailability of TCDD appears to be quite variable, depending on the site and material tested, and the species used as an assay system. (2). Laboratory contaminated samples yield different reactions than environmentally contaminated samples. It appears that TCDD added to soil in the laboratory is much more bioavailable, at least initially, than TCDD on materials contaminated in the environment. (3). Apparently the amount of time TCDD has been in contact with the substrate greatly affects its bioavailability and chemical extractablility. This effect may be a physiochemical ageing or a weathering phenomena.

Poiger and Schlatter (2) reported a series of experiments on the absorption by animals of TCDD from various materials contaminated in the laboratory. The percentage of the TCDD dose (tritiated TCDD in ethanol) found in the liver of treated animals varied with the amount of time between dosing and assay, and the size of the dose of TCDD. They found that TCDD added to soil in the laboratory was about one quarter as bioavailable as the pure compound, and that this bioavailability was reduced (from 24% to 16%) by increasing the time of contact between soil and TCDD before dosing (from 24 hours to 8 days). They also reported that TCDD in a mixture with activated charcoal was only slightly bioavailable.

Isensee and Jones (3) detected little uptake by oats and soybeans of TCDD from sprayed soil, and found that adult plants took up even less than young shoots. Further, no uptake from leaves was detected. Van der

Table I: Comparison of Literature Reports of the
Bioavailability of TCDD

| author | type of sample | species | assay | bioavailability (uptake, toxicity) |
|---|---|---|---|---|
| Poiger + Schlatter 1980 | soil or charcoal lab cont | rat | CA | charcoal <0.07% soil 10 hr = 24% soil 8 days = 16% |
| Isensee + Jones 1971 | soil cont in lab | plant | CA | 1.7% |
| van der Berg et al   1985 | fly ash | g.p. hamster rat | CA | 0.9-3.7% 1.7-2.4% <14% |
| Kuehl et al 1985a 1985b | fly ash sediment | fish aquar envir | CA CA | 0.024-2.1% >37.5% |
| Silkworth et al 1982 | PCB fire soot | g.p. | $LD_{50}$ | 80% |
| McConnell et al 1984 | Times Beach soil | g.p. rat | CA AHH | 60-85% 54-100% |
| Lucier et al 1986 | Times Beach soil | rat | AHH | 25-50% |
| Umbreit et al 1986a | Newark soil A soil B | g.p. | CA | 0.5% 21.3% |
| Cooper et al 1986 | Newark soil | fish embryo | Tox | ca. 0.1% |

Notes: g.p. = guinea pig. envir = environmental uptake.
cont = contaminated. lab = laboratory. CA = chemical
analysis. aquar = aquarium exposure. Tox = toxicity. AHH
= aryl hydrocarbon hydroxylase induction in liver
microsomes.

Berg et al (4) reported that uptake of TCDD and other
dioxins and furans from dietary fly ash was less than
14% in rats, 3.7% in guinea pigs, and 2.4 % in
hamsters. Kuehl et al (5) showed a minimum of 37.5%
uptake of TCDD from contaminated lake sediments into
carp. In an aquarium study, Kuehl et al (6) found a
maximum bioavailability of 2.1% to fish. Silkworth et
al (7) demonstrated toxicity of soot from a PCB fire;
however, the extremely low levels of TCDD in these
materials make it difficult to relate these results to
bioavailability of dioxins.

McConnell et al (8) studied the bioavailability of
TCDD from the dioxin contaminated soils at Times Beach,
Missouri. They reported a bioavailability (based on
toxicity data and aryl hydrocarbon hydroxylase
induction) of approximately 60-85% from soil from Times
Beach, Missouri. Lucier et al (9) examined the same
Missouri soils as reported by McConnell et al (8).
Using AHH induction in rat liver as a measure, they
estimated that TCDD was about 25-50% bioavailable from
these soils. These data demonstrated a clear dose
response for TCDD toxicity and AHH induction from the
contaminated soils.

We previously reported studies of TCDD
contaminated soils from a 2,4,5-T manufacturing site in
New Jersey (10). No lethality was seen in guinea pigs
treated with soils using doses as high as 12 ug TCDD/kg
body weight. The $LD_{50}$ in male guinea pig is ca. 0.6 ug
TCDD/kg. Bioavailability was determined by analysis of
liver samples and was estimated to be <0.5% from
contaminated soil from the 2,4,5-T manufacturing site.
A nearby metal scrap yard where the stills from the
manufacturing plant had been broken down for scrap
metal also had TCDD contamination in its soil. Tests of
this soil demonstrated a bioavailability of TCDD in
guinea pigs of ca. 21%. Cooper et al (11), examining
these same soils, reported that embryos of the Japanese
Medaka (Oryzias latipes) were extremely sensitive to
toxicity from TCDD contaminated soils; however, the
actual bioavailability of TCDD was still extremely low.
We completed a study in susceptible mice of the long
term and reproductive effects of the TCDD contaminated
soils from New Jersey (12-14). Whereas female mice
treated with TCDD in oil or TCDD added to
decontaminated soil just before use were unable to
reproduce, mice treated with TCDD contaminated soils
reproduced successfully. Some reproductive toxicity was
observed in females treated with contaminated soil;
however, this toxicity could not be attributed to TCDD.
The many other compounds present on these soils,
including potent teratogens and fetotoxins, may well
have caused the limited toxicities seen.

Because the various reports of bioavailability have involved different protocols and systems, we undertook a study of both the Times Beach and the Newark soils.

## METHODS

Soils were the identical samples previously studied, from Newark, New Jersey, (10-15) and Times Beach, Missouri (8,9) although they had been stored longer. TCDD (2,3,7,8 isomer) levels in the soils have been reported as approximately 2300 ppb at Newark and 770 ppb at Times Beach. Methods for the acute toxicity study of these soils in guinea pigs have been reported previously (15). Briefly, guinea pigs (ca. 200 g initially, 10 per sex per group) were given single doses of 10% soil suspensions in 5% aqueous gum Acacia by gavage and observed for up to 60 days following the single dose. Treatment materials included Times Beach soil, Newark soil, soil from Newark from which hydrocarbons had been stripped (designated "decontaminated soil"), and decontaminated soil to which pure TCDD in acetone was added shortly before use (designated "recontaminated" soil). Doses ranged from 1 to 10 ug TCDD/kg. All volumes administered were less than 15 ml. Animals that died during the course of the experiment were autopsied as soon as possible after death.

Rats were dosed with soil suspensions, by gavage, either once or for four consecutive days. Total TCDD dosages administered to rats were either 10 ug TCDD/kg or 40 ug/ TCDD/kg . Rats were sacrificed 24 hours after the final dose, autopsied, and hepatic microsomal fractions were collected. Aryl hydrocarbon hydroxylase (AHH) levels were determined in the microsomes, using the fluorescent assay of the product of the metabolism of benzo(a)pyrene to 3-OH benzo(a)pyrene (16).

## RESULTS

Cause and mean time of death of guinea pigs in each treatment group was noted (summarized in Table II). Cause of death was determined by autopsy. Characteristic signs of TCDD intoxication included wasting, thymic atrophy and atrophy of mesenteric lymph nodes. Other causes of death (including pneumonia, abdominal fibrosis, and undeterminable) were approximately evenly distributed among treatment groups. Overall, the Times Beach soil was toxic ($LD_{50}$ <10ug/kg) whereas the Newark soil was less toxic ($LD_{05}$ >10ug/kg), when approximately the same TCDD dosages were given in the soil. Somewhat smaller doses of TCDD on recontaminated soil were much more toxic. Further, deaths occurred most rapidly in the recontaminated soil

group, and almost as fast in the group treated with
Times Beach soil. The Newark soil death (1 death in 20
animals treated) occurred at the end of the observation
period, and the designation based on autopsy of this
death as induced by TCDD is questionable.

Table III presents the results of aryl hydrocarbon
hydroxylase (AHH) determinations in rat liver
microsomes. AHH levels were roughly equivalent for
males and females in each group except the negative
control. Times Beach soil and Newark soil induced AHH
activity in both sexes (Times Beach soil was ca. 2 to 4
times decontaminated soil, while Newark soil was ca. 2
to 5.5).

## DISCUSSION

The results of toxicity testing and liver analysis
support the conclusions on bioavailability of TCDD from
these soils previously presented by our group (10,12-
15) for the Newark soil, and by McConnell et al for
Times Beach soil (8). However, AHH induction in rats
treated with Newark or Times Beach soil was equivalent.

Several possible reasons for the difference
in bioavailability of TCDD from these soils can be
suggested. 1) Differences in the composition of the
soils may cause TCDD to be sorbed more tightly to one
soil than to another soil [results of physiochemical
characterization of the soils (unpublished) and of
extractions of TCDD from the soils support this
possibility (10)]. Therefore, it is less able to leave
the soil and be taken up by the animal. The differences
include the amount of highly absorptive material such
as carbon particles or clay, the size distribution and
total surface area of such particles, the amount and
types of humic acids present, and moisture content. 2)
The presence of various other compounds in the soil may
affect TCDD binding to soil (such as solvents or oils)
or interfere with TCDD binding to its receptor (such as
other dioxins or furans). The Newark soil has been
extensively analyzed and found to contain over fifty
different dioxins and furans, some in concentrations
almost as high as 2,3,7,8-TCDD. A wide variety of other
compounds were also found. Although no detailed
analysis of the Times Beach soil has appeared,
unpublished results show a much more limited range of
dioxins and furans present. Reports by Webster et al
(17) and Jackson et al (18) suggest that dissolved and
extractable organic matter influence leaching and
transport potential of TCDD. 3) Contamination occurred
by different mechanisms at the two sites: at Newark,
TCDD contamination was the result of manufacturing
processes, and the mixture reaching the soil contained
a large aqueous component which percolated through the

Table II. Summary of the Time and Cause of Death of
Guinea Pigs Treated With TCDD Contaminated Soils.

| Treatment | TCDD ug/kg | TCDD % | Deaths time (days) |
|---|---|---|---|
| Decont soil | 0 | 0 | - |
| Newark soil | 10 | 7 | 57 |
| Times Beach soil | 10 | 57 | $14.3 \pm 2.3$ |
| Recont soil | 6 | 95 | $9.8 \pm 3.2$ |

Notes: Recont soil = recontaminated soil, which was
clean soil to which TCDD was added. Decont soil = soil
from which chlorinated hydrocarbons had been removed.
Days are expressed as mean +/- standard deviation

Table III. Induction of Aryl Hydrocarbon
Hydroxylase (AHH) by TCDD Contaminated Soils in Rats.

| Treatment | AHH Activity (pmoles/min/ug protein) mean $\pm$ SD | | AHH/ background |
|---|---|---|---|
| Female 1 day | | | |
| decontaminated soil | 0.042 | 0.057 | 1.00 |
| recontaminated soil | 0.560 | 0.070 | 13.33 |
| Times Beach soil | 0.173 | 0.100 | 4.12 |
| Newark soil | 0.218 | 0.156 | 5.19 |
| Female 4 day | | | |
| decontaminated soil | 0.058 | 0.047 | 1.00 |
| recontaminated soil | 0.580 | 0.150 | 10.00 |
| Times Beach soil | 0.212 | 0.030 | 3.66 |
| Newark soil | 0.315 | 0.114 | 5.43 |
| Male 1 day | | | |
| decontaminated soil | 0.115 | 0.060 | 1.00 |
| recontaminated soil | 0.420 | 0.140 | 3.62 |
| Times Beach soil | 0.240 | 0.100 | 2.07 |
| Newark soil | 0.230 | 0.110 | 1.98 |
| Male 4 day | | | |
| decontaminated soil | 0.143 | 0.070 | 1.00 |
| recontaminated soil | 0.650 | 0.150 | 4.55 |
| Times Beach soil | 0.310 | 0.090 | 2.17 |
| Newark soil | 0.370 | 0.120 | 2.59 |

Notes: 1 day dose was 10 ug TCDD/kg body weight. 4 day
dose was 10 ug TCDD/kg body weight on each of 4
consecutive days for a total of 40 ug/kg. AHH was
determined as pmoles/min/ug protein of 3-OH-
benzo(a)pyrene formed, and reported as mean $\pm$ standard
deviation of individual assays on four animals per
treatment group. AHH/background = induction compared to
decontaminated soil for each treatment group.

soil for more than 10 years, while at Times Beach the
TCDD contamination occurred because of the spreading of
contaminated waste oil for dust control. It is possible
that the TCDD at Times Beach is really dissolved in an
oil matrix surrounding the soil particles, rather than
bound to the soil. Such solution in oil would make the
TCDD readily extractable and presumably more
bioavailable.

Both Times Beach and Newark soils induced AHH
activity in rats to similar levels despite the much
lower toxicity of the Newark soil in guinea pigs. The
amount of TCDD needed to cause AHH induction is
considerably less than that needed to cause toxicity,
and the low bioavailability of TCDD from the Newark
soil may have been sufficient to induce AHH without
being sufficient to cause toxicity. Another possible
explanation of this result is the fact that among the
numerous other compounds present on this soil were
several potent AHH inducers [such as benzo(a)pyrene and
benzo(a)anthracene (12)], that may have been
bioavailable to a greater extent than TCDD.
Importantly, the AHH induction in both groups implies
that the use of AHH induction as a primary marker for
TCDD exposure from environmental materials may be
unreliable.

The results presented, and the previous reports
confirmed by these results, demonstrate that soils from
different TCDD contaminated sites have different
toxicities and may represent quite different risks to
human populations. The exact factors that influence the
bioavailability of toxicants from soils remain to be
elucidated.

Funded in part by USEPA cooperative agreement
#CR812114-01-1.

## Literature Cited

1.   Safe, S.; Fujita, T.; Homonko, K.; Romkes,
     M.; Piskorska-Pliszczynska, J.; Denomme, M.A.
     Toxicologist 1986, 6, 309.

2.   Poiger, H.; Schlatter, C. Food Cosmet.
     Toxicol. 1980, 18, 477-81.

3.   Isensee, A.R.; Jones, G.J. J. Agr Food Chem. 1970,
     19, 1210-14.

4.   Van dan Berg, M.; de Vroom, E.; van Greevenbroek,
     M.; Olie, K.; Hutzinger, O. Chemosphere 1985, 14,
     865-69.

5.   Kuehl, D.W.; Cook, P.M.; Bateman, A.R. Fifth
     Internat. Symp. Chlorinated Dioxins, 1985, abstr.
     172.

6.   Kuehl, D.W.; Cook, P.M.; Bateman, A.R. Chemosphere
     1985, 14, 871-72.

7.   Silkworth, J.; McMartin, D.; DeCaprio, A.; Rej,
     R.; O'Keefe, P.; Kaminsky, L.; Toxicol. Appl.
     Pharmacol. 1982, 65, 425-39.
8.   McConnell, E.E.; Lucier, G.W.; Rumbaugh, R.C.;
     Albro, P.W.; Harvan, D.J.; Hass, J.R.; Harris,
     M.W. Science 1982, 223, 1077-79.
9.   Lucier, G.W.; Rumbaugh, R.C.; McCoy, Z.; Hass,
     J.R.; Harvan, D.; Albro, P. Fund. Appl. Toxicol.
     1986, 6, 364-71.
10.  Umbreit, T.H.; Hesse, E.J.; Gallo, M.A. Science
     1986, 232, 497-99.
11.  Cooper, K.R.; Schell, J.; Umbreit, T.H.; Gallo,
     M.A.; submitted, Environmental Health and Toxicol.
12.  Umbreit, T.H.; Hesse, E.J.; Gallo, M.A. submitted,
     Fund. Appl. Toxicol.
13.  Umbreit, T.H.; Hesse, E.J.; Gallo, M.A. submitted,
     Fund. Appl. Toxicol.
14.  Umbreit, T.H.; Hesse, E.J.; Gallo, M.A. in prep.
15.  Umbreit, T.H.; Hesse, E.J.; Gallo, M.A.
     Chemosphere, 1986, in press.
16.  Guengerich, F.P. In "Principles and Methods
     of Toxicology"; Hayes, A.W., Ed.; Raven Press: New
     York, 1982; pp. 615-16.
17.  Webster, G.R.B.; Muldrew, D.H.; Graham, N.J.;
     Sarna, L.P.; Muir, D.C.G. 5th International
     Symposium on Chlorinated Dioxins and Related
     Compounds 1985, Bayreuth, FRG. abstract 84.
18.  Jackson, D.R.; Roulier, M.R.; Grotta, H.M.; Rust,
     S.W.; Warner, J.S.; Arthur, M.F.; DeRoos, F.L.
     Land Disposal of Hazardous Waste. Barkley, N.P.
     Hazardous Waste Engineering Research Laboratory,
     Office of Res. and Dev., USEPA: Cincinnati, Ohio,
     1985; pp. 153-168.

RECEIVED November 25, 1986

# RISK ASSESSMENT: EVALUATION

# Chapter 11

# Epidemiology of Populations Exposed to Dioxins

M. A. Fingerhut, M. H. Sweeney, W. E. Halperin, and T. M. Schnorr

National Institute for Occupational Safety and Health, Cincinnati, OH 45226

A historical review of studies of human exposure to
dioxin-contaminated substances is presented, with
emphasis on 2,3,7,8-tetrachlorodibenzodioxin
(2,3,7,8-TCDD). Exposed populations include
production workers, herbicide sprayers, persons
exposed to Agent Orange, and residents of Missouri,
U.S.A. and Seveso, Italy. Published medical reports
have described chloracne, asthenia, neurological
problems, and hepatotoxicity, but some of these
studies have not had adequate comparison populations.
Some recent epidemiologic studies have concluded that
no outcomes could be attributed to dioxin exposure,
but others have found associations of exposure with
soft tissue sarcoma, lymphoma, nasal and stomach
cancer. These studies are described.

This paper presents a historical review of reports and clinical
studies of humans exposed to dioxin-contaminated substances.
Dioxins are chemical contaminants produced during the synthesis of
chlorophenols and certain other halogenated aromatic hydrocarbons.
There are 75 dioxin isomers of which 2,3,7,8 tetrachlorodibenzo-
p-dioxin (2,3,7,8-TCDD) is the most toxic in animal studies (1).
Table I illustrates some major substances contaminated with isomers
of dioxin. These manufactured products include 2,4,5-trichloro-
phenol (TCP) and its derivatives, such as 2,4,5-trichlorophenoxy-
acetic acid (2,4,5-T), which are contaminated with 2,3,7,8-TCDD, as
well as pentachlorophenol, which is contaminated with hexa-, hepta-,
and octachlorinated isomers of dioxin.

TABLE I.   The Relevant Substances

| MANUFACTURED PRODUCT | DIOXIN CONTAMINANT |
|---|---|
| 2,4,5-TRICHLOROPHENOL<br>2,4,5-T(ACID, ESTER, AMINE)<br>SILVEX (ACID, ESTER, AMINE) | 2,3,7,8-TETRACHLORODIBENZODIOXIN<br>(2,3,7,8-TCDD) |
| PENTACHLOROPHENOL | HEXACHLORODIBENZODIOXINS<br>HEPTACHLORODIBENZODIOXINS<br>OCTACHLORODIBENZODIOXINS |
| 2,4-D | NONE<br>DICHLORODIBENZODIOXINS<br>TRICHLORODIBENZODIOXINS<br>TETRACHLORODIBENZODIOXINS<br>(1,3,6,8 or 1,3,6,9) |

Figure I illustrates some major events which have occurred since production of the chlorophenols began in the United States in the mid-1930's . Although accidents have occurred periodically and adverse health effects related to dioxin exposure have been recognized in exposed workers, it was not until the 1970's that the problems received public attention.  During that decade, animal studies demonstrated the severe toxicity of 2,3,7,8-TCDD and it was realized that large numbers of people had potential exposure to 2,3,7,8-TCDD through the use of Agent Orange in the Vietnam war, the distribution of dioxin-contaminated wastes throughout Missouri, U.S.A. and the contamination of several communities after a  major explosion in Seveso, Italy.  This perception of a potential human crisis motivated rapid advances in analytic techniques, animal toxicology and the initiation of epidemiologic investigations of human health effects.

## The Early Period:  Descriptive Medical Reports (1937-1978)

From 1935 to 1978, workers world-wide were exposed during periodic explosions at trichlorophenol production facilities as well as during their daily production activities.  Table II illustrates some major industrial accidents which yielded published reports of health effects.  Table III lists some major health outcomes reported following exposures to products contaminated with 2,3,7,8-TCDD.  The primary dermal effect of exposure is chloracne, a persistent form of acne caused by exposure to a number of chlorinated organic compounds.  Chloracne occurred in some exposed persons in all accidents, as well as in children in Seveso (2-4).  Chloracne appeared with and without other health effects and persisted in some persons up to 28 years after exposure (5-6).

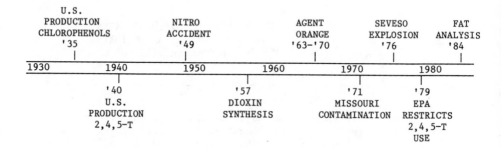

FIGURE 1.   Key Events in the History of Dioxin Exposures

TABLE II. Industrial Explosions

| YEAR | LOCATION |
|------|----------|
| 1949 | MONSANTO, NITRO, W.V., U.S.A. |
| 1953 | BASF LUDWIGSHAFEN, W. GERMANY |
| 1963 | PHILIPS-DUPHAR AMSTERDAM, NETHERLANDS |
| 1966 | RHONE POULENC GRENOBLE, FRANCE |
| 1968 | COALITE & CHEMICALS PROD. BOLSOVER, DERBYSHIRE, U.K. |
| 1976 | ICMESA SEVESO, ITALY |

Neurologic effects, including disturbances of both the peripheral and central nervous systems, were reported following every accident and in many industrial exposures. The neurologic effects almost always included profound weakness and fatigue, as well as pain and weakness in extremities. Other reported neurologic symptoms included headaches, irritability, sleep disturbances, peripheral neuropathy, depression, confusion, and personality changes (7-8).

Hepatotoxic effects were also reported in exposed workers. These included hepatitis, hepatomegaly, alterations in level of liver enzymes and porphyria cutanea tarda, a disturbance of liver metabolism in which excess porphyrins are produced and excreted. Some symptoms of porphyria cutanea tarda were exhibited as dermal effects, including hyperpigmentation, blistering, and an abnormal growth of hair on the face and body, also known as hirsutism (7,9-10).

Less frequently reported effects included gastrointestinal disturbances, renal, cardiovascular and respiratory problems, and abnormalities in lipid levels (11-13).

Case reports in 1977 and in 1978 from a clinic in Sweden noted that neoplasms (soft tissue sarcoma and lymphoma) were observed more frequently than expected in workers exposed to chlorophenols or phenoxy herbicides (14-15).

In a unique situation, three British laboratory workers who synthesized 2,3,7,8-TCDD in a laboratory experienced chloracne, asthenia, neurologic and gastrointestinal problems along with changes in lipid metabolism (12). Their medical effects were of special interest because they seem to have been associated only with pure 2,3,7,8-TCDD.

TABLE III.  Major Human Health Effects Following
2,3,7,8-TCDD Exposure, 1937-1978

| SYSTEM | EFFECT |
| --- | --- |
| DERMAL | CHLORACNE |
| NEUROLOGIC | PERIPHERAL NEUROPATHIES<br>FATIGUE<br>DEPRESSION<br>PERSONALITY CHANGES |
| HEPATIC | HEPATITIS<br>ENLARGED LIVER<br>ABNORMAL ENZYME LEVELS<br>PORPHYRIA CUTANEA TARDA |

Adverse health outcomes were also described among community
residents in Missouri and Seveso (2,16).  Although the conditions
of exposure of workers and the community residents differed, some of
the reported health outcomes in these groups were quite
similar (17).

In summary, many medical reports were published between 1937
and 1979 which described serious problems in multiple organ-systems
among individuals exposed to 2,3,7,8-TCDD.  However, during this 50
year period of exposure, no formal studies were conducted which
included a control group of non-exposed persons.

It is generally assumed that the affected workers experienced
heavy exposures.  Extrapolation to less severely exposed populations
from these reports was difficult because of the absence of
comparison groups of non-exposed persons, and because limited
information was provided about severity of the exposure and the
proportions of persons injured.

The Current Period:  Epidemiologic Studies (1979-1986)

The observations in the medical reports just described provided the
hypotheses for controlled epidemiologic studies of exposed human
populations.  With the exception of one study of herbicide workers
in 1974 (18), epidemiologic studies have been published only since
1979.  In the United States and in some other countries, most
industrial exposures to 2,3,7,8-TCDD had ceased by 1979 when
restrictions on uses of 2,4,5-T were issued by the U.S.

Overview of Basic Epidemiologic Study Designs.  Epidemiology is the
systematic study of the distribution and determinants of disease in
human populations (19).  Analytic research studies fall into several
designs such as cohort studies, case-control studies, proportional
mortality ratio (PMR) studies and cross sectional studies.  The
choice of a particular study design is determined by the

characteristics of the problem under investigation. However, all designs include requirements for accurate assessment of exposure, adequate sample size to detect an effect, and appropriately selected control groups. Although studies of human populations often cannot have an experimental design as strict as that of toxicologic studies of animals, a goal in designing epidemiologic studies is quite similar: to construct as much as possible a study group and a control group which differ only with respect to the variable of interest. Often the researcher can account for many confounding variables, such as age and sex, in the design or in the analysis of the study.

In a cohort mortality study design, the study population is chosen on the basis of exposure to a particular substance. The mortality rates in the exposed group are compared to mortality rates in an unexposed group. Often the unexposed comparison group is a standard population, such as the U.S. male population or an appropriate unexposed group such as unexposed workers in the same plant.

In a case-control design, the study population is selected on the basis of disease status of the individual cases. Controls are selected who are free of the disease of interest at the time of the study. To determine whether the disease is related to the exposure of interest, the frequency of the exposure is compared among cases and controls. Usually the cases and controls (or their next of kin) are interviewed about occupational, and environmental exposures as well as personal habits. Of particular concern in a case-control study is the correct or unbiased ascertainment of relevant exposure. Unintentional or intentional under-reporting or over-reporting of exposure by either the cases or the controls may produce erroneous results.

In proportional mortality ratio (PMR) studies, the observed proportions of deaths due to particular causes are compared to expected proportions calculated from the comparison group. There are two major limitations of this type of study. First, one must assume that the deaths studied are representative of the larger group, which may not be true. Second, proportions must add to one so a deficit in one cause of death category will necessarily produce excesses in other categories.

Epidemiologic studies which evaluate the long term effect of exposure on health generally have had a cross-sectional study design, in which the medical assessment of current workers or residents is made at one point in time. In such a design, one major concern is that sick individuals may not be included because they left the workplace or area before the time of the cross-sectional medical study.

In all epidemiologic studies, the statistical power is of special concern. A study of adequate statistical power has the ability to detect an excess outcome as statistically significant, if the excess is truly present. Studies which have too few subjects may be unable to detect an excess simply because the size of the study group is too small. Therefore, in studies with few subjects, excesses over the expected should not be ignored solely because the result was not statistically significant.

In evaluating the results of an epidemiologic study, it is
important to examine the extent of exposure of the subjects.
"Exposure" is defined by the researchers and is specific only to
that study.  For example, in some cohort studies of chemical workers
the exposure has been defined as assignment to the TCP or 2,4,5-T
production processes.  In other studies, the definition of exposure
has been less specific; for example, in some cohort studies of
herbicide sprayers, all sprayers have been considered "exposed" even
though the authors have no knowledge whether the various herbicides
sprayed by a particular individual included 2,4,5-T.

Cohort Studies.  To date, a number of cohort studies have been
conducted of chemical workers from the U.S. and Europe and of
herbicide sprayers from Sweden and Finland (20-28).  In general, the
studies have not demonstrated a definitive relationship between
mortality from any malignant or nonmalignant condition and exposure
to chlorophenols or phenoxy herbicides.  All of the studies lacked
sufficient statistical power due to the small number of individuals
in each cohort.

Table IV presents the cohort studies of chemical workers.  In
two cohort studies of U.S. chemical workers, statistically nonsignificant excesses in mortality were observed for the ICD categories
describing cancers of the lung, soft tissue sarcoma, stomach, male
genital organs and for non-Hodgkins lymphoma (21,23).  One soft
tissue sarcoma death was observed in the Zack study (21), but the
meaning of one death is difficult to interpret.  The Cook study (23)
updated two earlier studies, so those are not shown here (22,29).

Among European chemical workers, a statistically significant
increase in deaths from stomach cancer was observed in German
workers exposed to trichlorophenol (24).  Among Danish women workers
exposed to phenoxy herbicides, a statistically nonsignificant excess
in the incidence of cervical cancer was found.  Male workers exposed
to phenoxy herbicides showed a statistically significant excess of
lung cancer as well as an elevated but statistically nonsignificant
excess of rectal cancer.  A single case of soft tissue sarcoma was
also observed (25).  An excess incidence of STS which was not
statistically significant, was found also among manual service
workers, a group including maintenance and shipping workers who may
have had exposure to phenoxy herbicides.  One case of STS was
observed also among workers assigned to departments without phenoxy
herbicides.  Interpretation of these results was severely hampered
by the limited exposure assessment.

Cohort studies of herbicide sprayers are presented in Table V.
An excess of mortality from stomach cancer was statistically
significant in one small Swedish study (27).  No specific
malignancies were found in excess in the other studies.  All had low
statistical power and limited exposure assessments.  The researchers
had insufficient information about the types of phenoxy herbicides
to which the workers were exposed and limited data about the
intensity and duration of the exposures.  Some phenoxy herbicides do
not contain 2,3,7,8-TCDD.  Corroborating results from other studies
and additional observations obtained through further vital status
follow-up of the cohorts may reduce the ambiguity of the results.

TABLE IV.  Cohort Studies of Chemical Workers

| POPULATION | EXPOSURE | DEATHS/N | CANCER EXCESSES | OBS/EXP | CONCERN |
|---|---|---|---|---|---|
| Mortality Studies | | | | | |
| U.S.A. (21) | TCP | 32/121 | LUNG<br>STS | 5/2.85<br>1/? | P |
| U.S.A. (23) | TCP<br>2,4,5-T | 298/2189 | STOMACH<br>MALE<br>GENITAL<br>ORGANS<br>NON-<br>HODGKINS<br>LYMPHOMA | 5/3.2<br>6/3.8<br><br>5/2.1 | P |
| W. GERMANY (24) | TCP | 21/74 | STOMACH | 3/0.6** | P |
| Incidence Studies | | | | | |
| DENMARK (25) | PH Women | 0/240 | CERVIX | 5/1.82 | |
| | PH Men | 0/690 | LUNG<br>RECTAL<br>STS | 11/5.33**<br>4/1.49<br>1/0.50 | P,E |
| | MS Men | 0/988 | STS | 3/0.6 | |
| | O  Men | 0/1385 | STS | 1/0.8 | |

N, TOTAL NUMBER IN COHORT; P, POWER; E, EXPOSURE ASSESSMENT;
OBS/EXP, OBSERVED/EXPECTED; TCP, TRICHLOROPHENOL; STS, SOFT TISSUE
SARCOMA; PH, PHENOXY HERBICIDES; MS, MANUAL SERVICE WORKERS; O,
OTHER MANUFACTURING WORKERS; **p lt 0.05

TABLE V.  Cohort Mortality Studies of Herbicide Sprayers

| POPULATION | EXPOSURE | DEATHS/N | CANCER EXCESSES OBS/EXP | CONCERN |
|---|---|---|---|---|
| SWEDEN (27) | PH | 45/348 | STOMACH 3/.71** | P,E |
| SWEDEN (26) | 2,4,5-T | 29/158 | NO | P,L,E |
| FINLAND (28) | 2,4-D 2,4,5-T | 144/1926 | NO | P,L,E |

P, POWER; L, LATENCY; E, EXPOSURE ASSESSMENT; PH, PHENOXY
HERBICIDES; N, TOTAL NUMBER IN COHORT; OBS/EXP, OBSERVED/EXPECTED;
**p lt 0.05

Case-Control Studies.  The case control studies presented in Table
VI were conducted to assess the possible association between the
occurrence of soft tissue sarcoma, lymphoma, nasal and colon cancers
with exposure to phenoxy herbicides and chlorophenols.  No
statistically significant association was found between colon cancer
and such exposures (30), but an association was found with lymphoma
(31).  Nasal cancer was found to be associated with exposure to
phenoxy herbicides and chlorophenols in a Swedish study (32).
However, a Danish study found no association between nasal cancer
and exposure (33).  Differences in results between the studies may
be explained by the methods used for control selection.  The Swedish
controls were selected from the general population and the Danish
controls were selected from among other cancer cases.  Some critics
have suggested that as a group, cancer cases have heightened recall
of past exposures, thus increasing the likelihood of a positive
finding unless the controls have a similar heightened recall.
    In the past few years, there has been widespread interest in
the possibility that individuals exposed to phenoxy herbicides and
chlorophenols may be at greater risk of developing soft tissue
sarcomas.  Soft tissue sarcomas constitute a category of very rare
cancers with a total mortality rate of 1 STS per 100,000 persons per
year in the United States (34).  The soft tissue sarcomas are
malignant neoplasms of diverse histologic subtypes, which occur
throughout the body in mesenchymal connective tissue other than
bone (35).  Because of the diversity of histologic subtypes,
these malignancies are often not reported accurately on death
certificates (36) and may not be recognized accurately by general
pathologists (37).  These factors may lead to the incorrect
reporting of soft tissue sarcomas.

TABLE VI. Case-Control Studies

| STUDY | DISEASE | EXPOSURE | CASES/<br>CONTROLS | EXCESSES | CONCERN |
|-------|---------|----------|----------|----------|---------|
| SWEDEN (30) | COLON | PH, CL | 157/541 | NO | E |
| SWEDEN (31) | LYMPHOMA | PH<br>CL | 169/338 | 5-FOLD**<br>4-FOLD** | E |
| SWEDEN (32) | NASAL | PH<br>CL | 71/541 | 2-FOLD<br>7-FOLD** | E |
| DENMARK (33) | NASAL | CL | 146/2465 | NO | E |
| SWEDEN (38) | STS | PH, CL | 52/206 | 5-FOLD** | E |
| SWEDEN (39) | STS | PH, CL | 110/220 | 6-FOLD** | E |
| NEW ZEALAND (40) | STS | PH<br>CL | 82/92 | NO<br>5-7 FOLD**<br>(PELT<br>HANDLERS) | E |
| New York, USA (41) | STS | VIETNAM<br>SERVICE<br>AO | 281/410 | NO | E |

PH, PHENOXY HERBICIDES; CL, CHLOROPHENOLS; AO, AGENT ORANGE; E,
EXPOSURE ASSESSMENT; P, POWER; **p lt 0.05

Several studies have assessed the plausibility of the
association between soft tissue sarcomas and exposure to phenoxy
herbicides and chlorophenols. Table VI lists two case-control
studies conducted in Sweden, which selected controls from the general
population and concluded that exposure to the herbicides or to
chlorophenols resulted in a greater than 5-fold excess in soft
tissue sarcomas (38-39). A New Zealand study found no association
with exposure to phenoxy herbicides (40). This study drew controls
from other cancer cases in the National Cancer Registry of New
Zealand. However, in the New Zealand study, a 5-fold excess of STS
was noted in persons who handled animal pelts, which are sometimes
preserved with trichlorophenols containing isomers of dioxin.

Because of possible exposure to Agent Orange during tours of
duty in southeast Asia, Vietnam Veterans have been concerned that
they may have increased risk of developing soft tissue sarcomas.
Agent Orange was composed of equal parts of esters of 2,4,5-T and
2,4-D. Table VI presents results from an interview study of soft
tissue sarcoma cases from the New York State Cancer Registry with
controls selected from New York driver's license registration
files (41). Greenwald et al. found no association between STS and

a history of Vietnam service or reported exposures to Agent Orange.
The major limitation of the study was the assessment of exposure of
individuals to Agent Orange.

Studies Using National Census Data. Table VII lists four studies
with different epidemiologic designs which have utilized existing
computerized population data to evaluate soft tissue sarcoma. This
record-based type of study is valuable for generating hypotheses, but
generally provides weak evidence for confirming hypotheses because of
the absence of individual exposure information. Three of the studies
used broad occupational categories such as farmer or forester and
assumed that exposure to phenoxy herbicides occurred to the
group (42-44). Milham examined proportions of deaths due to STS
which were recorded on death certificates in Washington State (42)
and Balajaran used occupations recorded upon registration of the
cancer in the National Cancer Register of England and Wales (43).
Each found excess STS over expected in a category of farmer. Wiklund
matched Swedish census data for occupation to cancers in the cancer
registry. He found no excess soft tissue sarcoma in 6 categories of
agricultural and forestry workers (44). Kogan studied causes of
death listed on death certificates of veterans who died in
Massachusetts between 1972 and 1973 and found that the proportion of
deaths due to soft tissue sarcoma and to kidney cancer was
significantly higher among veterans who served in Vietnam when
compared to those who served elsewhere (45).

TABLE VII.   Studies of Soft Tissue Sarcoma from
National Census Data

| POPULATION | EXPOSURE | STUDY SIZE | EXCESSES (STUDY) | CONCERN |
|---|---|---|---|---|
| WASHINGTON STATE DEATHS (42) | FARMER | 429,926 | STS 1.5 FOLD** (PMR) | E |
| ENGLAND AND WALES (43) | FARMER | 1961/1961 | STS 1.7 FOLD** (CC) | E |
| SWEDEN (44) | FARMER FORESTER | 354,620 | NO (COHORT) | E |
| MASS. DEATHS 1972-73 (45) | VIETNAM SERVICE | 840 | STS 5 FOLD** KIDNEY 4 FOLD** (PMR) | E |

E, EXPOSURE; PMR, PROPORTIONAL MORTALITY RATIO STUDY; CC,
CASE-CONTROL STUDY; **p lt 0.05.

In summary, studies of STS have reported both positive and negative findings. All of the studies had limitations in statistical power or assessment of exposure. To date, no definitive answer exists as to whether STS is associated with exposure to phenoxy herbicides or chlorophenols. The situation is similar for lymphoma, stomach and nasal cancer.

Reproductive Outcome Studies. Studies of miscarriages and birth defects have been few in number and have considered male-mediated effects by examining pregnancy outcomes among the wives of exposed men (46-50). These studies are listed in Table VIII. The studies of Vietnam veterans had uncertain exposure data and considerable time between last exposure and conception. One study found no excess birth defects among Vietnam veterans (48). In two studies, excesses were noted of some birth defects: neural tube defects and cleft lip (47,50). These excesses appeared to be associated with probable Agent Orange exposure. However, the significance of the findings is questionable because of the large numbers of statistical tests performed. The reproductive studies among the wives of occupationally exposed men observed no excess of adverse reproductive outcomes. These studies had the potential for simultaneous occurrence of exposure and conception. However, the power of the studies is quite low and exposure assessments are inadequate (46,49).

TABLE VIII. Reproductive Studies

| POPULATION | COMPARISON | EXPOSURE | EXCESSES (STUDY) | CONCERN |
|---|---|---|---|---|
| NEW ZEALAND SPRAYERS 548 (46) | AGRICULTURAL CONTRACTORS 441 | 2,4,5-T | NO (COHORT) | E,P |
| WIVES CHEMICAL WORKERS 370 (49) | WIVES CHEMICAL WORKERS 345 | 2,4,5-T TCP | NO (COHORT) | E |
| ANATOMICAL BIRTH DEFECTS 5,000 (47) | NORMAL BIRTHS ATLANTA 3,000 | VIETNAM | SPINA BIFIDA** CLEFT LIP** (CC) | E |
| BIRTH DEFECTS AUSTRALIA 8517 (48) | NORMAL BIRTHS AUSTRALIA 8517 | VIETNAM SERVICE | NO (CC) | E |
| RANCH HAND PERSONNEL 1024 (50) | USAF PERSONNEL 1024 | AO | NEURAL TUBE DEFECTS+ (COHORT) | E,P |

E, EXPOSURE ASSESSMENT; P, POWER; AO, AGENT ORANGE; ** $p < 0.05$;
+ BASED ON PRELIMINARY ANALYSIS

Cross-Sectional Medical Studies.  Table IX lists the cross-sectional
studies.  In a study of active, retired, and former workers exposed
to TCP and 2,4,5-T, Singer observed a statistically significant
correlation between reduced nerve conduction velocity and length
of employment (51).  Bond found excesses of ulcer and digestive
system diseases in a survey of company bi-annual medical
examinations (52).  Four cross-sectional studies were conducted in
chemical workers who had been exposed at least ten years prior to
the study.  Suskind and Moses separately studied U.S. workers at a
West Virginia plant (53-54).  Suskind (53) observed excesses of
peptic ulcer, decreased libido, reduced lung function in current
smokers, and 3 cases of Peyronie's disease, a condition of internal
scarring of the penis.  In the study by Moses (54), all subjects had
been exposed to 2,4,5-T.  The group which had experienced chloracne
had increased levels of triglycerides and a liver enzyme, as well as
decreased sensation to pinprick, decreased libido and increased
sexual dysfunction.

Pazderova examined Czech workers about ten years after exposure
and found sustained neural and psychiatric problems and arterio-
sclerosis in the Czech workers, as well as glucose intolerance and
increases in cholesterol (55).  In a laboratory study of British
workers ten years after exposure, Martin found increases in some
liver enzymes as well as increased levels of cholesterol and
triglycerides in exposed workers (56).  Whether a health risk
results from the enzyme and lipid changes is not known, but one
concern is that lipid abnormalities may confer increased risk of
coronary vascular disease.

Several medical studies are presented in Table X which have
been conducted in groups outside of the industrial sector.  In a
medical study of exposed Seveso subjects, the prevalence of
peripheral neuropathy was three times higher among those exposed
persons with chloracne (57).  In a study of Missouri residents from
a mobile home park with soil contamination with 2,3,7,8-TCDD, some
parameters of immune response were reported to differ between the
exposed and unexposed (58).  The U.S. Air Force completed a
comprehensive medical study of the personnel of Operation Ranch
Hand, the individuals who sprayed Agent Orange in Vietnam (50).
Increased prevalence of enlarged livers and an increase of basal and
squamous cell carcinomas was observed.

In summary, the epidemiologic medical studies conducted after
1979 have had limitations such as inadequate exposure assessment,
limited participation, or limited control of confounding factors,
such as age and socioeconomic status of the comparison group.
Consequently, they have not provided definitive conclusions
regarding the persistence of medical effects of exposure to phenoxy
herbicides and chlorophenols or the risk of disease among
populations with low-level exposures.  They do suggest that
chloracne, ulcer, neurologic disease and elevations of triglycerides, cholesterol and liver enzymes persist in some exposed
persons.

TABLE IX. Medical Studies of Chemical Workers

| AUTHOR | EXPOSURE | EXCESSES | CONCERN |
|--------|----------|----------|---------|
| (51) | TCP 2,4,5-T | SLOWED NERVE CONDUCTION VELOCITIES | PN, CG |
| (52) | TCP 2,4,5-T | ULCER (2,4,5-T) DIGESTIVE SYSTEM DISEASES (2,4,5-T) | PN |
| (53) | TCP | PEPTIC ULCER PEYRONIE'S DISEASE REDUCED LUNG FUNCTION DECREASED LIBIDO | E,PN |
| (54) | 2,4,5-T | TRIGLYCERIDES ALTERED LIVER ENZYMES DECREASED SENSATION DECREASED LIBIDO SEXUAL DYSFUNCTION | E,PN |
| (55) | TCP | POLYNEUROPATHY ARTERIOSCLEROSIS PSYCHIATRIC DISORDERS GLUCOSE INTOLERANCE CHOLESTEROL | CG |
| (56) | TCP | D-GLUCARIC ACID GAMMA GLUTAMYL TRANSFERASE DECREASED SERUM CALCIUM CHOLESTEROL, TRIGLYCERIDES | E |

TCP, TRICHLOROPHENOL; E, EXPOSURE ASSESSMENT; PN, PARTICIPATION; CG, COMPARISON GROUP

Table XI lists several current epidemiologic studies which improve upon earlier design limitations such as statistical power and exposure assessment. Researchers at the National Institute for Occupational Safety and Health (NIOSH) are nearing completion of a large cohort mortality study of 7,000 U.S. chemical workers from 14 companies which produced trichlorophenol, 2,4,5-T and pentachlorophenol. A particular asset of this study is the availability of good information on type and duration of exposure of the workers. The International Agency for Research on Cancer (IARC) is preparing a worldwide registry of data on chemical workers and sprayers with exposure to phenoxy herbicides and chlorophenols. The NIOSH data base will be included in the IARC International Dioxin Registry. Case control studies are also underway for soft tissue sarcoma and lymphoma at the National Cancer Institute (NCI), Veterans Administration (VA) and the Centers for Disease Control (CDC). These studies will assess possible associations of these cancers with use of phenoxy herbicides in Kansas, with Vietnam service, and with exposure to Agent Orange.

Table XII lists medical studies to be completed in the next few years. NIOSH researchers will conduct a comprehensive medical examination study of chemical workers who made trichlorophenol and 2,4,5-T, and Northwestern University is conducting a medical study of workers who made pentachlorophenol. Good exposure information is available for both of these studies.

TABLE X. Non-Industrial Medical Studies

| AUTHOR | POPULATION/ COMPARISON | EXPOSURE | EXCESSES | CONCERN |
|--------|------------------------|----------|----------|---------|
| (57)   | +/- CHLORACNE 319/380  | TCP      | PERIPHERAL NEUROPATHY | E |
| (58)   | MISSOURI 154/155       | TCDD     | ANERGY T CELL RATIO | E,P |
| (50)   | RANCH HAND/ USAF PERSONNEL 1024/1024 | AO | ENLARGED LIVER NON-MELANOTIC SKIN CANCER | E |

TCP, TRICHLOROPHENOL; TCDD, 2,3,7,8-TCDD; AO, AGENT ORANGE;
E, EXPOSURE ASSESSMENT; P, POWER

TABLE XI. Current Epidemiological Studies

| STUDY | AGENCY* | POPULATION | COMPARISON | EXPOSURE |
|-------|---------|------------|------------|----------|
| COHORT MORTALITY | NIOSH | CHEMICAL WORKERS 7,000 | U.S. MALE POPULATION | PHENOXY HERBICIDES CHLOROPHENOLS |
| DIOXIN REGISTRY | IARC | CHEMICAL WORKERS/SPRAYERS 17,000 | NATIONAL POPULATIONS | PHENOXY HERBICIDES CHLOROPHENOLS |
| CASE/ CONTROL | NCI | STS 200 LYMPHOMA 400 | KANSAS POPULATION | PHENOXY HERBICIDES |
| CASE/ CONTROL | VA | STS 250 | PATHOLOGY 750 | VIETNAM AO |
| CASE/ CONTROL | CDC | STS 400 LYMPHOMA 1,300 | NATIONAL POPULATION 1,300 | VIETNAM AO |

\*   Full names are found in text.

TABLE XII. Current Medical Studies

| AGENCY | POPULATION | COMPARISON | EXPOSURE | COMPLETION |
|--------|------------|------------|----------|------------|
| NIOSH | CHEMICAL WORKERS 450 | NEIGHBORS 450 | 2,4,5-T TCP | 1989 |
| NORTH- WESTERN UNIV. | CHEMICAL WORKERS 500 | WORKERS 500 | PCP 2,4,5-T | 1987 |
| USAF | RANCH HAND PERSONNEL 1024 | AIR FORCE PERSONNEL 1024 | AGENT ORANGE | PHASE II 1987 |
| CDC | AO EXPOSED VIETNAM VETS 2000 | VIETNAM VETS NOT EXPOSED 2000 | AGENT ORANGE | 1989 |
| CDC | VIETNAM VETS 2000 | NON-VIETNAM VETS 2000 | VIETNAM SERVICE | 1989 |

To assess the potential health effects from exposure to Agent Orange, the Air Force is conducting the second phase of the Ranch Hand Health Study, and a large medical study of army veterans is underway at the Centers for Disease Control. The comparison groups for these studies are non-exposed military personnel.

## Conclusions

What conclusions can be drawn from the epidemiologic studies of persons exposed to dioxin-contaminated products?
1. Epidemiologic studies have been conducted within a very short time, between 1979 and 1985. All have been limited in exposure assessment or statistical power.
2. Chloracne is a consequence of exposure to dioxin in some people and is persistent for many years in some workers.
3. Acute medical consequences following exposure to dioxin-contaminated substances in industrial accidents included peripheral neuropathy, weakness, cardiovascular disease, liver dysfunction, abnormalities in liver enzymes and lipid levels. Symptoms of these medical consequences have persisted in some workers when examined in several studies conducted many years after exposure. No clear understanding yet exists of the severity or persistence of these health problems. Additionally, there is no clear information regarding medical risks for populations with low exposures to phenoxy herbicides and chlorophenols.
4. To date, exposure to phenoxy herbicides and chlorophenols has been shown in some studies to be associated with soft tissue sarcoma, lymphoma, stomach cancer, and nasal cancer, but no outcome has been conclusively established or rejected.
5. Some current studies have better statistical power and improved designs for assessing exposure. Recent successes with chemical analyses of human adipose tissue suggest that it may soon be possible to analyze biological levels of 2,3,7,8-TCDD in human adipose tissue, or better yet, in serum. Success in these efforts could contribute greatly to the accuracy of current studies of health outcomes in exposed persons.

## LITERATURE CITED

1. Esposito MP, Tierman TO, and Dryden FE: Dioxins, EPA-600/2-80-197, November, 1980.
2. Reggiani, G. Medical Problems Raised by the TCDD Contamination in Seveso, Italy. Arch Toxicol 40:161-188 (1978).
3. Butler MG: Acneform dermatosis produced by Ortho (2 chloro-phenyl) Phenol Sodium and Tetrachlorophenol Sodium. Arch Derm Syph 35: 251-254, 1937.
4. Kimmig J and Schulz KH: Occupational chloracne caused by aromatic cyclic ethers. Dermatologica 115: 540-546, 1957.
5. Goldman PJ: Critically acute chloracne caused by trichloro-phenol decomposition products. Arbeitsmed Sozialmed Arbeit-shygiene 7:12-18, 1972.
6. May G,: Chloracne from the accidental production of tetrachlor-odibenzo-dioxin. Br J Ind Med 30:276-283, 1973.

7. Bleiberg J, et al: Industrially acquired porphyria. Arch Dermatol 89:793-97, 1964.
8. Jirasek L, et al: Chronic poisoning by 2,3,7,8-tetrachlorodibenzo-p-dioxin. Cesk Dermatol 49:145-157, 1974.
9. Cholak J, Schafer LJ, Yeager D: "Reports on clinical and environmental surveys at Monsanto Chemical Co. Nitro, West Virginia, 1953." Department of Environmental Health, University of Cincinnati, Unpublished.
10. Strik JJTWA: The occurrence of chronic-hepatic porphyria in man caused by halogenated hydrocarbons. In: "Chemical Porphyria in man"; Strik JJTWA and Koeman JH (eds); Elsevier/North-Holland: New York, 1979.
11. Bauer H, et al: Industrial poisoning in the manufacture of chlorophenol compounds. Arch Gewerbepath Gewerbehyg 18:538-555, 1961.
12. Oliver RM: Toxic effects of 2,3,7,8-tetrachlorodibenzo 1,4 dioxin in laboratory workers. Br J Ind Med 32:49-53, 1975.
13. Poland A, et al: A health survey of workers in a 2,4-D and 2,4,5-T plant. Arch Environ Health 22:316-27, 1971.
14. Hardell L: Malignant mesenchymal tumors and exposure to phenoxy acids-a clinical observation. Lakartidningen 74:2853, 1977.
15. Hardell L: Soft tissue sarcomas and exposure to phenoxyacetic acids-a clinical observation. Lakartidningen 74:2753-2754, 1977.
16. Kimbrough RD, Carter CD, Liddle JA and Cline, RE. Epidemiology and pathology of a tetrachlorodibenzodioxin poisoning episode. Arch Environ Health 32:77-85, 1977.
17. IARC. "Long Term Hazards of Polychlorinated Dibenzodioxins and Polychlorinated Dibenzofurnas". IARC Technical Report No 78/001. International Agency for Research on Cancer. Lyon, 1978.
18. Axelson O and Sundell L: Herbicide exposure, mortality and tumor incidence: an epidemiological investigation on Swedish railroad workers. Work Environ Health 11:21-28, 1974.
19. Mausner JS and Kramer S: "Epidemiology - An Introductory Text". W.B. Saunders Co., Philadelphia, 1985.
20. Zack J and Suskind R: The mortality experience of workers exposed to tetrachlorodibenzodioxin in a trichlorophenol process accident. J Occup Med 22:11-14, 1980.
21. Zack JA and Gaffey WR: A mortality study of workers employed at the Monsanto Company plant in Nitro, West Virginia. Environ Sci Res 26:575-591, 1983.
22. Cook R, Townsend J, Ott MG and Silverstein L: Mortality experience of employees exposed to 2,3,7,8-tetrachlorodibenzo-dioxin (TCDD). J Occup Med 22:530-532, 1980.
23. Cook RR, Bond GG, Olson RA, Ott MG, and Gondek MR: Evaluation of the mortality experience of workers exposed to the chlorinated dioxins. Fifth International Conference on Dioxin, Bayreuth, West Germany, 1985.
24. Thiess AM, Frentzel-Beyme R, and Link R: Mortality study of persons exposed to dioxin in a trichlorophenol-process accident that occurred in the BASF AG on November 17, 1953. Am J Ind Med 3, 179-189, 1982.
25. Lynge E: A follow-up study of cancer incidence among workers in manufacture of phenoxy herbicides in Denmark. Br J Cancer 52:259-270, 1985.

26. Hogstedt C. and Westerland B:  Cohort study of causes of death of forestry workers with and without exposure to phenoxy acid preparations. Lakartidningen 77:1828-1831, 1980.

27. Axelson O, Sundell L, Andersson K, Edling C, Hogstedt C, and Kling H:  Herbicide exposure and tumor mortality. Scand J Work Environ Health 6:73-79, 1980.

28. Riihimaki V, Asp S, and Hernberg S:  Mortality of 2,4-dichlorophenoxyacetic acid and 2,4,5-trichlorophenoxyacetic acid herbicide applicators in Finland. Scand J Work Environ Health 8:37-42, 1982.

29. Ott MG, Holder BB, Olson RD:  A mortality analysis of employees engaged in the manufacturer of 2,4,5-trichlorophenoxyacetic acid. J Occup Med 22:47-50, 1980.

30. Hardell L:  Relation of soft tissue sarcoma malignant lymphoma and colon cancer to phenoxy acids or chlorophenol and other agents. Scand J Work Environ Health 7:119-130, 1981.

31. Hardell L, Eriksson M, Lenner P, and Lundgren E:  Malignant lymphoma and exposure to chemicals, especially organic solvents, chlorophenols and phenoxy acids:  a case control study. Br J Cancer 43:169-176, 1981.

32. Hardell L, Johansson B, Axelson O:  Epidemiological study of nasal and nasopharyngeal cancer and their relation to phenoxy acid or chlorophenol exposure. Am J Ind Med 3:247-257, 1982.

33. Olsen JH and Jensen OM:  Nasal cancer and chlorophenols. Lancet 2:47-48, 1984.

34. Young JL, Percy CL, and Asire AJ, et al:  SEER:  Incidence and Mortality Data, 1973-1977. Nat Cancer Inst Monograph 57:1-1082, 1981.

35. Russell WO, Cohen J, Enzinger F, Hajdu S, Heise H, Martin RG, Meissner W, Miller WT, Schmitz RL, Suit HD:  A clinical and pathological staging system for soft tissue sarcomas. Cancer 40:1562-1570, 1977.

36. Percy C, Stanek E, and Gloekler L:  Accuracy of cancer death certificates and its effect on cancer mortality statistics. Am J Pub Health 71:242-250, 1981.

37. Fingerhut MA, Halperin WE, Honchar PA, Smith AB, Groth DH, and Russell WO:  An evaluation of reports of dioxin exposure and soft tissue sarcoma pathology in U.S. chemical workers. Scand J Work Environ Health 10:299-303, 1984.

38. Hardell L and Sandstrom A:  Case-control study:  soft tissue sarcoma and exposure to phenoxyacetic acids or chlorophenols. Br J Cancer 39:711-717, 1979.

39. Eriksson M, Hardell L, Berg N, Moller T, and Axelson O:  Soft tissue sarcomas and exposure to chemical substances:  a case-referent study. Br J Ind Med 38:27-33, 1981.

40. Smith AH, Pearce NE, Fisher DO, Giles HJ, Teague CA, and Howard JK:  Soft tissue sarcoma and exposure to phenoxyherbicides and chlorophenols in New Zealand. JNCI 73:1111-1117, 1984.

41. Greenwald P, Kovasznay B, Collins DN, Therriault G:  Sarcomas of soft tissues after Vietnam service. JNCI 75:1107-1109, 1984.

42. Milham S:  Herbicides, occupation, and cancer. Lancet i:1464-1465, 1982.

43. Balarajan R and Acheson E:  Soft tissue sarcomas in agriculture and forestry workers. J Epidemiol Comm Health 38:113-116, 1984.

44. Wiklund K and Holm L: Soft tissue sarcoma risk in Swedish agricultural and forestry workers. JNCI 76:229-234, 1986.
45. Kogan M and Clapp R: Mortality among Vietnam veterans in Massachusetts 1972-1983. Abstract, Am J Epidemiol 122:523, 1985.
46. Smith A H, et al: Congenital defects and miscarriages among New Zealand 2,4,5-T sprayers. Arch Environ Health 37:197-200, 1982.
47. Erickson JD, Mulinare J, McClain PW, et al: Vietnam veterans' risks for fathering babies with birth defects. JAMA 252: 903-912, 1984.
48. Donovan JW, Adena MA, Rose G, Battistutta D: "Case-Control Study of Congenital Anomalies and Vietnam Service (Birth Defects Study)". Report to the Minister for Verterans' Affairs. Australian Government Publishing Service, Canberra, 1983.
49. Townsend JC, Bodner KM, VanPeenen PF, Olson RD, and Cook RR: Survey of reproductive events of wives of employees to chlorinated dioxins. Am J Epidemiol 115:695-713, 1982.
50. Lathrop GD, Wolfe WH, Albanese RA, Moynahan PM: "An epidemiologic investigation of health effects in air force personnel following exposure to herbicides: Baseline morbidity study results." U.S. Air Force School of Aerospace Medicine, Aerospace Medical Division, Brooks Air Force Base, Texas, 1984.
51. Singer R, et al: Nerve conduction velocity studies of workers employed in the manufacture of phenoxy herbicides. Environ Res 29:297-311, 1982.
52. Bond GG, Ott MG, Brenner FE, and Cook RR: Medical and morbidity surveillance findings among employees potentially exposed to TCDD. Br J Ind Med 40:318-324, 1983.
53. Suskind RR and Hertzberg VS: Human health effects of 2,4,5-T and its toxic contaminants. JAMA 251:2372-2380, 1984.
54. Moses M, Lilis R, Crow KD, Thornton J, Fischbein A, Anderson HA, and Selikoff IJ: Health status of workers with past exposure to 2,3,7,8-tetrachlorodibenzo-p-dioxin in the manufacture of 2,4,5-trichlorophenoxyacetic acid: comparison of findings with and without chloracne. Am J Ind Med 5:161-182, 1984.
55. Pazderova-Vejlupkova J, et al: The development and prognosis of chronic intoxication by tetrachlorodibenzo-p-doxin in men. Arch Environ Health 36:5-11, 1981.
56. Martin JV: Lipid abnormalities in workers exposed to dioxin. Br J Ind Med 41:254-256, 1984.
57. Filippini G, Bordo B, Crenna P, Massetto N, Musicco M, and Boeri R: Relationship between clinical and electrophysiological findings and indicators of heavy exposure to 2,3,7,8-tetra-chlordibenzo-dioxin. Scand J WorK Environ Health 7:257-262, 1981.
58. Hoffman RE, Stehr-Green PA, Webb KB, et al: Health Effects of long-term exposure to 2,3,7,8-tetrachlorodibenzodioxin. JAMA 255:2031-2038, 1986.

RECEIVED November 25, 1986

Chapter 12

# Human Breast Milk Levels of Dioxins and Dibenzofurans: Significance with Respect to Current Risk Assessments

Arnold Schecter[1] and Thomas A. Gasiewicz[2]

[1]Department of Preventive Medicine, Clinical Campus at Binghamton,
State University of New York, Health Science Center at Syracuse, 88 Aldrich Street,
Binghamton, NY 13903
[2]Environmental Health Sciences Center, Department of Biophysics,
University of Rochester Medical Center, Rochester, NY 14642

While the partitioning of the lipophilic chlorinated
dibenzodioxins and dibenzofurans into breast milk fat
represents a mode of excretion and detoxification for
the lactating female, this may not be without impact on
nursing infants. This study examined whether the levels
of these compounds in human breast milk from Vietnam and
North America exceeded the recommended intake values
currently employed by the United States Environmental
Protection Agency and the United States Public Health
Services Centers for Disease Control. Based on a number
of assumptions, these calculations suggest that many
nursing infants from the south of Vietnam may have
consumed, and are continuing to consume, amounts of these
contaminants that are much greater than currently
recommended intake values. Although concentrations of
these compounds in mother's milk samples from North
America are much lower, they are still near or slightly
greater than the recommended amounts. Analyses of milk
samples from areas of northern Vietnam showed levels of
contamination that are below employed standards.
Further study is needed to determine if there is any
real short- or long-term clinical risk to the nursing
infants in these populations.

Elevated human tissue dioxin levels found in certain areas after
environmental contamination were described in previous publications
(1-3). The highest levels were noted in human breast milk lipid a few
years following heavy 2,3,7,8-tetrachlorodibenzo-p-dioxin (2,3,7,8-
TCDD) contamination from herbicides, especially Agent Orange, sprayed
in Vietnam. Elevated levels in this tissue from individuals living
in the south of Vietnam decreased with time but were still above levels
observed in samples from the North American continent (3). It was
hypothesized that the relatively low human tissue levels of dioxins
observed in individuals living in the north of Vietnam may be attributed

to the absence of use of synthetic chemicals in that region and to the fact that no spraying of dioxin contaminated herbicide occurred in the north. Previous results also presented evidence of penta- through octa-chlorinated dioxin contamination of human tissue in the south of Vietnam and North America that was suggestive of the characteristic isomer pattern seen in technical grade pentachloro-phenol (PCP), a commonly used wood preservative (3).

In the present study we estimated whether the intake of dioxin and dibenzofuran contaminated breast milk presents a potential risk to the health of the nursing infants in these populations. This was performed using "virtually safe" or "acceptable daily intake" values which various governmental agencies in the United States currently employ in their risk assessments for these compounds.

Methods and Assumptions

The recommended daily intake values as estimated by the United States Environmental Protection Agency (EPA) (4) and the Centers for Disease Control (CDC) (5,6) have been used for the present calculations. For the EPA the "Acceptable Daily Intake" (ADI) for 2,3,7,8-TCDD is $1 \times 10^{-12}$ g/kg/day. This value is based on the lowest-observed-adverse-effect-level (LOAEL) of $1 \times 10^{-9}$ g/kg/day for a reproductive effect in rats (7,8), a 10-fold uncertainty factor because a LOAEL is used as the basis of the calculation rather than a no-observed adverse effect level (NOAEL), and an additional uncertainty factor of 100 based on the existence of lifetime animal studies and lack of knowledge of the effects in man. (4). For a $10^{-6}$ (1/1,000,000) cancer risk, the EPA has estimated a 95% lower-limit criteria for a lifetime intake of $6.3 \times 10^{-15}$ g/kg/day (9). For this same cancer risk, the CDC has estimated a "virtually safe dose" of $28 \times 10^{-15}$ g/kg/day (hereafter, CDC1) (5,6). These estimates are based on a linear-derived multistage extrapolation model that is usually used for genotoxic agents such as ionizing radiation. However, the results to date indicate that 2,3,7,8-TCDD is a tumor promoter rather than an initiator (10,11). Therefore, the CDC estimate for a $10^{-6}$ cancer risk of $636 \times 10^{-15}$ g/kg/day (hereafter CDC2), which is based on a non-linear model for tumor promoters (5,6), has also been considered. The present paper takes no position as to the validity of these values, but cites them as figures which appropriate government agencies have published or prepared for regulatory purposes or to make health risk estimates.

For the calculation of the relative intake of chlorinated dioxins (PCDDs) and dibenzofurans (PCDFs) by a nursing infant, some of the assumptions that have been made include: 1) the infant is breast-fed for 1 year, 2) the average infant weight for 1 year is 10 kg (12), 3) 100% of the dioxin and dibenzofuran isomers are absorbed through the gastrointestinal tract of the infant, and 4) approximately 3% of human breast milk is fat (2,3,13). For the % of lipid in adipose tissue, we have used the mean of determined values for the individual populations under study. For the population in North America we have assigned a value of 80% (2), while for the south and north Vietnam populations these values are 62% and 56%, respectively (3). We have also used a value of 850 ml/day for the average amount of milk consumed (12). A number of studies have reported values from 650 to 1000 ml/day for infants 1 to 8 months of age (12-15).

Values previously reported (1-3,16,17) for concentrations of dibenzodioxin and dibenzofuran isomers in breast milk either measured directly or calculated from adipose tissue were used for these analyses. For the sake of clarity some of these values are reported here again.

## Results

Recalling levels of the PCDD and PCDF isomers previously reported in adipose tissue from a North American population (Tables I-II) (16,17), the most toxic isomer, 2,3,7,8-TCDD, is found in the lowest concentration, whereas the octachlorodioxin is found in the highest concentration. We and others have reported similar results of analysis of separate sample populations in the United States (1,18,19). These results emphasize the need to consider other dioxin and dibenzofuran isomers, in addition to the 2,3,7,8-TCDD isomer, when an evaluation of potential human health risk is performed.

Table II indicates the qualitative and quantitative similarity of the dioxin and dibenzofuran isomers in human milk on a lipid basis as compared to those present in adipose tissue. The 4.5 ppt value for 2,3,7,8-TCDD in milk derived from a pooled sample from 200 mothers is close to the mean value of 7.1 ppt of 2,3,7,8-TCDD from individual adipose tissue samples. The lower mean value in breast milk compared to adipose tissue may be due to the lack of inclusion of the nondetectable values from individual adipose tissue specimens in calculating the mean. For adipose tissues the geometric mean of the positives for 2,3,7,8-TCDD is 6.0 ppt and the arithmetic mean is 4.4 if calculated by including the nondetected specimens at a value of one-half the detection level. The other isomer values are comparatively similar for fat or milk, except for the octachlorodibenzo-p-dioxin which, for unknown reasons, is markedly lower in the milk than in the adipose samples from these two unmatched populations. When reported on a lipid basis, the similarity of these values in milk and adipose tissue is expected because of the lipophilic nature of these compounds. This relationship has been reported for other lipid soluble chemicals as well (20). Similar levels of these isomers in human breast milk samples from European populations have been reported recently (21-3).

Table III summarizes some of the reported and calculated levels of PCDD and PCDF isomers in human breast milk from populations in the south and north of Vietnam (3), and the United States (16). It is noteworthy that analysis of 9 adipose tissue samples taken in 1984 from individuals living in the north of Vietnam showed no detectable concentrations of 2,3,7,8-TCDD at a detection limit of 2 ppt (3). As expected, the milk pattern and levels on a lipid basis are similar to that reported for adipose tissue (2,3,16) (Tables I and II).

Many health organizations world-wide are currently estimating risks of the halogenated dibenzo-p-dioxins and dibenzo-furans to humans in terms of "2,3,7,8-TCDD equivalents," i.e., the amount of the specific chemical or mixture which would cause the same degree of toxicity at 2,3,7,8-TCDD. Tables IV and V present values currently assigned to various PCDD and PCDF isomers found in human tissues in an attempt to relate them to 2,3,7,8-TCDD (24-6). These values are subject to change, and may well be assigned different numerical values as new toxicology studies provide more data and toxic end points upon which to provide a less speculative basis of assigment. The concept of toxic equivalents

TABLE I
Average Concentration of PCDD and PCDF Isomers in Adult Human
Adipose Tissue from a North American Population[a]

| Isomer | Concentration[b] | Range[b] |
|--------|-----------------|----------|
| 2,3,7,8-TCDD | 5.0 | (ND-10) |
| 1,2,3,7,8-PeCDD | 32 | (ND-180) |
| HxCDD | 72 | (7.9-330) |
| 1,2,3,4,7,8,9-HpCDD | 87 | (ND-390) |
| OCDD | 560 | (64-1250) |
| 2,3,7,8-TCDF | 9.1 | (ND-32) |
| 2,3,4,7,8-PeCDF | 27 | (ND-77) |
| HxCDF | 18 | (2.9-35) |
| 1,2,3,4,6,7,8-HpCDF | 18 | (ND-55) |
| OCDF | 60 | (ND-360) |

[a]  Data from (16)
[b]  Values as the mean of 46 composite samples from 900 individuals,
as  pg/g, or parts per trillion (ppt).


TABLE II
PCDDs and PCDFs in Human Milk and Adipose Tissue
from a Canadian Population

| | Milk[a] | | Adipose Tissue[a] |
|--------|---------|------------|-------------------|
| Isomer | Wet Wt. Basis | Lipid Basis | Lipid Basis |
| 2,3,7,8-TCDD | 0.17 | 4.5 | 7.1[b] |
| 1,2,3,7,8-PeCDD | 0.38 | 10 | 11 |
| HxCDD | 2.6 | 69 | 97 |
| 1,2,3,4,6,7,8-HpCDD | 5.3 | 138 | 151 |
| OCDD | 10.3 | 271 | 951 |
| 2,3,7,8-TCDF | 0.16 | 4.2 | ND (2) |
| 2,3,4,7,8-PeCDF | 0.44 | 12 | 17 |
| HxCDF | 0.46 | 12 | 14 |
| 1,2,3,4,6,7,8-HpCDF | 0.50 | 13 | 36 |
| OCDF | ND (0.2) | | ND (4) |

[a]  Results for milk are from a single pooled sample of 200 human
milk samples collected across Canada in 1981.  Results for human
adipose tissues from Canada in 1976 from 46 accident victims.
Data from (17).  Data are presented as mean values for adipose
tissue samples, pg/g.

[b]  Average of 25 positive out of 46 samples; geometric mean is 6.0
and the arithmetic mean is 4.4 pg/g if NDs are estimated at one-
half the detection limit.

TABLE III
Reported and Calculated Concentration of PCDDs and PCDFs
in Human Milk on a Wet Weight or Whole Milk Basis

| Population | Isomer | Concentration[a] | | Reference for Original Data |
|---|---|---|---|---|
| | | Mean[b] | Ranges | |
| south of Vietnam (1973) | 2,3,7,8-TCDD | 4.2 | (2.3-6.9) | (3) |
| | 2,3,4,7,8-PeCDF | 0.7 | (ND-0.8) | |
| | OCDD | 7.9 | (3.4-12) | |
| south of Vietnam (1984) | 2,3,7,8-TCDD | 0.68 | (ND-3.1) | (3) |
| | 1,2,3,7,8-PeCDD | 0.44 | (ND-1.3) | |
| | HxCDD | 3.0 | (0.7-10.4) | |
| | 1,2,3,4,6,7,8-HpCDD | 5.3 | (0.41-21.3) | |
| | OCDD | 39.8 | (4.2-102.3) | |
| | 2,3,4,7,8-PeCDF | 0.63 | (0.13-1.4) | |
| | HxCDF | 1.7 | (0.41-5.0) | |
| | 1,2,3,4,6,7,8-HpCDF | 0.9 | (0.13-2.2) | |
| north of Vietnam (1984) | 2,3,7,8-TCDD | ND | | (3) |
| | 1,2,3,7,8-PeCDD | .039 | (ND-0.11) | |
| | HxCDD | 0.24 | (ND-0.72) | |
| | 1,2,3,4,6,7,8-HpCDD | 0.59 | (ND-1.7) | |
| | OCDD | 2.8 | (ND-6.2) | |
| | 2,3,4,7,8-PeCDF | 0.31 | (ND-0.88) | |
| | HxCDF | 0.32 | (ND-0.6) | |
| | 1,2,3,4,6,7,8-HpCDF | 0.09 | (ND-0.32) | |
| United States | 2,3,7,8-TCDD | 0.19 | (ND-0.38) | (16) |
| | 1,2,3,7,8-PeCDD | 1.2 | (ND-6.8) | |
| | HxCDD | 2.7 | (0.3-12.4) | |
| | 1,2,3,4,7,8,9-HpCDD | 3.3 | (ND-14.6) | |
| | OCDD | 21 | (2.4-46.9) | |
| | 2,3,7,8-TCDF | 0.34 | (ND-1.2) | |
| | 2,3,4,7,8-PeCDF | 1.0 | (ND-2.9) | |
| | HxCDF | 0.68 | (0.11-1.31) | |
| | 1,2,3,4,6,7,8-HpCDF | 0.68 | (ND-2.1) | |
| | OCDF | 2.3 | (ND-13.5) | |

[a] Values are as mean, pg/g, (range). Results from the south of Vietnam (1973) are reported values (3). Other values presented have been calculated from previously published data and using reported values for the % of lipid in adipose tissue as 80, 62, and 56 for the United States (1,2), south of Vietnam (3), and north of Vietnam (3), respectively, An estimated value of 3% lipid in human milk was also used.

[b] None detectibles were included in the calculation of arithmetic means as one-half of the detection limits.

TABLE IV
Estimation of Relative Toxicities (2,3,7,8-TCDD Equivalents)
of Various Chlorinated Dibenzo-p-dioxins

| Isomer | EPA (24) | New York State (25) | California (26) |
|---|---|---|---|
| 2,3,7,8-TCDD | 1 | 1 | 1 |
| Other TCDDs | 0.01 | 0 | 0 |
| 2,3,7,8-PeCDDs | 0.5 | 0.5 | 1 |
| Other PeCDDs | 0.005 | 0 | 0 |
| 2,3,7,8-HxCDDs | 0.04 | 0.03 | 1 |
| Other HxCDDs | 0.0004 | 0 | 0 |
| 2,3,7,8-HpCDDs | 0.001 | 0 | 1 |
| Other HpCDDs | 0.00001 | 0 | 0 |
| OCDD | 0 | 0 | 1 |

TABLE V
Estimation of Relative Toxicities (2,3,7,8-TCDD Equivalents)
of the Chlorinated Dibenzofurans

| Isomer | EPA (24) | New York State (25) | California (26) |
|---|---|---|---|
| 2,3,7,8-TCDF | 0.1 | 0.33 | 1 |
| Other TCDFs | 0.001 | 0 | 0 |
| 2,3,7,8-PeCDFs | 0.1 | 0.33 | 1 |
| Other PeCFs | 0.001 | 0 | 0 |
| 2,3,7,8-HxCDFs | 0.01 | 0.01 | 1 |
| Other HxCDFs | 0.0001 | 0 | 0 |
| 2,3,7,8-HpCDFs | 0.001 | 0 | 1 |
| Other HpCDFs | 0.00001 | 0 | 0 |
| OCDF | 0 | 0 | 0 |

assumes that all of the isomers have a similar mechanism of action and that total "dioxin" toxicity may be calculated by adding the weighted factors for the individual isomers present. Table VI shows the result of simple arithmetic calculations going from measured PCDD and PCDF values to their "dioxin equivalents." Although the value of 2,3,7,8-TCDD remains 5.0, the value of total equivalents varies from 27.8 to 35.3 to 828, depending on the weighting values assigned to the various isomers. The ratio of added risk for all of the PCDD and PCDF isomers compared to 2,3,7,8-TCDD alone varies from 5.6. to 7.1 to 166, again based on the reported levels in adipose tissue from individuals in the United States. This uncertainty or lack of agreement between governmental agencies must be considered when any conclusions as to the health consequences of these compounds in breast milk are presented. Notably, the penta- and not the tetra-chlorinated dioxins and dibenzofurans appear to give the greater amount of toxic equivalents compared to all other isomers.

Table VII compares the calculated average total dioxin toxic equivalents in human breast milk (or extrapolated from adipose tissue data) from populations in Vietnam and the United States. These numbers are based on the EPA equivalency values shown in Tables IV and V. For purposes of comparison and since the equivalent value for the north of Vietnam is the lowest we know of world-wide at the present time, we have defined this level as one. On this basis, the levels in the United States are on the average approximately 16-fold higher, while the values for south of Vietnam for 1973 and 1984 are approximately 67- and 17-fold higher respectively. It should be noted that the values for the south of Vietnam would be higher still were the data from the breast milk samples collected in 1970 (27) included in these calculations. By either calculation, there existed a population in the south of Vietnam and nursing during the early 1970's, whose consumption of these contaminants in breast milk was quite high, and higher than any other population of nursing infants. Values from industrial countries such as the United States, Canada (Table II), or in Europe (21-23) are well above those seen in such nonindustrialized areas as the north of Vietnam, but below what was seen in heavily contaminated areas such as the south of Vietnam in 1973.

Using the average values for the total dioxin equivalents (Table VII) the daily intake of these equivalents by a nursing infant can be estimated (Table VIII). Notably, all values are considerably greater than the ADI of one pg/kg/day from the USEPA, and even much greater than the recommended daily intakes for $10^{-6}$ risk of cancer as estimated by the EPA or the CDC. However, these recommended intakes have been estimated considering a lifetime of exposure to the contaminants. If it is assumed that the infants in the United States nurse for 1 year, then during this year the child will have consumed above the lifetime (70 years) recommended intake, the factor of excess being from 2 to 201 fold, depending on the standard and the agency cited. If it is further assumed that the child has no further intake (or excretion) of these contaminants from other sources for the remainder of his/her lifetime, and the weight increases to 70 kg (i.e., a dilution of the body burden of dioxin equivalents), then these factors of excess will be from 0.3 to 29. Table VIII also presents results of similar calculations for the Vietnam populations, using however a 55 kg body weight attained at 70 years of age. Thus, for a 1973 nursing infant

TABLE VI
Estimation of Total "2,3,7,8-TCDD Equivalents"
in Adipose Tissue from Residents of the United States

| Isomer | Mean Concentration (pg/g)[a] | 2,3,7,8-TCDD Equivalents EPA | NYS | Cal |
|---|---|---|---|---|
| 2,3,7,8-TCDD | 5.0 | 5.0 | 5.0 | 5.0 |
| 1,2,3,7,8-PeCDD | 32 | 16 | 16 | 32 |
| HxCDD | 72 | 2.9[b] | 2.2[b] | 72[b] |
| 1,2,3,4,7,8,9-HpCDD | 87 | 0.87 | 0 | 87 |
| OCDD | 560 | 0 | 0 | 560 |
| 2,3,7,8-TCDF | 9.1 | 0.91 | 3.0 | 9.1 |
| 2,3,4,7,8-PeCDF | 27 | 2.7 | 8.9 | 27 |
| HxCDF | 18 | 0.18[b] | 0.18[b] | 18[b] |
| 1,2,3,4,6,7,8-HpCDF | 18 | .018 | 0 | 18 |
| OCDF | 60 | 0 | 0 | 0 |
| Total 2,3,7,8-TCDD Equivalents | | 27.8 | 35.3 | 828 |
| Ratio of Total Equivalents/2,3,7,8-TCDD Alone | | 5.6 | 7.1 | 166 |

[a]  Data from (16), Table I.
[b]  Assuming all HxCDDs and HxCDFs are as the 2,3,7,8-isomer.
Similar values for 2,3,7,8-HxCDD and 2,3,7,8-HxCDF have
been reported (1-3).


TABLE VII
Comparison of Total 2,3,7,8-TCDD Equivalents
in Human Milk in Vietnam and United States

| Population | Total 2,3,7,8,-TCDD Equivalents (pg/g)[a] |
|---|---|
| south of Vietnam (1973) | 4.27 |
| south of Vietnam (1984) | 1.11 |
| north of Vietnam (1984) | 0.064 |
| United States | 1.04 |

[a]  Calculated from data presented in Table III and using the USEPA
equivalency values presented in Tables IV and V.

TABLE VIII
Estimated Average Daily and First Year Intake of
Total 2,3,7,8-TCDD Equivalents by Nursing Infants from Vietnam and
the United States, and the Ratio of these First Year Intakes to the
Recommended Lifetime Intake Values for 2,3,7,8-TCDD

| Population | Daily Intake[a] (pg/kg/ day) | First Year Intake (pg/kg) | Ratio of First Year Intake to Recommended Lifetime Intake Values | No Age[c] Correction | Age[d] Correction |
|---|---|---|---|---|---|
| south of Vietnam (1973) | 362 | 132,477 | EPA[b] | 828 | 150 |
| | | | CDC1[b] | 184 | 33 |
| | | | CDC2[b] | 8 | 1.5 |
| south of Vietnam (1984) | 94.4 | 34,456 | EPA | 215 | 40 |
| | | | CDC1 | 54 | 9.1 |
| | | | CDC2 | 2.2 | 0.4 |
| north of Vietnam (1984) | 5.4 | 1,971 | EPA | 12 | 2.2 |
| | | | CDC1 | 3.1 | 0.5 |
| | | | CDC2 | 0.1 | .03 |
| United States | 88.4 | 32,266 | EPA | 201 | 29 |
| | | | CDC1 | 50 | 6 |
| | | | CDC2 | 2 | 0.3 |

[a]  Calculated from data in Table VII.

[b]  For a cancer risk of $10^{-6}$ the lifetime (70 year) recommended intake values of 2,3,7,8-TCDD are $1.6 \times 10^{-10}$, $6.4 \times 10^{-10}$ and $1.6 \times 10^{-8}$ g/kg for EPA, CDC1 and CDC2, respectively. See Methods and Assumptions.

[c]  Assuming 10 kg infant.

[d]  Assuming growth to a 70 kg adult for United States and a 55 kg adult for Vietnamese residents for a 70 year lifetime, and exposure to no other source of PCDDs and PCDFs.

from the south of Vietnam the factors of fold-excess intake are 1.5 to 150 (age and weight corrected). For the Vietnam population in the north, these factors are much lower, .03 to 2.2.

Discussion

Although the neonatal body burden of lipid-soluble exogenous chemicals is likely much less than that of the mother, the transfer of these contaminants to milk is likely to be very efficient due to the high proportion of milk fat. Breast milk is considered the ideal food for a certain, but not fully characterized, time interval after birth of the infant. Against the beneficial aspects of human breast milk must be weighed the risks posed by the chemicals, in this case the chlorinated dioxins and dibenzofurans. This may be especially true for populations known to be heavily contaminated with these compounds. In animal models, these chemicals have been shown to increase the risk of developing certain tumors, immune deficiency, adverse reproductive effects including congenital malformations and fetal lethality, hepatic damage, and gastrointestinal and genitourinary system epithelial cell disorders. While it is clear that some toxic effects have been observed in humans exposed to the dioxins, an unequivocal effect on more subtle and/or longer term parameters such as cancer development and alterations of immune function has not yet been conclusively demonstrated. This may reflect unusual, but certainly not unique, species differences between human and other mammalian species. Alternatively, this may be a reflection of inadequacies of epidemiological design and analysis. If dioxins do cause human health effects at the levels seen in industrial countries or in the south of Vietnam, clinical and epidemiologic studies in Vietnam, with its extreme levels of dioxins in human tissues, high in the south and low in the north, may more readily reveal this than elsewhere.

We have used the human tissue levels of PCDDs and PCDFs in the north of Vietnam as a reference value, believing that this area has had little environmental contamination from synthetic, industrial, and agricultural chemicals. The United States, Canada, and Europe represent highly industrialized areas with a substantial use, disposal, and combustion of a variety of synthetic, especially halogenated chemicals, The south of Vietnam, because of the herbicides used for military purposes during the 1960's and 1970's, has had a significant contamination with 2,3,7,8-TCDD as well as other PCDD and PCDF isomers.

Our calculations suggest that levels of these contaminants in breast milk from individuals from the south of Vietnam may exceed recommended standards currently employed by governmental agencies in the United States. Although concentrations of these compounds expressed as TCDD equivalents in North American populations are lower as compared to the south of Vietnam, nursing infants may be consuming levels which are near or above these recommended values. It must be noted that these calculations are based on mean tissue values for which there are wide ranges of variation. We have also made necessary assumptions regarding infant weight, duration of nursing, the average amount of milk consumed, and for the gastrointestinal absorption of these isomers, all of which may or may not be relevant for individual situations. However, we have also assumed that breast milk represents the only lifetime source of exposure to these environmental contaminants. This latter assumption appears unlikely given the use, disposal, and combustion of chemicals which may lead to the continued input of these specific toxins into the environment.

## Conclusions

The findings of the chlorinated dibenzo-p-dioxin and dibenzofuran isomers in persons residing in contaminated areas and both measured and calculated levels of these compounds in breast milk in the United States presents a possible cause for concern regarding health effects in the nursing infant. Further study is indicated to determine if there is any real clinical risk at the levels found.

Breast fed infants represent a population with daily exposure to dioxins and related chemicals. This population may have an increased theoretical risk for PCDD and PCDF induced cancer and other dioxin induced illnesses. This is especially true for contaminated populations in the south of Vietnam. However, the theoretical risk is based on an extrapolation from animal models and varies considerably on the model chosen. We do not know whether there will actually be an increased cancer incidence at these levels of contamination.

Curtailment of breast feeding is not recommended at this time. However, infant populations consuming elevated levels of the chlorinated dioxins and related chemicals in breast milk (especially in the south of Vietnam) should be followed for longer term effects of dioxin exposure.

## Acknowledgments

The authors gratefully acknowledge the use of unpublished data from Dr. J.J. Ryan (17), generously provided for this manuscript.

Financial assistance from the Reynolds Foundation, the Samuel Rubin Foundation and the CS Fund for the work of one of us (A.S.) is gratefully acknowledged.

## Literature Cited

1. Schecter, A.J.; Ryan, J.J.; Gitlitz, G. In "Chlorinated Dioxins and Dibenzofurans in Perspective"; Rappe, C.; Choudhary, G.; Keith L., Eds.; Lewis Publishers Inc.: Chelsea, Michigan, 1986; pp. 51-65.
2. Schecter, A.J.; Ryan, J.J.; Gross, M.; Weerasinghe, N.C.A.; Constable, J. In "Chlorinated Dioxins and Dibenzofurans in Perspective"; Rappe, C.; Choudhary, G.; Keith, L., Eds.; Lewis Publishers Inc.: Chelsea, Michigan, 1986; pp. 35-50.
3. Schecter, A.J.; Ryan, J.J.; Constable, J. Chemosphere 1986, 15, 1613-20.
4. "Health Assessment Document for Polychlorinated Dibenzo-p-dioxins," United States Environmental Protection Agency, EPA/600/8-84/014F, 1985.
5. Kimbrough, R.D.; Falk, H.; Stehr, P. J. Toxicol. Environ. Hlth. 1984, 14, 47-93.
6. Morbidity and Mortality Weekly Report 1984, 33, 25-7.

7.  Murray, F.J.; Smith, F.A.; Nitschke, K.D.; Humiston, C.G; Kociba, R.J.; Schwetz, B.A. Toxicol. Appl. Pharmocol. 1979, 50, 241-51.
8.  Nisbet, I.C.T.; Paxton, M.B. Am. Stat. Vol. 1982, 36, 290-8.
9.  "Ambient Water Quality Criteria for 2,3,7,8-Tetrachlorodibenzo-p-dioxin," United States Environmental Protection Agency, EPA/440/5-84-007, 1984.
10. Poland, A.; Palen, D.; Glover, E. Nature 1982, 300, 271-3.
11. Pitot, H.C.; Goldsworthy, T.; Campbell, H.A.; Poland, A. Cancer Res. 1980, 40, 3616-20.
12. International Commission on Radiological Protection in "Report on the Task Group on Reference Man"; Pergamon Press: New York, 1975.
13. Butte, N.F.; Garza, C.; Stuff, J.E.; Smith, E.O.; Nichols, B.L. Am. J. Clin, Nutr. 1984, 39, 296-306.
14. Whitehead, R.G.; Paul, A.A. Lancet 1981, 2, 161-3.
15. Hofvander, Y.; Hagman, U.; Hillervik, C.; Sjolin, S. Acta Ped. Scand. 1982, 71, 953-8.
16. Stanley, J.S.; Boggess, K.E.; Onstot, J.; Sack, T.M.; Remmers, J.C.; Breen, J.; Kutz, F.W.; Carra, J.; Robinson, P.; Mack, G.A. Chemosphere 1986, 15, 1605-12.
17. Ryan, J.J. Report of a World Health Organization Planning Meeting on PCBs, PCDDs and PCDFs in Human Milk, Norway, 1986.
18. Graham, M.; Hileman, F.D.; Orth, R.G.; Wendling, J.M.; Wilson, J.D. Chemosphere 1986, 15, 1595-600.
19. Patterson, D.G.; Hoffman, R.E.; Needham, L.L.; Roberts, D.W.; Bagby, J.R.; Pirkle, J.L.; Falk, H.; Sampson, E.J.; Houk, V.N. JAMA, 1986, 256, 2683-6.
20. Wolff, M.S. Am. J. Ind. Med. 1983, 4, 259-81.
21. Rappe, C.; Bergqvist, P-A.; Hanson, M.; Kjeller, L-O.; Lindstrom, G.; Marklund, S.; Nygren, M. In "Biological Mechanisms of Dioxin Action"; Poland, A.; Kimbrough, R.D., Eds.; BANBURY REPORT 18, Cold Spring Harbor Laboratory; Cold Spring Harbor, 1986; pp. 17-26.
22. Rappe, C.; Nygren, M.; Lindstrom, G.; Hansson, M. Chemosphere 1986, 15, 1635-40.
23. Tarkowski, S.; Yrjanheikki, E. Chemosphere 1986, 15, 1641-8.
24. Barnes, D.G.; Bellin, J.; Cleverly, D. Chemosphere 1986, 15, 1895-903.
25. Eadon, G. et al., New York State Department of Health, 1982.
26. Gravitz, N. et al., California Department of Health Services, 1983.
27. Baughman, R.W. Ph.D. Thesis, Harvard University, Cambridge, MA, 1974.

RECEIVED February 24, 1987

# Chapter 13

# Uncertainties in Dioxin Risk Assessment

**Vernon N. Houk**

**Center for Environmental Health, Centers for Disease Control, and Agency for Toxic Substances and Disease Registry, Public Health Service, U.S. Department of Health and Human Services, Atlanta, GA 30333**

An evaluation of human health hazards posed by dioxin-contaminated soil in certain areas of Missouri illustrates specific uncertainties in dioxin risk assessment. These uncertainties include the relationship of studies in animals to effects in humans, the level and extent of contamination in the soil, the level of exposure to humans, and the character of the dose-response curve. Uncertainties in assessing risks posed by toxic substances in general are viewed from the standpoint of a 1985 report prepared by the Task Force on Risk Assessment and Risk Management for the Secretary, Department of Health and Human Services. The Task Force listed nine commonly used assumptions--which may also be called uncertainties.

In 1981, the Environmental Protection Agency (EPA), through its regional office in Kansas City, Missouri, and the State of Missouri, asked the Centers for Disease Control (CDC) to evaluate the human health hazards posed by dioxin-contaminated soil in certain areas of Missouri. Industrial wastes containing dioxin (2,3,7,8-tetrachloro-dibenzodioxin or dioxin) had been mixed with salvage oil, and in 1971 the mixture was sprayed on riding arenas and dirt roads in eastern Missouri to control dust. An outbreak of poisoning in horses and other animals followed. In 1974, CDC established that the riding arenas had been contaminated with dioxin. Recently, however, investigators have found that the soil in several other areas--many of them residential--was also contaminated. Concentrations in the more recently examined soil samples have ranged from less than 1 to more than 1,000 parts per billion--measured in micrograms of dioxin per kilogram of soil.

Details of the Center for Environmental Health's assessment of the risk to human health of dioxin-contaminated soil in residential areas are in an article in the Journal of Toxicology and Environmental Health (1). A shorter version appeared in the CDC

Morbidity and Mortality Weekly Report (2). The uncertainties in the
Missouri study are covered in these two reports.

## Missouri Study:   Uncertainties

Since no information was available on the specific doses of dioxin
that caused or did not cause health effects in humans, we reviewed
the data from studies in animals. These studies show that some
animal species are more susceptible to the toxic effects of dioxin
than others, but we do not know which species responds most like
humans.

Some scientists have claimed that humans must not be very
susceptible to the toxic effects of dioxin because, despite all the
exposures in the workplace, the main health effect in humans is
chloracne. Although worker populations have had most of the heavy
exposures, they may not fully reflect the risks for the general
population. In estimating the risks for the general population, we
must consider other groups—children, women of childbearing age, the
aged, and the infirm.

Another uncertainty is the effect of long-term exposure. Many
short-term tests of dioxin's acute effects have been conducted in
animals, but at the low levels of contamination in Missouri, acute
effects are not as important as chronic effects that might follow
long-term daily exposure. Studies that provide information on the
chronic effects of dioxin include a few conducted in rodents to
determine whether or not dioxin is a carcinogen. We used the
results of these studies to calculate a dose that might represent a
reasonable risk of exposure for humans.

The estimate of how much dioxin humans take up after exposure
to contaminated soil was also based on uncertainties, that is, on
assumptions that have not been verified. We estimated how much
dioxin people exposed to contaminated soil adjacent to their homes
would absorb via the skin or gastrointestinal or respiratory
tracts. We assumed that each daily dermal contact with soil would,
in most instances, result in a 1 percent uptake of dioxin from
1 gram of soil. We also estimated how frequently adults and older
children would come in direct contact with soil.

As for small children, we assumed that when they played outside
they might eat as much as 10 grams of soil per day, although they
were more likely to eat 1 gram. We assumed that 30 percent of the
dioxin bound to the ingested soil might be absorbed from the
gastrointestinal tract, and then we estimated how often a child
would play outside and for how much of his or her lifetime the child
would ingest soil.

Since we were evaluating residential areas with abundant
vegetation, and consequently not much dust, we did not think that
inhaling dioxin-contaminated dust would be a significant problem.

Another uncertainty was the level and extent of contamination.
An entire area is not contaminated at the highest level found
anywhere in the area. Furthermore, dioxin contamination is more
likely to be limited to a percentage of the total area. We
calculated what the dose would be if only 10 or 20 percent of the
soil in an area were contaminated. In addition, the dioxin was
applied in an oil mixture, so it might not have been bound to the
soil as tightly as it would have been had it not been applied in the

mixture.  Recent studies have shown that without the oil, the dioxin
would have been bound much tighter.

No one knows whether the dose-response curve for carcinogens
like dioxin is linear--that is, that the response is directly
proportional to the dose.  Nevertheless, we assumed a linear
relationship, and this could have caused us to overestimate the
risk.  Further, as suggested above, we assumed that a chemical shown
to be a carcinogen in animals is also a carcinogen in humans.

Despite these uncertainties, in 1983 CDC advised Missouri that,
in two residential areas, levels above 1 part per billion of dioxin
per kilogram of soil could result in an unreasonable risk to human
health.  Later on June 28, 1983, a group of outside consultants
reviewed this assessment and concurred.

## Task Force Report:   Uncertainties

The uncertainties in any risk assessment were addressed in the April
1985 report to the Secretary, Department of Health and Human
Services (3).  In January 1985, Secretary Margaret Heckler asked
Dr. James O. Mason, Chairman of the Executive Committee of the
Department's Committee to Coordinate Environmental and Related
Programs (CCERP), to analyze the Department's policies and practices
on assessing and managing risks posed by toxic substances.  As a
result, the Task Force on Risk Assessment and Risk Management was
formed.  It was made up of senior scientists from the Centers for
Disease Control, the Food and Drug Administration, and the National
Institutes of Health.  A group established by CCERP's Executive
Committee guided the Task Force, and I was Chairman of this group.

The final product of any risk assessment generally produces
numbers that appear to have precision, but the Task Force emphasized
that a risk assessor should clearly define the differences in the
elements that go into the process as scientific fact, consensus,
assumption, and "science policy"--or the agency decision on how it
is going to handle controversial issues.  The Task Force listed nine
commonly used assumptions--which may also be called uncertainties:
(1) When human data are not adequate, adverse effects in
experimental animals are regarded as indicative of adverse effects
in humans; (2) results obtained with dose-response models can be
extrapolated outside the range of experimental observations to yield
estimates or estimated upper bounds on low-dose risk; (3) when an
appropriate standardized dosage scale is used, observed experimental
results can be extrapolated across species; (4) there is no
threshold for the production of cancer, but threshold effects may
apply for other toxicologic outcomes; (5) when dose rates are not
constant, average doses give a reasonable measure of exposure;
(6) in the absence of pharmacokinetic data, the effective target
dose is assumed to be proportional to the administered dose;
(7) risks from many exposures and from many sources of exposure to
the same chemical are usually assumed to be additive; (8) in the
absence of evidence to the contrary and regardless of the route of
exposure, 100 percent absorption across species is assumed; and
(9) results associated with a specific route of exposure are
potentially relevant for other routes of exposure.

The Task Force cautioned that in any risk assessment, an
attempt should be made to clearly identify all of the main

assumptions made and to indicate their probable effect on the risk assessment.

As the Task Force stated, risk assessment is not a static process and its "evolutionary nature is, perhaps, best characterized by the increasing emphasis . . . on identifying and reducing the uncertainties associated with the process." Various organizational units in the Department are attempting to improve or expand data bases on human exposures and health effects and to further characterize the toxicologic profiles of hazardous agents. Some units are conducting basic and applied research in toxicology and other fields that bear on some of the uncertainties.

The Task Force also developed, in concept, a problem-solving approach to risk management that provides a framework for overcoming difficulties by analyzing the risk assessment, analyzing options, promoting understanding and acceptance of risk-management decisions, and evaluating the effectiveness of the options chosen. This is a framework through which policy makers can assess information, determine risks faced by the public, and allow for the democratic process to decide the acceptability of each risk on an incremental basis. In this approach, each risk management action can be seen as a solution to a problem--a solution from which we can learn.

## Conclusion

The uncertainties in dioxin risk assessment in Missouri are many--and there are many in the risk assessment and risk management of any toxic substance anywhere. But, we are working to reduce these uncertainties and, as this is done, our assessments of risks and our management of risks should continue to improve.

## Literature Cited

1.  Kimbrough, R. D.; Falk, H.; Stehr, P. J. Toxicol. Environ. Health. 1984, 14, 47-93.
2.  Centers for Disease Control. MMWR 1984, 33, 25-27.
3.  Risk Assessment and Risk Management of Toxic Substances: A Report to the Secretary, Department of Health and Human Services (DHHS), from the Executive Committee, DHHS Committee to Coordinate Environmental and Related Programs (CCERP): April 1985; DHHS [Centers for Disease Control]: [Atlanta, GA], 1985.

RECEIVED December 15, 1986

# Chapter 14

# Assessing the Potential Human Health Hazards of Dioxin-Contaminated Soil

D. J. Paustenbach, H. P. Shu, and F. J. Murray

Environmental Health and Safety, Syntex (USA), Inc., 3401 Hillview Avenue, Palo Alto, CA 94303

Regulatory agencies worldwide are currently considering environmental standards for 2,3,7,8-tetrachlorodibenzo-p-dioxin (dioxin, TCDD). This paper assesses the validity of assumptions which underlie the proposed approaches to setting limits for TCDD in the soil of residential and industrial sites. This paper also offers alternatives to these assumptions which are more justifiable scientifically, which profoundly affect the conclusions of the risk assessment, and which alter the magnitude of the recommended limits. Specifically, these assumptions concern 1) the quantities of soil typically ingested by children, 2) TCDD's nongenotoxicity, 3) the extent of dermal contact with soil, 4) the concentration of airborne soil particles, 5) dioxin's bioavailability in soil, 6) extrapolation of the dose response curve, and 7) appropriate risk criteria for small exposed populations. Two case studies are presented which illustrate the quantitative effect of these assumptions on the exposure estimates. Non-U.S. regulatory agencies which have incorporated TCDD's nongenotoxicity in their approach have estimated the virtually safe dose (VSD) or acceptable daily dose (ADI) for TCDD at up to 10 pg/kg/day (10,000 fg/kg/day). The approaches of these agencies are compared and contrasted with the method used by the United States EPA whose risk estimates are higher and whose VSD is approximately 1,000-fold lower. An alternative analysis of the cancer data, which is more valid scientifically than approaches which have been based on regulatory policy, estimates a VSD of 130 pg/kg/day. In light of these many considerations, in residential areas a soil concentration of TCDD considerably in excess of 1 ppb should be acceptable. Soil concentrations in excess of 100 ppb in non-residental settings should amply protect the environment and public health.

0097-6156/87/0338-0178$10.00/0
© 1987 American Chemical Society

Public and regulatory attention in the United States and Europe
has focused on setting limits for 2,3,7,8-tetrachlorodibenzo-
p-dioxin (TCDD or dioxin) in soil, water, air, fly ash, fish and
other foods.  In 1982, the U.S. Centers for Disease Control (CDC)
developed a risk assessment to evaluate the hazard posed by soil
contaminated with low levels of dioxin.  The closing sentence in
the abstract of the CDC publication summarizes its principal
conclusion:  "One part per billion of 2,3,7,8-TCDD in soil is a
reasonable level at which to *begin consideration* of action to
limit human exposure for contaminated soil." (emphasis added)
(1) This manuscript discusses various assumptions which underlie
the assessments by CDC and the U.S. Environmental Protection
Agency (EPA)  (2) and recommends refinement of the assumptions.

Kimbrough et al noted that to apply accurately the
methodology they suggested for assessing risk, at least seven
caveats should be heeded (1,3);  namely, [a] the 1 ppb level for
surface soil was intended to be only a guideline, developed for
only one set of conditions, not a standard to be applied anywhere
TCDD is present in soil; [b] this guideline would not apply to
industrial sites; [c] the 1 ppb guideline assumes that 100% of
the soil surface area is contaminated with TCDD; [d] the
recommendation assumes that persons would spend a lifetime
(70 years) in the contaminated area; [e] one must consider the
ease of human access to the contaminated area; [f] dietary uptake
should be considered, when appropriate; and [g] whenever new or
better data become available, these should be incorporated into
the assessment methodology.  The EPA described similar caveats in
its risk assessment for dioxin contaminated soil (2).

Despite CDC's caveats, regulatory agencies within the United
States have in many cases adopted the CDC's 1 ppb guideline as a
generic standard for clean-up *regardless* of the circumstances
at the site.  For example, EPA has functionally implemented a 1
ppb standard for clean-up at most of its remediation sites within
Missouri, regardless of the potential for human exposure (4,5).
It is critically important that regulatory agencies responsible
for establishing *clean-up* levels be familiar with the
underpinnings of the methods and assumptions used in any risk
assessment of TCDD contaminated soil.  The primary reason is that
the cost of remediation varies dramatically with the degree of
clean-up and excessive remediation would not make optimal use of
America's limited financial resources.  For example, the cost of
removing and disposing of soil containing more than 1 ppb at the
Castlewood site in Missouri, was estimated to be $17,000,000
(Figure 1).  To illustrate the dramatic effect of the criteria
for clean-up on cost, if 10 ppb were the clean-up level, the cost
would drop to $6,000,000, and minimal action would be required at
100 ppb (using EPA estimates for clean-up costs of $1500 per
cubic yard of soil excavated and incinerated).  Other sites, such
as Times Beach, Missouri show an even more dramatic relationship
between the cost of clean-up and the degree of remediation.

The following discussion addresses both the CDC and, to a
lesser degree, the EPA risk assessments.  We suggest specific
alternative assumptions which appear more consistent with the

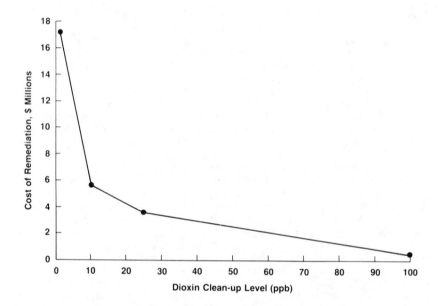

Figure 1: Estimated cost of soil removal and destruction (clean-up) for various target soil contamination levels at the Castlewood site in Missouri. Plot is based on EPA estimates of the number of yards of soil contaminated at various concentrations of dioxin and their estimated cost for incinerating. Reproduced with permission from ref. 108. Copyright 1986, Academic Press.

current scientific data. Although there are many factors to consider when evaluating the health hazards posed by contaminated soil, this paper will address a few of the most critical ones, including exposure from soil ingestion, inhalation and dermal contact, bioavailability of soil-bound dioxin via ingestion, dermal contact, and inhalation, dioxin distribution at a site, human access to residential vs industrial sites, genotoxicity, the dose-response extrapolation, and the appropriate risk criteria for situations where only small numbers of persons are exposed.

EXPOSURE FROM INGESTION OF SOIL

Exposure is clearly one of the most important aspects of a risk assessment. In CDC's assessment, its estimates indicated that the primary route of exposure was soil ingestion (Table I). CDC predicted that about 95% of the average lifetime uptake of TCDD would occur as a result of soil ingestion; about 3% of the lifetime dose would be absorbed through the skin as a result of contact with contaminated soil (associated with gardening and poor hygiene); and no more than 2% of the total dose would be due to inhalation of TCDD-contaminated dust. Based on the information presented in CDC's manuscript, it was implied that a daily uptake of about 636.5 fg/kg/day of TCDD did not pose a health hazard since, using CDC's assumptions, this is the estimated amount which could potentially be absorbed (lifetime average) by persons living in communities which contain soil contaminated with 1 ppb of TCDD. CDC's figure of 636.5 fg/kg/day was selected based on consideration of both the upper bounds and fitted model values on the cancer risks estimated by mathematical models used for extrapolation of the data obtained in two bioassays of dioxin (6,7) as discussed by Portier et al (8).

TABLE I: CDC Estimates of TCDD Uptake by Route of Exposure (1 ppb in soil)

| Route | Avg. daily dose (fg/kg/day) | % Lifetime uptake |
|---|---|---|
| Ingestion of soil | 606 | 95 |
| Dermal uptake of soil | 20 | 3 |
| Uptake of soil inhaled | 10 | 2 |

In its calculations, CDC assumed that as much as 10 grams per day of soil would be ingested by children aged 1.5 to 3.5 years and that during other periods ingestion would be much less, depending on age (Table II). Persons older than 5 years were assumed to ingest 100 mg/day through incidental ingestion (1).

If these assumptions are used, the resulting calculations
indicate that about 80% of the entire lifetime dose occurs during
the first 5 years of life.

TABLE II: Ingestion of Dirt* (CDC Assumption)

| Age group | Soil ingested | % Lifetime uptake |
|-----------|---------------|-------------------|
| 0-9 Months | 0 mg/day | 0 |
| 9-18 Months | 1000 mg/day | 2.6 |
| 1.5-3.5 Years | 10,000 mg/day | 70.0 |
| 3.5-5 Years | 1000 mg/day | 5.2 |
| 5-70 Years | 100 mg/day | 22.6 |

*Adjusted for seasonal variations

In light of the critical role which soil ingestion plays
when estimating human exposure to contaminated dirt, a survey of
the literature was undertaken to identify the typical amount
consumed by children and adults. Walter and co-workers (9) have
estimated that a normal child typically ingests very small
quantities of dust or dirt between the ages of 0-2, the largest
quantities between ages 2-7, and nearly insignificant amounts
thereafter. In the classic text by Cooper (10), she notes that
the desire of children to eat dirt or place inedible objects in
their mouths "becomes established in the second year of life and
has disappeared more or less spontaneously by the age of four to
five years." A study by Charney et al (11) indicated that
mouthing tends to begin at about 18 months and continue through
72 months depending on several factors such as nutritional and
economic status as well as race. Work by Sayre et al (12) also
showed that the ages 2-6 years are the ones of primary concern.
    An important subtlety that is often lost in the scientific
literature is that mouthing tendencies and the ingestion of very
small quantities of dirt associated with poor hygiene should not
be called pica. Children who intentionally eat dirt, plaster or
paint chips and, as a consequence, have developed chronic health
problems can be said to suffer from the disease known as pica
(10). If the craving is for dirt alone, this disease is known as
geophasia. Further, the incidence of pica in the general
population has often been overstated because some of the best
studies were conducted in children who already suffered from lead
poisoning due, in part, to their strong desire to eat dirt and
other small objects. In such populations, the incidence of pica
has been reported at about 20% (10,16). In contrast, in the
general population the incidence of pica is probably in the range
of 1-3% (11) while geophasia is more rare.
    Duggan and Williams (13) have summarized the literature on
the amount of lead ingested through dust and dirt. In their
opinion, a quantity of 50 µg of lead was the best estimate for

daily ingestion by children from dust.  Assuming, on the high side, an average lead concentration of 1000 ppm, this would indicate an ingestion of 50 mg/day of soil and dust per day. Lepow and co-workers (14,15) estimated a rate of ingestion equal to 100 mg/day (specifically, 10 mg ingested 10 times a day). Barltrop (16) also estimated that the potential uptake of soils and dusts by a toddler is about 100 mg/day.  A report by the National Research Council which addressed the hazards of lead (17) suggested a figure of 40 mg/day.  Day et al (18) also suggested a figure of 100 mg/day (based on eating soiled candy) and Bryce-Smith (19) estimated 33 mg/day.  In their document addressing lead in air, EPA (20) assumed that a child ate 50 mg/day of household dust, 40 mg/day of street dust, and 10 mg/day of dust derived from their parents' clothing (i.e., a total of 100 mg/day).

More recently, Hawley (21) reviewed the available literature on soil ingestion and concluded that uptake was approximately 100 mg/day but he developed a more complex lifetime exposure schedule than had been proposed by others (Table III).  Bellinger et al (22) have suggested a figure of 20 mg/day.  Binder et al (23) conducted a pilot study which employed a rigorous experimental approach involving the analysis of trace elements in children's stool samples.  Their data indicated that children 1 to 3 years of age ingest about 180 mg/day of soil (geometric mean) based on the quantity of silicon, aluminum and titanium found in the feces.  The limitations of this study and the difficulties encountered in the interpretation of the titanium data have been reviewed by Clement Associates (24).

TABLE III: Other Estimates for Ingestion of Soil by Humans

| Age group (years) | Lepow et al. (14) [a] (mg/day) | Duggan and Williams (13) (mg/day) | Baltrop (14) (mg/day) | Hawley (21) (mg/day) | Van Wijnen et al. (25) (mg/day) |
|---|---|---|---|---|---|
| 0-2 | — [b] | — | — | Negligible | — |
| 2-6 | 100 | 50 | 100 | 90 | 56 |
| 6-18 | — | — | — | 21 | — |
| 18-70 | — | — | — | 57 | — |

[a] Used in EPA TCDD risk assessment.
[b] —Indicates the researchers did not discuss these age groups.

In a very recent study, van Wijnen et al (25) reported the results of a study of 2-4 year old children wherein the feces were analyzed for titanium, aluminum, and acid soluble residue (air).  The results showed that the data were approximately normally distributed.  Estimates of 105 mg/day for nursery school children and 49 mg/day for the hospitalized children were obtained.  Even with the limited number of samples in the study (n = 24), the difference between the two populations was significant (p < 0.01).  If the value for the hospitalized

children is assumed to be the background due to intake of these
substances from non-soil sources (e.g., diet and toothpastes),
the estimated average soil ingestion of this group of nursery
school children would be 56 mg/day. This value is in the lower
range of the estimates in the literature and supports the use of
100 mg/day as a reasonable daily average uptake of soil by
toddlers (ages 2-4 or ages 1.5 - 3.5).

For the majority of persons beyond the age of 5-6, the daily
uptake of dirt due to intentional ingestion should be quite low.
One route by which adults ingest dirt is presumably fruits and
vegetables; and nearly all of it is due to leafy vegetables
(20,26). Another source of ingestion is poor personal hygiene
(31). Investigations at nuclear weapons trials have shown that
particles which exceed 45 um are seldom retained on leaves (27).
In addition, the superficial contamination by the smaller
particles is readily lost from leaves; either by mechanical
processes or rain, and certainly by washing (26,29).

It has been estimated that the deposition rate of dust in
rural environments is about 0.008 ug/cm$^2$-day (20) assuming that
rural dust contains about 500 ug/g of lead (the substance for
which these data were obtained). EPA (20) also estimated that
even at relatively high air concentrations (i.e., 0.45 mg/m$^3$
total dust), it is unlikely that surface deposition alone can
account for more than 1.0-2.5 mg dust per gram of lettuce
(2-5 ug/g lead) on the surface of lettuce during a 21-day growing
period. Based on EPA upper worst case estimates for lead uptake
via gardens (100 µg lead/day), the corresponding value for
ingestion of dust would be 10 mg/day (at 1000 µg/g lead).
These data suggest that the daily ingestion of dirt and dust by
adults is unlikely to exceed 0-5 mg/day even if all of the 137 g
of leafy and root vegetables, sweet corn and potatoes consumed by
adult males each day were replaced by family garden products.
This figure is much lower than the 100 mg/day figure used by CDC
to describe average daily soil ingestion by adolescents and
adults (ages 6-70). The actual uptake by adults from vegetables
should be virtually zero since this estimate assumes that all
dust is contaminated with dioxin, that persons don't wash the
vegetables, that photodegradation does not occur, and that garden
vegetables are eaten throughout the year rather than only during
the growing season.

When all this published information on soil ingestion is
considered, the data indicate that a consensus estimate for soil
ingestion by children (ages 1 1/2 - 3 1/2) is about 100 mg/day.
This figure was adopted by the EPA in its risk assessment (2),
and in the Superfund Health Assessment Manual (30). The likely
average uptake of contaminated soil by adults should also be much
less than that estimated by CDC, perhaps as low as 0-5 mg/day.
Most persons wash their vegetables before ingestion and the
hygienic practices of most persons are not so poor as to make
this route of uptake very significant. The impact of these
assumptions regarding soil ingestion by children and adults on
the risk estimates is dramatic. Depending on the site on which a
risk assessment is conducted, as will be shown later in this

paper, the use of 100 mg/day for those aged 2-4, rather than 10,000 mg/day, and 0-5 mg/day rather than 100 mg/day for ages 6-70 years, will significantly change the estimates of risk.

## EXPOSURE FROM INHALATION

Although some persons have been concerned about inhaling dioxin, either as a vapor or as a contaminant of ambient dust, both the EPA, CDC and other assessments have demonstrated that inhalation does not constitute a significant route of entry for TCDD.  If, as assumed by CDC, the average air concentration of total suspended particulates (TSP) is 0.14 mg/m$^3$ and 100% of this amount (by weight) is respirable, then the average daily uptake over a lifetime is estimated at 10 fg/kg/day – roughly 2% of the amount taken up by ingestion, according to the CDC calculations (Table 1).

Inhalation is actually a less important route of entry than assumed by CDC, if other data are considered.  For example, the EPA has estimated that the average concentration of total suspended particulates (TSP) in Missouri is about one-half the level assumed by CDC, or about 0.070 mg/m$^3$ (32,33).  Secondly, only a fraction (about 30%) of the total amount of airborne dust is respirable (less than 10 μm aerodynamic diameter) (32).  The percentage of TSP which is respirable has been estimated by EPA to be no more than 50% (2).  Also, the assumption that all of the airborne particles are derived from dioxin-contaminated soil is overly conservative.  Actually, about 50% of the inhaleable particles are respirable and the remainder are between 10 and 50 μm.  Further, about 83% of the non-respirable particles are from crustal material (e.g., soil) and only 47% of the respirable particles are from soil (32).  Larger studies conducted by the U.S. EPA have suggested that the portion of inhaleable dust due to soil can often be much less (34).

## EXPOSURE FROM DERMAL CONTACT

To estimate daily TCDD uptake via the skin, CDC assumed that dermal exposures would follow "an age-dependent pattern of deposition similar to soil ingestion" as shown in Table IV (1). There are several subsequent assumptions which would over estimate the degree of dermal exposure.  CDC assumed that dirt would remain on the hand for a period long enough to bring about 1% absorption (1) – the percent absorption determined in rats exposed for 24 hours (35).  A 24-hr duration is almost certainly longer than what is likely for humans under normal conditions. Secondly, human skin has generally been shown, for a diverse class of chemicals, to be less permeable to xenobiotics than the skin of rabbits and rats (36-38).

TABLE IV: Amount of Soil Deposited on Skin (CDC Assumption)

| Age group | Soil on skin (day) |
|---|---|
| 0-9 Months | 0 g |
| 9-18 Months | 1 g |
| 1.5-3.5 Years | 10 g |
| 3.5-5 Years | 1 g |
| 5-70 Years | 100 mg |

In both assessments, CDC and EPA assumed that the likelihood for dermal exposure would be affected by weather conditions, and consequently, made adjustments. In the CDC calculations, it appears that CDC assumed that persons would come into contact with soil or garden for about 180 days per year for 64 years [70 minus 6]. This estimate is almost certain to overestimate exposure since [a] not everyone in the community gardens; [b] many persons wear gloves when working intimately with dirt; [c] gardeners work directly with the soil primarily during planting and weeding; and [d] most people do not garden each day.

EPA, in its risk assessment, used an alternative set of assumptions which, because they are based, in part, on actual field investigations, seem more realistic than CDC's assumption in Table IV. A study by Roels et al (38) has indicated that about 0.5 mg of soil per $cm^2$ of skin adheres to a child's hand after playing in and around the home. This is similar to that reported by Day et al (18) who observed that 5-50 mg of dirt transferred from a child's hand to a sticky sweet. Brunekreef et al (39) found similar results. Using table values for skin surface area (40), uptake can be estimated by multiplying this value by the 1% absorption rate and the amount of dirt on the skin. Depending on the conditions of exposure, this alternative approach - which could be based on skin surface area, duration of exposure (time), and the amount of dirt on the skin - could predict a markedly different, often lesser, degree of dermal uptake than CDC's assumptions.

## BIOAVAILABILITY:  DERMAL ABSORPTION

Bioavailability is an important parameter in any risk assessment of dioxin. Throughout this discussion, bioavailability will be used to describe the percentage of TCDD in soil which is absorbed by humans (as suggested in animal studies) following exposure via inhalation, ingestion or dermal contact. There are a number of parameters which are likely to influence the degree of bioavailability of dioxin when it is on soil including aging (time following contamination), soil type (e.g., silt, clay and sand), co-contaminants (e.g., oil and other organics), and the dioxin concentration on the soil. Poiger and Schlatter (35) have conducted the only published study on dermal bioavailability. They dosed rats dermally with laboratory contaminated soil and observed that as the dose increased, the liver concentration of TCDD increased from 0.05 to 2.2%. The authors did not estimate a value for dermal bioavailability. On the basis of this study, Kimbrough and co-workers estimated a dermal bioavailability of 1% for humans (1). The use of a 1% dermal absorption factor (bioavailability) almost surely overestimates the actual uptake of TCDD on soil through human skin since investigators in the dermal field generally agree that rodent skin is approximately 10 times more permeable than human skin. As discussed in the next section, dermal bioavailability (like oral bioavailability) is also likely to decrease with the "age" of the soil. (41,42)

## BIOAVAILABILITY:  INGESTION

Poiger and Schlatter (35) published the first study on this topic. They dosed rats orally with laboratory prepared TCDD contaminated soil and monitored the % of administered dose in the liver. Their data suggest that as the time of contact between the soil and TCDD (known as aging) increased, the oral bioavailability decreased. Other investigators have also observed that aging may decrease bioavailability (41,42).

McConnell et al. (43) studied Missouri soil contaminated with TCDD. They looked at the liver concentration of TCDD in the guinea pig and rat, and arylhydrocarbon hydroxylase (AHH) induction in the rat, following soil ingestion. They concluded that TCDD absorption from soil by test animals is highly efficient, but that they had difficulty in arriving at an exact percentage for bioavailability. In the CDC assessment, Kimbrough et al. (1) used a 30% bioavailability value and cited McConnell et al. (43) as the reference. Lucier et al. (44) republished some of the original data from McConnell et al. (43) and concluded the oral bioavailability was 50%. However, the data of Lucier et al. (44), suggested the bioavailability was dose dependent – 24% at 1 µg/kg and 50% at 5 µg/kg TCDD. Lucier et al. estimated oral bioavailability by comparing the liver TCDD concentration of control rats dosed with TCDD in corn oil with experimental rats dosed with TCDD on Missouri soil.

In a 1985 abstract, Umbreit et al. (45) reported bioavailability of less than 0.05% for a New Jersey manufacturing site. This work was subsequently published (46) wherein they reported oral bioavailability of 0.5% for soil at a manufacturing site and 21% for a salvage yard in Newark. In this paper, Umbreit et al attributed an oral bioavailability of 85% to the data presented in the 1984 paper by McConnell et al. Umbreit et al. did not discuss how they defined or calculated bioavailability for their own data or in their interpretation of McConnell et al's data. Work by Umbreit et al (47) has shown that the bioavailability of TCDD in contaminated soil samples from Times Beach and New Jersey can not be reliably assessed using AHH induction due to the presence of co-contaminants.

Some of the confusion concerning the value for oral
bioavailability undoubtedly arises because of the ways
investigators have calculated bioavailability.  Apparently, some
may have used AHH induction as the basis for calculation, while
others have used actual liver levels of TCDD.  The difficulties
in using AHH induction to assess the bioavailability of
dioxin-bound soil has been discussed (47).  Thus far, no one has
used a total material balance, including the amount in all
tissues and in excreta, as the basis for comparison; an approach
which would yield a much more useful estimate of uptake.
Recently, officials of the EPA (48) and CDC (49) cited 85% as the
bioavailability of dioxin in soil, based on the available data,
in spite of the apparent differences between testing methods and
methods for defining bioavailability.
        Bonaccorsi et al. (50) have also published a paper on oral
bioavailability in the rabbit.  They compared liver levels of
dioxin 7 days after an oral dose of Seveso soil or a comparable
TCDD dose in alcohol.  They reported that absorption of
soil-bound TCDD from Seveso was 32% that of TCDD in alcohol.
        The divergent results on oral bioavailability reported in
the literature may occur for several reasons, which will be
discussed below.  Umbreit and co-workers (46) and Poiger and
Schlatter (33) have also offered explanations for the
discrepancy.  The dioxin concentrations in the soil samples for
the various laboratories were similar, but other conditions were
quite different.  For example, the bolus size (the amount of soil
administered to the animal) varied markedly among the studies, as
did the amount of TCDD taken up in the liver.  The data from the
three studies suggest that the larger the quantity of soil (i.e.,
larger dose of dioxin) given to the animal, the larger percentage
of uptake by the liver.  There are a number of physiological
(e.g., residence time and G.I. motility), biochemical (e.g.,
liver enzyme induction) and physical (e.g., low concentrations
bind more tightly to soil, soil type, co-contaminants) reasons
why this might be expected.  The guinea pig data suggest that
when the amount of soil ingested is low (on a mg/kg basis) - a
condition which more closely resembles that seen in children -
the percent GI absorption is lower than the 30% figure used by
CDC.  Due to a lack of experimental data, a similar inference
cannot be drawn for the rat.
        The level of organic matter in soil may also be an important
variable.  The New Jersey soil used by Umbreit et al (45)
contained a high organic loading in the form of asphalt-like
residues, as well as natural organic content.  Interestingly,
when this soil was stripped of its organic loading, and the
dioxin was reapplied, bioavailability approached 23% (45), which
supports the hypothesis that increasing amounts of organics in
the soil may decrease the bioavailability of TCDD.
        In summary, 30% bioavailability of TCDD in soil in the G.I.
tract may represent an upper estimate.  Given the low
concentrations of TCDD usually encountered in the environment and
the small daily oral dose anticipated among residents, a figure
of 10% may be a reasonable estimate of the average oral

bioavailability that might be anticipated for many contaminated sites.

## BIOAVAILABILITY:   INHALATION

Because TCDD has a very low volatility, TCDD uptake via inhalation is directly related to the concentration of airborne dust due to wind-blown soil.  It has been estimated that of all airborne, respirable particulates, only about 30-50% comes from soil, while the rest is apparently due to products of combustion, tire wear and other sources (32).  Of the total suspended particulates, usually no more than 50% are respirable (i.e., particles less than 10 um).  Of these, about 50% of the respirable particles are deposited in the upper airways and ultimately swallowed while the rest reach the alveoli or are expired.  An analysis of CDC's data indicates that CDC assumed that 100% of the TCDD present on all the inhaled particles would be retained and absorbed in the respiratory tract.  In contrast, the EPA assessment (2) assumed that only 25% of the inhaled particles would be absorbed in the lower airways since at least 50% of the particles would be non-respirable (especially by weight) and these will be swallowed due to impaction in the throat and only about 50% of the respirable particles would be absorbed.  In any assessment, it is important to recognize that of those particles swallowed, no more than 10-30% should be absorbed since they will pass through the G.I. tract (assuming 10-30% oral bioavailability).

## EFFECTS OF TCDD DISTRIBUTION AT THE SITE

Kimbrough et al (1) observed that of all the assumptions used in their risk analysis, the "most prominent of these is the assumption of uniform levels of contamination throughout the living space (environment)".  CDC was especially sensitive to this issue and generated a very interesting plot which illustrates the relationship between the magnitude of the risk and the percent of the surface area of the land that has been contaminated (Figure 2).  It is important to recognize that the degree of human exposure (ingestion, inhalation and dermal) is almost always a function of the TCDD concentration at the soil surface (top 1-2 cm) rather than the concentration at lower depths.  This is significant since recent research suggests that within 18 months, nearly all of the TCDD in the top 1/4 cm of soil, and most of it within 1/2 cm,  is no longer present due to photodegradation and volatilization (51-53).  Photodegradation of TCDD in soil may require the presence of a hydrogen donor, e.g., a solvent or humic soil (52).

## RESIDENTIAL VERSUS INDUSTRIAL SITES

Probably the most overlooked of the many caveats in the CDC assessment is the one involving the setting of different clean-up

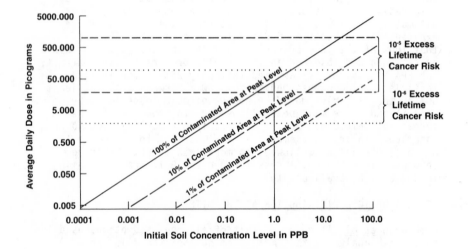

Figure 2: Effect of the degree (prevalence) of dioxin soil contamination at a residential site versus the estimated risk (from Kimbrough et al, 1984). This plot is based on an acceptable daily lifetime dose of 636 fg/kg/day (CDC's best estimate of a dose which would increase the individual cancer risk by 1 in 1,000,000). Reproduced with permission from ref. 108. Copyright 1986, Academic Press.

and health alert guidelines for residential versus industrial
sites.  As noted in CDC's publication, "in all of these scenarios
(factories, farms, residential sites), these decisions must be
made on a site-specific basis".  The most prominent difference
between a residential and an industrial setting, with respect to
the hazard to human health, is the lack of access by the public,
and, in particular, children to industrial sites.  In the absence
of such access, at least 95% of the potential exposure to dioxin
is eliminated (Table I).  In light of the characteristics of
industrial sites, the CDC suggested that *unless* soil "levels
are very high - e.g., above 100 ppb - more extensive remedial
action" than paving may not have to be considered (1).  The
implication is that soil levels at or below 100 ppb at a
non-residential site may be acceptable.

## APPLICATIONS OF THE CDC METHODOLOGY

As noted in both the CDC and EPA assessments, the process of
setting standards for clean-up should be done on a site-specific
basis.  The task of setting "clean-up levels" and assessing the
risk of contaminated soil on a case-by-case basis need not be a
process so complex, or cumbersome, as to be impractical for
regulatory agencies.  Certainly, an algorithm which incorporates
all of the important variables could be developed, as illustrated
by Hawley (21) and Schaum (2), and these calculations can easily
be handled by a desk top computer.

   The following case studies illustrate how the CDC methodology
could be applied, on a site-specific basis, incorporating some of
the data we have described on soil ingestion and bioavailability.
These examples illustrate the effect of altering only a few of
the critical assumptions in the CDC assessment and the effect of
following CDC's advice concerning site-by-site analyses.  In
developing a comprehensive risk assessment, it is important to
acknowledge the uncertainties, as recommended by the National
Academy of Science (54).  CDC recognized the fragility and
uncertainty of many of the assumptions it used and specifically
noted that "it must be stressed that the exposure assessments
used in estimating risks for carcinogenicity and reproductive
health effects contain critical assumptions that are not likely
to be actually encountered."  Although not addressed in detail in
this paper, other critical issues, including the use of classic
cancer risk models to estimate TCDDs carcinogenic potency in
humans at low doses (despite its lack of genotoxicity) and the
incorporation of the generally favorable epidemiology data should
be examined in any comprehensive review of a risk assessment of
dioxin (55-58).

## CASE I (A RESIDENTIAL SITE)

In this example, a hypothetical residential site will be
evaluated.  For the sake of this discussion, 10% of the soil
surface in this community is assumed to be contaminated with 10
ppb TCDD.  Altering only three different assumptions in the CDC

assessment process, would the analysis suggest that clean-up is needed at this site if only a few of the CDC values were updated?

Using the methods described by the CDC and the EPA, a preliminary evaluation of the need for clean-up at a given site can be readily conducted. In Case I, we followed the CDC assessment procedure but updated a few of their values. Specifically, in these calculations we used: [a] a soil uptake of 100 mg/day (ages 2-6), and negligible soil ingestion for the rest of the lifetime: [b] 10% oral, and 1% dermal bioavailability; [c] quantitative assumptions on dermal exposure, [d] actual field data on the concentration of respirable dust in air; and [e] corrections for the differences in bioavailability between particles that are swallowed vs. those retained in the lung (Table V).

TABLE V: Exposure Assumptions Used in Case I Calculations (Lifetime Average)

| Route | CDC | Alternate |
|-------|-----|-----------|
| Oral | 0.21 g/day ingested (lifetime ave.)<br>30% absorption | 0.0028 g/day ingested (lifetime ave.)<br>10% absorption |
| Dermal | 0.21 g/day of soil on the skin<br>Dose is weighted by age over lifetime<br>1% absorption | 0.5 mg soil/$cm^2$ skin<br>1400 $cm^2$ exposed surface<br>8 hr/day, 90 days/year<br>1% absorption |
| Inhalation | Total suspended particulates<br>is 0.14 mg/$m^3$<br>15 $m^3$/day<br>100% in lungs<br>100% bioavailable | Total suspended particulates<br>is 0.075 mg/$m^3$<br>15 $m^3$/day<br>Of particles inhaled, assume 50%<br>ingested and 50% in lungs<br>Bioavailability weighted for differences in absorption for respirable and nonrespirable particles.<br>Only 50% of the particles are from the contaminated site. |

As shown in Table VI, using the alternate assumed values, the oral dose would not be expected to be greater than 2.8 fg/kg/day. If a 30% oral bioavailability were assumed, the average daily dose increases to 16.7 fg/kg/day. CDC's assumed values would suggest an oral uptake of about 606.5 fg/kg/day. The alternate method estimated dermal uptake of 2.7 fg/kg/day, in contrast to 20 fg/kg/day using CDC's assumed values. Lastly, CDC assumptions would suggest that 10 fg/kg/day might be inhaled versus 5.6 fg/kg/day. In summary, use of the alternative assumptions predicts that the most likely uptake of TCDD will, in this example, be 11.1 fg/kg/day. In contrast, the assumptions in the CDC assessment led to an estimate for total TCDD uptake of 636.5 fg/kg/day (which CDC considered acceptable when recommending the 1 ppb guideline).

TABLE VI: Residential Site [a] (Case I)

| Route | TCDD Uptake (fg/kg/day) | |
|---|---|---|
| | CDC | Alternate |
| Oral | 606.5 | 2.8 |
| Dermal | 20.0 | 2.7 |
| Inhalation | 10.0 | 5.6 |
| Total | 636.5 | 11.1 |
| | | (16.7) [b] |

[a] Ten percent of land contaminated (10 ppb TCDD).
[b] Using a 30% oral bioavailability.

This analysis indicates that remediation would not be indicated at this site. Of course, in any isolated instances where children or adults might be exposed to TCDD soil concentration in excess of 500-1000 ppb, e.g., hot spots, clean-up of these would need to be considered. Concentrations as high as 1000 ppb in soil, assuming 1% dermal bioavailability, would not be expected to cause chloracne with repeated exposure, based on the work of Kligman who dermally applied TCDD to human volunteers (<u>57,59</u>).

## CASE II (INDUSTRIAL SITE)

The CDC methodology can also be used to assess the potential hazards at an industrial site. In this example, assume that 20% of the site has been contaminated with 100 ppb TCDD. Because it is an industrial site, children have virtually no access. Is remediation necessary? The assumptions and factors used here are shown in Table VII.

TABLE VII: Exposure Assumptions Used in Case II Calculations (Lifetime Average)

| Route | CDC | Alternate |
|---|---|---|
| Oral | Not relevant | Not relevant |
| Dermal | Exposure is almost same as oral exposure<br>15 m³/day<br>100% in lungs | 0.5 mg/soil<br>1400 cm² exposed skin<br>8 hr/day, 40 years exposure |
| Inhalation | 0.14 mg/m³ (dust)<br>15 m³/day<br>100% in lungs<br><br>100% bioavailable | Total suspended particulates are 0.075 mg/m³ (Springfield, Mo.)<br>Of particles inhaled, assume 50% ingested and 50% in lungs<br>50% of respirable particles from contaminated soil<br>Adjust bioavailability for ingestion and inhalation |

Because children are not exposed, the oral route of exposure becomes insignificant. As shown in Table VIII, calculations based on the CDC assumed values indicate that an average lifetime dose of 590 fg/kg/day TCDD could potentially be absorbed by those who work at this site (lifetime average). This value is still less than 636 fg/kg/day, the daily dose which CDC considered acceptable (Table I). Further, use of the alternative assumptions indicates that the more likely daily uptake is 135 fg/kg/day. These calculations suggest, since the daily intake is less than 636 fg/kg/day, that 20% contamination of soil by 100 ppb TCDD at an industrial site poses no health hazard to workers or the community. Further, at many industrial sites it may be acceptable to permit soils contaminated with TCDD at levels greater than 100 ppb to remain in place, especially where soil erosion is not a problem and where the contamination is at the soil surface (where it is available for photodegradation if in the presence of solvents). Based on these factors, CDC noted that unless the levels of TCDD are greatly in excess of 100 ppb, paving should be an adequate remediation at many sites (1).

TABLE VIII: Industrial Site [a] (Case II)

| Route | TCDD uptake (fg/kg/day) | |
| | CDC | Alternate |
| --- | --- | --- |
| Oral | 0 | 0 |
| Dermal | 390 | 78 |
| Inhalation | 200 | 57 |
| Total | 590 | 135 |

[a] 20% of land contaminated (100 ppb TCDD)

## PROMOTER VERSUS INITIATOR

It is generally well accepted within the scientific community that tumor initiation involves a change to cellular DNA which is an irreversible and heritable event. Tumor promotion, on the other hand, involves reversible and nonheritable event(s). Promoters provide a favorable environment for tumor growth. When a promoter is taken away from a tumor, the environment becomes inhospitable, and tumor growth is adversely affected. In contrast, the alterations to DNA produced by initiators remain with that cell and are passed on to successive progeny cells during cell division.

The distinction between initiation and promotion as the mechanism of carcinogenesis is critical. Many in the scientific community would agree that one of the most critical aspects in the risk assessment of a carcinogenic substance is whether the substance acts through a genotoxic or non-genotoxic mechanism. Weisburger and Williams (58) point out the importance of this distinction: "The action of epigenetic agents of the promoter class is highly dose-dependent and reversible, and thus, a distinctly different risk analysis is required to take account of their quantitatively lesser hazard."

The discussion of the calculations in the previous sections is based on CDC's conclusion that an average daily uptake of about 636 fg/kg/day is a reasonable level at which to begin consideration of limiting exposure.  In view of dioxin's lack of genotoxicity (60-64), however, this VSD seems excessive since it is based on the upper bound of risks estimated from models which assume linearity at low doses.  Further, the arguments for linearity are frequently based on the chemical being genotoxic.  Tumor promoters constitute a small percentage of the chemical carcinogens which have been studied or regulated.  Regulatory agencies have much more experience in dealing with chemical initiators.  Thus, the temptation is to regulate all carcinogens as initiators.  However, if regulations are to be based on scientific fact and not on tradition, the cancer risk assessment for TCDD must reflect the fact TCDD is only a tumor promoter in animals.  In fact, government bodies in Ontario, Germany and the Netherlands, many eminent scientists in Western Europe, and the U.S. Food and Drug Administration (FDA) regard TCDD as a promoter in animals and have estimated, accordingly, a lower potential risk to human health (see table 9).

By assuming TCDD is an initiator when the data attest to the contrary, EPA and CDC are not incorporating all the available data into their assessments.  In EPA's "Proposed Guidelines for Carcinogen Risk Assessment" (65), they stipulate that models used in risk assessment should reflect data on mechanism of carcinogenesis:

> The choice of low-dose extrapolation models *should be consistent with current understanding of the mechanisms of carcinogenesis* . . . .   When pharmacokinetics or metabolism data are available, or when other substantial evidence on the mechanistic aspects of the carcinogenesis process exists, a different low dose extrapolation model (than linear multi-stage) might be considered more appropriate on biological grounds.  When a different model is chosen, the risk assessment should clearly discuss the nature and strength of the evidence that lead to the choice (emphasis provided).

For dioxin, there is evidence that its mechanism of action is receptor-mediated (66) and, to describe this mechanism, a low dose extrapolation model other than the linearized multi-stage is more appropriate.  The linearized multi-stage model forces linearity at low doses - a trait which should not be forced for chemicals which act through a receptor mediated event.  Further, the linearized  models do not account for the reversible behavior of promoters or the possibility of a dose at which no increased risk would be expected.

## TCDD LACKS INITIATOR ACTIVITY

The ability of TCDD to interact with genetic material has been examined by over 20 studies.  Wassom et al. (60), Kociba (61-63), and Shu et al (64) have reviewed much of this data.  Mutagenic

studies using the Salmonella/Ames bacteria test alone encompass
13 different strains with tests performed in 9 laboratories,
including the National Toxicology Program.  Of these
independently conducted studies, all have been negative with the
exception of two early studies by Hussain et al. (67) and Seiler
(63).  As has been discussed by Shu et al (64), there is good
scientific reason to question the results of Hussain et al. and
Seiler.  These two early positive studies do not meet current
criteria for demonstrating positive mutagenic response.  For
example, the studies did not demonstrate a dose response
relationship; nor were the results reproducible by later
studies.  Moreover, in these studies, the TCDD used was greatly
in excess of TCDD solubility in water, and the bacterial survival
rates were extremely low.
     In assessing the mechanism by which TCDD induces tumors in
animals, regulatory agencies are expected to evaluate the largely
negative mutagenesis findings on TCDD against the documented
reliability which short term tests have for detecting mutagens
and carcinogens.  Several scientific panels have stated that it
can be reasonably concluded that the negative mutagenic data on
TCDD are real and not false negatives resulting from inadequate
testing (69-70).  The Salmonella/Ames test is extremely
sensitive, and usually responds to micrograms, and in some cases
even nanograms, of material.  Given the sensitivity of the test,
TCDD's lack of mutagenic activity is all the more convincing when
it has been inactive in test after test.  The importance of
classifying a chemical as genotoxic in risk assessments has been
quantitatively addressed in Squire (56), Park and Snee (71) and
Longstreth and Hushon (55).

## CANADIAN AND EUROPEAN VSD's

As early as 1981, Rodricks (72) suggested that in light of TCDD's
lack of genotoxicity, the safety factor approach would be
appropriate for setting an acceptable daily intake (ADI); using
this approach, he calculated a 10 pg/kg/day figure.  More
recently, the Province of Ontario and several Western European
countries, as well as European scientists, have estimated TCDD
risk to humans that is significantly less than EPA's estimate.
For example, the Ontario risk assessment uses a no observable
effect level (NOEL) of 0.001 ug/kg/day (6,73) and a safety factor
of 100 to obtain a maximum allowable daily intake of $1 \times 10^{-11}$
g/kg/day (= 10 pg/kg/day) for humans (74).  In contrast, EPA has
used a value of $6.4 \times 10^{-15}$ g/kg/day which suggests cancer
risks that are 1670 fold higher.  The United States Food and Drug
Administration (FDA) has, on the other hand, accepted risks
associated with the ingestion of up to 13 pg/kg/day.  (Table IX).
     The fundamental difference between the EPA and Canadian
analyses is how each treats the data on TCDD's mechanism of
action.  Scientists from Canada and Western European countries
regard TCDD as a tumor promoter in animals whereas EPA regards
TCDD as a tumor initiator (75).  The large body of data which
indicate TCDD does not possess initiator activity but does
possess promoter activity in animals has been discussed (60-64).
The rather strong evidence that TCDD is a promoter rather than an

TABLE IX: TCDD Cancer Risk Estimates by Different Agencies

| Agency | Acceptable risk | Model | Reference |
|---|---|---|---|
| Ontario | 10,000 fg/kg/day | Safety factor (100) | Ontario, 1984 (74) |
| USEPA [a] | 6.4 fg/kg/day | Linear multistage | EPA, 1985b (51) |
| CDC [b] | 28-1428 fg/kg/day | Linear multistage | Kimbrough *et al.*, 1984 (1) |
|  | 632.6 fg/kg/day | (Best estimate) |  |
| FDA | 13,000 fg/kg/day | Safety factor (77) | Cordle, 1981 (107) |
|  |  | Linear multistage ($10^{-5}$ risk, mle) |  |

[a] Acceptable defined as $10^{-6}$ risk (upper bound).
[b] Based on mouse and rat bioassay ($10^{-6}$ risk).

initiator, and the likelihood that current dose-response models may overstate the actual risks, were acknowledged by Kimbrough et al (1).

## Extrapolating To Very Low Doses

As discussed by Sielken (76), the method used to extrapolate the dose-response curve can be an important part of any risk assessment.  The scientist responsible for selecting the most appropriate method for extrapolating the dose-response curve faces a multitude of uncertainties which require several choices, assumptions and judgments during that selection process.  These decisions generally will have serious impact on the results and have a marked effect on the risk management decision.  In short, the choice of model, tumor type, species, bounding procedures, etc. can radically impact the results of the extrapolation process.  These decisions are often driven more by policy than by the available scientific information.  Before the results of the extrapolation process are allowed to influence risk management decision, a thorough analysis of the quantitative impact of the particular choices made in an assessment should be presented and the scientific merit of these particular choices should be carefully explained (54).

The interpretation of the dose-response curve for dioxin, like the dose-response relationship for other chemicals, requires careful thought since numerous subtleties can dramatically affect the results.  For example, false impressions can arise from fitting quantal response models to very high administered doses. In the Kociba et al study (6), the highest experimental dose level (0.1 ug/kg/day) is one hundred times larger than the lowest non-zero experimental dose level (0.001 ug/kg body wt/day).  Even the second highest experimental dose level (0.01 ug/kg body wt/day) is ten times the lowest non-zero experimental dose level.  As noted by Sielken (76), the trade-offs inherent in curve fitting may lead to questionable fits in the low-dose region of primary concern.

The fitted models in Figure 3 reflect trade-offs both in the sense that the fitted models are shaped differently from the experimental data and in the sense that the fitted model response rates, relative to the observed rates, are too large at the lowest non-zero experimental dose level and too small at the intermediate non-zero level.  Furthermore, the need to accommodate the highest experimental dose forces the fitted

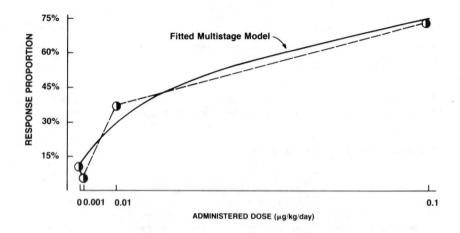

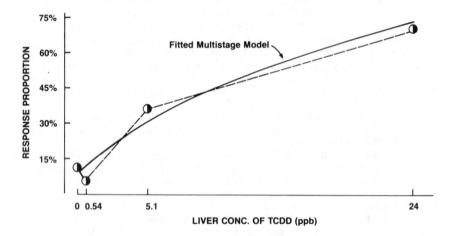

Figure 3:   Regardless of whether the dose is expressed as
ADMINISTERED DOSE or LIVER CONCENTRATION, when the
multistage model is fit to the experimental data on
hepatocellular neoplastic nodule or carcinoma in female
rats in the Kociba et al (1978) study, the fitted models do
NOT reflect the observed behavior at the lower experimental
doses (From ref. 76).   Reproduced with permission from
ref. 108.   Copyright 1986, Academic Press.

models to be very non-responsive to whatever is observed at the lowest non-zero dose level.  For example, as illustrated in Figure 4, the presence or absence of the experimental data at the lowest experimental dose has very little effect on the overall shape of the fitted models and makes only a relatively small effect (factor of 2) on the fitted model values for the VSD.

For several years, it has been acknowledged that whenever possible bioassay data should be corrected for early death.  In both CDC's and EPA's analysis of Kociba et al (6), the individual animal pathology results were not available.  Recently, these data were made available and the analysis showed some interesting results (76-77).  The nonparametric Kaplan-Meier estimates of the probability of a female rat developing a hepatocellular neoplastic nodule or carcinoma by the end of 25 months, the duration of the Kociba study, are shown in Figure 5.  These estimates are computed separately for each dose level and take into account the observation times of each rat.  The values of these estimates for the two highest dose levels are 0.81 at 0.01 ug/kg/day and 1.00 at 0.1 ug/kg/day.  Thus, by the end of the experimental period the number of rats that could develop a hepatocellular response is completely saturated at 0.1 ug/kg/day and nearly saturated at 0.01 ug/kg/day (76).  It is impossible for the multi-stage model to portray both this type of saturation phenomenon and the observed nonlinearity at the lowest experimental dose levels (0, 0.001, and 0.01 ug/kg/day).  The conflict caused by the model's inability to reflect both behaviors is dealt with in the fitting process by essentially ignoring the lower dose behavior and focusing on depicting the relative flatness at higher doses.

As discussed by Sielken (76), the flattening out or leveling off of the observed dose-response relationship at high doses causes the fitted models to modify dramatically their lower dose shape in order to have a relatively flat higher dose shape.  This change in the shape of the fitted models at the lower doses is illustrated in Figure 6 where the fitted multi-stage model on the administered dose scale is relatively linear if 0.1 ug/kg body wt/day is included in the fitting process and is upward curving in the lower dose region if 0.1 ug/kg body wt/day is excluded.  These two fits have very different shapes in the lower dose region, particularly between 0 and 0.001 ug/kg/day.  Consequently, the use of the very high dose data here leads to fitted models with an unsupported false impression of linearity in the lower dose region.  This pitfall is lessened by fitting the models to the observed proportions excluding the highest dose level.

When the very highest experimental dose level is not allowed to dominate the shape of the fitted multi-stage model for hepatocellular neoplastic nodule or carcinoma in the Kociba study, the nonlinearity in the fit of the multi-stage model to the three lower experimental dose levels is much more consistent with the observed nonlinearity in the fitted multi-stage model for the same carcinogenic response in the NTP study (Figure 7).  Contradictory shapes arise (Figure 8) if the data at the high dose in the Kociba study are allowed to dominate the fit.

In short, the availability of the time-to-early-death data for the animals in the Kociba study, recognition of the inability

**Results when the Experimental Data at Lower Dose Level are EXCLUDED**

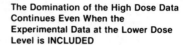

**The Domination of the High Dose Data Continues Even When the Experimental Data at the Lower Dose Level is INCLUDED**

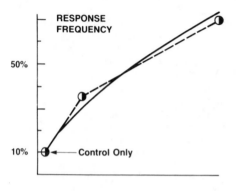

$$V\hat{S}D = 4.1 \times 10^{-8} \ \mu g/kg/day$$

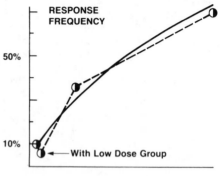

$$V\hat{S}D = 8.1 \times 10^{-8} \ \mu g/kg/day$$

**The NON-RESPONSIVENESS to the Inclusion of the Experimental Data at the Lower Dose Level**

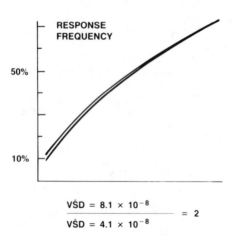

$$\frac{V\hat{S}D = 8.1 \times 10^{-8}}{V\hat{S}D = 4.1 \times 10^{-8}} = 2$$

Figure 4: Both the fit of the multistage model to the Kociba et al (1978) experimental data on hepatocellular neoplastic nodule or carcinoma in female rats and the corresponding estimate of the virtually safe dose (VSD) are dominated by the higher experimental dose levels and are ESSENTIALLY UNAFFECTED by the results obtained at lower doses (From ref. 76). Reproduced with permission from Paustenbach et al. Copyright 1986, Academic Press.

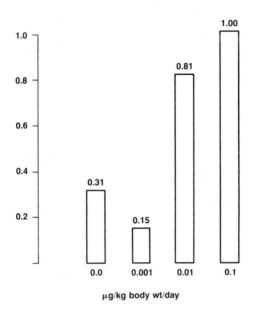

Figure 5:  The Kaplan-Meier estimates of the probability of
a female rat developing a hepatocellular neoplastic nodule
or carcinoma in the Kociba et al (1978) study suggest that
the dose-response relationship resembles one with a
saturation-like phenomenon occurring at the highest
experimental dose level (From ref. 76).  Reproduced with
permission from Paustenbach et al.  Copyright 1986,
Academic Press.

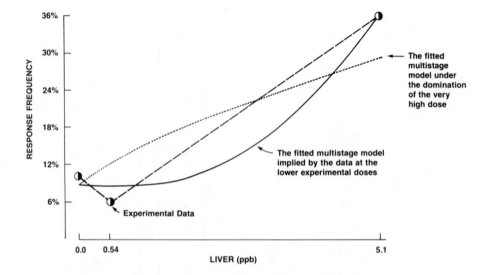

■ The VŜD under the domination of the very high dose is 0.00008 ng/kg/day.

■ The VŜD implied by the data at the lower experimental doses is 0.14 ng/kg/day.

Figure 6:  The fit of the multistage model and the
estimated virtually safe dose (VSD) for the Kociba et al
(1978) data on hepatocellular neoplastic nodule or
carcinoma in female rats are substantially different (1750
fold) if the domination of the very high dose is removed
(From ref. 76).  Reproduced with permission from
Paustenbach et al.  Copyright 1986, Academic Press.

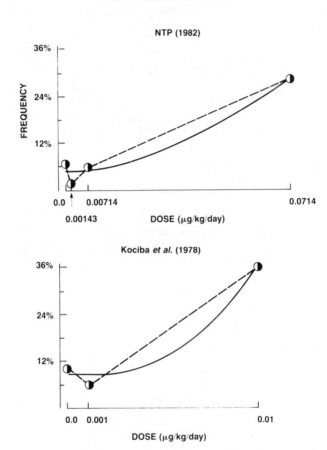

Figure 7: The shape of the fitted multistage model for the experimental data on hepatocellular neoplastic nodule or carcinoma in female rats in the NTP (1982) study SUPPORTS the NONLINEARITY in the shape of the fitted multistage model for the experimental data on hepatocellular neoplastic nodule or carcinoma in female rats at the lower doses in the Kociba et al (1978) study (From ref. 76). Reproduced with permission from Paustenbach et al. Copyright 1986, Academic Press.

**DIFFERENT SHAPES**

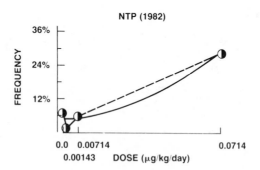

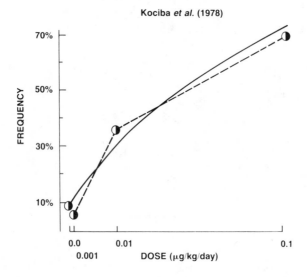

Figure 8: The shape of the fitted multistage model for the experimental data on hepatocellular neoplastic nodule or carcinoma in female rats in the NTP (1982) study does NOT SUPPORT the LINEARITY in the shape of the fitted multistage model for the experimental data on hepatocellular neoplastic nodule or carcinoma in female rats in the Kociba et al (1978) study if the data at the very high dose is allowed to dominate the fit (From ref. 76). Reproduced with permission from Paustenbach et al. Copyright 1986, Academic Press.

of the multi-stage model to respond to the data and the
domination of the highest dose in the model provides grounds for
re-evaluating the prior mathematical analysis of the cancer
bioassay data. Specifically, the corresponding estimated
virtually safe dose (VSD) for an increase of 0.000001 (one in a
million) in the probability of hepatocellular neoplastic nodule
or carcinoma in a female rat is 140 pg/kg/day (140,000 fg/kg/day)
in the diet using the Kociba data at 0.001 and 0.01 ug/kg/day and
is 130 pg/kg/day in the diet using the NTP data. The
corresponding estimated VSD's for male rats are higher, as are
those for hepatocellular carcinoma alone.

## UPTAKE BY CROPS

The likelihood that crops will take-up (absorb) appreciable
quantities of TCDD from contaminated soil is negligible (51).
Oats and soybean plants grown to maturity in soil contaminated
with 0.06 ppm 2,3,7,8-TCDD showed less than 1 ppb of 2,3,7,8-TCDD
in the seeds (78). Cocucci et al. (79) measured the level of
contamination in kitchen garden plants (carrot, potato, onion and
narcissus) grown in soil from the contaminated Seveso area
containing 1000-4000 mg/m$^2$ of 2,3,7,8-TCDD. Although dioxin
was found to be 3-5 times higher in foliage than in fruits, these
results have been questioned because others have not made similar
observations. Wipf et al. (80) failed to detect any measurable
2,3,7,8-TCDD in the flesh of fruits and vegetables collected from
the contaminated area in Seveso during 1977-1979, although the
soil 2,3,7,8-TCDD concentration was 10 ppb. These authors
concluded that 2,3,7,8-TCDD does not appear to be translocated
from soil to the plants. A similar conclusion was reached by
Pocchiari et al. (81) from their uptake experiments with plants.
As noted by EPA, it can be concluded from these studies that
2,3,7,8-TCDD will not accumulate in plants grown in contaminated
soils (51).

## EXPOSURE OF DOMESTIC ANIMALS

The uptake and translocation of TCDD in plants used for animal
feed is not an important route of animal exposure (82). Although
Fries has noted that residues of TCDD are occasionally reported
in the aerial parts of plants grown in contaminated soil (82),
the more usual finding has been that there is little or no TCDD
in the aerial parts and seeds of crops grown in contaminated soil
(83,84). Results from work on TCDD are substantially in
agreement with more extensive work on other halogenated
hydrocarbons (80). The latter studies generally indicate that
contamination of the aerial parts of the plant is mainly from
surface contamination due to dust or redeposition of volatilized
material from soil. Field experience with PBB indicates that
surface contamination from dust gathered during harvest of forage
crops makes a negligible contribution to residues in feed as
harvested. This concentration was less that 1% of that present
in soil (85).
        The ingestion of soil by grazing animals is apparently the

main route by which livestock take up many environmental
contaminants which are contained on particles (e.g., granular
pesticides and contaminated dust). This is in contrast with the
belief that the primary hazard is due to the ingestion of
contaminated foods or crops. Soil ingestion by cattle and sheep
has been studied under a variety of conditions (86-92). It has
been shown that soil ingestion is inversely related to the
availability of forage (82). The amount is as low as 1-2% of dry
matter intake in seasons of lush plant growth and it rises as
high as 18% in periods when forage is sparse. Under New Zealand
conditions, where animals can graze 365 days a year, average soil
intake was about 6% of the estimated dry matter intake for cattle
and 4.5% of the dry matter intake for sheep (93). The amount of
soil ingested is reduced more than 50% when animals are offered
harvested feed as a supplement to pasture (88-89).
    Farm animals also ingest soil when they are confined to
unpaved holding areas (86,91). Under typical U.S. farm
conditions, lactating cows may consume as much as 1% of their dry
matter intake as soil whereas nonlactating cattle, who have
greater exposure and are less intensely fed, may consume up to 4%
of their dry matter intake from this source. Pigs because of
their habit of rooting will tend to have higher values, which can
be as great as 8% of dry matter intake (86). Since pigs never
subsist on pasture alone, this value may be considered an upper
limit for the amount of soil ingested by pigs.
    The relationship between the concentration of TCDD in soil
and the ultimate food product is determined largely by the amount
of soil ingested by animals and this is determined in large part
by the animal management system. Farmers who primarily eat their
own livestock will be the population who will be exposed to the
highest levels of TCDD and many of them will have other sources
of meat. When estimating the amount of TCDD which could be
detected in meat or milk, several basic factors must be
considered: [a] amounts of soil ingested by the animal (yearly
averages), [b] the fat:diet ratio is usually 5:1 for milk and
body fat, [c] the amount of soil ingested should be averaged over
a year when animal access is less than a full year, [d] the
half-life of TCDD in growing cattle is 115 days, [e] the
degradation of TCDD-contaminated soil at the soil surface,
[f] rate of metabolism by the animal, and [g] soil
bioavailability in the animal. (94-99).
    Fortunately, the practical significance of soil ingestion as
a potential route of animal exposure is greatly mitigated under
the U.S. agricultural conditions. (82) Lactating dairy cows are
rarely pastured and some form of supplemental feeding is always
employed. Consequently, it is unlikely that soil ingestion would
ever exceed 1 or 2% of dry matter intake in actual farm
situations. While Fries has noted that cattle raised for beef
might often be on pastures with little other feed, it is the
general practice to fatten these animals in feed lots before
slaughter. This period of time may be as long as 150 days and
animals can gain as much as 60 to 70% in body weight. (87) TCDD
concentrations would also be reduced by dilution in the expanding
body fat pool. The role of metabolism is very important for

animals which might be eaten.  Recent data from Texas A&M (100)
indicate that the cow readily and thoroughly metabolizes TCDD - a
trait not possessed by most other species.

Most hogs destined for slaughter are confined and would
never be exposed to contaminated soil.  Thus, as noted by Fries
(82) only cull breeding cattle and pigs might be expected to go
directly from soil to slaughter and these are not the animals
ordinarily used for home consumption by farmers who raise them.
In short, for most domestic animals in the United States, few
will ever be exposed to contaminated soil without having been
provided with ample feed.  In general, only when they graze upon
soil where the dioxin level exceeds 1-20 ppb might it pose a
hazard to those persons who primarily eat their own meat
products.  For nearly all others, due to dilution with other
meats from numerous sources, as well as the other factors which
we have discussed, the risk will be de minimus.  Due to the many
factors that need to be considered, the setting of an acceptable
soil level should be done on a site specific basis.

## DISCUSSION

The selection of the most appropriate assumptions is critical in
any environmental risk assessment.  Often, as few as one, two or
three assumptions or factors can dominate the results of the
assessment.  Clearly, in the health assessment of dioxin in soil,
the most critical parameters are the quantity of soil ingested by
children and adults, the results of the mathematical modeling of
the bioassay data, consideration for dioxin's lack of
genotoxicity, and dioxin's lower bioavailability in a soil
matrix.  Other assumptions used in the assessment are also
important but generally they do not alter the results by 2-3
orders of magnitude as do those which have been discussed.

The application of more sophisticated approaches to
quantitative risk assessment for cancer and other toxic effects
such as physiological-pharmacokinetics should markedly reduce the
uncertainties in the health hazard assessment process for dioxin
(102) and these should be incorporated when available.  In
addition, regulatory decisions regarding the appropriateness of
adopting risk criteria such as 1 in 1,000,000 must be carefully
considered with respect to dioxin contaminated soil in light of
the relatively small number of persons exposed to significant
levels.  For example, most environmental and occupational
regulations that have been promulgated thus far, tend to accept
cancer risks in the region of 1 in 1,000 to 1 in 100,000 since it
is recognized that these risk assessment models are believed to
overestimate the true risks (based on human data) or because the
exposed population is so small that cost/benefit criteria
indicate that lower risks are financially impractical (102,103).

EPA has recently found the maximum individual risks and
total population risks from a number of radionuclide and benzene
sources to be too low to be properly described as "significant".
Specifically, benzene emissions from maleic anhydride process
vents created maximum individual risks of 7.6 in 100,000 and an
aggregrate yearly cancer incidence of twenty-nine thousandths of

a case (104). Radionuclides from the Dept. of Energy facilities would expose a person who accrued lifetime exposure to a plant's most concentrated emissions to a risk of 1 to 8 in 10,000, while, in the aggregate, only eight-hundredths of a cancer would be predicted to occur yearly (105). EPA found these risks to be insignificant and eventually withdrew the proposed regulations (106).

CDC, in its written assessment and in all of its public discussions on the topic, has urged that regulatory agencies understand the underpinnings of the methodology and its assumptions before clean up measures are decided upon. Use of the more justifiable assumptions, which we have discussed, should assist regulatory agencies in developing a more rational and scientifically supportable approach to the remediation of TCDD-contaminated sites (108).

In summary, the CDC assessment proposed a site-specific recommendation, not a universal standard for clean-up. CDC's analysis assumed a uniform contamination of the entire soil surface in residential neighborhoods, a situation not known to exist in Missouri or elsewhere in the United States. Further, the CDC 1 ppb guideline and risk assessment methodology were intended for application only to residential sites--not to industrial sites or other areas where the exposure to children would not occur. The present assessment indicates that, depending on the site characteristics and the use patterns, a soil concentration of TCDD considerably in excess of 1 ppb is acceptable for residential areas. Soil concentrations greater than 100 ppb in non-residential areas should amply protect the environment and public health.

Literature Cited

1.  Kimbrough, R.; Falk, H.; Stehr, P.; Fries, G. J Toxicol Env Health 1984, 14, 47-93.
2.  Schaum, J. "Risk Analysis of TCDD Contaminated Soil"; Office of Health and Environmental Assessment, U.S. Environmental Protection Agency; Washington, D.C., 1983.
3.  Houk, V. Chemosphere 1986, 15, 1875-1881.
4.  St. Louis Globe-Democrat. "Castlewood dioxin site clean-up to cost more than $12.7 million." July 20, 1985.
5.  Kay, M. Abstract 32. 196th meeting of the American Chemical Society. (Symposium on Solving Hazardous Waste Problems.) 1986.
6.  Kociba, R.J.; Keyes, D.G.; Beyer, J.E.; Carreon, R.M.; Wade, C.E.; Dittehber, D.A.; Daknins, R.P.; Frauson, L.E.; Park, C.N.; Barnard, S.D.; Hummel, R.A.; Humiston, C.G. Toxicol Appl Pharmacol, 1978, 46, 279-303.
7.  "National Toxicology Program, Technical Report #209", Research Triangle Park, NC, 1980.
8.  Portier, C.J.; Hoel, D.G.; Van Ryzin, J. In "Public Health Risks of the Dioxins", W.W. Lowrance, ed. William Kaufmann, publishers, Los Altos, Calif, 1984: Chapter 7.
9.  Walter, S.D.; Yankel, A.J.; von Lindern, I.H. Arch Env Health 1980, 35, 53-58.

10. Cooper, M. "Pica"; Charles C. Thomas Publishers. Springfield, IL, 1957; p. 65-66.
11. Charney, E.; Sayre, J.; M. Coulter; Pediatrics 1980, 65, 226-231.
12. Sayre, J.W.; Charney, E.; Vostal, J.; Pless, B. Am J Dis Child 1974, 127, 167-170.
13. Duggan, M.J; Williams, S. In "The Science of the Total Environment", 1977, 7, 91-97.
14. Lepow, M.L.; Bruckman, L.; Robino, R.A.; Markowitz, S.; Gillette, M.; Kapish, J. Environ Health Perspectives 1974, 6, 99-101.
15. Lepow, M.L.; Bruckman, L.; Gillette, M.; Markowitz, S.; Robino, R.; Kapish, J. Env Res 1975, 10, 415-426.
16. Barltrop, D. "Proceedings Inter Symp Env Health Aspects of Lead". Published by Commission of European Communities, Center for Information and Documentation, Luxembourg, 1973.
17. "Lead in the human environment". National Academy Press, 2101 Constitution Avenue NW, Washington, DC. 20418, 1980.
18. Day, J.P.; Hart, M.; M.S. Robinson. Nature 1975, 253, 343-345.
19. Bryce-Smith, D. Phys. Bull., 1974, 25: 178.
20. "Air Quality Criteria for Lead". Vol. II. U.S. Environmental Protection Agency, 1984, EPA-600/8-83-028A.
21. Hawley, J. Risk Analysis 1985, 5, 289-302.
22. Bellinger, D.; Leviton, A.; Rabinowitz, M.; Needleman, H.; C. Waternaux. Pediatrics 1986 (Submitted).
23. Binder, S.; Sokal, D.; Maughan, D. Arch. Env. Health 1987 (in press).
24. Clement Assoc., Inc. "Endangerment assessment for the Smuggler Mountain site, Pitkin County, Colorado". Prepared for the U.S. EPA (Region VIII), under Contract No. 68-01-6939, 1986.
25. O. Clausing; A.B. Brunekreef; van Wijnen, J.H.. Inter. Arch. Env. Occ. Health 1987 (in press.)
26. Russell, R.S. In "Radioactivity and human diet". (R.S. Russell, ed.) Pergamon Press Inc.: Long Island City, New York, 1966; Chapter 5.
27. "Airborne lead in perspective". National Academy of Science: Washington, D.C., 1972.
28. Romney, E.M.; Lindberg, N.G.; Hawthorne, H.A.; Bystrom, B.B.; Larson, K.H. Ann. Rev. Plant Physiol. 1963, 14, 271-279.
29. Martin, W.E. Radiation Bot. 1964, 4, 275-281.
30. Superfund Health Assessment Manual (draft). Submitted to The Office of Emergency and Remedial Response, U.S. Environmental Protection Agency. Produced by ICF Incorporated under EPA contract 68-01-6872, 1985.
31. Wolfe, H.R.; J.F. Armstrong; W.F. Durham. Mosquito News, 1974, 34, 263-267.
32. Trijonis, J.; Eldon, J.; Gins, J.; Berglund, G. Analysis of the St. Louis RAMS Ambient Particulate Data. Produced by Technology Service Corporation under EPA contract 68-02-2931 for the Office of Air, Noise, and Radiation of the U.S. Environmental Protection Agency. EPA report 450/4-80-006a, 1980.

33. Environmental Protection Agency (EPA) of Region VII.
    Correspondence from John Helvig, 1985.
34. Environmental Protection Agency (EPA). Air quality criteria
    for particulate matter and sulfur oxides. Volume 2. U.S.
    Environmental Protection Agency, Office of Environmental
    Criteria and Assessment. Research Triangle Park, N.C.
    EPA-600-8-82-029bF. 1982. P. 5-106 to 5-112.
35. Poiger, H.; C. Schlatter. Food Cosmetic Toxicol., 1980,
    18, 477-481.
36. Bartek, M.J.; LaBudde, J.A. Percutaneous absorption, in
    vitro. In "Animal Models in Dermatology". H. Maibach, ed.
    Churchill Livingston: New York, 1975; pp 103-120.
37. Wester, R.C.; Noonan, P.K. Int. J. Pharm., 1980, 7, 99-110.
38. Roels, H.; Buchet, J.P.; Lauwerys, R.R. Environ. 1980, 22,
    81-94.
39. Brunekreef, B.; Noy, D.; Biersteker, K.; Boleij, J. J. Air
    Pol Control Assn 1983, 33, 872-876.
40. Snyder, W.S. "Report of the Task Group on Reference Man".
    International Commission of Radiological Protection No. 23.
    Pergammon Press: NY, 1975.
41. Philippi, M.; Krasnobagew, V.; Zeyer, J.; Huetter, R. In
    "Microbial Cultures and Soil Under Laboratory Conditions".
    Fems Symp 1981, 12, 2210-2233.
42. Huetter, R.; Philippi, M. Pergammon Ser Environ Sci 1982, 5,
    87-93.
43. McConnell, E.; Lucier, G.; Rumbaugh, R.; Albro, P.; Harvan,
    D.; Hass, J.; Harris, M. Science 1984, 223, 1077-1079.
44. Lucier, G.W.; Rumbaugh, R.C.; McCoy, Z.; Hass, R.; Harvan,
    D.; Albro, P. Fund. Appl. Tox. 1968, 6, 364-371.
45. Umbreit, T.H.; Hesse, E.J.; Patel, D.; Gallo, M.A. Presented
    at the annual meeting of the Society of Toxicology, San Diego,
    CA (Abstract 249), 1985.
46. Umbreit, T.H.; Hesse, E.J.; Gallo, M.A. Science 1986, 232,
    497-499.
47. Umbreit, T.H.; Hesse, E.J.; Gallo, M.A. Presented at the
    annual meeting of the Society of Toxicology, New Orleans, LA
    (Abstract 1273), 1986.
48. Environmental Reporter. Bioavailability said to vary.
    June 28, 1985, p. 328.
49. Chemical Regulation Reporter. "Some assumptions used in risk
    assessment for Missouri areas were incorrect, Houk says."
    (March 18th), 1986, p. 63.
50. Bonaccorsi, A.; di Domencio, A.; Fanelli, R.; Merli, F.;
    Motta, R.; Vanzati, R.; Zapponi, G.A. Arch Toxicol. Suppl.
    1984, 7, 431-436.
51. "Health Assessment Document for Polychlorinated
    Dibenzo-p-dioxins. (Final Report)". U.S. Environmental
    Protection Agency, Office of Env. Assessment, Cincinnati,
    Ohio. EPA-600/8-84-014F, 1985b, P. 5-8 and 5-10.
52. Yanders, A.F. Presented at the Maine Department of
    Environmental Protection Dioxin Workshop. Augusta, Maine
    (Feb. 4th), 1986.
53. Di domenici, A.; Silano, V.; Viviano, G.; Zapponi, G.
    Ecotoxicol Environ Safety, 1980, 4, 298-320.
54. "Risk Assessment in the Federal Government: Managing the

Process". National Academy of Sciences, National Academy Press: Washington, DC, 1983.
55. Longstreth, J.D. and Hushon, J.M. In: Tucker, R.E., Young, A.L., Gray, A.P. eds. "Human and Environmental Risks of Chlorinated Dioxins and Related Compounds", Plenum Press: NY, 1983, p. 639-664.
56. Squire, R.A. Science 1981, 214, 877-880.
57. Tschirley, F.H. Scientific American 1985, 254, 29-35.
58. Weisburger, J.H.; Williams, G.M. Fd Cosmet Toxicol 1981, 19, 561-566.
59. Young, A. Bull Environ Contam Toxicol 1984, 33, 702-709.
60. Wassom, J.S. Mutat. Res. 1977, 47, 141-160.
61. Kociba, R.J. In: "Banbury report 18: Biological mechanisms of dioxin action". A. Poland, R. Kimbrough, ed. Cold Springs Harbor, NY, 1984, P. 73-84.
62. Kociba, R.J. Abstract #78. 5th Inter. Symposium on Dioxin and Related Compounds(Bayreuth, Germany), 1985.
63. Kociba, R.J. Chemosphere 1986, in press.
64. Shu, H.P.; Paustenbach, D.J.; Murray, F.J. Regul Toxicol Pharm. 1987, (in press).
65. EPA Proposed Guidelines for Carcinogen Risk Assessment. Federal Register 51 CFR 29844, Sep. 24, 1986, p. 33992-34003.
66. Poland, A. 1st Annual Burroughs Welcome Lecture, Meeting of the Society of Toxicology, New Orleans, LA; March 6, 1986.
67. Hussain S.; Ehrenberg, L.; Lofroth, G.; Gejvall, T. Ambio 1975, 1, 32-33.
68. Seiler, J.P. Experientia 1973, 29, 622-623.
69. California Scientific Review Panel Discussions (1985). Health effects of 2,3,7,8-tetrachlorodibenzo-p-dioxin and related compounds: Response to public comments. Department of Health Services, Berkeley, California, 1985.
70. EPA Science Advisory Board, Environmental Health Committee Transcripts. Nov. 29, 1984.
71. Park, C.; Snee, R. Fund Appl Toxicol 1983, 3, 320-333.
72. Rodricks, J.V. In "Human and Environmental Risks of Chlorinated Dioxins and Related Compounds". Tucker, R.G., Young, A.L. and Gray, A.P., Eds. Plenum Press: New York, 1983.
73. Murray, F.J.; Smith, F.A.; Nitschke, K.D.; Humiston, C.G.; Kociba, R.J.; Schwetz, B.A. Toxicol Appl Pharmacol 1978, 50, 241-251.
74. "Scientific Criteria Document for Standard Development No. 4-84: Polychlorinated Dibenzo-p-dioxins (PCDD's) and Polychbrinated Dibenzofurans (PCDF's)". Ontario Ministry of the Environment. September, 1985.
75. Whittemore, A.S.; S.C. George; Silver, A. Fund Appl Toxicol 1986, 7, 183-190.
76. Sielken, R.L. Food And Chemical Toxicology 1987, (in press).
77. Sielken, R.L.; Carlborg, F.W.; Paustenbach, D.J.; Shu, H.P.; Murray, F.J. (Abstract 1133). Presented at the 25th Annual Meeting of the Society of Toxicology. New Orleans, LA, 1986.
78. Isensee, A.R.; G.E. Jones. J. Agric. Food Chem. 1971, 19, 1210-1214.
79. Cocucci, S.; F. Di Gerolamo; A. Verderio, et al. Experientia. 1979, 35(4), 482-484.

80. Wipf, H. K.; Homberger, E.; Neimer, N.; Ranalder, U.B.; Vetter, W.; Vuilleumeir, J.P. In: "Chlorinated Dioxins and Related Compounds: Impact on the Environment", O. Hutzinger, et al., Ed. Pergamon Press: NY, 1982, p. 115-126.

81. Pocchiari, F.; A. DiDomenico; V. Silano; G. Zapponi. In "Accidental Exposure to Dioxins: Human Health Aspects", F. Coulston and F. Pocchiari, Ed. Academic Press: NY, 1983, p. 5-35.

82. Fries, G. F. (Abstract GL-02), 6th Inter. Symposium on the Chlorinated Dioxins and Related Compounds. (Fukuoka, Japan), 1986.

83. Jensen, D.J.; Getzendaner, M.E.; Hummel, R.A.; Turley, J. J. Agric. Food Chem. 1983, 31, 118-122.

84. Sundstrom, G.; Jensen, S.; Jansson, B.; K. Erne. Arch. Environ. Contam. Toxicol. 1979, 8(4), 441-448.

85. Fries, G.F.; Jacobs, L.W. Mich. State Univ. Agric. Exp. Sta. Res. Report. 1986, 477.

86. Fries, G.F.; Marrow, G.S.; Snow, P.A. Environ. Toxicol. Chem. 1982, 1,201-204.

87. Healy, W.B. N.Z. J. Agric. Res. 1968, 11,487-499.

88. Healy, W.B.; Cutress T.W.; Michie C. N.Z. J. Agric. Res. 1967, 10, 201-209.

89. Healy, W.B.; Drew, K.R. N.Z. J. Agric. Res. 1970, 13, 940-944.

90. Healy, W.B.; Ludwig, T.G. N.Z. J. Agric. Res. 1965, 8, 737-752.

91. Fries, G.F.; Marrow, G.S.; Snow, P.A. J. Dairy Sci. 1982, 65, 611-618.

92. Mayland, H.F.; Florence, A.R.; Rosenau, R.C.; Lazar, V.A.; Turner, H.A. J. Range Manage 1975, 28, 448-452.

93. Fries, G.F. J. Toxicol. Environ. Health 1985, 16, 565-579.

94. Jensen D.J.; Getzendaner, M.E.; Hummel R.A.; Turley, J. J. Agric. Food Chem. 1983, 31, 118-122.

95. Jensen D.J.; Hummel, R.A.; Mahle, N.H.; Kocher C.W.; Higgins, H.S. J. Agric. Food Chem. 1981, 29, 265-268.

96. Jensen, D.J.; Hummel, R.A. Bull. Environ. Contam. Toxicol. 1982, 29, 440-446.

97. Kocher, C.W.; Mahle, N.H.; Hummel, R.A.; Shadoff, L.A.; Getzendaner, M.E. Bull. Environ. Contam. Toxicol. 1978, 19, 229-236.

98. Jensen D.J.; Hummel, R.A.; Mahle, N.H.; Kocher C.W.; Higgins, H.S. J. Agric. Food Chem. 1981, 29(2), 265-268.

99. Fries, G.F. J. Environ. Qual., 1982, 11, 14-20.

100. Safe, S.; Ivie, D. (Abstract BP-20). 6th Inter. Dioxin Symposium (Fukuoka, Japan), 1986.

101. Andersen, M.E.; Gargas, M.; Reitz, R.A. Toxicol. Appl. Pharm 1987, in press.

102. Ruckelshaus, W.D. Vital Speeches of the Day. City News Publishing Co.: Southold, NY, April 1st, 1984.

103. Bartman, T.R. In "Quantitative Risk Assessment in regulation". L.B. Lave, Ed. The Brookings Institution Press: Washington, D.C., 1982.

104. "National Emission Standards for Hazardous Air Pollutants; Benzene Emissions from Maleic Anhvdride Plants,

Ethylbenzene/Styrene Plants, and Benzene Storage Vessels; Proposed Withdrawal of Proposed Standards", 49 Fed. Reg. 8386, 8388 (March 6, 1984) ("Benzene NESHAPS Withdrawal Notice")
105. "National Emission Standards for Hazardous Air Pollutants; Regulation of Radionuclides; Withdrawal of Proposed Standards", 49 Fed Register 43906, 43910 (Oct. 31) ("Radionuclides NESHAPS Withdrawl Notice").
106. Wreen, G. Asbestos ban and phaseout proposal. Testimony before OSHA (June 29th). Transcript available from Environ Corp, 1000 Potomac, The Flour Mill, Washington, D.C., 1986.
107. Cordle, F. Regul Toxicol. Pharm. 1981, 1,379-387.
108. Paustenbach, D.J.; Shu, H.P.; Murray, F.J. Regul Toxicol Pharm 1986, 6, 284-307.

RECEIVED February 4, 1987

# RISK MANAGEMENT: SOCIETAL FACTORS

# Chapter 15

# Solving Dioxin Contamination Problems in Missouri

**Morris Kay and Ralph Hazel**

**U.S. Environmental Protection Agency, Region VII, 726 Minnesota Avenue, Kansas City, KS 66101**

This paper discusses measures taken by U. S. Environmental Protection Agency (EPA) Region VII, to deal with the problem of dioxin contamination in Missouri. Investigations which were carried out to identify the sites of contamination are described, along with temporary measures which were taken to protect public health and the environment from the dioxin contamination. The Region's participation in an accelerated research effort to find solutions to the problem is detailed, particularly a project whereby the EPA mobile incinerator was brought to a farm site in Southwest Missouri to demonstrate its effectiveness in destroying dioxin. Finally, the paper describes cleanup activities which have been completed or are well underway as the Agency moves rapidly toward a comprehensive, final solution to the Missouri dioxin problem.

The Environmental Protection Agency (EPA) working with the state and other federal agencies has moved rapidly to clean up dioxin contamination in Missouri. Since the buy out of Times Beach in 1983, EPA has developed safe clean-up technology to remove dioxin-laden soil and destroy the dioxin by incineration. In addition, EPA has successfully removed dioxin materials from residences and streets and rehabilitated previously contaminated property.

More than 40 sites have been identified in the state of Missouri where soil is contaminated with 2,3,7,8-tetrachlorodibenzo-p-dioxin (2,3,7,8-TCDD) at levels above 1.0 parts per billion. Many of the sites resulted from dioxin-containing wastes being mixed with waste oil and sprayed as a dust suppressant. Other sites such as the Minker residential area were contaminated by using soil as fill dirt which had been sprayed for dust control and excavated and moved from a horse arena.

Knowledge of the dioxin spraying activities did not fully become known to Region VII EPA until 1982 when a full investigation was

started.   Since that time two hundred fifty-two (252) potential sites
have been investigated in the State.   In the course of these investigations, 13,593 soil samples have been collected and analyzed by
Region VII.

As dioxin contamination was found, the Region immediately proceeded with temporary measures to ensure that:   (1) People would have
very minimal contact, if any, with the dioxin-contaminated soil;
(2) Barriers were put in place to prevent contact with or subsequent migration of the contaminated soils.   Initially, families
were relocated and at Times Beach and Minker the State purchased
the properties using Superfund money;   (3) EPA Region VII immediately began studies to remove and/or destroy the dioxin and at
subsequent sites the dioxin-contaminated material was removed
safely (gathered and contained) by cleaning and vacuuming.

The contaminated sites are located in two general areas of
the State; Southwest Missouri, where the facility which was the
origin of the waste is located, and the St. Louis area in Eastern
Missouri.   The sites are located in a wide variety of residential,
industrial and rural settings, with diverse topographical and
geological compositions.   These variations combined with the
massive volumes of contaminated materials (possibly more than two
hundred thousand cubic yards) have posed a massive challenge to
EPA and the state of Missouri.

However, cleanup projects are underway in Missouri.   Cleanup
activities have been safely completed at several sites and are
well underway at a number of sites; still others are on the
drawing board with mitigation plans moving ahead rapidly.

This emerging success story is due to the efforts and talents
of several organizations.   These include the EPA, The Centers for
Disease Control, The National Institutes of Occupational Safety
and Health, the Federal Emergency Management Agency, the Missouri
Department of Natural Resources (MDNR), the Missouri Division of
Health, and several contractors including Riedel International,
IT Enviroscience, Roy F. Weston, Battelle-Northwest and $CH_2M$ Hill
in Eastern Missouri, and IT Enviroscience, Foster Wheeler Envire-
sponse and Cornejo and Sons in Southwest Missouri.

At sites in the St. Louis area where cleanup efforts are well
underway the work is being carried out under hazard mitigation
plans developed and peer reviewed as team efforts by the agencies
and firms mentioned previously(1).These plans list as key components:

Community Relations - a comprehensive effort to ensure
that affected residents, elected officials and the
public in general are kept informed of all activities
at the sites.   Initiatives such as moving an incinerator
to Southwest Missouri took a massive comprehensive
effort to ensure that citizens received consistent,
accurate technical information on a process with which
they were unfamiliar.   Components included briefings
for neighbors of the Denney Farm and local elected
officials.   A special brochure and slide show detailed
the burning process and fact sheets and photographs
gave tangible evidence of what EPA planned to do.   All
major civic organizations were included in an intensive

speaking tour. Additionally, an EPA Information
Center was established at the Denney Farm to answer
questions posed by the public. A series of Information
Center trailers at Castlewood, Quail Run, and Minker/
Stout in Eastern Missouri serve similar functions.
Regular business hours are maintained, with EPA personnel
also available on Saturday mornings (2).

Relocation - During the initial months of discovery of
individual sites, there was no alternative other than
possible relocation of some affected families to protect
human health. As EPA has learned more about the characteristics of dioxin, mitigation is now possible through
various alternatives, without long-term interruption of
family life.

Cleanup, Excavation, Transportation and Storage - Based
on health advisories from the Centers for Disease Control,
and the state health agency, contaminated materials are
excavated until no dioxin is left behind in the soil at
a cleanup level of 1 ppb and, where excavation takes
place, clean soil is put down so that people will not
come in contact with dioxin-contaminated soil. The
basic approach involves innovative excavation of 4- to
6-inch layers of contaminated material. Then the area
is sampled in a statistically verifiable manner to
assure cleanup below 1 ppb at the 95 percent confidence
level. Excavated soil is loaded into specially designed,
lined polypropylene containers and placed on plastic
sheeting for subsequent loading by crane into lined
trucks. Then loaded containers are transported to central
storage facilities. Where excavation is completed that
area is then filled back in with clean soil and revegetated.
      These storage structures meet all pertinent require-
ments of the Resource Conservation and Recovery Act
(RCRA). Each building has a concrete foundation and
catch basin, a 1,000 psi rolled asphaltic concrete
floor with sealer applied and each wood frame, steel-sided
building encloses the entire foundation area. These buildings are secured with fences which will be posted, locked
and inspected regularly by MDNR personnel. Thus, safe,
secure, temporary storage is assured until a permanent
disposal method can be planned and implemented.
      All cleanup, transportation and storage procedures
are conducted safely with methodologies to prevent
fugitive emissions or spillage. A fundamental concept
to any activity is: disturb the dioxin area only,
preserving trees and other vegetation and the general
environment wherever possible. The opened area is then
restored with clean soil and a vegetation cover.

Health and Safety - Plan prescribes the workplace practices and controls required to prevent employee exposure
to 2,3,7,8-TCDD during handling of dioxin-contaminated
materials.

Air Monitoring - An air sampling network for worker
protection and general population exposure is established as part of cleanup activities. The network
collects samples for the identification of total suspended solids and dioxin.

Contingency Plan - Outlines the procedures to be
followed in the unlikely event of any unplanned release
of hazardous materials at the site.

Structure Decontamination - Outlines a sampling plan
for contaminated buildings. Subsequently describes
cleanup procedures so that facility is cleaned until
no dioxin is detected at analytical detection levels
of 0.3 ppb or less.

Cost Summary - Outlines the budget for the project.

Concurrent with these efforts in Eastern Missouri, EPA embarked
on an accelerated research and development program to find permanent
solutions to the dioxin contamination problem. Paramount to this
effort is a project whereby the Agency's mobile incinerator was
transported from its home base in Edison, New Jersey, to the Denney
Farm site in Southwest Missouri in December 1984.
    The Denney Farm was selected for the incinerator because
approximately 90 drums of waste containing dioxin from the production
of hexachlorophene was buried in a trench on the farm. That material
had been excavated and stored on site and was readily available for
incineration. The initial mitigation of the site was performed by
EPA. Syntex, the owner of the facility where the dioxin originated,
is located only a few miles from the farm site and was willing to
do the site preparation work plus provide other dioxin-contaminated
materials for this research-oriented project.
    The mobile incinerator passed a series of trial burns (conducted
between February 25 and April 8, 1985) and attained destruction and
removal efficiencies exceeding 99.999 percent as required by RCRA
for 2,3,7,8-TCDD-contaminated materials burned in the system.
Furthermore, the waste process streams, consisting of kiln ash and
quench water, were successfully delisted.
    Following the successful completion of the trial burns, an
operating permit was issued for a full-field demonstration at the
site. On July 23, 1985, this demonstration began by feeding dioxin-
contaminated liquids and solids into the incinerator (3).
    In addition to the Denney Farm wastes, four other dioxin sites
in Southwest Missouri have been cleaned. The sites include Tally,
Rusha, Erwin and Neosho. These cleanups were carried out using
procedures similar to those previously described for sites in
Eastern Missouri. The wastes from all the Southwest Missouri sites

were taken to Denney Farm for incineration.  To date, more than two
million pounds of solids and 180,000 pounds of liquids contaminated
with 2,3,7,8-TCDD have been safely burned in the incinerator.  The
operation was temporarily halted awaiting additional Superfund
dollars.  Once burning resumes, only a few weeks are needed to
complete the materials at the Denney Farm Site.  During the
interim period an engineering study has been conducted evaluating
ways to increase the throughput and efficiency of the incinerator.
Based on the results of this study, a decision was made to make
modifications to the unit involving enlargement of the feed
system, addition of a cyclone separator, replacing the particulate
filter with a more efficient system and converting the air supply
in the secondary combustion chamber to a pure oxygen system.
     EPA is sensitive to the concerns of those residents whose
communities have been contaminated with dioxin.  We are moving
forward with cleanup activities and tremendous progress has
already been made toward our overall goal, which is a comprehensive,
final solution to the Missouri dioxin problem.

Literature Cited

(1)  Keffer, W.G.; Wurtz, S.; Newbore, G.; Howard, D.; Exner, J.H.;
     "Quail Run Hazard Mitigation Plan," U.S. EPA Region 7 Report,
     Kansas City, KS, 1984.

(2)  "Community Relations Plan, EPA Mobile Incinerator Project," U.S.
     Environmental Protection Agency, Office of Public Affairs,
     Region 7, May 1984.

(3)  Proc. 1986 Haz. Materials Spills Conference St. Louis, Mo,
     May 1986.

RECEIVED November 25, 1986

# Chapter 16

# Case Study and Proposed Decontamination of a Closed Herbicide Plant in the Federal Republic of Germany

### H.-J. Jürgens and R. Roth

Dekonta GmbH, Lotharstrasse 26, D-6500 Mainz, Federal Republic of Germany

This chapter describes the background to the closing of a $50 million chemical plant in Hamburg, Federal Republic of Germany, and proposed decontamination steps.

History

The plant, on the outskirts of Hamburg, began in 1923 as a branch for chemical pharmaceutical production of morphine and codeine. In 1951, production of herbicides began with the manufacture of hexachlorocyclohexane (HCH) and the corresponding isolation of lindane. The inactive isomers from this production were stored on site.

In 1953, recycling efforts for these waste isomers began, and thermal decomposition of these residues led to integration of several process steps (see figure). Thermal decomposition of the HCH isomers led to a 75% yield of 1,2,4-trichlorobenzene, which opened the process for production of 2,5-dichlorophenol and the corresponding bromination product. In addition to 2,5-dichloro-4-bromophenol production, the recycled trichlorobenzene was converted to 1,2,4,5-tetrachlorobenzene which could then be converted to 2,4,5-trichlorophenoxyacetic acid.

Formulation of insecticides and herbicides was carried out also.

The residues from the thermal decomposition were significantly smaller than the inactive HCH isomers. Although 2,3,7,8-TCDD content in 2,4,5-T production was known, the presence of polychlorinated dioxins in the residue from the thermal decomposition of HCH isomers was not demonstrated until 1984 (Table I).

0097-6156/87/0338-0221$06.00/0
© 1987 American Chemical Society

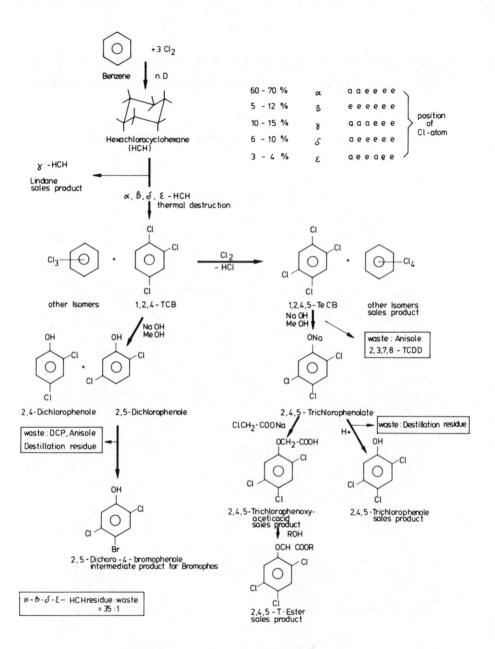

Figure 1. Recycling production of the Hamburg chemical plant.

Table I:  Analysis of the
Thermal Destruction Residue of HCH (1)

| Compound | Concentration (ppm) |
|---|---|
| 2,3,7,8-TCDD | 0.3 |
| other isomers | 12 |
| | |
| 1,2,3,7,8-Penta-CDD | 7 |
| other isomers | 200 |
| | |
| 1,2,3,4,7,8-Hexa-CDD | 45 |
| 1,2,3,6,7,8- | 150 |
| 1,2,3,7,8,9- | 65 |
| other isomers | 680 |
| | |
| 1,2,3,4,6,7,9-Hepta-CDD | 1400 |
| 1,2,3,4,6,7,8- | 3000 |
| | |
| Octa-CDD | 7600 |
| | |
| | |
| 2,3,7,8-TCDF | 13 |
| other isomers | 10 |
| | |
| 1,2,3,7,8-Penta-CDF | 1-2 |
| 2,3,4,7,8- | 15 |
| other isomers | 40 |
| | |
| 1,2,3,4,7,8-Hexa-CDF | 65 |
| 1,2,3,6,7,8- | 17 |
| 2,3,4,6,7,8- | 13 |
| other isomers | 230 |
| | |
| 1,2,3,4,6,7,8-Hepta-CDF | 370 |
| 1,2,3,4,6,7,9- | 15 |
| 1,2,3,4,6,8,9- | 100 |
| 1,2,3,4,7,8,9- | 10 |
| | |
| Octa-CDF | 200 |

Therefore, an exceptional recycling process, which converted waste HCH isomers
to useful product, led to the closing of
the lindane plant.

Plant Closing

How did it happen? The production facilities were not
outmoded since the production plant was continually
modernized according to best available technology, and
between 1980 - 1984 a total of 30 million DM were inve-
sted in environmental protection.

A major reason for the closing was pressure by the public
on government. The plant is separated by a road from a
neighborhood with many small vegetable gardens. Increased
air emissions of HCH, which led to increases of HCH in
vegetables, gained extensive media attention in 1979, although the HCH content in vegetables was not demonstrated
to be hazardous to health.

In 1981, a spectacular occupation of a stack in the plant
by Greenpeace led to the beginning of the pressure by
public interest groups and ecologists (Green Party) on the
plant and on the appropriate agencies of the Free and
Hanseatic City of Hamburg. In 1983, the attention resulting from the 41 drums of waste from Seveso, lost during
transport, led to prohibition of transport of residues
containing 2,3,7,8-TCDD in Germany. In this manner, incineration of the liquid residues at sea became eliminated
as a disposal option. Consequently, the Hamburg-Moorfleet
plant stopped production of 2,4,5-T, for which a new
building and process had been erected  in 1978. The newly
founded department of environmental protection in Hamburg
increased its search for dioxin in production, waste,
aqueous discharges, and in soil. After soil from the
plant was found to contain about 30 ppb of 2,3,7,8-TCDD,
and because of the known TCDD contents in residues from
2,4,5-T production, the company remained in the headlines.

References to the company appeared in almost every publication relating to TCDD, either municipal incinerators,
landfills, or residues in fish. When it was demonstrated
that the residue from the thermal decomposition of HCH
contained, unexpectedly, 2,3,7,8-TCDD and other polychlorinated dioxins and furans, the company was required
by the Hamburg environmental protection department to
meet the following effluent limits: TCDD contents in
residue 1 µg/kg, in air 1 pg/m³ and in aqueous discharge
1 ng/l(2).These limits, which had been suggested by Epstein
and others at the Georgswerder-Symposium, in June 1984,
were opposed by the company but upheld by the Hamburg
courts. Since these limits represented analytical detection limits in Germany, and since future lowering of the
detection levels was probable, it was uncertain whether
these values could ever be met. Consequently, production
was stopped at the site. For comparison, at the same time
the allowed emissions from two Hamburg municipal incinerators were 200 pg/m³ and 650 pg/m³ (3).

## Cleanup Plans

Dekonta is engaged in planning and carrying out appropriate measures for converting the plant site into a reusable industrial site. The project is divided into two parts, decontamination of soil and underlying areas, and cleaning and dismantling of buildings and equipment.

We are operating under the following guidelines:

- Liquid wastes containing dioxins are not allowed in normal landfills.

- Incineration in land-based facilities that are capable of destroying dioxins is not allowed by local authorities.

- Incineration at sea also cannot be permitted.

- If permits for disposal in a secure landfill could be obtained, transportation of wastes containing dioxin above 10 µg/kg is prohibited. Exceptions to this transportation prohibition are possible but not specified. Therefore, on-site destruction of liquid wastes remains the only alternative, however, specific procedures are not defined.

- Solid wastes containing dioxins can be disposed in one secure landfill, an old salt mine located at Herfa-Neurode in Hessen. There are three major restrictions:

  1. Only wastes from the Federal Republic of Germany are accepted.

  2. The landfill imposes special packaging restrictions which, in case of our wastes, double the disposal weight.

  3. The possible exception of the transportation prohibition is tied to specific packaging requirements. A distinction is made between those wastes containing greater than 10 µg/kg and those below that number.

## Soil and Groundwater

The 80,000 sq meter area has been divided into a grid and, since May 1985, 46 exploratory drillings to 30 to 60 meters and 118 drillings to 8 meter depths have been carried out. In addition, 32 wells are being drilled to 30 meter depth in the immediate vicinity of the plant site. The soil samples are being analysed for total extractable halide, specific production materials by gas chromatography,

and total PCDD's. The geological and hydrogeolocial knowledge from this investigation, coupled with the analytical results, will be the basis for a decontamination plan.

Preliminary results from the exploratory borings are:

- The plant area contains areas that are highly contaminated, with EOX values up to 284,000 ppm.

- The pollution result from chlorobenzenes, HCH,
  chlorophenols and 2,4,5-T-acid.

- A few samples from the surface area contain 2,3,7,8-
  TCDD. One sample contains 9 ppm.

- Groundwater below contaminated soil is also contaminated, 2,3,7,8-TCDD has been not detected.

- Contamination decreases markedly outside the plant.
  EOX-values in soil are generally less than 20 ppm.

- Geologic conditions limit the groundwater contamination to a reasonably well-defined plume towards
  the South.

14% of the borings at depth contain EOX at greater than
20 ppm, whereas 40% of the shallow borings have similar
contamination levels.

Soil contaminated with levels of TCDD up to 9 ppm are
subject to immediate response. About 2,000 m³ of such
soil will be excavated and placed into an interim storage
area upon approval by the Hamburg authorities. These
contaminated soils will be stored until a destruction
method becomes available. Such a method will be proposed
upon conclusion of the drilling test program. Soil decontamination methods must also take account of the building and equipment cleanup procedures.

Buildings and Equipment

Equipment is to be cleaned for off-site reuse or scrapping. Buildings are to be cleaned or demolished.

The degree of contamination of the buildings and the
equipment is being determined according to the principle
of worst case. Selection of samples from areas most likely to be contaminated will lead to the establishment of
personal protection measures and to the appropriate decontamination method. Four levels of worker protection have
been established with appropriate protective equipment:

0   no chemical contamination
ea requires normal work clothing.

A   Chemical contamination and 2,3,7,8-TCDD equivalents
< 0,01 ppm
Work in this area will be carried out in coated
Tyvex, safety shoes with booties, chemically resistant gloves, partial face mask with particulate
and organic vapor respirators, and safety glasses.

B   Chemical contamination and 2,3,7,8-TCDD equivalents
between 0,01 - 1,0 ppm
In this area, the area A procedures will be expan-
ded to include full face mask and more frequent
clothing changes.

C   2,3,7,8-TCDD equivalents greater than 1 ppm. Work
will be carried out in air-supplied suits.

Workers in the project are being monitored by a comprehensive occupational health examination on a 6-month-basis.

A comprehensive sample tracking procedure has been developed. For example, the computerised system assigns a
number which contains a sequential sample number, day and
date, coordinates according to a site grid (length,
width, level), building number, and sample type such
as:

| Sequential sample number | Day+Date | Grid-Coordinates | | | building number | sample typ |
|---|---|---|---|---|---|---|
| 200002 | MI 13.02.85 | L 272 | B 102 | H 4,6 | B250 | 02 |

Additional information is added to define the specific
piece of equipment and sample location. This procedure
will also contain information about decontamination procedures, demolition, disposition of residues, and disposition of cleaned equipment for reuse or scrapping.

Target levels were established for cleaning equipment surfaces.
These levels for normal products were proposed based on a
simple evaluation of toxicological data, such as ADI (allowable daily intake) or $LD_{50}$, and estimates of dermal contact
and potential skin adsorption (Table II).

Table II. TARGET LEVELS FOR EQUIPMENT DECONTAMINATION

| Compound | Concentration $mg/m^2$ | | |
|---|---|---|---|
| HCH | 18 | – | 77 |
| 1,2,4-Trichlorobenzene | 2000 | – | 8800 |
| 2,4,5-T-acid | 107 | – | 462 |
| 2,4,5-Trichlorophenol | 89 | – | 385 |
| 2,3,7,8-TCDD | 0,000004 | – | 0,000155 |

Cleaning and dismantling of the lindane plant will begin this summer. Although this unit contains no PCDD,
worker protection and decontamination procedures will be
established as training for cleanup of PCDD-containing
plants. Cleaning water and surface runoff will be collected and treated by filtration through an activated carbon
system that is being constructed by Dekonta. We expect to
meet or exceed the discharge criteria to the Hamburg waste
water treatment plant of 1 ng/l of TCDD.

## Literature Cited

1) Analysis was made by:

   Dr. H.R. Buser, Eidgenössische Forschungs-
   anstalt, CH-8820 Wädenswil, Schweiz

2) Freie und Hansestadt Hamburg
   Behörde für Bezirksangelegenheiten, Natur-
   schutz und Umweltgestaltung
   -Amt für Umweltschutz-
   Nachträgliche Anordnung nach § 17 BImSchG-zu den
   Genehmigungsbescheiden der Fa. C.H. Boehringer Sohn
   vom 18.06.1984

3) Bürgerschaft der Freien und Hansestadt Hamburg
   Drucksache 11/3159 vom 30.10.1984
   Mitteilung des Senats an die Bürgerschaft

RECEIVED November 25, 1986

# Chapter 17

# Military Sites Contaminated with 2,3,7,8-Tetrachlorodibenzo-p-dioxin

## Permitting Remedial Action Research

Judy N. Casanova[1] and Robert F. Olfenbuttel[2]

[1]EG&G Idaho, P.O. Box 1625, Idaho Falls, ID 83415
[2]Headquarters, Air Force Engineering Services Center, Research & Development Directorate, Environics Division, Tyndall Air Force Base, FL 32403

Recent amendments to the 1984 Hazardous and Solid Waste Act have discouraged the disposal of dioxin-containing wastes on land and encouraged the development of unique treatment technologies. The 1984 Amendments make provisions for the waiver of research development and demonstration (RD&D) permit requirements by Environmental Protection Agency regional administrators to facilitate and expedite critically needed research (pilot-scale and prototype testing). Although these regulations have been established, they have done little to speed up the permitting process. Problems and costs of RD&D permitting are discussed, together with the related issue of hazardous waste delisting. Recommendations are made to expedite the RD&D process and meet the intent of the 1984 Amendments.

The Air Force Engineering and Services Center, located at Tyndall Air Force Base, Florida, has the lead responsibility within the Air Force for conducting research and development (R&D) in a wide spectrum of environmental problem areas. Chief among these challenges is hazardous waste reduction, control, and site cleanup.

The R&D program has two thrusts: 1) Basic research and laboratory studies to establish the technical base from which innovative and cost-effective hazardous waste site cleanup technologies can be developed, and 2) field testing of promising technologies for which no performance "track record" is available. The latter includes pilot and prototype-scale demonstrations, and is the focus of this paper as it applies to 2,3,7,8-tetrachlorodibenzo-p-dioxin (TCDD).

Identifying candidate innovative and alternative technologies for dioxin-contaminated soil cleanup has not been a difficult process. Many organizations, ranging from small entrepreneurial individuals and businesses to established waste management firms, have unique approaches and ideas for solving contamination problems. The challenge has not been in selecting the most promising technologies, but in conducting field tests and evaluations (T&E)

0097-6156/87/0338-0229$06.00/0
© 1987 American Chemical Society

in a reasonable, timely fashion. Unfortunately, the current
regulatory permitting process is inconsistent, often costly, and
time consuming.

This paper discusses, through case studies, the U.S. Air
Force's (USAF) experiences with the activities, time, and costs
involved in meeting regulatory requirements to conduct small- and
large-scale technology demonstration projects under two different
governing acts and four different programs. The analysis is limited
to those activities that were part of the hazardous waste permitting
process. The results indicate a lack of economic considerations in
the current regulatory program for research, development and
demonstration (RD&D) projects for hazardous waste management.

The basic goal of environmental laws is to induce people to
withdraw, use, reuse, and discharge materials in amounts and ways
that take proper account of the damages that discharges can do to
human welfare(1). This also includes taking care of past problems
in a manner that will prevent further damage to the environment and
human health. The inefficiencies and costs currently encountered in
an effort to correct an environmental problem act as disincentives
for commercial development and application of new and better
technologies to remedy environmental problems. Furthermore, they
retard rather than expedite technology demonstration and site
rehabilitation.

## Background

During the Vietnam conflict of the 1960s and 1970s, the Department
of Defense (DOD) launched a massive defoliation program to eliminate
the vegetation used by the enemy for concealment. A herbicide
commonly known as Agent Orange was used for this program in which 11
million gallons were sprayed over 0.5 million acres of Vietnam
between 1965 and 1970.

Agent Orange was formulated to contain a 50:50 mixture of two
active ingredients: 2,4-D (2,4-dichlorophenoxyacetic acid) and
2,4,5-T (2,4,5-trichlorophenoxyacetic acid). In 1970, studies were
published which indicated that 2,4,5-T was a teratogen (a substance
which causes defects of fetal development)(2). Subsequent studies
revealed that the teratogenic effects resulted from a toxic
contaminant which was inadvertently formed in the production of
2,4,5-T. This substance was identified as TCDD.

In 1970, the Secretaries of Agriculture; Health, Education, and
Welfare; and the Interior jointly announced the suspension of
certain uses of 2,4,5-T. Subsequently, the DOD suspended use of
Agent Orange. At the time of the suspension, the USAF had a 0.85
million gallon inventory of the herbicide at the Naval Construction
Battalion Center (NCBC) in Gulfport, Mississippi. The 1.37 million
gallons in South Vietnam were moved to Johnston Island, Pacific
Ocean, in 1972.

In 1977, the USAF disposed of the entire stockpile of Agent
Orange by high-temperature incineration at sea. The disposal
project was accomplished according to requirements of the U.S.
Environmental Protection Agency (EPA) under ocean-dumping require-
ments promulgated under the Federal Water Pollution Control Act.
The approximate cost of disposal was $70 million(3).

At this time, regulation of dioxin was piecemeal and fragmented between authorities who were functioning under the Insecticide Act of 1910, the Federal Insecticide, Fungicide and Rodenticide Act of 1972, the Federal Water Pollution Control Act as amended by the Clean Water Act of 1977, the Clean Air Act as amended, the Occupational Safety and Health Act, the Consumer Product Safety Act, and the Toxic Substances Control Act of 1976 (TSCA).

Following destruction of the Agent Orange in 1977, the USAF committed to EPA a program of follow-up storage site reclamation and environmental monitoring. (Due to leakage during storage or spillage from handling, the old storage sites were contaminated with undetermined quantities of Agent Orange.) In an attempt to restore the storage sites to beneficial use, the USAF entered programs which included the following:

1. Conducting sampling and analysis programs to determine the vertical and horizontal extent of contamination of the old storage sites at Johnston Island and NCBC.

2. Selecting, field testing, demonstrating, and evaluating different dioxin destruction technologies.

3. Determining the best technology to be used for eventual cleanup of dioxin-contaminated sites.

## RD&D Experiences

**Small-Scale Demonstrations Under TSCA.** As a result of a competitive procurement, the USAF selected two promising technologies for test and evaluation at the dioxin-contaminated site on the NCBC, in Gulfport, Mississippi. The site is a USAF responsibility. These two technologies were a thermal desorption/U.V. destruction system developed by International Technologies, Inc. (IT Corporation), and an advanced electric reactor developed by the J.M. Huber Corporation. In early 1985, these two technologies were tested at the NCBC, governed by regulations promulgated under the Toxic Substances Control Act (TSCA), under the authority of the EPA's Dioxin Disposal Advisory Group. To meet the regulatory requirements for this effort, a document was assembled which explained the purpose of the project, description of the two technologies to be tested, and plans for protection of human health and the environment.

As indicated in Table I, it took a little more than two months to get the necessary approvals for conducting the experiments. Total cost for planning, preparing, and obtaining the approvals was approximately $60,000.

**Resource Conservation and Recovery Act of 1976 (RCRA) as amended by the Hazardous and Solid Waste Amendments of 1984 (HSWA).** In 1976, RCRA was passed to provide a multifaceted approach toward solving problems caused by solid waste. Salient aspects of RCRA were the expansion of the role of the federal government in the field of solid waste disposal management with particular emphasis on regulation of hazardous wastes(4).

TABLE I.   Permitting Costs for Small-Scale Demonstrations (NCBC)

Governing Act:   Toxic Substances Control Act

Regulatory Authority:   EPA Dioxin Disposal Advisory Group
                        EPA Region IV Office

| Activity | Approx. Cost* |
|---|---|
| Planning Meetings | $ 9,712 |
| Preparing Document | 34,000 |
| Preparing Presentations | 2,000 |
| Conducting 3 Presentations | 8,500 |

Lag Times:   The activities for obtaining                6,000
approvals were initiated in March 1985 and the
demonstrations began in May 1985, resulting in
a lag-time equipment lease cost of $6,000.

                              Total Cost:    $60,212

*Cost estimates include labor, G&A, overhead, materials, and travel
costs.   They do not include contractor fees, which were not applicable.

    In 1984, the President signed HWSA into law.   The Amendments
made many changes to the existing EPA hazardous waste management
program developed under the Resource Conservation and Recovery Act
(RCRA) of 1976.   Significantly, the Amendments reflect the intent of
Congress to encourage innovative research and development of
advanced technology for destroying hazardous wastes.   Section
3005(g) gives EPA the authority to issue research, development and
demonstration (RD&D) permits, without promulgation of permitting
regulations (under Part 264) that would establish standards for
technologies or processes that treat hazardous waste in an
innovative and experimental manner.   In addition, the EPA may modify
or waive the permitting and technical requirements applicable to
other types of hazardous waste management facilities as long as:   1)
human health and the environment are protected; 2) financial
responsibilities are maintained; and 3) public participation
requirements are fully adhered to.
    In 1985, management of dioxins was transferred from TSCA to
authority under RCRA, as amended by HSWA.   The new Amendments also
added paragraph 3001(f), establishing specific criteria and
procedures for delisting petitions.   In addition, permitting
authority was delegated to the Regional EPA Offices.
    As codified in 40 CFR 270.65, these RD&D permits were conceived
to aid in the development of safe alternatives to land disposal of
hazardous waste, a primary goal of the Amendments, by expediting the
permitting process to demonstrate the technical and/or economic
feasibility of experimental and innovative technologies and
processes.   Indeed, the EPA Director of the Office of Solid Waste
stated that processing RD&D permits is "one of our highest

priorities, as indicated in both the National Permits Strategy and the RCRA Implementation Plan for FY86"(5).

The goal of expediting everything, however, has not been realized in a consistent manner. The USAF changed its program to comply with these regulations and to continue with testing and demonstrating technologies that would develop the most effective and cost-beneficial method to clean up the dioxin contamination. This resulted in inconsistent response among regional EPA offices, extraordinary delays in permitting some activities, and concomitant high costs which threaten the viability of some projects. The problems described below also apply to the EPA R&D community as well, and must be resolved if the intent of Congress is to be realized and the challenge of contaminated sites restoration is to be effectively met.

Case Study 1: A Small-Scale Demonstration Under RCRA. As discussed previously, two technologies were tested and evaluated at the NCBC, Mississippi in mid-1985. The approval process went smoothly and quickly under TSCA. Preliminary data indicate that the systems were capable of reducing the level of dioxin in soil to less than 1 part per billion.

The apparent success of the systems led to a decision to continue testing the IT Corporation technology at Johnston Island, in the Pacific Ocean, as originally planned. The Johnston Island site offered a different soil matrix and further opportunity to characterize the maintainability and reliability of the system.

Permitting of this single technology demonstration fell under the jurisdiction of EPA Region IX and the RCRA system. Table II presents the activities and costs to date (September 1986) under RCRA requirements. The following discussion refers to activities listed in Table II and is instructive with regard to requirements and difficulties.

1. (See 1, Table II)   Under RCRA, generators of hazardous waste must obtain an identification number from the appropriate EPA Regional Office (EPA Form 3510-1).

2. (See 2, Table III)   Under RCRA, certain projects can be designated as RD&D projects (Hazardous and Solid Waste Amendments of 1984). Specific requirements to obtain a permit for an RD&D project are up to the discretion of each EPA region. Therefore, requirements can vary greatly from region to region, or where applicable, from state to state.

3. (See 4, Table II)   Each project is assigned a permit writer in the appropriate EPA Regional Office. For an RD&D permit, EPA is not required to respond within legal time limits. Because of the time constraints placed on the assigned permit writer, and the low priority given RD&D projects in this region, it became necessary to use a large portion of the budget for travel in order to meet with the permit writer in efforts to expedite the permit process.

4. (See 6, Table II)   This activity is the result of regulatory complications. EPA published regulations in 1985(6) which specifically required that dioxin-contaminated soil which had been thermally treated to remove dioxin would still be considered a hazardous waste (F027 and F028 wastes). This meant that the treated soil would have to be placed into appropriate containers and sent to

TABLE II.  Permitting Costs for Small-Scale Demo (Johnston Island)

Governing Act:  Resource Conservation & Recovery Act, (as amended)

Regulatory Authority:  EPA Regional Office

| Activity | Approx. Cost* |
|---|---|
| 1. Submit application for notification of Hazardous Waste Activity | $ 2,000 |
| 2. Assemble and submit Research, Development, and Demonstration permit application | 17,500 |
| 3. Obtain EPA comments | 2,000 |
| 4. Respond to EPA comments/requests | 17,250 |
| 5. Revise and resubmit permit application | 2,000 |
| 6. Submit application for waste storage facility | 300 |
| 7. Respond to Freedom of Information (FOI) request | 1,000 |
| 8. Respond to additional EPA comments/requests | 6,250 |
| 9. Revise and resubmit permit application | 1,000 |
| 10. Resubmit Notification of Hazardous Waste Activity and interim storage application forms | 500 |
| 11. Efforts expended to expedite permit issuance | 2,000 |
| 12. Meet with Region IX to discuss draft permit | 5,000 |
| 13. Revise and resubmit permit application | 1,000 |
| 14. Participate in public hearings | 24,500 |
| 15. Respond to Regional Counsel on FOI request | 4,300 |
| 16. Time lags:  The permitting activities listed above were begun in April 1985.  The start date will be June 1986.  Thus, costs to transport equipment, associated equipment rental, and additional costs incurred to reschedule and replan were $48,080. | 48,080 |

Total Cost:  $134,680

*Cost estimates include labor, G&A, overhead,  materials, and travel
costs.   They do not include contractor fees, which were not applicable.

TABLE III:   Permitting Costs for a Full-Scale Demonstration

Governing Act:   Resource Conservation and Recovery Act of 1976
                 (as amended)

Regulatory Authority: EPA Region IV Office
                      EPA Headquarters, Office of Solid Waste
                      Mississippi State Bureau of Pollution Control

| Activity | Approx. Cost* |
|---|---|
| 1. Planning Meetings for RD&D permit | $ 19,325 |
| 2. Meeting to initiate delisting activities | 11,325 |
| 3. Preparation of RD&D permit application | 22,500 |
| 4. Preparation of Delisting Petition form | 25,000 |
| 5. Meet with State officials | 4,500 |
| 6. Meet with EPA Regional officials | 4,500 |
| 7. Meet with EPA Headquarters officials | 4,500 |
| 8. Submit Notification of Hazardous Waste Activity | 1,000 |
| 9. Prepare Environmental Assessment | 10,000 |
| 10. Resolve EPA and State comments | 4,250 |
| 11. Revise and resubmit permit application | 2,000 |
| 12. Support public information activities | 8,382 |
| 13. Continue resolution of issues and submission of information for delisting process | 25,000 |
| 14. Incorporate delisting criteria into RD&D test plans | 7,000 |
| 15. Lag time | |
| Total Cost: | $149,282 |

*Cost estimates include labor, G&A, overhead, materials, and travel
costs.  They do not include contractor fees, which were not applicable.

permitted hazardous waste disposal facilities for final disposal.
These rules create the following problems:

a.   Although EPA has published rules to allow the disposal
of dioxin-containing waste at interim status facilities, to our
knowledge there are no disposal facilities which are currently
accepting such waste. This creates another permitting impass.

b.   Without the ability to dispose of treated soil, a
storage permit must be obtained to allow for storage of the treated
soil until an appropriate disposal facility is established or until
regulations are adjusted. EPA Form 3510 was submitted to Region IX.

Because no "de minimus" limit has been established as to when
something contaminated with dioxins is considered "clean," there is
no method to prove the material has been treated to an acceptable
limit. Therefore, there is no economic benefit to clean up a large
quantity of soil contaminated with F027 wastes if it must be managed
as a hazardous waste after treatment. The only recourse available
is to pursue "delisting" of the treated soil through EPA
Headquarters, Office of Solid Waste - that is, to go through a
petitioning process in which one attempts to prove to EPA that the
soil can be placed back on the ground without harm to human health
or the environment.

c.   The delisting process usually takes a minimum of one
year to complete. As of September 1986, EPA had approved nine
delisting petitions, including the EPA's Mobile Incineration System
use at Denney Farms in McDowell, Missouri(7).

At the moment, an RD&D permit must be obtained to legally
perform this technology demonstration. In order to perform the
demonstration, a storage permit must be obtained to legally store
wastes until the wastes can be legally disposed of or legally
delisted or until the regulations are changed, whichever comes
first.

5.   (See 7, Table II)  A copy of the USAF RD&D permit
application was requested from the EPA by another party under the
Freedom of Information (FOI) Act. To protect confidential process
information, a Confidentiality Claim was filed with Region IX.

6.   (See 8,9, Table II)  Five months after the resubmission of
the permit application, the EPA Regional Office submitted a second
set of comments and requirements. The permit application was
revised and submitted a third time.

7.   (See 10, Table II)  The application forms from Items 1 and
6 could not be located at the Regional Office. Both were
resubmitted.

8.   (See 13, Table II)  Following the meeting with Region IX
to discuss the draft permit, it was agreed that the permit
application would be revised and resubmitted; and that another
version with the revisions and confidential information blacked out
would also be submitted.

9.   (See 15, Table II)  In June 1986, notification was received
that the response to the FOI request submitted in August 1985 had
been submitted for review to the Regional Counsel's Office. Considerable effort was expended responding to questions and reevaluating
information to obtain approval for the "confidentiality" claim.

10.  (See 16, Table II)  After review of the second submittal
of the permit application, a draft permit was estimated to be

forthcoming in October 1985. Because equipment transport to
Johnston Island takes about one month, the equipment was en route to
the project site before the numerous delays occurred; therefore,
equipment rental costs have been incurred since September 1985.
Since additional transport costs have been incurred because of the
significant permit process delay, these additional costs are
included in the permit process.

Discussion

The total costs in Tables I and II may be misleading in that Table I
is the total cost for conducting two technology demonstrations, and
the total costs in Table II are for only one demonstration. If the
regulatory programs had been somewhat consistent, one could expect
the costs in Table II to be about one-half of those in Table I.
However, the costs are 2.2 times higher.

The goal of such regulatory programs is to protect human health
and the environment. Because we believe that efforts to protect
human health and the environment were equivalent under both the TSCA
and RCRA demonstrations, it does not appear that accomplishing this
goal is more effective under RCRA than TSCA.

Additionally, based on the preceding data, the goals of the RD&D
permit process, which are to expedite the development of land
disposal alternatives and simplify the permit application and
issuance process, are not being met. Not only are the goals not
being met, it would seem fair to say that the complexity of the
present hazardous waste management system is promoting economic
inefficiencies which cannot be justified.

Case Study 2: Full-Scale Demonstration. A third technology demonstration project is currently being pursued. Although similar in
nature to the previously mentioned demonstrations, different
regulatory problems are being encountered with this RD&D project.

Thermal treatment appears to be the most readily available
remedial action technology for dioxin. However, no data are available to confirm the maintainability, reliability and cost-effectiveness of transportable commercial systems. Through a competitive
process, the USAF selected ENSCO Corporation for a full-scale field
test of their rotary-kiln combustor. The test will be conducted at
the NCBC, Mississippi and will involve treatment of approximately
9000 cubic yards of contaminated soil. An intense analytical
program and engineering failure mode analysis will support the
project. Testing is planned for November 1986 - March 1987.

Permitting of this single technology demonstration fell under
the jurisdiction of EPA Region IV, whose staff has been outstanding
in attitude and actions. Table III summarizes the actitivies and
costs as of September 1986.

The following provides additional information on selected
activities listed in Table III.

1. (See 1, Table III) The cost for the planning meetings is
somewhat misleading in that the original planning meetings took
place on Johnston Island, where the full-scale demonstration was
originally planned to take place. However, because of the problems
already encountered, and the associated costs with Region IX and the

higher costs of conducting a demonstration on Johnston Island, the
demonstration was replanned for NCBC.

2. (See 2, Table III)  As mentioned in Table II, dioxin-
contaminated soil which has undergone thermal treatment must still
be managed as a hazardous waste (i.e., properly disposed of at a
permitted hazardous waste facility).  The only alternative available
for this project was to petition EPA Headquarters, Office of Solid
Waste for delisting of the treated soil.  Because the draft guidance
manual for RD&D Permits places a ceiling on the maximum amount of
hazardous waste stored at any time for experimental purposes,
obtaining a storage permit pending delisting would not be useful;
therefore, delisting must be obtained.  However, to follow delisting
procedures, test burns of the machine and feedstock must be
conducted and data from those tests evaluated before issuance of
delisting.  This would mean a downtime of several months from test
burn to official delisting.

3. (See 9, Table III)  Because of the size of the full-scale
demonstration project, an Environmental Assessment was prepared to
fulfill National Environmental Policy Act requirements.

4. (See 15, Table III)  The RD&D permit application was
submitted to Region IV and the State of Mississippi on January 21,
1986.  The final permit was received July 2, 1986.  Lag-time costs
will be incurred for this project.  However, these costs will be a
result of the delisting process, rather than the RD&D permit
process.

Table IV compares the costs and time involved in the RD&D
permitting process in two different EPA regions.

TABLE IV.  PERMITTING PROCESS COMPARISON

|  | Small Scale Demo<br>Region IX | Large Scale Demo<br>Region IV |
|---|---|---|
| Permit application (original) | $17,500 | $22,500 |
| Comment resolution | 19,250 | 4,250 |
| Resubmission | 2,000 | 2,000 |
| Comment resolution | 6,250 | ----- |
| Resubmission | 1,000 | ----- |
| Comment resolution | 5,000 | ----- |
| Resubmission | 1,000 | ----- |
| (does not include public<br>hearing process) | $52,000 | $28,750 |
| Notification of Hazardous<br>Waste Activity) | 2,000 | 1,000 |
| Resubmittal | 250 | ----- |
| TOTAL | $54,250 | $29,750 |
| TIME: | 13 Months | 5 Months |

## Delisting: A Serious Issue Requiring Change

Researchers face significant potential time delays and costs associated with "delisting" the output of the treatment systems. As already mentioned, HSWA added paragraph (f) to section 3001 establishing specific criteria and procedures for delisting petitions. This requires the EPA to consider additional factors, such as constituents other than those for which the waste was listed, if the Agency believes there is a reasonable likelihood that the additional factors could cause the waste to be hazardous.

Although the delisting petition process was established around regular RCRA treatment operations and/or production facilities, it is presently being applied to RD&D with adverse consequences. Delisting is of particular concern because we are dealing with: 1) soils containing listed F027 substances and constituents which are identified as acutely hazardous wastes; and 2) the treated soil resulting from the demonstration which is specifically listed as an F028 waste, i.e., residues from the incineration or thermal treatment of soil contaminated with dioxin(6).

The rationale for requiring delisting is reasonable in relation to regular treatment operations. However, for RD&D the process must be streamlined and the risk for investors reduced. Currently, a demonstration project must be stopped soon after it has started in order to submit laboratory data on the products of the treatment process, via a formal "delisting petition" to HQ EPA. The downtime engendered by this sequence is expensive, particularly when it involves a full-scale incinerator at a cost of thousands of dollars per day. Added to this is the uncertainty of criteria for the delisting and the fact that EPA has up to 24 months to grant or deny the petition. Taken together, these factors create the potential for pushing the proposed demonstration beyond acceptable cost risk. It will take very few experiences of this type to discourage further contributions to technology development by investors both within government agencies and the entrepreneurs upon whom society depends for innovative ideas.

The issue of delisting is currently being considered on a specific and generic basis by legal counsel and the Waste Identification Branch at HQ EPA. Delisting could be expedited by the following suggested process: EPA establish a delisting standard in advance of the demonstration start. This standard can be based on laboratory and pilot scale data. The delisting standard would be published in the Federal Register and subject to a formal public comment period. The EPA reviews the comments and issues a formal delisting action that would be contingent on the petitioner demonstrating that the treated soil did, in fact, meet the delisting standard. This scenario would minimize the downtime of equipment at the demonstration site since the formal process involved with delisting would be completed prior to project start. Verification of waste residues' quality would be the only step necessary and should be accomplished rapidly by EPA.

As of September 1986, EPA's guidance on delisting was contained in EPA publication 530-SW-85-003(8).

Contents of RD&D Permit Applications

When the permit application was submitted to Region IX, guidance did
not exist on contents of an RD&D permit application.  For the
purpose of the first technology demonstrations, an outline was
submitted to EPA's Dioxin Disposal Advisory Group (DDAG) for the
proposed contents.  This outline was acceptable to both DDAG and the
State of Mississippi, and was therefore used as a guide for the
contents of the RD&D permit application to Region IX.

This resulted in some problems with the EPA.  EPA believed that
some items in the application were extraneous, while others were
omitted.  Because reviews were performed by different offices within
EPA and at different times, several rounds of comments required
resolution.

Table V presents the major sections from the Table of Contents
of the USAF RD&D permit applications.  It contains all the
significant information required by the draft guidance document for
RD&D permits issued from EPA Headquarters(5).

The most recent permit guidance (September 1986) is contained
in Office of Solid Waste and Emergency Response (OSWER) Policy
Directive No. 9527.00-1A(9).

TABLE V.  Major Headings for Contents of RD&D Permit Application

---

Executive Summary

Introduction and Background (includes site description)

Process Description (includes process monitoring, inspection and
    maintenance, and test plan)

Process Validation (includes technology assessment and process
    confirmation)

Emergency and Contingency Plan

Health and Environmental Protection

Monitoring Plans (includes independent verification and QA/QC
    plans)

Financial Responsibility

Closure and Equipment Decontamination Plan

Public Relations

Personnel Qualifications

Appendices Sampling and Analysis Matrix and Assessment of Part 264
    requirements

---

## Conclusions

The difficulties experienced in seeking RD&D permits are related to a number of factors. The EPA Administrator has delegated permit authority to each of the Regional Administrators. However, a demonstrated inconsistency among these authorities and/or their staffs regarding their willingness to issue or waive permits indicates that regional sensitivities are sufficiently strong to override the national intent of the HSWA legislation. It also indicates that guidance from HQ EPA is not firm enough to foster an equal opportunity for obtaining permits around the country.

In addition, it appears that the size and capabilities of some staffs are insufficient to handle the permit process in a timely manner. To apparently mitigate this difficulty, HQ EPA has arranged for assistance from both the Alternative Technologies Division at the Office of Research and Development in Cinncinnati, Ohio and the Headquarters Permit Assistance Team (PAT). Although these resources add expertise to permit application reviews, they also can add time to a process which is already too long. As discussed in these case studies, the turnaround time from original application to issuance of a draft permit in Region IX took 13 months. Contrast this with the office in Region IV which had the willingness and staff capability to process and award a permit in 150 days.

The expense involved in waiting for permit application approval is significant; in addition, the wait endangers the availability of funds for the project and creates a veritable logjam of other hazardous waste treatment projects scheduled for test and evaluation.

The major problem is that broad preliminary requirements were issued in the beginning. The dioxin research program was developed in a "crisis" atmosphere, resulting "in instability and some hasty decisions that, in hindsight, may need to be changed."(10,11) In a similar way, the regulated community's approach to dioxin management was developed under a framework of "hurry-up" legislation. In attempting to live with these regulations, researchers find that they have been written into a corner shared by authorities who are also struggling for guidance and well-defined direction. Unless effective changes are made to the permitting and delisting process, not only will we find it difficult to meet our own environmental cleanup requirements, but such major programs as EPA's proposed Superfund Innovative Technology Evaluation (SITE) may never get off the ground.

Because of the rapidly evolving hazardous waste regulations, it is difficult if not impossible, to predict the effects each new rule or promulgation of regulations will have on a particular project. Dioxins and similar compounds have been hit especially hard by several iterations of new rulemaking. Perhaps the best lesson to be learned from the subject technology demonstrations is that a very careful assessment of the regulatory authorities involved should be a first step in initiating a new project. Personnel involved, their willingness to work with people, and general policy and atmosphere of the Region and/or State involved can be a very good indicator of the potential of overcoming regulatory problems which, at this time, determine whether or not a project can occur.

## Recommendations

The difficulties discussed in this paper are certainly the product
of an immature program and participants must provide constructive
recommendations to improve the system wherever possible.  Therefore,
the following recommendations are offered to EPA for promoting RD&D
projects:
 1. Centralize RD&D permitting at HQ EPA Office of Research and
Development (EPA/ORD); or adopt a mandatory guideline for regional
RD&D permitting.
 2. Modify the RCRA regulations to accommodate timely issuance
of RD&D permits including a shortened timeframe for final permit
award (e.g., 90-120 days).
 3. Modify RD&D permit requirements to allow federal agencies
to conduct RD&D on federal property.  The federal agencies would
comply with the "intent" of RCRA without participating in the formal
permitting process.
 4. Modify "delisting" procedures and criteria to expedite the
RD&D process.
 Centralization of RD&D permitting at EPA/ORD would add a
national perspective to the RD&D permitting process, something that
is currently missing.  Additionally, shifting the permitting to HQ
EPA would eliminate much of the regional sensitivities and politics.
Realistically speaking, this approach has little chance of
adoption.
 The adoption of a mandatory permitting suspense of 90-120 days
would greatly shorten the time required in some regions to obtain an
RD&D permit.  Adequate staffing must be provided to accomplish this
option.  Federal agencies, including EPA's own research groups,
should be allowed to conduct timely, problem solving research and
development on federally owned facilities without the need for
formal RCRA permitting.  The federal agencies should only be tasked
to comply with the intent of RCRA to protect the environment and
public health, while allowing for adequate public participation.
Allowances for RD&D should also be made in other associated
regulations.
 The delisting change would minimize the expensive downtime of
equipment and dedicated manpower at the demonstration site since the
lengthy formal process involved with delisting would be completed
prior to project start.
 The alternatives discussed will significantly improve the time-
liness of RD&D permitting under RCRA.  Without these changes we will
not have sufficient innovative, proven cost-effective technolology
options to choose from when a ban on land disposal takes effect.

## Literature Cited

1. Mills, E.S., The Economics of Environmental Quality, W.W. Norton
 & Company, Inc., New York, 1978.
2. Doull, J., Klaassen, C.D., Amdur, M.O., eds., Casarett and
 Doull's Toxicology.  MacMillan Publishing Co., Inc., New York,
 1980.
3. Goldstein, E.C., ed., Social Issues Resources Series, Pollution,

Vol. 3, Articles 1-100, 1980-1984, SIRS Inc., Boca Raton, Florida, 1985.

4.  Arbuckle, J.G., Frick, F.W., Miller, M.L., Sullivan, T.F.P., and Vanderver, T.A., Jr., Environmental Law Handbook, Sixth Edition, Government Institutes, Inc., Washington D.C., 1979.

5.  Memorandum from Marcia E. Williams, Director, Office of Solid Waste, to Hazardous Waste Division Directors, Hazardous Waste Branch Chiefs, Hazardous Waste Section Chiefs, Regions I-X, Oct 3, 1985, Subject: Research, Development, and Demonstration (RD&D) Permits.

6.  Federal Register, Monday, January 14, 1985, Part II, Hazardous Waste Management System; Dioxin-Containing Wastes; Rule.

7.  The Bureau of National Affairs, Environmental Reporter, August 22, 1986, EPA Grants Final Exclusion From RCRA for Wastes Generated at Eight Facilities, p. 611, BNA, Washington D.C., 1986.

8.  U.S. EPA Office of Solid Waste, Petitions to Delist Hazardous Wastes - A Guidance Manual, EPA/530-SW-85-003, April 1985, NTIS Number PB85-194488.

9.  U.S. EPA Office of Solid Waste, Guidance Manual for Research, Development, and Demonstration Permits Under 40 CRD Section 270.65, EPA/530-SW-86-008, July 1986, NTIS Number PB86-229192.

10. The Bureau of National Affairs, Environmental Reporter, February 7, 1986, Research, p. 1838, BNA, Washington D.C., 1986.

11. Hazardous Waste News, Vol. 8, No. 7, February 17, 1986, Business Publishers, Inc., Silver Spring MD, 1986.

RECEIVED November 25, 1986

# RISK MANAGEMENT: TECHNOLOGY

# Chapter 18

# Risk-Qualified Mapping of Polychlorinated Dibenzodioxin Contamination

R. C. Bryan[1] and D. E. Splitstone[2]

[1]Geostat Systems, Inc., P.O. Box 1193, Golden, CO 80402
[2]International Technology Corporation, Regional Office, William Penn Plaza, 2790 Mosside Boulevard, Monroeville, PA 15146-2792

Nonparametric geostatistics is a useful tool for the adequate assessment of the magnitude and spatial distribution of alleged contamination at a potential hazardous waste site. The resulting mappings of expected contamination as well as risks of making incorrect remedial decisions can support the development of effective and cost-controlled site remediation. Because of the nature of 2,3,7,8-tetrachlorodibenzo-p-dioxin (TCDD) in soils, traditional geostatistical techniques provide little assistance in producing risk qualified mappings of site contamination. Nonparametric geostatistical techniques used to estimate the conditional probability distribution of an unknown concentration provide the means to produce such meanings. Using an "indicator" transformation of actual site TCDD data, these techniques are illustrated. This approach has several outstanding features:

o   It is distributed free and resistant to outlier data; hence, it can be applied to data sets whatever the shape of the site data histogram.

o   It results in confidence intervals which are not only data configuration dependent but also data values dependent.

o   It is reasonably simple in its application and has performed well in the example site investigation.

An industrial site contaminated with polychlorinated dibenzodioxin (PCDD) presents a set of complex problems to those charged with the assessment of site contamination and the development of a remediation plan. In the suite of PCDD compounds, TCDD is of particular concern. The U.S. Environmental Protection Agency (U.S. EPA) has designated TCDD as a potent animal carcinogen and very acutely toxic(1).

0097-6156/87/0338-0246$06.00/0

The first decision to be made from the results of a site assessment and subsequent risk analysis is whether to remediate a site or leave the contamination in situ. Frequently, site remedial alternatives may result in greater environmental risks than in situ containment. The evaluations of remedial alternatives often hinge on one's ability to accurately map the magnitude and extent of contamination at a site. Such mappings should also support an assessment of the risk or probability of not remediating a contaminated area of the site and the risk of unnecessarily remediating a noncontaminated area. The former probability may be associated with public health consequences; the latter can be linked to the unnecessary expenditure of remediation dollars. The application of geostatistical techniques to the mapping of site contamination can provide mappings which satisfy these desired objectives.

Zirshky, et al.(2), present an extensive review of classical geostatistical concepts as they apply to hazardous waste investigations. The basic concept of geostatistics is often referred to as the theory of regionalized variables. Briefly summarized, this theory states that observations which are close together are similar and the similarity between observations decreases as the distance between points of observation increases. The geostatistical measure of similarity among observations is one-half of the square of the difference between measurements taken a fixed distance apart. If the measure of similarity is averaged over all pairs of points a fixed distance apart and calculated over a range of distance separations between points, a graphical representation of the spatial similarity among observations can be constructed. This graphical representation is known as the variogram. An idealized variogram is presented in Figure 1.

Because some understanding of the information and geostatistical concepts presented by the variogram is required for an understanding of the application presented in this paper, a few of these concepts will be briefly presented. The idealized variogram presented in Figure 1 clearly illustrates the concept of spatial similarity mentioned above. As it is unlikely that observations taken close together will be exactly the same, the variogram model does not reach the distance axis (zero variation between points) at zero distance separation. This portion of the variation among observations is commonly referred to as the nugget and represents random variation which may be due in part to sampling and measurement variability. As the distance between observations becomes larger, the variogram approaches the "sill" which represents the total variability among the observations over the entire site. The distance at which the variogram reaches the sill is known as the "range."

Characterization of the variogram from actual observations permits the estimation of concentrations at points on the site which were not sampled by application of generalized least-squares type statistical regression algorithms. This type of estimation has come to be referred to as "kriging"(2). Thus, once the similarity of observations with distance has been described in terms of the variogram, contamination across the site can be estimated and mapped.

For the typical site, characterization of the spatial similarity relationship among TCDD concentrations in soils in terms of the variogram is complicated by the very nature of TCDD. TCDD is tightly bound to soils containing a high organic content and is therefore not mobile in soil. Kearney, et al.(3), observed that the mobility of TCDD decreased with increasing organic content of soil. Similar conclusions were reached by Matsumura and Benezet(4) who showed that the mobility of TCDD is much slower than that of dichlorodiphenyltrichloroethane (DDT). Ward and Matsumura(5) observed that the concentrations of TCDD in waters separated from a contaminated lake bottom sediment exceeded its water solubility (0.2 parts per billion [ppb]). The report suggests this may be due to the binding or adsorption of TCDD onto organic matter or suspended sediment particles.

Jackson, et al.(6), examined the leaching potential of TCDD-contaminated soils from various sites. Soil partition coefficients were large (the mean log $K_d$ for two samples was 5.9 and 6.02), indicating that TCDD is only very slightly soluble and that only very small amounts of TCDD will be released into water. The authors concluded that the rates of TCDD movement in soils are so slow that other transport mechanisms such as wind and water erosion are likely to be more significant.

Once TCDD reaches the soil, it will not spread in the absence of a solvent other than by some mechanical means. On an industrial site, the initial deposition of TCDD in soil quite likely resulted from accidental spills. Thus, it is easy to envision a situation where measurement of TCDD concentrations across the site reveals very few "high" concentrations and many concentrations are observed as "low" or not detected. Further, one can easily envision that both "high" and "low" measured concentrations might occur within a confined spatial volume of soil. Such is the case with the industrial site used as an example here.

The example site is located in the northeastern United States in an area that has been industrialized since the 1870s. The site occupies approximately four acres and is surrounded by other industrial facilities. Since the early 1900s, agricultural chemicals have been produced on the site by several manufacturers. For a period of time in the 1950s and 1960s, these chemicals included 2,4,5-trichlorophenoxyacetic acid (2,4,5-T). TCDD is a by-product of 2,4,5-T production and in reality is a product contaminant. Thus, it is plausible to consider TCDD being deposited at the site in the course of product spills and leaks. A major industrial accident occurred at the site some 20 years ago and subsequent reconstruction activities can be hypothesized to have a significant effect on the current deposition of TCDD at the site.

Samples of soil from the site indicated that TCDD concentrations of over 10,000 ppb were present. This discovery initiated further sampling to ascertain the extent and magnitude of contamination. Thirty near-surface (0 to 2 feet) borings were taken across the site to investigate the vertical and horizontal extent of TCDD contamination. Several deeper borings were also performed. The sampling program was designed to locate borings in areas suspected of contamination. Over 100 analyses for TCDD were performed which indicated that TCDD concentrations ranged from 0.02 to 19,500 ppb.

The frequency distribution of the TCDD concentration data from the example site is presented in Figure 2. Note that the concentration scale in this figure is logarithmic, implying that a highly skewed frequency distribution is represented.

While the frequency distribution presented in Figure 2 might suggest that geostatistical analysis may be applied to the data after a logarithmic transformation, a closer examination of the data indicates that this is not the case. The observed concentrations for pairs of observations at the same depth and within as little as 60 feet of each other vary by orders of magnitude. The unhappy consequence of this is that the large variability among observations which are close together is reflected in the nugget of the variogram. This is true even if the logarithmic transformation is applied to the data. Thus, the geostatistical description of the similarity relationship among observations as a function of their distance apart would appear to be compromised. In addition, the use of "block kriging" to estimate the average concentration within a reasonable size remediation unit or "block" would appear to be inappropriate as the estimated "block" average would not reflect the physical reality unless the "block" size was chosen to be very small. Attempts at describing the within-block variability in terms of a convenient distributional assumption, say of a log-normal distribution, would also appear to be fruitless as the within-block variation is not proportional to the mean block concentration. Therefore, standard geostatistical techniques appear to be of little value in accomplishing the objective mapping of contamination in this situation.

Journel[7-9] provides a means for generating the desired mappings in situations such as the example site which are free from any undue assumptions regarding the distributional form of concentrations within blocks. This approach simply transforms the data into the sample cumulative probability distribution. This nonparametric geostatistical approach is sometimes called "indicator kriging."

The objective of indicator kriging is to estimate the local distribution of TCDD concentrations rather than the concentrations themselves. To apply indicator kriging, the data must be transformed from the original measurements of concentrations into indicator variables. This is accomplished by letting $z(x_a)$, a=1, N represent the initial data set

where

$z(x_a)$ = the TCDD concentration at datum location $x_a$, which is interpreted as a realization of the random variable, $Z(x_a)$

$x_a$ = the location of the datum in space, given in three-dimensional coordinates, and

N = the total number of data.

The indicator transform of the datum, $z(x_a)$, is defined as:

$$i(x_a:z) = \begin{cases} 1, & \text{if } z(x_a) \text{ F } z \\ 0, & \text{if not} \end{cases}$$

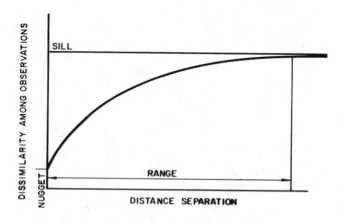

Figure 1. Idealized variogram.

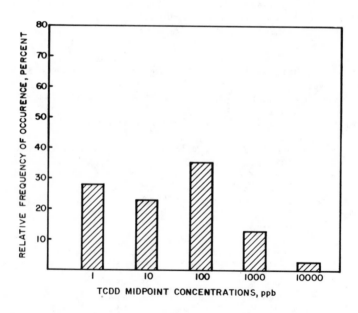

Figure 2. Histogram of TCDD concentrations at the example site.

where
$$z = \text{a "cutpoint" concentration.}$$

The indicator transform was completed for six cutpoints. Table 1 presents these cutpoint concentrations, the number of observations between consecutive cutpoints, and the mean concentration for each class.

**TABLE 1**
**INDICATOR CLASSES**

| CLASS | CUTPOINT CONCENTRATION | NUMBER OF OBSERVATIONS | CLASS MEAN CONCENTRATION (ppb) |
|-------|------------------------|------------------------|--------------------------------|
| 1 | - | 56 | 9.8 |
| 2 | 50 | 26 | 135.3 |
| 3 | 275 | 13 | 398.6 |
| 4 | 675 | 7 | 874.1 |
| 5 | 1,700 | 3 | 2,240.0 |
| 6 | 2,700 | 2 | 2,715.0 |
| 7 | 3,500 | 4 | 8,937.5 |
|   |   | 111 |   |

The distribution of the random variable, $I(x_{az})$, associated with $i(x_a:z)$ is called a Bernoulli distribution, and its mean and variance are given by:

$$E[I(x:z)] = 1 \quad \text{prob}[z(x) \le z] + 0 \quad \text{prob}[z(x) > z] = F(z)$$

$$\text{Var}[I(x:z)] = F(z) \quad [1 - F(z)]$$

where
$$F(z) = \text{prob}[z(x) \le z] \text{ is the stationary cumulative}$$
distribution function of the random variable $Z(x)$.

In practice, $F(z)$ is estimated by the cumulative histogram, $F*[z(x_a)]$, of all the N data. If each datum receives the weight $1/N$, the cumulative histogram is given by:

$$F*[z(x_a)] = (1/N) \quad t_a, \text{ for } a = 1, \ldots, N$$

where $t_a$ is the rank order of the datum $z(x_a)$ which is an integer ranging from 1 (for the smallest datum) to N (for the largest datum).

The goal of indicator kriging is to estimate the conditional distribution function of the unknown concentrations, $Z(x)$ at location x, given "n" data within its neighborhood. Symbolically, this is represented as:

$$F_x[Z| (n)] = \text{prob}[Z(x) \le z| (n)]$$

An estimate of the conditional distribution of $Z(x)$ can be
obtained by an ordinary kriging of the indicator transformed data.
The indicator kriging estimator, $I*(x:z)$, appears as a linear
combination of the indicator data, $i(x_a:z)$, in the neighborhood,
"n," surrounding the point for which a prediction is to be made.
This can be symbolized as:

$$I*(x:z) = S_n \; w_a \; i(x_a:z)$$

where the weights, $w_a$, are derived from the variogram description of
regional continuity. $I*(x:z)$ is an estimate of the conditional
distribution function of $Z(x)$ given the data. Note that there are
as many kriging estimators as there are cutpoints. In the present
case, there are six such estimators.

## Variogram Description of Continuity

The spatial continuity relationship (correlation) for each
indicator, $I(x:z_k)$, was characterized by an empirical variogram
model of the apparent continuity within the near-surface soil in
each of two dimensions. The construction of such a model is based
on the assumption that the value of the indicator at location x,
i.e., $I(x:z_k)$, may be greatly influenced by values of that indicator
at nearby locations and less influenced by more distant values.
This degree of relationship between points a specified distance, h,
apart may be measured by:

$$q(h) = 1/2 \; [I(x:z_k) - I(x+h:z_k)]^2$$

Averaging all differences between pairs of points separated by a
distance, h, gives rise to the variogram.
The function $q(h)$ is directly related to the coefficient of
correlation, $r(h)$, between two indicator values a distance h apart
by:

$$r(h) = 1 - \frac{q(h)}{Var}$$

where Var represents the total variance among the indicator
values.
The experimental variogram models constructed for each of the
six cutpoints indicated that a simple omnidirectional variogram
model was an appropriate descriptor of the continuity relationship
for each of the six cutpoints. Figure 3 presents the variogram
model appropriate for the 50 ppb cutpoint.
This variogram shows a nugget ($Co$) of 0.12 with a sill of
0.253. The indicator variogram reaches the sill at a range, A, of
90 feet.

## Indicator Kriging

The characterization of the spatial distribution of TCDD
concentrations was performed by obtaining estimates of the
conditional probability distribution function, $I*(x:z_k)$, for each of
the six concentration cutpoints, $z_k$, k=1,. . .,6. These estimates

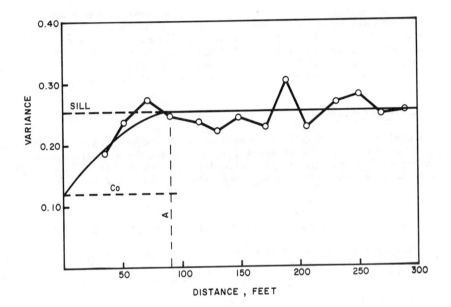

Figure 3. Indicator variogram appropriate for the 50-ppb cutpoint.

of the probability that a cutpoint concentration will not be exceeded were obtained at each node of a 40-by-40-foot grid system superimposed on the site.

In practice, the conditional probability distribution function, $F_x[z \mid (n)]$, is estimated by a discrete set of k values, $I*(x:z_k)$, one of each of the k cutpoints. In this case there are six such values. Since each estimate is determined individually, there is no guarantee that $I*(x:z_k)$ will verify the order-relations of a cumulative distribution function, i.e.:

$$I*(x:z_{k-1}) \ F \ I*(x:z_k) \text{ for } k=2,\ldots,6$$

In cases where order relation problems presented themselves, correction estimates were obtained using a simple averaging of the points in the region of the problem. This is consistent with the procedure recommended by Isaaks(10) and the results are nearly identical to more sophisticated averaging algorithms. Once these ordering problems are resolved, several types of data presentations are possible.

Data Presentations
‾‾‾‾‾‾‾‾‾‾‾‾‾‾‾‾‾

The conditional probability of an unknown TCDD concentration in an area being less than a threshold, T, can be found by simple linear interpolation from the estimated conditional probability distribution function. This interpolation is of the form:

$$prob[Z(x) \ F \ T \mid (n)] = I*[x:z_{k=1} \mid (n)] +$$

$$[I*[x:z_k \mid (n)] - I*[x:z_{k-1} \mid (n)] \quad (T-z_{k-1})/(z_k-z_{k-1})$$

The conditional probability of an unknown TCDD concentration being greater than the threshold, T, is just one minus the probability given by the previous equation, i.e.:

$$prob[Z(x) > T \mid (n)] = 1.0 - prob[Z(x) \ F \ T \mid (n)]$$

The isopleths of the probability that an unknown TCDD concentration exceeds 50 ppb and 675 ppb are presented in Figures 4 and 5, respectively.

The expected value of an unknown concentration of TCDD, $Z(x)$, can be estimated using the following approximation to its conditional expectation:

$$E*[Z(x) \mid (n)] = \sum_1^{k+1} u_k [I*[x:z_k \mid (n)] - I*[x:z_{k-1} \mid (n)]$$

where:

$$I*[x:z_{K+1} \mid (n)] = 1.0$$

$$I*[x:z_0 \mid (n)] = 0.0$$

and

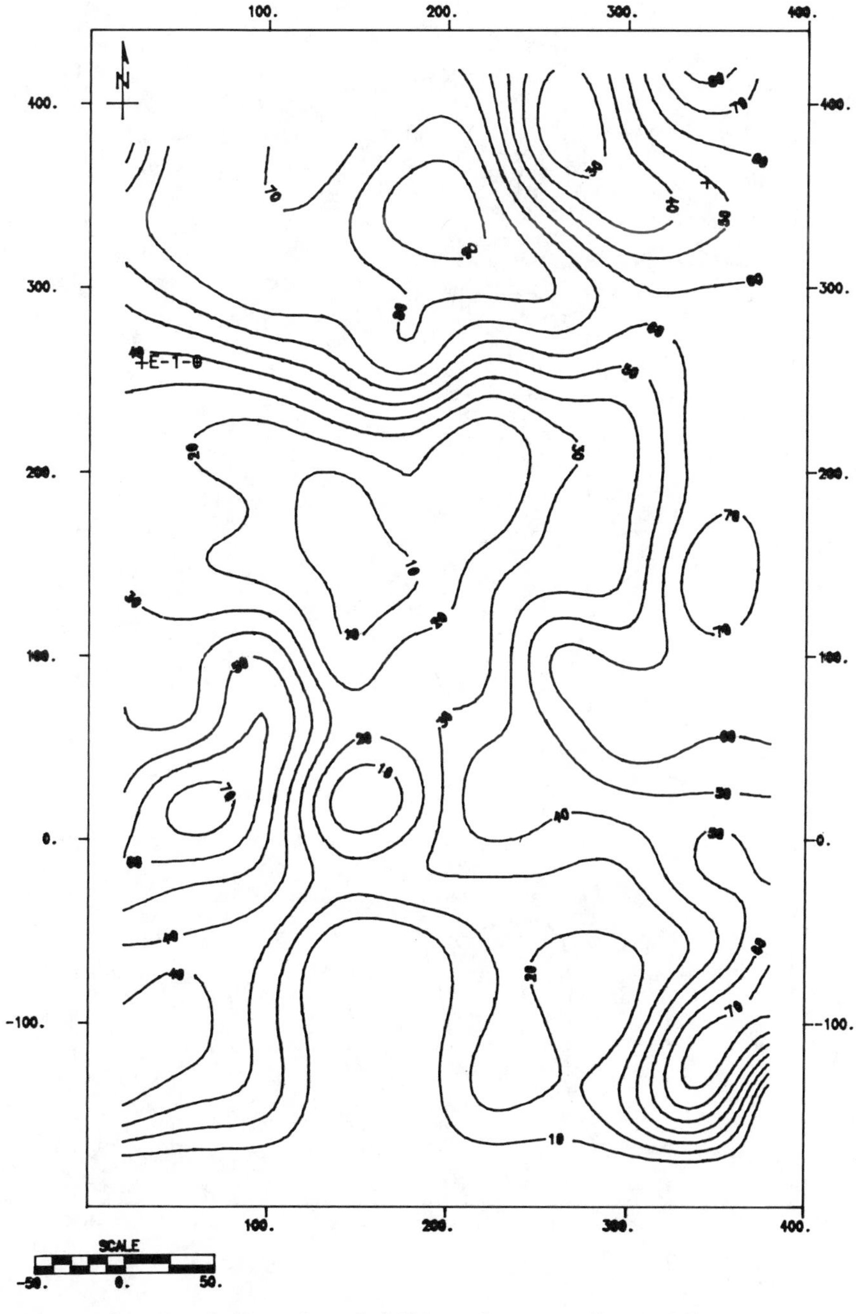

Figure 4.    Isopleths of probability that an unknown TCDD concentration exceeds 50 ppb.

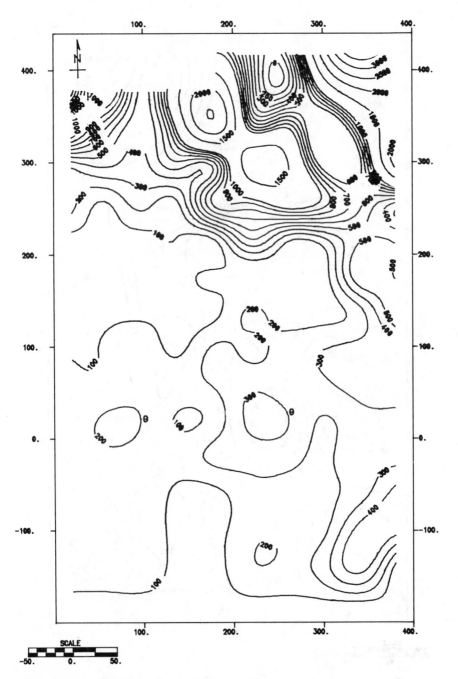

Figure 5.  Isopleths of probability that an unknown TCDD concentration
exceeds 675 ppb.

$u_k$ = the mean concentration of the class of data between cutpoint concentrations $z_k$ and $z_{k-1}$. The class mean concentrations for the seven classes are given in Table 1.

For instance, at the point 180 East, 380 North, the probability that the TCDD level is below the concentration cutpoint of 50 ppb is 0.21 and the probability that the TCDD level is below the concentration cutpoint of 2,700 ppb is 0.89. After generating the probability estimate for each cutpoint at this location, the conditional expectation for the TCDD concentration can be calculated as 882.42 ppb. Table 2 illustrates this calculation.

Performing similar calculations for all points on the 40-by-40-foot grid permits the mapping of the expected values of TCDD concentrations across the site. Such a map is presented in Figure 6.

TABLE 2
**PROBABILITIES AND ESTIMATE OF TCDD AT 180 EAST, 380 NORTH**

| THRESHOLD | CUTOFF CONCENTRATION CLASS | CONDITIONAL PROBABILITY | PROBABILITY WITHIN CLASS | CLASS MEAN CONCENTRATION | AVERAGE PROBABILITY TIMES CONCENTRATION |
|---|---|---|---|---|---|
| | 0 ppb | | | | |
| | | | 0.21 | 9.8 | 2.06 |
| 1 | 50 ppb | 0.21 | | | |
| | | | 0.21 | 135.3 | 28.41 |
| 2 | 275 ppb | 0.42 | | | |
| | | | 0.16 | 398.6 | 63.78 |
| 3 | 675 ppb | 0.58 | | | |
| | | | 0.15 | 874.1 | 131.12 |
| 4 | 1,700 ppb | 0.73 | | | |
| | | | 0.16 | 2,240.0 | 358.40 |
| 5 | 2,700 ppb | 0.89 | | | |
| | | | 0.11 | 2,715.0 | 298.65 |
| 6 | 3,500 ppb | 1.00 | | | |
| | | | 0.00 | 8,937.5 | 0.00 |
| | 99,999 ppb | 1.00 | | | |
| TOTAL | | | 1.00 | | 882.42 |

Conclusions

The indicator approach to estimation of spatial distributions of
TCDD concentrations consists in estimating first the conditional
probability distribution of any unknown concentration. Estimates of
the unknown concentration are then derived, together with their
confidence intervals. This approach has several outstanding
features:

o  It is distribution free and resistant to outlier data; hence,
   it can be applied to data sets whatever the shape of the site
   data histogram.
o  It results in confidence intervals which are not only data
   configuration dependent but also data values dependent.
o  It is reasonably simple in its application and has performed
   well in the example site investigation.

Literature Cited

1.  U.S. Environmental Protection Agency (U.S. EPA), 1984, "Health
    Assessment Document for Polychlorinated Dibenzo-p-Dioxins," EPA
    600/8-84-014A.
2.  Zirshky, J., G. P. Kary, R. O. Gilbert, and J. E. Middlebrooks,
    1985, "Spatial Estimation of Hazardous Waste Site Data,"
    Journal of Environmental Engineering, Vol. III, No. 6, December
    1985, pp. 777-789.
3.  Kearney, P. C., A. R. Isensee, C. S. Helling, E. A. Woolser,
    and J. R. Plimmer, 1973, "Environmental Significance of
    Chlorodioxins," Advances in Chemistry, Series 120, pp. 105-111.
4.  Matsumura, F. and H. J. Benezet, 1973, "Studies on the
    Bioaccumulation and Microbial Degradation of 2,3,7,8-
    Tetrachlorodibenzo-p-dioxin," Environmental Health
    Perspectives, Vol. 5, pp. 253-258.
5.  Ward, C. and F. Matsumura, 1978, "Fate of 2,3,7,8-TCDD in a
    Model Aquatic Environment," Archives of Environmental
    Contamination and Toxicology 7 (3) pp. 349-357.
6.  Jackson, D. R., M. H. Roulier, H. M. Grotta, S.W. Rust, J. S.
    Warner, M. F. Arthur, and F. L. DeRoos, 1985, "Leaching
    Potential of 2,3,7,8-TCDD in Contaminated Soils," Proceedings
    of the Eleventh Annual Research Symposium, EPA-600/9-85-013,
    pp. 153-168.
7.  Journel, A. G., Non-Parametric Estimation of Spatial Distribu-
    tion, Math. Geol., 1983, 9, No. 6, pp. 563-586.
8.  Journel, A. G., New Ways of Assessing Spatial Distributions of
    Pollutants, in Environmental Sampling for Hazardous Wastes,
    G. Schweitzer, Ed., Amer. Chem. Soc. Press, 1984, pp. 109-118.
9.  Journel, A. G., Indicator Approach to Toxic Chemical Sites, EPA
    Project Report No. CR-811235-02-0, EPA Exposure Assessment
    Division EMSL, Las Vegas, 30 p., 1984.
10. Isaaks, E. H., Risk Qualified Mappings for Hazardous Waste Sites.
    A case study in distribution-free geostatistics, MSc. thesis,
    Applied Earth Sciences Department, Stanford University, 1984.

RECEIVED December 2, 1986

# Chapter 19

# Analytical Support During Remedial Action at Sites Contaminated with 2,3,7,8-Tetrachlorodibenzo-p-dioxin

Robert Kleopfer, Mary Gerken, Angelo Carasea, and Debra Morey

U.S. Environmental Protection Agency, 25 Funston Road, Kansas City, KS 66115

The U.S. Environmental Proection Agency (EPA) has identified more than 40 sites in Missouri which are contaminated with 2,3,7,8-tetrachlorodibenzo-p-dioxin (2,3,7,8-TCDD) at levels above one part per billion (micrograms per kilogram) in soil. Remediation at some of these sites began in 1985, with excavation and temporary storage of the contaminated soil. Timely analytical support was needed to optimize the utilization of field resources while monitoring for potential exposure to local residents. Standard analytical procedures used during the preliminary site investigations were not suitable for the remedial phase due to unacceptable turnaround time in reporting validated data. Analytical procedures were consequently modified to reduce data turnaround time. Procedures were also developed for semi-automated data validation and electronic data transmission from the analytical laboratories to EPA.

The U.S. Environmental Protection Agency has identified more than 40 sites in Missouri which are contaminated with 2,3,7,8-TCDD at levels above one part per billion (micrograms per kilogram) in soil. In each case, the contaminant originated from the manufacture of hexachlorophene at a chemical plant in Southwestern Missouri (1). In most instances, the contamination occurred during the application of waste oil for the purpose of dust control. Sites include an entire town (Time Beach), a mobile home park (Quail Run), residential streets, rural roads, horse arenas, small farms, streams (Romaine Creek and Spring River), and parking lots. Although most of the contamination is limited to soil, 2,3,7,8-TCDD has also been found in house dust, mobile home insulation material, concrete slabs, tree bark, stream sediment, and biota (worms, fish, etc.).

The public health implications required a rapid, yet reliable assessment of these sites. A cost-effective procedure was developed to analyze for 2,3,7,8-TCDD down to 1 part per billion (ppb) in hundreds of soil samples (2). From late 1982 thru 1985, over 13500 samples were analyzed by 50 different laboratories using procedures based on isotope dilution and high resolution gas chromatography with low resolution mass spectrometry. A comprehensive quality assurance program was implemented to assure the reliability of data generated during this massive monitoring effort (3).

## Remediation Options

A number of different options have been proposed for remediation of the Missouri sites (4). The two basic proposals are removal and in-place treatment. Post-removal options include:
1. Immediate treatment or detoxication of the excavated soil,
2. Temporary storage of all contaminated soils, and
3. Long-term storage in an approved landfill, concrete bunker, or abandoned mine. In-place treatment proposals have included biodegradation, chemical degradation, photolysis, and chemical stabilization.

In 1980, Syntex, Inc., utilized a process based on photolysis to destroy approximately 13 pounds of 2,3,7,8-TCDD contained in 4300 gallons of oily trichlorophenol still-bottom residues (5). In 1984, EPA began to use a transportable rotary kiln incinerator to detoxify solid and liquid waste which were contaminated with 2,3,7,8-TCDD (6). Concurrent with the incineration activities, EPA began removing soils and other contaminated materials from a number of sites including a mobile home park near Grays Summit, Missouri. These activities required the application of extensive compositing techniques and statistical treatment of the data to assure the removal of 2,3,7,8-TCDD down to acceptable levels (7).

## Analytical Requirements

During remedial operations, large costs can be incurred if cleanup operations are delayed by slow response in the analysis of samples. Thus, analytical techniques must be available to verify that a cleanup criterion has been achieved and to indicate during cleanup efforts whether to stop or proceed. Preliminary discussions of proposed excavation approaches led to the requirement of 20 to 25 analyses within a 24-hour period. The standard EPA contract laboratory procedure required a minimum of 72 hours elapsed time including data reporting and data validation by EPA. Unfortunately, available protocols such as the EPA Contract Laboratory (CLP) mechanism, typically required two weeks or longer to produce verified data. Alternatives were needed to meet the unique demands of site remediation.

## EPA Contract Laboratory Procedure

This procedure (2) has been used since 1982 by EPA for routine investigations. The analytical protocol requires complete extraction of the sample followed by liquid chromatographic cleanup and isomer-specific 2,3,7,8-TCDD analysis by high resolution gas chromatography/low resolution mass spectrometry. The extraction begins with ten grams of soil which is spiked with internal ($^{13}C_{12}$-2,3,7,8-TCDD) and surrogate ($^{35}Cl_4$-2378-TCDD) standards. A drying agent (anhydrous sodium sulfate) is added and the mixture is allowed to stand for a total of six hours. After this period, 170 ml of (methanol/hexane) is added to the sample and the mixture is shaken for at least three hours. The sample is filtered and the jar and soil are thoroughly rinsed with additional solvent. The combined rinses and original extracts are concentrated to about 1 ml by Kuderna-Danish evaporation. The concentrated extract is then cleaned up by elution in series through a neutral/ acidic/basic silica gel column and an alumina column. The eluted fraction containing dioxin is collected and concentrated. Cleanup by carbon column chromatography is required as a final polishing step. Further separation of the sample components uses a fused-silica capillary column (SP-2340 or equivalent) before entering the mass spectrometer for analysis. Data reports are prepared and shipped (generally by air express) to EPA for review and data validation. The elapsed time requirements for these processes are summarized in Table I.

## Modified LRMS Procedure

The previously described contract laboratory procedure was modified to permit faster data turnaround. The major changes included the following:
1. The six hour drying time requirement was deleted. Anhydrous sodium sulfate was still required however.
2. The extraction solvent was changed from 12% methanol/hexane to 10% acetone/hexane and the extraction time was reduced from three hours to one hour. A sonication step was added, however.
3. A three concentration level (1, 5, and 25 ppb) calibration curve is required rather than five.
4. The requirement to verify isomer specificity was deleted since TCDD isomer interference was not a problem at the Missouri sites (1).

## Tandem Mass Spectrometry Procedure

The application of GC/MS/MS to the analysis of 2,3,7,8-TCDD in soil was first demonstrated in 1983 (8) and later refined (9,10,11).

Five grams of anhydrous sodium sulfate is placed in a 10 ml serum vial and the vial, with cap and septum, is weighed. Approximately five gram of a soil sample is added and the vial is reweighed. The sample is spiked with internal and surrogate

standards of isotopically labeled 2,3,7,8-TCDD. The sample is
mixed by shaking and extracted with 5 ml of 67% acetonitrile/
dichloromethane in the closed vial. An aliquot of the extract is
taken and, after separation from acetonitrile, the dichloromethane
is used directly for GC/MS/MS analysis. Cleanup should usually
not be necessary, but a cleanup procedure is included for those
samples which do not meet quality assurance criteria. A short
capillary column (15m DB-5) is used which allows for separation
of TCDD from the bulk sample matrix and measurement of TCDD in
the extract. Quantification is based on the response of native
TCDD relative to the isotopically labeled TCDD internal standard.

The method employs a tandem quadrupole mass spectrometer
(MS/MS) as the final detector. The specificity of detection
inherent in such a system significantly reduces the need for
sample cleanup. This, in turn, improves productivity and
cost-effectiveness relative to other high resolution and low
resolution GC/MS analysis techniques. The aparatus and methods
described are designed for use in a mobile laboratory, which
permits on-site analyses.

## Data Handling/Data Review

The Contract Laboratory Program procedure required delivery of
specified documents included data summary forms, calibration
data, chromatograms, and mass spectra and were generally shipped
by air freight. Upon receipt by EPA, the documents were reviewed
for data usability which was based on consideration of completeness of documentation and adherence to quality control requirements
(3). Due to the nature of the remedial projects, these procedures
had to be modified to allow for quicker turnaround.

To achieve this quicker turnaround, EPA Region VII needed a
method that not only allowed for the quick transfer of raw data,
but a system to quickly review, validate, and transmit the data.
To support this goal, a computer system was developed which
allowed for the circular transfer of information via computers
from the EPA field team to the lab; the raw data from the lab to
EPA; and validated results from EPA back to the field team.

The laboratory portion of the computer system was made up of
a series of computer programs written in dBASE III. These
programs were designed to work on any IBM portable, XT, or AT
computer or compatible models. The actual data software is
composed of three to four inter-related dBASE files (labs using
GC/MS require three files while labs using GC/MS/MS require
four files) linked together through the use of a common file
name. A different extention is given to each file name for
distinction among the files for a particular set of samples.

Each of the inter-related dBASE files allows for specific
data entry for a particular aspect of the sample set. Data are
entered into individual files for the Initial Calibration;
Blank Response (GC/MS/MS only); Continuing Calibration; and

actual sample results. Raw data entries are made into the respective files using screen driven monitor prompts. The software programs then compute all calculations required by the method. For example, initial calibration data are entered into the Initial Calibration file where it is used to calculate the native TCDD and surrogate RRFs; ion ratios; mean RRFs; %RSDs; and standard deviations. The computer program then compares these results to established criteria. Any data not meeting the criteria are flagged. Each of the other files work in the same manner by flagging unacceptable data. Not only does this flagging of data assist the EPA data reviewer in spotting unacceptable data, it gives the lab an opportunity to rerun any samples not meeting criteria prior to turning it in.

The inter-related dBASE files representing the data set are transmitted to EPA via Crosstalk software over regular commercial phone lines. The EPA data reviewer will print out the data files looking for unacceptable data or anomalies which may be present. Since the computer program has done all the data calculations, these will not be verified by the data reviewer, saving much time. Data are reviewed much the same way as for routine work with the exception that only the computer transmitted raw data will be used for the initial qualification of the data. The actual mass chromatograms and spectra are received seven days later at which time they are also reviewed. Any discrepancies between the two sets of data are immediately rectified. Data are qualified based on adherence to the method criteria plus the results of the field blank, fortified sample, and performance evaluation sample. Data are qualified as either valid or invalid for remedial site work.

The computer programs allow for the qualification of data and other data editing by EPA. The qualified data results are then fed into a dBASE text file which forms a memorandum which will be used to formally transmit the data to the field team. This dBASE text file containing the data transmittal memorandum is sent electronically to the field team.

## Method Performance

Before implementation of the proposed procedures, a round-robin comparison study was performed which involved three different soils, three different methods, and five different laboratories. These results are summarized in Table II. Although the modified procedures gave somewhat lower mean results, the differences were not statistically significant. The MS/MS procedure displayed similar performance characteristics during its utilization in 1985 at a remedial site in Eastern Missouri. Those results are summarized in Table III.

## Conclusions

By modifying analytical procedures and relying on modern PC based data management and communications technology, we have succeeded in providing timely analytical data to support hazardous waste

site cleanup activities. The system described was used to
assist in the cleanup of one mobile home park in Eastern Missouri
over a two year period. Numerous other applications have been
started or are planned.

Table I.  Analytical Turn Around Times For 2,3,7,8-TCDD
                    Determinations*

|  | | PROCEDURE | |
|  | | MODIFIED | |
| STEP | CLP | CLP | MS/MS |
|---|---|---|---|
| SAMPLE EXTRACTION[a] | 12 | 3 | 1 |
| CLEANUP OF EXTRACT[b] | 10 | 4 | 3 |
| GC/MS ANALYSIS[c] | 12 | 12 | 6 |
| DATA REDUCTION/TRANSMISSION[d] | 25+ | 1 | 1 |
| DATA VALIDATION[e] | 4 | 1 | 1 |
| TOTALS[f] | 63+ | 21 | 12 |

*Estimated elasped times in hours for processing, analyzing,
and reporting one batch of 24 soil samples.
a.  Assumes two workers.  Includes all weighing, drying, and
extraction steps.
b.  Assumes two workers.  Includes all column chromatography and
extract concentration steps.
c.  Assumes that GC/MS/DS instrument has been previously cali-
brated.  Assumes one instrument only.
d.  Requires electronic or hard copy delivery of data in EPA
specified format.
e.  Includes data review and EPA decision on data usability.
f.  The totals assume that each step is done sequentially.  In
practice, the processing steps may overlap thus reducing the
total turn around times.

Table II.  Methodology Comparison Data For 2,3,7,8-TCDD
                    Contaminated Soils[a]

| METHOD (LAB) | SOIL A | | SOIL B | | SOIL C | |
|  | MEAN | RSD | MEAN | RSD | MEAN | RSD |
|---|---|---|---|---|---|---|
| CLP (1) | .81 | 20% | 16.6 | 6% | <.053 | N.A. |
| CLP (2) | .75 | 29% | 15.8 | 13% | <.024 | N.A. |
| CLP (3) | .83 | 11% | ---- | | ---- | |
| RAPID LRMS(1) | .63 | 8% | 15.5 | 6% | <.035 | N.A. |
| RAPID LRMS(2) | .57 | 12% | 13.6 | 4% | <.035 | N.A. |
| RAPID LRMS(3) | .53 | 23% | 13.4 | 13% | <.14 | N.A. |
| MS/MS (4) | .51 | 27% | 14.1 | 14% | <.3 | N.A. |
| MS/MS (5) | .88 | 40% | 15.7 | 10% | <.04 | N.A. |

a.  Data are in micrograms per kilograms (ppb) based on six
replicate runs by each laboratory and each soil.  The Missouri
soils were dry and well-homogenized.
RSD  =  Relative Standard Deviation
N.A. =  Not applicable

Table III.  Summary Of QC Results For Tandem Mass Spectrometry
Procedure[a]

| QC TYPE | MEAN | RSD | N |
|---------|------|-----|---|
| Soil A | .59 | 24% | 24 |
| Soil B | 13.5 | 6% | 26 |
| Soil D | .91 | 20% | 22 |
| Soil Spike[b] | 1.02 | 7% | 64 |
| Soil Blank[c] | <.03 | NA | 64 |

a.  Data generated during 1985 remedial support.
b.  Clean soil spiked at 1.0 PPB by laboratory.
c.  Soil provided by EPA known to be uncontaminated by 2,3,7,8-
TCDD.
N = Number of samples analyzed

References

1.  R.D. Kleopfer, Chemosphere 14, 739 (1985).
2.  R.D. Kleopfer, K. Yue, and W.W. Bunn, Chapter 27 in
Chlorinated Dioxins and Dibenzofurans in the Total Environment-
Volume II, L. H. Keith, C. Rappe, and G. Choudhary, Eds. (Stoneham,
MA:  Butterworth Publishers, 1985).
3.  R.D. Kleopfer and C. Kirchmer, Chapter 26 in Chlorinated
Dioxins and Dibenzofurans in the Total Environment-Volume II,
L. H. Keith, C. Rappe, and G.  Choudhary, Eds. (Stoneham, MA:
Butterworth Publishers, 1985).
4.  "Final Report of the Missouri Dioxin Task Force," submitted
to Governor Christopher S. Bond (State Capitol, Jefferson City,
MO    65101) October 31, 1983.
5.  Exner, J. H., J. D. Johnson, O. D. Ivins, M. N. Wass, and
R. A. Miller, Chapter 17, in Detoxication of Hazardous Waste
(Ann Arbor, Michigan:  Ann Arbor Science Publishers, 1982).
6.  R. D. Kleopfer, F. J. Freestone, R. Hazel, and P. desRosiers,
"Destruction of Dioxin Containing Wastes In a Mobile Incineration
System," Chapter 34 in Chlorinated Dioxins and Dibenzofurans
in Perspective, C. Rappe, G. Choudhary, and L. H. Keith, Eds
(Chelsa, MI:  Lewis Publishers, Inc., 1986).
7.  J. H. Exner, W. J. Keffer, R. O. Gilbert, and R. R. Kinnison,
"A Sampling Strategy for Remedial Action at Hazardous Waste
Sites: Cleanup of Soil Contaminated by Tetrachlorodibenzo-p-
dioxins," Chapter 10 in Chlorinated Dioxins and Dibenzofurans in
Perspective" C. Rappe, G. Choudhary, and L. H. Keith, Eds (Chelsa,
MI: Lewis Publishers, Inc., 1986).
8.  Unpublished Report by Roy F. Weston, Inc., West Chester, PA.
(1983).
9.  "The Application of Flash Chromatography-Tadem Mass Spectrom-
etry to the Analysis of Complex Samples for Chlorinated Dioxins
and Dibenzofuran," T. Sakuma, N. Gurprasad, S. D. Tanner, A.
Ngo, W. R. Davidson, H. A. McLeod, and B. Lau, Chapter 12 in
Chlorinated Dioxins and Dibenzofurans in the Total Environment-
Volume II, Chapter 12 (1985). L. H. Keith, C. Rappe, and G.
Choudhary, Eds. (Stoneham, MA:  Butterworth Publishers, 1985).

10.  B. Shushan and S. D. Tanner, Chemosphere 14, 843 (1985).
11.  "Comparison of a New Rapid Extraction GC/MS/MS and the
Contract Laboratory Program GC/MS Methodologies, for the Analysis
of 2,3,7,8-TCDD," J. S. Smith, D.  Ben-Hur, M. J. Urban, R. D.
Kleopfer, C. J. Kirchmer, W. A. Smith and T. S. Viswanethan,
Chapter 25 in Chlorinated Dioxins and Dibenzofurans in
Perspective, C. Rappe, G. Choudhary, and L. H. Keith, Eds.
(Chelsa, MI: Lewis Publishers, Inc., 1986).

RECEIVED November 25, 1986

# Chapter 20

# Ambient Air Monitoring During the Cleanup of Hazardous Waste Sites Contaminated by Polychlorinated Dioxins

Tony Babb

International Technology Corporation, Air Quality Services Group,
3028 East Magnolia Avenue, Knoxville, TN 37914

Ambient air monitoring during the cleanup
of hazardous waste sites contaminated by
polychlorinated dioxins is done because of
potential hazards associated with dioxin
exposure. An effective ambient air monitoring program can document the exposure
levels on site and the potential migration
of contamination off site. The method
validation data described herein provides
a basis for concluding that the PUF high-
volume sampler effectively collects dioxin
with no observed breakthrough in a 24-hour
sampling period. The PUF sampler with its
first-stage particulate filter allows for
quick, low cost determination of suspended
particulate concentrations. This data,
in many cases, may enable screening of
samples for dioxin analysis based on the
assumption that the higher the suspended
particulate matter concentration at the
site, the higher the potential for measurable levels of dioxin. Much more data is
needed to further evaluate the effectiveness of the PUF sampler for measuring
ambient levels of dioxin and to evaluate
sample screening techniques which can be
used to provide high quality data at a
much lower cost.

For some animal species 2,3,7,8-tetrachlorodibenzo-p-
dioxin (2,3,7,8-TCDD, dioxin) is one of the most toxic
synthetic compounds known to man ($\underline{1}$). In addition to
being toxic, 2,3,7,8-TCDD is also a suspected carcinogen.
Dioxins can enter the environment in a variety of ways,
generally as a contaminant of a product, as a waste byproduct, or as a product of combustion. For these rea-

sons, there is an immediate concern of the contamination
of our environment with dioxins. Remedial action is
ongoing to remove dioxin contaminated soil and debris
from identified sites to safe storage until procedures
to detoxify the material are available.

Due to the hazards associated with dioxin exposure,
remedial action at dioxin contaminated sites presents
a potential hazard to the general populace in the vicinity of the sites and to the personnel actually performing the remedial activity. As an issue of major
concern to the public, regulators, industry, and scientists, the need to evaluate and control this potential
exposure during remediation may be as important as the
remedial action itself. An effective ambient air monitoring program can provide documentation of the exposure
levels on site and of the potential migration of contamination off site. It can be used to assess the effectiveness of dust suppression techniques being used on site.
It can identify and document meteorological conditions
which may represent high potential for exposure. This
paper summarizes information which has been used in the
development and operation of several ambient air monitoring programs during the cleanup of sites contaminated
with dioxin.

## Ambient Air Monitoring Survey Design

The proper development of a cost-effective air monitoring survey involves not only air quality monitoring
but also meteorological monitoring, quality control,
quality assurance, and data evaluation. Failure to recognize this fact at the outset results in a design
based on many practical compromises that may fail to meet
the sampling objectives. A cost-effective system should
reflect both the realities of current air quality monitoring system technology and the ultimate application
for which the measurement system is intended. It is
especially important to develop a systematic plan for the
implementation of the system in advance of choosing specific pieces of hardware (2).

Before developing a working air monitoring survey,
specific general information about the contaminated site
is needed. 1) What is there? It is important to know
all the pollutants present because of the possibility of
additive health effects and the possibility of tracking
several parameters by monitoring only a few because of
their chemical and/or physical characteristics. 2) How
much is there? The answer to this question will aid in
the determination of the type of monitoring equipment
needed in terms of detection limits, averaging times,
and estimating potential emission rates. 3) Where is
the contamination? 4) What are the prevailing meteorological conditions? 5) Where are the receptor locations? This information will help to determine the physical size of the air monitoring survey, the number of
air monitoring stations, the monitoring station locations
and the duration of the survey.

There are seven basic steps in the design of an air monitoring survey:

(1)  Clearly define the objectives,
(2)  Determine the parameters to be measured,
(3)  Site selection,
(4)  Determine sampling schedules and sampling duration,
(5)  Determine sampling and analytical methods,
(6)  Develop a quality control and quality assurance program, and
(7)  Data management and reporting.

Objectives
The starting point is the setting of objectives. When monitoring during the cleanup of sites contaminated by dioxin, these objectives may include the following:

(a)  Evaluating the potential for airborne migration of dioxin contamination off-site (general population exposure).
(b)  Evaluating the potential for worker exposure on-site during remedial activities.
(c)  Evaluating the potential for recontamination of areas already "cleaned".
(d)  Evaluating the adequacy of methods being employed to contain contamination on site as a function of site activity and site-specific meteorological conditions.

Translating the study objectives into clear meaningful statements will serve as the cornerstone for the rest of the air monitoring plan.

Parameters To Be Measured
Once the objectives are clearly defined, the second step is to determine the physical parameters to be measured. In order to achieve any one or a combination of the previously listed objectives, it is necessary to measure ambient air concentrations of dioxin. In order to interpret variations in the distribution of air pollution concentrations, the on-site measurement of meteorology and a basic understanding of the role of the atmosphere in transporting and dispersing air pollutants is needed.

Sampling Site Selection
Step three is the selection of sampling sites. In choosing a technically suitable location for an air quality monitoring site, one must consider the representativeness of the site in terms of its exposure to air pollutants and prevailing meteorological conditions. Site exposure is heavily dependent on the relative location of pollutant sources and the effects of terrain on meteorological conditions. Where the maximum background concen-

trations are expected to occur and where the maximum
project contribution to air quality is expected to occur
should be considered when locating specific sites.  The
location of human receptors should be taken into account.
It should be recognized that site selection is a critical
element in the survey design.  If the wrong site is pick-
ed or if a critical site is missed, no amount of accurate
data collection will allow the objectives of the study
to be fully realized.

The meteorological exposure of an air monitoring
site should be representative of either area-wide meteorology or localized meteorological regimes that will
affect the dispersion of air pollutants.  Localized
meteorological regimes result from irregular terrain
features which can cause increased mecanical turbulence
or localized drainage winds.

The number of monitoring sites that should be used
in the study depends on the diversity of the land use
patterns, meteorological regimes, source configurations,
and sensitive receptors.  This number is limited by the
number of technically suitable sites available, the
constraints of money and manpower available, and the
level of statistical significance or confidence desired
in the results.

Sampling Schedules and Sampling Duration

The fourth step is to determine the sampling schedules
and duration.  Due to the concern about hazards associated with dioxin exposure, the sampling schedule and
duration should be continuous during the period in which
there is remedial activity on site.  This practice will
probably continue until information pertaining to the
hazards of exposure to dioxin indicate it is not necessary.

Sampling and Analytical Methods

The fifth step in the design of this air monitoring survey is determining the sampling and analytical methods to
be used.  The criterion generally used as an acceptable
level of exposure to dioxin is in the very low picogram
per cubic meter range.  In order to monitor for the
concentration of dioxin in ambient air at these levels,
it is necessary to obtain sufficient sample volumes.
The Environmental Protection Agency has developed a high
volume sampler, referred to as a PUF Sampler, which
through testing and actual field use appears to be suitable for this task (3) (4).  Figures 1 and 2 show dia-
grams of the sampler and sampling module, respectively.
The sampler utilizes a dual-chambered aluminum sampling
module which contains both particulate and vapor phase
collection media.  The upper chamber supports a four-inch
diameter airborne particulate glass-fiber filter.  The
lower chamber houses a glass cartridge which contains the
polyurethane foam plug for vapor entrapment.  This glass
cartridge may readily be used with several different
types of solid sorbents.  Air flow is provided by a high
pressure blower.  Air flow rate is monitored with a

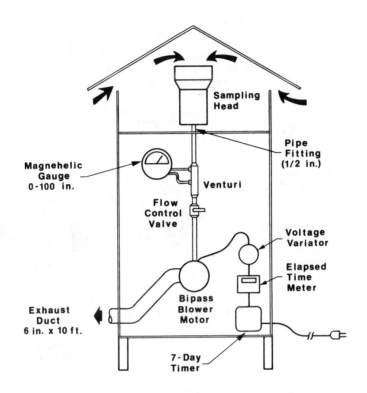

Figure 1.   Modified Hi-Vol Sampler (General Metal
Works, Inc., Model PS-1) Used To Collect
Suspended Particulate Matter (PM) and
2,3,7,8-TCDD Samples

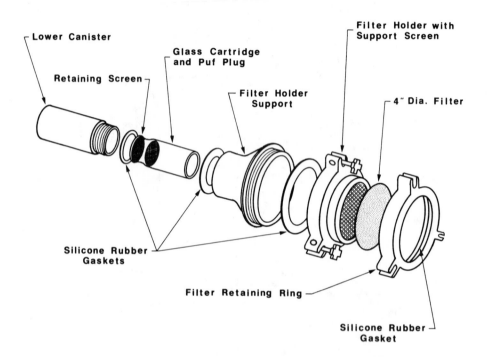

Figure 2.   A Detailed Illustration Of The Sampling
Head Module Showing The Fiberglass Filter
Used To Collect Particulates And The
Glass Cylinder and PUF Used To Collect
Vapors

magnehelic gauge hooked to a venturi. The sampler is
equipped with an elapsed-time indicator to provide actual
sampling time and a seven-day timer to allow the sampler
start and stop time to be pre-set.

The two-stage module of the PUF sampler enables determination of suspended particulate matter concentrations
by pre- and post-weighing of the four inch glass-fiber
filter. Because relative differences in suspended particulate matter are of concern, this evaluation can be
performed immediately upon the collection of the samples
and can be used to aid site personnel in the assessment
of dust suppression techniques and evaluation of meteorological conditions. This technique for the determination
of suspended particulate matter concentrations should not
be directly compared to national ambient air-quality
standard for Total Suspended Particulate (TSP) because
the filter size, sample flow rate, and sample volume do
not conform to the sampling procedures outlined in the
Code of Federal Regulation 40, Part 50.11, Appendix B
for TSP sampling, however, it does provide accurate results.

Quality Control and Quality Assurance

The sixth step in the design of an air monitoring survey
is the development of a quality assurance and quality
control plan. This plan should include specific sampling
procedures, calibration procedures and frequency, sample
custody, analytical procedures, data reduction, internal
quality control checks, performance and system audits,
completeness, and corrective action.

Data Management and Reporting

The final step in the development of an air monitoring
survey is determining the methodology to be used for data
management and reporting. Detailed evaluation of this
step is beyond the scope of this paper; however, data
management and reporting should be developed to meet the
overall objectives of the air monitoring survey which
were clearly stated in step one.

Sampling Method Validation

To add validity to the air monitoring survey, it is important to know the effectiveness of the sampling and
analytical technique used for the specific compounds in
question. Questions as to the effectiveness of the PUF
sampler for collection of $2,3,7,8$-TCDD have come up
during the course of its use. Table 1 illustrates the
results of a study conducted to investigate the adsorption efficiency of the PUF sampler for dioxin. This
study consisted of spiking known amounts of dioxin
($2,3,7,8$-TCDD) in solution (approximately 100 nanograms)
on the 1st stage filter of a PUF sampler. Three individual runs were performed with sample durations of 17.5
min., 144 min., and 24 hours. The filters and the PUF
plugs were analyzed separately to evaluate potential
dioxin breakthrough. The average percent recovery of
dioxin for the three samples was 112.5% with a standard
deviation of 1.3%. The analytical recoveries of dioxin

were consistant for the three samples. Recoveries were slightly high but within the expected precision of the analytical method. The decreasing amount of dioxin found on the filter and the increasing amount of dioxin found in the PUF with increasing sample duration, in conjunction with consistant overall recovery percentages, indicates that dioxin is being air stripped off the filter and being adsorbed in the PUF with no observed breakthrough.

Table 1
Dioxin Method Validation Study Results

| Run # | Duration (min) | Volume ($m^3$) | Relative Filter (%) | Recovery PUF (%) | Total Recovery (%) |
|---|---|---|---|---|---|
| 1 | 17.5 | 4.66 | 100 | 0.0 | 111 |
| 2 | 144 | 46.9 | 96.5 | 3.5 | 113.3 |
| 3 | 1440 | 480.8 | 81.8 | 18.8 | 113.2 |

The above described study was also performed to evaluate the effectiveness of the PUF sampler for collecting 2,3,7,8-tetrachlorodibenzo-p-furan. As is shown in Table 2, the overall furan recoveries were not as consistent as the results for the dioxin but were increasing with run duration. This increase indicates that the variation is not due to breakthrough but possibly due to analytical variation. One interesting difference in the furan results is that the furan appears to air strip off the filter much more readily than dioxin. During the 17.5 minute run almost 40 percent of the furan placed on the filter had migrated to the PUF. Ninety percent had migrated from the filter to the PUF after 2.4 hours, and 100 percent after less than 24 hours.

Table 2
Furan Method Validation Results

| Run # | Duration (min) | Volume ($m^3$) | Relative Filter (%) | Recovery PUF (%) | Total Recovery (%) |
|---|---|---|---|---|---|
| 1 | 17.5 | 4.66 | 62.7 | 37.3 | 81.6 |
| 2 | 144 | 46.9 | 10.2 | 89.8 | 87.3 |
| 3 | 1440 | 480.8 | 0.0 | 100 | 102.2 |

Sample Screening to Reduce Cost
Sample screening techniques, which provide high quality data by enabling low cost routine analysis of all samples

and a logical procedure by which to determine samples to be analyzed for dioxin, are important and cost effective. A majority of the remedial activities now in progress and planned for in the near future involve the removal of dioxin contaminated soil and debris. Based on the nature of these sites, it seems possible that migration of the contamination, and therefore potential exposure due to remedial activities, may be related to suspended particulate concentrations. Determination of particulate matter concentrations can be done quickly and at very low cost. By analyzing for suspended particulate matter concentrations at all monitoring stations and analyzing on-site wind data, an upwind or background sample can be identified. This value can be subtracted from all the samples collected to determine the above background particulate matter concentrations. These values should represent the concentrations due to activities on the site. After 20-30 samples have been analyzed, it is expected that a relationship between above background particulate matter (PM) concentration and TCDD concentration may be established. It is expected that the concentration of TCDD in airborne particulate matter will be quite variable depending on factors such as the level of contaminant in the soil being removed, the amount of dust attributable to other sources, the particle size being suspended (function of meteorological conditions and on site activity), and whether vapor phase dioxin is evaporated from exposed contaminated soil. Even though the expected dioxin level in airborne particulate matter may be variable, this methodology may prove useful to establish an upper bound or maximum concentration of dioxin measured in airborne particulate matter. This data can be used to screen samples for dioxin analysis. Dioxin analysis would then be performed only on those samples with PM levels that exceed a predetermined threshold level, below which previous results indicate that dioxin would be nondetectable. This type of evaluation should be site specific, and may not be applicable in some cases.

Figure 3 is a graph showing the relationship between particulate matter and dioxin concentrations at one site. A total of 75 samples were collected at this site with 9 of the highest above background particulate matter concentrations being analyzed for dioxin. Of these 9 samples, four showed positive results for dioxin. The data is limited; nevertheless, there appears to be a trend of increasing dioxin concentration with increasing particulate matter.

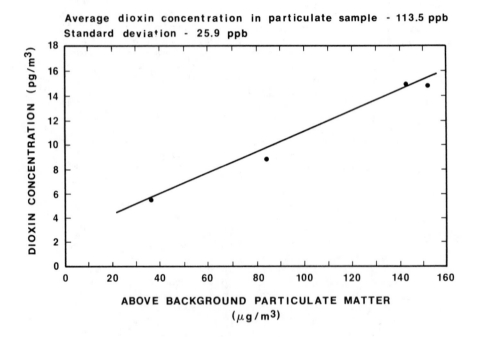

Figure 3.    Trend Between Particulate Matter
             Concentration and Dioxin Concentration At
             One Ambient Air Sampling Site

## Literature Cited

1. Esposito, M. P., Drake H. M., Smith, J. A., Owens, T. W., "Dioxins: Sources, Exposure, Transport and Control," Volume I, Report No. EPA-600/2-80-156, Industrial Environmental Research Laboratory, Office of Research and Development, U. S. EPA, Cincinnati, Ohio 45268 147-199.

2. Noll, K. E. and Miller, T. L. Air Monitoring Survey Design, Ann Arbor Science Publishers, 1977.

3. Lewis, R. G. and Jackson, M. D., "Modification and Evaluation of High Volume Air Sampler for Pesticides in Semivolatile Industrial Organic Chemicals," Analytical Chemistry, Vol. 54, No. 3, PP. 592-594, (March, 1982).

4. Lewis, R. G., "Monitoring Strategy for 2,3,7,8-Tetrachlorodibenzo-p-dioxin in Ambient and Source Related Air", Appendix D, Research Triangle Park, N. D., July 21, 1983.

RECEIVED November 25, 1986

# Chapter 21

# Remediation of a Dioxin-Contaminated Surface Impoundment

Ray K. Forrester[1], Leland Marple[2], and C. P. Carson, Jr.[3]

[1]Syntex Agribusiness, Inc., Syntex (USA), Inc., P.O. Box 1246 SSS,
Springfield, MO 65805
[2]Syntex Analytical and Environmental Research, Syntex (USA), Inc.,
3401 Hillview Avenue, Palo Alto, CA 94303
[3]Carson–Mitchell, Inc., 601 North Glenstone, Springfield, MO 65801

The complete remedial plan for cleanup of an unlined
surface impoundment containing dioxin and solvent
contaminated waste contains a brief history,
preliminary sampling, pertinent scientific studies,
development of a plan, site preparation, excavation of
dioxin and solvent contaminated sludges and soils,
on-site storage of wastes and ultimate disposal
plans. Special emphasis is given to techniques for
removal of dioxin from wastewater streams and a method
of dewatering organic chemical sludge. The design and
permitting of an on-site dioxin storage facility is
described. Environmental and personal monitoring,
safety, special protective equipment, decontamination
procedures and other general considerations are
briefly discussed.

In 1982, Syntex Agribusiness, Inc. (Syntex) ceased use of an unlined
surface impoundment (Lagoon) at its Springfield, Missouri plant
site. Shortly thereafter, the company began RCRA closure of the
Lagoon. Early in the closure process, a series of samples were
taken from the sludge deposited in the Lagoon's bottom and these
samples were submitted to exhaustive chemical analysis. As soon as
the results of the chemical analysis became available, Syntex sent
the results to the United States Environmental Protection Agency
(USEPA) and the Missouri Department of Natural Resources. The
analysis of the sludge showed significant levels of common plant
solvents and low parts per billion levels of 2,3,7,8
tetrachlorodibenzo–p–dioxin (dioxin). Syntex then began a removal
of the standing water in the Lagoon to reduce the hydrostatic
pressure (head) which might force contaminants into the ground
water. The standing water in the Lagoon was processed through
activated carbon, analyzed to verify that it contained no detectable
dioxin, and discharged to the municipal treatment system. This
removal and treatment of the standing water was done on a continual

0097–6156/87/0338–0278$06.00/0
© 1987 American Chemical Society

basis until the sludge from the Lagoon was excavated in the fall of 1985. Simultaneous to the removal of the standing water, a plan for assessing the Lagoon began to be developed.

## Plan Development

A series of monitoring wells was installed on the plant site around the perimeter of the Lagoon to monitor the alluvial groundwater. Also, a series of near surface bedrock wells was installed in the bedrock (less than 75 feet in depth) to monitor the upper most aquifer.

As previously mentioned, chemical analysis of samples of the Lagoon sludge showed relatively high levels of several solvents and other organic chemicals. Based on these results and the low levels of dioxin previously determined, it seemed desirable to remove these chemical sludges to eliminate a future potential point source of contamination to the groundwater.

The Lagoon was located immediately adjacent to one of the plant's production buildings (approximately 15 feet away) and the plant's wastewater aeration basin. The foundation of the production building and the wall of the wastewater aeration basin was of particular concern since the excavation of the Lagoon sludge could induce caving of the adjacent soil embankments and put these structures at risk. To assess this potential hazard, a series of core borings was made around the Lagoon perimeter. These soil borings were also analyzed for dioxin and various solvents. Soil properties adjacent to these structures were determined to be particularly poor and the chemical analysis of these soils indicated the presence of significant quantities of toluene and xylene. No dioxin was found in any of the borings. A close study of the analytical results and plant history showed that much of the soil contamination was due to an abandoned plant sewer which was located between the Lagoon and the production building. This sewer had evidently leaked for some time and had saturated this area with solvents. This new data required plans which were a significant modification of the relatively straightforward Lagoon excavation that had been contemplated.

In order to excavate the Lagoon and protect the structures mentioned above, a procedure called "benching" was devised. Benching consists of removing a quantity of soil adjacent to the Lagoon and controlling the slope of this excavation to produce an approximately 1.5 to 1 slope. A slope of 1.5 to 1 is not as likely to suddenly fail and endanger the structures. This procedure prevented non-dioxin contaminated soil from falling into the chemical sludge and also allowed the excavation of the majority of the solvent contaminated soils along the path of the abandoned sewer.

The final work plan, which began with various site modifications, followed by benching, sludge excavation, sampling, installation of a french drain system, backfilling, and capping was then developed, reviewed by MDNR (lead agency at the site) and USEPA, and approved in August of 1985. Numerous site preparations had to be implemented prior to commencement of the actual Lagoon remediation.

## Site Preparations

Water Treatment Process. Prior to the development of the final
plan, certain site preparations were required. A long term means of
efficiently processing contaminated water had to be developed to
continue to treat rainfall and infiltration to the Lagoon. During
analytical work, it was discovered that all dioxin contamination of
this water was due to attachment of the dioxin to suspended solids
which, when filtered, removed all of the dioxin contamination in the
water. Based on this discovery, a very efficient alum flocculation
process was developed to remove suspended dioxin bearing
particulates prior to further processing by activated carbon
columns. Dioxin removal prior to  carbon treatment gave extra
capacity for organics removal. Furthermore, the spent carbon could
be returned to the manufacturer for regeneration since it was no
longer contaminated with dioxin. The carbon was then reused for
further organics removal.

Storage Facility. Prior to the finalization of the remedial plan,
it was determined that the excavated sludge contaminated with TCDD
would need to be stored on site until an ultimate disposal method
could be developed. Once measurements were made to assess the
quantity of contaminated sludge (approximately 800 cubic yards), an
on-site storage facility was designed and built. Plan
specifications and actual installation were approved and monitored
by MDNR and USEPA. The facility was sited after geotechnical
borings were conducted. The facility which is approximately 36 feet
wide, 120 feet long, and 8 feet deep, was constructed with one foot
thick reinforced concrete walls and floor. Three equal-sized,
sloped segments of the facility were drained to their own sump. The
storage facility was installed over compacted clay with an
underdrainage system connected to three sumps corresponding to the
three segments of the facility. A second underdrainage system was
then installed inside the concrete facility and the entire facility
lined with 100 mil. high density polyethylene. Perforated pipes
were installed at each sump to allow water to be removed from the
facility once the sludge was in place. The bottom of the stand
pipes was held in place with gap-graded concrete and the entire
stand pipe was covered with filter fabric. The facility was  then
covered with pre-stressed concrete roofing panels. In the bottom of
the facility a six inch layer of spent, activated carbon was
installed and then covered with a geotextile membrane to allow a
drainage area and to further protect the liner during filling. This
storage facility was added to the plant's RCRA permit, a closure and
inspection plan was written, a liner compatibility study was
performed and the liner was dye tested and certified to be leak free
prior to sludge being placed into the storage facility. This
facility was designed to become eventually an equalization tank for
the plant's wastewater treatment system once the sludge is removed
for ultimate disposal and the structure is decontaminated.

<u>Staging Pad</u>. A soil staging pad was constructed adjacent to the Lagoon to accept the non-dioxin, solvent contaminated soil for temporary storage prior to shipment to a hazardous waste landfill. This staging pad was constructed with a one foot high curb and built from reinforced concrete. The pad was situated on top of a 30-mil. high density polyethylene liner with an underdrainage system installed in between the liner and the pad. The pad was covered with a steel frame and canopy and has since been enclosed to provide a RCRA-approved drum storage area for hazardous waste. A closure and inspection plan has been developed for the storage area and the area has been added to the plant's RCRA permit.

<u>Crane Pad</u>. Along one side of the Lagoon a pad for the 100-ton crane was constructed by benching approximately 3 feet of soil and filling the area with shot-rock with a finish of small gravel on top to facilitate foot traffic. This pad allowed the large, tracked crane to maneuver the entire length of the Lagoon to enhance the excavation process.

<u>Hopper and Conveyors</u>. A hopper was built and located at one corner of the crane pad with a concrete wash down area under the hopper. The hopper was used to remove large debris on its bar grate and then used to fill the mixing trucks. It was designed with a pneumatically operated dumping device to assist the cleaning of the bar grate and a pneumatic slide gate to load the mixing trucks. An inclined conveyor was installed at one end of the storage facility and a horizontal conveyor installed on the top of the storage facility which was fed by the inclined conveyor. Both conveyors were belt-type conveyors designed to convey and place concrete. The bottom side of each conveyor was enclosed with a drip-catcher to prevent the return side of the belt from contaminating the work area. Additionally, the inclined conveyor's loading hopper was placed in a separate basin to catch any spills during the loading operation. The horizontal conveyor was designed with a diverter device which allowed the conveyor to be unloaded at any point along its length. This feature was used to place the sludge uniformly into the storage facility through holes sawed into the concrete roofing panels.

Finally, a large 100-ton crane fitted with a clam shell bucket was leased, along with a small track-type front loader. Two used, standard 10 cubic yard concrete trucks were acquired to mix and transport the sludge. A backhoe and other miscellaneous equipment which have previously been used in other remediation activities supported the cleanup. Once all the site preparation activities were completed the site cleanup could begin.

<u>Site Cleanup</u>

<u>Sludge Treatment</u>. The Lagoon chemical sludge was very waxy and did not readily give up entrained water. A pretreatment process was developed by our laboratory which allowed this sludge to be readily dewatered. The result was conversion of this difficult-to-transport material into a relatively dry, sandy textured material. The

pretreatment process involved the addition of a small quantity of
calcium oxide followed by vigorous mixing.  A slaking process then
occurred which rendered the waxy sludge a fluid slurry which, upon
standing, readily dewatered in place.

Dewatering.  Geologic and hydrologic analyses conducted by our
consultant suggested that a groundwater mound existed in conjunction
with Lagoon ponding.  Such a mound was a concern because of possible
(a) Lagoon slope instability prior to dissipation of soil pore
pressure and (b) excessive recharge to the Lagoon during sludge
excavation.  Recharge rates up to 100 gallons per minute were
projected.

Initial efforts focused on removal of free water from the
Lagoon.  Standing water resulting from rainfall was regularly pumped
to the treatment process.  For a period of time prior to excavation,
dewatering of sludge was attempted via pumping from an excavated
sump in the northwest corner of the Lagoon.  Due to the naturally
high water content of the sludge and the absence of monitoring wells
directly adjacent to the Lagoon, verification of mound
existence/dissipation was not possible.

It was generally thought that groundwater inflow to the Lagoon
would be greater through the floor than through the sideslopes
because of the relative permeabilities of the materials.  In order
to approximate the amount of inflow to be expected, a
percolation-type test was devised.  For this test, a 66-inch
diameter corrugated metal pipe, ten feet long, was placed vertically
in the Lagoon.  The clamshell bucket was used to drive the pipe to
refusal in the Lagoon floor.  Following evacuation of sludge and
water from the pipe, the unit recharge rate through the floor would
be quantified and projected for the total Lagoon area.  This
procedure found that water did not rise to a level within the pipe
but, rather, stabilized within an inch of the Lagoon floor.  These
results suggested that; (a) groundwater inflow would not be a
significant problem during excavation of sludge and (b) the Lagoon
floor lay above the shallow water table level.

These observations held true throughout the course of sludge
excavation.  No groundwater problems were encountered, although
surface water from abnormally high rainfall (20.31 in. actual versus
8.64 in. normal for the period 10/1/85 through 12/31/85) greatly
increased the quantity of water handled by the water treatment
system.

Benching.  In light of previously discussed soil stability problems
adjacent to the Lagoon, several precautionary measures were
implemented in conjunction with closure activities to ensure slope
stability.  These measures included:

    a) Benching of Lagoon slopes.  The top Lagoon slope was
       excavated to a depth of two to four feet to produce a
       bench approximately ten feet wide.  This action
       relieved slope surcharge (reduced the driving force)
       and provided a surface to contain upper slope
       sloughing.  Solvent contaminated soil adjacent to the
       production building was placed on the staging pad for
       future disposal.

b) Construction of a crane pad.  A 30 ft. X 90 ft. area adjacent to the Lagoon was excavated to a depth of two feet and backfilled with 4 - 6 inch crushed limestone.  The crushed limestone was topped with a 6-inch gravel layer to facilitate foot traffic.  This pad provided a solid working surface for the crane and distributed crane loads to an acceptable level. Excavated soils for the crane pad were free of contamination and were placed on the clean fill stock pile to be used as back fill once the Lagoon was excavated.

c) Monitoring of Process Building.  Due to the close proximity of the process building to the Lagoon, survey monuments were established along the east wall and monitored daily for displacement.  No such displacement was observed.

d) Protection of completed slopes.  Following excavation of sidewalls, polyethylene sheeting was placed on finished slopes to prevent subsequent contamination and provide protection from rainfall.

e) Visual inspection of slopes.  During the course of Lagoon closure, slopes were inspected daily for any signs of slope instability.

Lagoon slopes performed satisfactorily during the duration of the project.  Although abnormally high rainfall occurred, erosion/sloughing of slopes was minimal.

Excavation Sequence.  Excavation commenced with scraping of exposed Lagoon slopes above the sludge level to a depth of six inches.  This material was considered potentially contaminated and added to the Lagoon.  After the slopes were scraped, benching of adjacent non-dioxin, solvent-contaminated soil was performed by the front loader.  This material was transported by clamshell and placed on the staging pad.

After these activities, excavation of sludge began.  The sludge was excavated with the clamshell and placed in the elevated hopper. Materials not passing the bar grate on top of the hopper and other materials removed directly from the Lagoon were drummed and stored on the staging pad.  Prior to discharging the hopper, a measured quantity of calcium oxide was added to hopper.  The contents of the hopper was then dumped into the concrete mix truck and vigorously mixed for approximately five minutes.  Upon mixing, the truck was moved to the inclined conveyor and contents discharged to the conveyor loading hopper.  The inclined conveyor then fed the horizontal conveyor which was diverted to a series of holes cut into the storage facility roof.

This procedure was utilized successfully until the majority of sludge was removed from the Lagoon.  At this point, however, the shallow depth of sludge, approximately six inches, and greatly decreased percentage of solids, made clamshell excavation inefficient. To complete removal of sludge, a quantity of calcium oxide was added to the Lagoon and mixed with the track loader. The track loader was then used to pile the thickened material for clamshell excavation. This operation was repeated until all sludge was removed from the Lagoon. A section of the removable concrete roof was set aside to allow the clamshell to drop the treated sludge directly into the storage facility.

After the sludge was removed, the Lagoon bottom and slopes were scraped until no visible contamination remained. A rubber-tired backhoe was committed to the Lagoon to supplement the track loader for this activity. The Lagoon bottom was found to be firm and readily supported vehiclular traffic. No groundwater inflow to the Lagoon occurred. Excavated material was again piled by the two loaders and clamshelled directly to the storage facility.

Once the contaminated materials were placed inside the storage facility, the treated sludge rapidly dewatered to the three sumps. Water was pumped from the sumps in the storage facility as the dewatering occurred. This process will continue until no water remains in the sumps. Any water pumped from the facility is treated, analyzed and discharged to the municipal sewer system.

## Sampling

Following sludge excavation, the Lagoon bottom was sampled in accordance with the approved sampling protocol. Eighteen discrete samples were obtained and composited into three samples representing the north, middle, and south sections of the Lagoon floor. Discrete sample coordinates and elevations were tabulated. The highest levels of dioxin and total organics were 0.14 ppb and 875 ppm, respectively. The detected levels of dioxin are well below the 1 ppb level recognized by CDC as acceptable for residential exposure with one hundred percent surface contamination. The remaining organics will be addressed in the groundwater remediation program.

## French Drain

To recover any remaining organic contamination from the adjacent soils a french drain system was installed in the bottom of the excavated Lagoon.The french drain design used a granular layer over the entire Lagoon floor, allowing capture of water migrating upward through the floor (such as with naturally fluctuating watertable conditions) in addition to any rare seepage entering through the Lagoon walls. In conjunction with the drainage layer, a stainless steel well was constructed at the low point on the Lagoon floor to accommodate monitoring and recovery of fluids. Since the well could draw fluids from all directions, no supplementary piping was required.

The large crushed rock from the crane pad was pushed into the Lagoon to provide the porous drainage area of the french drain. In order to ensure absolutely free drainage to the monitoring/recovery well, a 24-inch wide perimeter trench was excavated in the crane pad

material and backfilled with clean 5/8-inch crushed limestone. The
monitoring/recovery well, sited in the southeastern portion of the
Lagoon, utilized an additional quantity of 5/8-inch crushed
limestone as gravel pack. Following construction of the french
drain, geotextile fabric and a one-foot thick layer of base course
were placed above the porous drainage area for protection during
backfill.

## Backfill

Backfill of the Lagoon proceeded with soil earlier stockpiled on
site. This material, derived from offsite construction excavations,
consisted of dark red residual clay native to the Springfield area.
Laboratory analyses certified this material to be free of dioxin and
other contaminants.

To ensure that the required cap permeability ($1.0 \times 10^{-7}$
cm/sec) could be achieved, laboratory testing of the remolded virgin
soil was conducted. These results confirmed that the required
permeability could be achieved utilizing virgin soil compacted to
approximately 95% Standard Proctor Density.

The backfill was placed in a maximum of one-foot lifts and
compacted to approximately 95% Standard Proctor Density using the
track loader and rubber tired backhoe. This procedure effectively
produced a 10-foot thick seal exhibiting $1.0 \times 10^{-7}$ cm/sec
permeability and precludes the possibility of appreciable
settlement. Field compaction tests were performed during the
backfilling to assure that proper compaction was achieved.

Once the backfill was completed it was graded to a two percent
slope for rapid stormwater drainage. The final graded area was then
covered with gravel.

## CONCLUSION

This paper described the process through which a team of
environmental engineering, geotechnical engineers, analytical
chemists, and other scientists addressed the cleanup of a dioxin and
solvent contaminated site. The remediation program used here was
successfully completed without posing a hazard to the community or
the workers, yet it was completed in a timely manner at a small
fraction of the cost normally reported for cleaning less complex
sites. The entire excavation was completed in 21 days using a crew
of six remediation workers. Every structure and piece of equipment
is designed to provide a future long term use or can be
decontaminated through proven methods and resold to minimize cost.
All contaminated materials were handled and stored in bulk to
eliminate costly bagging or drumming of the materials. This bulk
handling of materials can dramatically reduce cleanup costs.

Experience, planning, training and careful project
implementation provide the ingredients for a remediation project
that meets or exceeds all environmental and budget goals. This
remediation package should be a useful model for regulatory agencies
and firms faced with the evaluation and cleanup of similar lagoons
or landfills contaminated with dioxin and/or organic chemicals.

RECEIVED November 25, 1986

# Chapter 22

# Removal of 2,3,7,8-Tetrachlorodibenzo-*p*-dioxin from Waste Water and Well Water

## Coagulation and Flocculation with Aluminum Salts

Leland Marple, Dale Dei Rossi, and Lewis Throop

Syntex Analytical and Environmental Research, Syntex (USA), Inc.,
3401 Hillview Avenue, Palo Alto, CA 94303

At various times, water in a wastewater lagoon
contained several parts per trillion
2,3,7,8-tetrachlorodibenzo-p-dioxin (dioxin). A
process was developed for the removal of trace amounts
based on coagulation and flocculation with aluminum
salts. On site treatment utilized a batch process in
which suspended solids were coagulated with 1200 mg/l
aluminum sulfate. A polymer modified alum flocculation
process was developed for the removal of dioxin from
well water. The modification of the floc surface by
the adsorption of an uncharged, high molecular weight
polymer intensifies the adsorption of dioxin on the
floc.

One of the major problems involved in the remediation of the Dioxin
contaminated surface impoundment (lagoon) discussed earlier ([1]) was
the treatment of the water to insure complete removal of any
2,3,7,8-tetrachlorodibenzo-p-dioxin (Dioxin) that may be present.
Initially, suspended matter was removed by filtration through ground
corncobs, and residual organics were removed by treatment with
activated carbon. Although this treatment was effective, the
processing time per batch coupled with groundwater seepage and
periods of heavy rainfall prolonged the drainage of the lagoon for
over a year.

The selective removal of very low levels of dioxin from large
volumes of process wastewater has become a concern to a number of
companies and municipalities. Very little has been reported on how
dioxin behaves in conventional water treatment processes ([2-3]). The
work of Thebault, Cases, and Fiessinger suggested that alum
flocculation would be marginally effective for the removal of
dioxin. Our need to remove up to several parts per trillion dioxin
from water in the lagoon prompted us to evaluate flocculation as a
faster and more cost effective treatment for dioxin removal.

0097-6156/87/0338-0286$06.00/0

As it turned out, dioxin was readily removed by alum flocculating in the presence of suspended organic matter. The successful treatment of lagoon water prompted work on two related problems. Firstly, we needed to find a way to dewater the asphaltum like lagoon sludge, and secondly, we needed to find a way to treat wellwater, having little suspended solids, to remove dioxin that might be present. This paper describes our experimental work on these problems and application of our findings to treatment at the plant site.

EXPERIMENTAL

The amount of aluminum needed to produce rapid flocculation of lagoon water with a suspended solids content of about 3200 ppm was determined by 100 ml jar tests. A 0.002 uCi spike of 14-C dioxin (Kor Inc.) was added to the water and equilibrated for 2 hours before flocculation. Ammonium sulfate, 500 ppm, was added to increase the ionic strength and promote coagulation. The buffer capacity of the water was sufficient to precipitate the aluminum added, and the final pH of the water was about 8. The amount of dioxin spike remaining in solution was determined by centrifuging the sample, withdrawing a 50 ml aliquot of the clear supernatant and extracting the dioxin with hexane. The hexane extract was reduced in volume in a rotary evaporator, then transferred to a glass scintillation vial along with 5 ul of n-tetradecane. The extract was reduced to near dryness with a stream of nitrogen, diluted with scintillation fluid, then counted in a Packard TriCarb scintillation counter.

The flocculation process was scaled up to treat 20,000 gallons per batch. The supernatant from each batch was analyzed for dioxin, then treated with activated carbon for removal of residual organics The settled floc was returned to the lagoon for dewatering.

The coagulation of lagoon sludge by lime was followed by a simple jar test. A 40 g sample of sludge was mixed with water to bring the volume to 200 ml. Increments of 0.10 g calcium oxide were added and mixed well. The mixture was allowed to settle for 5 minutes after each addition, and the extent of coagulation estimated from the clarity of the supernatant. The dewatering of coagulated sludge was demonstrated by building a 4 inch by 6 foot column in 12-6 in. increments over a period of 9 days. The lime was added directly to the sludge and mixed by inversion of the container. The coagulated sludge was retained by a 2 inch bed of activated carbon held in place by a perforated stainless steel screen. Water draining from the column was pooled until the last addition was made, then it was collected on a daily basis.

The removal of dioxin from water by modified alum flocculation was monitored by the disappearance of a 0.08 uCi spike of 3-H labeled dioxin (obtained from A. Poland, repurified by silica column chromatography) in jar type experiments. A conventional uncharged Garratt-Callahan polymer #7882 was used for floc modification. The labeled dioxin spike, dissolved in hexane-methylene chloride, 80:20, was introduced into 200 ml of water in several ways. The spike was added directly to the water, it was added to water containing the

modifying polymer, and it was evaporated as a film on the inside of
the beaker used to hold the water sample prior to flocculation.
After the alum was added, the water was flash mixed for two minutes,
then stirred slowly for 5 minutes while the floc formed.  The floc
was allowed to settle for 15 minutes, then the supernatant was
analyzed for dioxin by withdrawing a 50 ml aliquot, extracting the
dioxin with hexane, and working up the extract as described above.


RESULTS/DISCUSSION

The removal of 14-C dioxin from lagoon water by flocculation with
varying amounts of aluminum followed by centrifugation is
illustrated in Table I.


Table I.  Removal of 14-C Dioxin spike from Lagoon Water by
          Flocculation with Aluminum Salts

| AlCl$_3$ | 44 ppm Al | (u) % |
|----------|-----------|-------|
|          | 87        | 99.8  |
|          | 87        | 99.7  |
|          | 100       | 99.7  |
|          | 130       | 99.6  |
| Alum     | 89 ppm Al | 98.5  |
|          | 89        | 99.5  |

      (u) unmeasured as coagulation was incomplete


The removal was calculated from the counts remaining in solution
compared to the counts added to the system.  Although there is very
little information in the literature on removal of chlorinated
organics by alum or lime flocculation, our results are consistent
with available data.  For example, Saleh, Lee and Wolf (4) removed
about 95% of combined DDT isomers from an activated sludge effluent
upon coagulation/flocculation with a 23 ppm/165ppm lime/alum
mixture.  One would expect a greater adsorption of dioxin compared
to DDT, owing to the lower water solubility of dioxin.
          Scale-up of the treatment process proceeded smoothly.  Table
II summarizes the levels of dioxin found in the supernatant for
batches processed at the plant site.
While low levels of other soluble organics, such as mixed xylenes,
ethylbenzene and toluene, are also adsorbed by the floc, data are
not available for their removal at the site.
                 Since the major difference, in principle, between water
in the lagoon and the sludge in the bottom was the peptized solids
content, coagulation appeared to be the logical route for sludge
dewatering.  This was demonstrated by suspending a sample in water,
and titrating suspension with alum until the solids coagulated.
Since coagulation with lime is generally more cost effective than
alum, we determined the amount needed by a simple jar test.
Although the coagulation appeared to be complete at 1% lime, we
allowed for variation in sludge composition by using a 25% excess

Table II. Removal of Dioxin from Lagoon Water at Plant Site by Alum Flocculation

| Batch # | Influent | Effluent |
|---------|----------|----------|
| 021-R-1 | 3.1 ppt | 0.35 ppt |
| 021-R-2 | * | 0.17 |
| 022 | * | 0.20 |
| 022 | | 0.21 |
| 023 | | 0.17 |
| 024 | | 0.16 |
| 025 | | 0.27 |
| 026 | | 0.93 |
| 027 | | 0.70 |
| 028-1 | | 0.42 |

*undetermined, but from the same source as 021-R-1

for the preparation of a dewatering test column. The total weight of the treated sludge put in the column was 22.89 Kg. Water drained from the column over the course of sludge addition amounted to 7.00 Kg, representing 98% of the water ultimately drained from the bed. Dioxin could not be detected in the pooled water sample, nor could it be detected (< 0.6 ppt) in water subsequently drained from the sludge bunker at the plant site.

We did not expect that the removal of dioxin from well and runoff water by alum coagulation and flocculation would be effective, as there is little or no suspended organic phase to act as a carrier for dioxin. This problem was solved by adding a high molecular weight polymer that would be adsorbed to and carried down with the floc. Partition of dioxin into the polymer is so favored that parts per million levels of polymer should remove most of the dioxin. The results of jar tests to find the optimum level of polymer, at a fixed 100 ppm level of aluminum are given in Table III.

Table III. Removal of 3-H Dioxin Spike from Tap Water by Polymer Modified Alum Flocculation

| Conc. Polymer, #7882 | % Dioxin Removed at 100 ppm Al |
|----------------------|--------------------------------|
| 12.3 | 86.1 |
| 18.5 | 92.8 |
| 18.5 | 89.0 |
| 24.6 | 68.0 |
| 24.6 | 73.8 |
| 30.8 | 84.6 |

If one assumes that the partition of dioxin between polymer and water is equivalent to the partition between octanol and water, the amount of dioxin in solution should drop by at least 94%. The penalty for this process is an additional solids waste loading of about 2.5 pound per 1000 gal. treated water.

The effect of introducing dioxin into the system by different routes is given in Table IV.

Table IV. Summary of Dioxin Removals by Modified Alum Flocculations

| Method | % Initial Spike Dissolved | % Soluble Spike Removed | Polymer/Al Ratio ppm |
|---|---|---|---|
| Solid Dioxin Residue | 65 | 85 | 18/100 |
| | | 25 | 0/100 |
| Dioxin to Water with Polymer | 30 | 86 | 12/100 |
| | | 93 | 18/100 |
| Dioxin to Water | 60 | 89 | 18/100 |
| | | 90 | 18/80 |
| | | 75 | 18/80 |

The various routes were used to avoid artifacts arising from adsorption at surfaces in the equilibrating system. It is clear from these data that the removal of dioxin by a 12-18 ppm polymer modified alum floc was very close to 90%. Verification of the removal of dioxin by the floc was obtained by recovering the floc and measuring the tritium activity. This was needed in order to rule out the possibility that the polymer merely enhanced the loss to the system. As it turned out, the amount of dioxin that was trapped by the floc was greater than that calculated from the decrease in soluble dioxin in solution, so some of the dioxin originally lost to the system was recovered by the floc. Consequently, scale up of this process at the plant site has the potential of being more efficient at removing dioxin from water than we predict from laboratory experiments.

LITERATURE CITED

(1)  Forrester, R.F., Marple, L.W. Carson Jr., C.P., in "Solving Hazardous Waste Problems: Dioxins," Exner, J.H., Ed.; ACS Symposium Series No.___, American Chemical Society, Washington, D.C. 1987, P.___.

(2)  Robeck, C.G., Dostal, K.A., Cohen, J.M., Dreissel, J.F., J. Am. Water Wks. Ass. 1965, 57, 181-199.

(3)  Thebault, P., Cases, J.M., Fiessinger, F., Water Research 1982, 15, 183-189.

(4)  Saleh, F.Y., Lee, G.F., Wolf, H.W., Water Research 1982, 16, 479-488.

RECEIVED November 25, 1986

# Chapter 23

# Comparison of Laboratory and Field Test Data in the Chemical Decontamination of Dioxin-Contaminated Soils

R. Peterson[1], E. Milicic[1], C. Novosad[1], and C. Rogers[2]

[1]Galson Research Corporation, 6601 Kirkville Road, East Syracuse, NY 13057
[2]U.S. Environmental Protection Agency, 26 West St. Clair, Cincinnati, OH 45220

A series of patented ([1]) processes have been developed for chemical decontamination of soils contaminated with halogenated aromatics, including polychlorinated dibenzo-p-dioxins (PCDD), chlorinated benzenes, polychlorinated biphenyls and similar materials. These processes allow reduction of PCDD levels to less than 1 part per billion (ppb) in as little as two hours at moderate temperatures and pressures.

Chemical decontamination is an alternative to thermal processing or landfilling of soils contaminated with polychlorinated dibenzo-p- dioxins (PCDD) or other aromatic halides such as chlorobenzenes or polychorinated biphenyls (PCB). Chemical decontamination, like incineration, involves changes to the chemical structure of the dioxin molecule. While chlorinated dioxins are thermally stable, they readily dechlorinate to water soluble compounds under relatively mild conditions of temperature and pressure. For example, chlorinated dioxins in oil are reduced to the ppt level within 60 minutes at 150 degrees C. by reacting them to a compound which is no longer oil soluble. In soils processing, the dioxin is dechlorinated to a water soluble form which is then leached from the soil using countercurrent extraction with water. Dechlorination also affects the toxicity of the dioxin, with dioxins containing fewer than three chlorine atoms generally showing low toxicity ([2]).

## Process Chemistry

The proposed mechanism for these reactions is shown in Figure 1 using 2,3,7,8 tetrachlorodibenzo-p-dioxin as an example. An alkali metal hydroxide, usually potassium hydroxide (KOH) is treated with an alcohol or glycol such as polyethylene glycol 400 ( PEG 400) to form an alkoxide. The alkoxide reacts with one of the chlorine atoms on the chlorinated dioxin to produce an ether and the alkali metal salt.

The reaction may proceed to complete dechlorination, although replacement of a single chlorine is sufficient to make the reaction products water soluble.  The ether formed by the dechlorination may  degrade to a phenol form or may remain as the ether, depending on the reaction conditions.  The processing is carried out using dimethyl sulfoxide (DMSO) as a solvent, which increases the base strength of the alkoxide.  In addition, the DMSO aids in the extraction of the PCDD from the soil.

Toxicity Considerations

Chemical decontamination of soil is a two-stage process;

1.  Dechlorinate PCDD to lower toxicity/ water soluble form
2.  Wash excess reagents and PCDD products from soil

A major concern in this type of processing involves the toxicity of any reagents and/or reaction products which may inadvertently be left in the decontaminated soil after treatment.  Some toxicity data on reagents used in the process  are shown in Table I, along with comparison values for sodium chloride and 2,3,7,8-TCDD.

Table I - Toxicity of Reagents and Comparison Materials

| Material | LD50, Oral-rat (3) |
|---|---|
| polyethylene glycol 400 | 27,500 mg/kg |
| dimethyl sulfoxide | 17,500 mg/kg |
| sodium chloride (comparison value) | 3,000 mg/kg |
| 2,3,7,8-TCDD       (comparison value) | 0.022 mg/kg |

The reagents used in this process are some five times less toxic than table salt, and roughly six orders of magnitude less toxic than 2,3,7,8 TCDD, the dioxin isomer of major concern.  Polyethlyene glycol 400 is an FDA approved material for use in foods and cosmetics.  Dimethyl sulfoxide is a naturally occurring material in foods such as potatoes, milk and coffee at the part per million level.  Expected residual levels of these materials in soil are not expected to be a serious concern.
Toxicity testing of the converted aromatic halides is currently underway with EPA sponsorship.  Structural assessment of the theoretical toxicity of the reaction products is favorable, ie the known reaction products would not be expected to show significant toxicity.  Results of the Ames test for mutagenicity are negative, ie the reaction products do not demonstrate carcinogenic potential.  Bioaccumulation tests also produced negative results, which is not surprising given the water solubility of these reaction products.  Acute toxicity tests are currently in progress, with intial results showing low toxicity .

## Process Description

The decontamination of soil proceeds in a series of six process steps.

1. Combine equal masses of soil and reagent to form a slurry
2. Mix and heat soil/reagent slurry to 100-180 °C
3. Allow to react 1-5 hours
4. Decant excess reagent
5. Wash soil 2-3 times with water
6. Discharge decontaminated soil

This process is shown in diagram form in Figure 2.  All of the process steps can be conducted in a single reactor equipped with an agitator.  The number of wash steps required depends on the effectiveness of each wash step and on the degree of reagent recovery required.

## Results of Tests to Date

Three series of tests using dioxin contaminated soil have been conducted to date:  laboratory tests at high and low rates of agitation and field tests at low agitation only.  Each set is discussed separately.

Laboratory Testing - High agitation.  Initial laboratory tests used 250 g. soil samples spiked to a  nominal  concentration  of 2000 parts per billion (ppb) of 1,2,3,4-TCDD.  The 1,2,3,4 isomer was used in place of the 2,3,7,8-TCDD isomer to simplify experimental and safety procedures.  Tests with both isomers in liquid solution show similar reaction rates.  These tests used an electrically heated 1000 mL three neck flask equipped with a reflux condenser and high torque agitator to provide a high degree of mixing.

In the initial series of experiments a fluorocarbon paddle was used with the agitator.  Analysis of the treated soil samples revealed the presence of an unknown halogenated contaminant which was later determined to be partially decomposed fluorocarbon.   The combination of reagent and erosion from the soil had broken down the fluorocarbon used in the agitator. This interference required some additional sample cleanup.  Changing to a glass paddle solved the problem for laboratory testing.

Treated samples were analyzed by three different labs using either gas chromatography/mass spectroscopy (GC/MS) or GC/MS/MS methods. Analysis by gas chromatography alone was unsuccessful, partly due to the fluorocarbon interferences previously noted. The results of this initial testing are summarized in Table II.

These tests indicated that while reaction rates for soils were lower than those obtained in oil tests, the overall reaction times were reasonable for large scale application.

Laboratory Testing - Low Agitation.  After design of the field test equipment, it became apparent that the degree of agitation obtained in the initial laboratory tests was not going to be achieved in the field.  Therefore,  tests were conducted at a low rate of agitation to provide a prediction of the

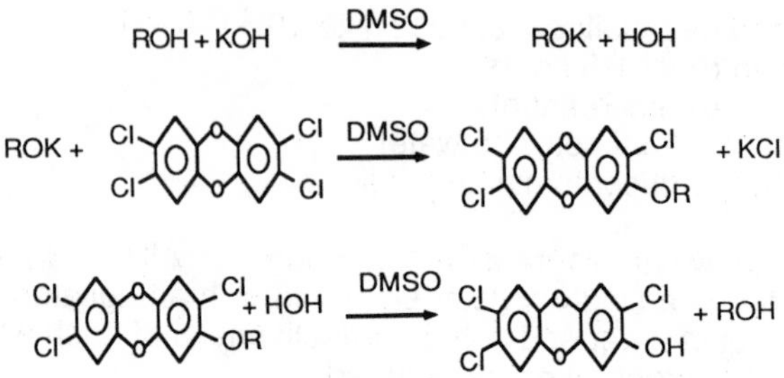

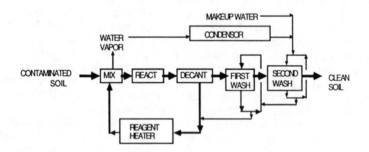

Figure 1. Proposed reaction mechanism.

Figure 2. Process diagram.

Table II - Results of Laboratory Testing with High Agitation
Initial Concentration 2200 ppb 1,2,3,4-TCDD

| Reaction Temperature, °C | Reaction Time, Hours | Final TCDD Concentration, ppb |
|---|---|---|
| 260 | 4 | <1 |
| 150 | 2 | <1 |
| 100 | 2 | <0.2 |
| 70 | 0.5 | 15 |
| 70 | 2 | <1 |
| 50 | 2 | 29 |
| 25 | 2 | 36 |

probable results of field testing. This testing used a flask equipped with a condenser and inserted into a heated oil bath. Agitation was provided by manually swirling the flask and contents at periodic intervals. Soil for this test was the same soil to be used for field testing, and contained "native" 2,3,7,8 TCDD. Analyses were made using GC/MS/MS techniques. The results of testing are shown in Table III.

Table III - Results of Laboratory Testing at Low Agitation, 125 °C
Initial concentration approximately 300 ppb 2,3,7,8 TCDD

| Reaction time, hours | TCDD level, ppb |
|---|---|
| 0 | 175 |
| 1.5 | 15.1 |
| 4.25 | 2.06 |
| 7.0 | 0.3 |

These data indicate that the reaction time for samples with low rates of mixing are on the order of 2-3 times longer than those for samples with high rates of mixing, but still well below 8 hours.

Field Test Results. Field testing for this test series consisted of a series of runs using 30 kg. soil samples taken from a dioxin site in Mississippi. Herbicide Orange had been stored at this site, with some spillage, causing soil contamination.

Test equipment for this series of tests is shown in Figure 3. A 55 gallon drum was modified by the addition of a steel plate halfway down the drum. The plate was pierced by a valve and by a tap to allow pumping of liquids out of the reservoir. The steel plate was sealed with a silicone sealant around the perimeter of the plate. Contaminated soil and reagents were added to the drum by weight. The drum was then covered and a vent line attached between the drum and a carbon filter. A heat tape was wrapped around the drum, and the entire drum was insulated with fiberglass.

The insulated drum was placed on a drum rocker and rocked from side to side to mix the soil and reagent during heating and reaction.   The results of the testing are shown  in Table IV.

Table IV - Results of Field Testing, 2,3,7,8-TCDD

| Reaction time, hours | TCDD level, ppb | |
|---|---|---|
|  | Initial | Final |
| 1.0 | 154 | 37.3 |
| 2.5 | 356 | 10.7 |
| 6.5 | equipment failure | |

The equipment failure occurred at the seal around the perimeter of the steel plate holding the soil/reagent slurry out of the reservoir.  In the 6.5 hour run this seal failed,  which caused the reagent to separate from the soil and stop the reaction.  As noted in the laboratory testing, the reagent is very corrosive to polymers, including fluorocarbons.  Seal material selection will be studied in depth prior to scaleup of this process.

Discussion of Laboratory and Field Data

The data from the three series of tests is summarized in Figure 4.  Three points can be noted from these data;

1.  For each reaction, an initial rate of reaction is followed by a second lower rate of reaction, vs. the single line reaction plot expected for a single order reaction.
2.  The laboratory data for the high mixing case indicate a higher rate of reaction than for the lower rate of mixing. This difference is primarily in the initial reaction rate, while the secondary reaction rate is closer to that for the low mixing case.
3.  The rates of reaction for field tests and for laboratory tests at low agitation rates are very similar.

The bimodal reaction rate is characteristic for soils treated by this process but not for oil treatment, in which a single line reaction plot is observed.  This dual reaction rate may be due to the heterogeneity of soils. Organics on soils may be adsorbed on the surface of the soil particles, in the micropores of the soil or even wrapped up in the helical humic structures present in some soils.  A bimodal reaction rate would be consistent with a process in which extraction of the dioxin from the soil into the reagent is the rate-limiting step.  Extraction of dioxin from the micropores would be expected to be much slower than from the surface of the soil particles.   This hypothesis is consistent with overall rate data showing that the rate of reaction is much higher for liquids than for soils, indicating an extraction limited process.

The micropore/soil surface phenomenon may also explain why the high mixing case shows a much greater difference in initial and final reaction rates than those for the low mixing case.  Despite the fact that the soil for all tests came from the same site, the soils for the high mixing case were spiked

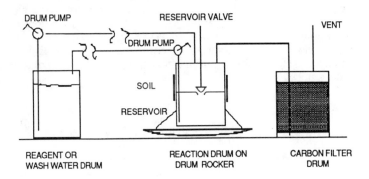

Figure 3. Apparatus for field soils processing.

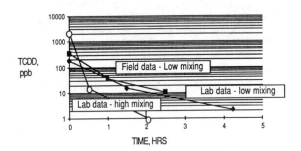

Figure 4. Results of soils processing.

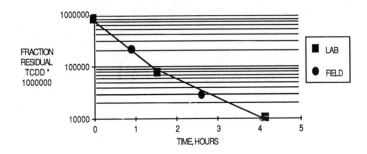

Figure 5. Comparison of laboratory and field data at low agitation.

with dioxin on the same day as the soil was processed.   By contrast, the low mixing case soils had weathered for more than five years.   It may be that weathering may change the micropore/soil surface distribution of the adsorbed dioxin, possibly by differential volatilization of the dioxin from the surface or by successive displacement of the dioxin by other materials.

The low mixing data for laboratory and field data show a very high degree of correlation.  If placed on a normalized graph, these data fall on a single line, as shown in Figure 5.  This indicates that the 100:1 scaleup of the process was successful in demonstrating that the procedure is not strongly dependent on sample size.

## Conclusions

The results of this study can be summarized as follow;

> 1.  Chemical decontamination of dioxin contaminated soils can reduce dioxin levels to < 1 ppb under laboratory conditions using either high or low rates of agitation.
> 2.  Increasing rates of agitation yield increasing rates of reaction, although other factors may also be involved.
> 3.  Field test data at low rates of agitation are very comparable to laboratory data at low rates of agitation.

## Acknowledgments

This work has been sponsored by the United States Air Force and by the United States Environmental Protection Agency under EPA contract 68-03-321.

## Literature Cited

1. Peterson, R. L. U. S. Patent 4 574 013,  1986.
2. Esposito, M. P.; Tiernan, T. O.; Dryden, F. E., "Dioxins", EPA-600/2-80-197, p. 187
3. "Niosh Registry of Toxic Effects of Chemical Substances", U.S. Department of Health and Human Services, 1981-2

RECEIVED December 12, 1986

Chapter 24

# Destruction of Dioxin Contamination by Pyrolysis Techniques

Jimmy Boyd[1], H. D. Williams[2], R. W. Thomas[2], and T. L. Stoddart[3]

[1]J. M. Huber Corporation, P.O. Box 283, Borger, TX 79008
[2]EG&G Idaho, P.O. Box 1625, Idaho Falls, ID 83401
[3]Headquarters, Air Force Engineering Services Center, Research & Development Directorate, Environics Division, Environmental Engineering Branch, Tyndall Air Force Base, FL 32403

The J. M. Huber Corporation Advanced Electric Reactor (AER) pyrolysis process was field-demonstrated in a proof-of-principle test to show that dioxins in contaminated soil could be destroyed to less than 1 ppb. Testing was conducted at a former Herbicide Orange storage site at the Naval Battalion Construction Center (NCBC) in Gulfport, MS, during June 1985. Sample analysis of treated soil shows total isomer classes of tetra-, penta-, and hexapolychlorinated dibenzo-p-dioxins and tetra-, penta-, and hexapolychlorinated dibenzofurans to be less than 0.12 ppb. Herbicide compounds 2,4-D and 2,4,5-T and 2,4-di and 2,4,5/2,4,6-trichlorophenol compounds in the soil feedstock were also destroyed in the treated soil to levels below detectability. NCBC treated soil meets the Environmental Protection Agency delisting characteristic requirements. Lead and zinc are enriched in the baghouse material, which suggests that the process can be used for recovery of inorganic materials from contaminated soils that volatilize at the AER operating temperature. Test results clearly demonstrate the extremely high destruction capabilities of the AER process.

Dioxin contamination of soils has occurred throughout the world. Herbicide Orange (HO), primarily composed of two compounds, 2,4-D (2,4-dichlorophenoxyacetic acid) and 2,4,5-T (2,4,5-trichlorophenoxyacetic acid) and various esters of these two compounds, was sprayed

as a defoliant in Vietnam during the 1960s and at Eglin Air Force
Base, FL, between 1962 and 1970 (1,2). 2,4,5-T was subsequently
identified as teratogenic in mice and rats, with tetrachlorodibenzo-
p-dioxin (2,3,7,8-TCDD) shown to be the toxic containment (3,4).
During the early 1970s, unpaved roads and riding arenas in Times
Beach, MO, were sprayed with salvage oil believed to have been mixed
with waste material containing 2,3,7,8-TCDD in high concentrations
(5). In 1976, an explosion in a trichlorophenol production plant at
Seveso, Italy, caused significant 2,3,7,8-TCDD contamination to the
surrounding area (6). Dioxins have also been identified as combustion products released from municipal and industrial incinerators
through the combustion of chlorinated precursors present in the fuel
or by reaction of organic compounds with inorganic chlorine both
present in the fuel (7-12). Through long-term release, these incinerator emissions of dioxins can contaminate downwind soils to reach
levels of concern to the public health. Exposure from dioxin-
contaminated soil conditions as shown in these examples may place
the public health at risk.

The U.S. Environmental Protection Agency (EPA) presently has no
limits on dioxin contamination levels in soil. After studying the
risks, however, the Centers for Disease Control (CDC) of the U.S.
Department of Health and Human Services in Atlanta, GA, has concluded
that residual soil contamination levels at or above 1 ppb of 2,3,7,8-
TCDD in residential areas cannot be considered safe and represent a
level of concern (5). Uniform contamination levels are assumed. CDC
also recommends low levels for pasture lands because of food chain
accumulation. However, CDC concludes that, in certain commercial
areas, higher levels in soils may represent an acceptable risk to
nonoccupationally exposed individuals, but that level has not been
defined.

In September 1983, the J. M. Huber Corporation of Borger, TX,
embarked on a program to demonstrate the capability of the Advanced
Electric Reactor (AER) to detoxify 2,3,7,8-TCDD contaminated soil.
This program also includes the treatment of soils contaminated with
polychlorinated biphenyls (PCBs), carbon tetrachloride, and
octachlorodibenzo-p-dioxin (OCDD). A field demonstration of 2,3,7,8-
TCDD contaminated soil at a former HO storage site at the Naval Construction Battalion Center (NCBC) in Gulfport, MS, represents a
continuation of this demonstration process. This testing was performed to demonstrate innovative technologies as part of the Air
Force Environmental Restoration Program for former HO sites. A specific goal of this technology testing was to reduce the total concentration of all isomers of tetra-, penta-, and hexa-CDD and
respective isomers of chlorodibenzofurans to less than 1 ppb.

## Method

AER Process. The AER employs a new technology to rapidly heat material to approximately 2200°C, using intense thermal radiation in the
near infrared region (Figure 1). The reactions, which can be gaseous, liquid, or solid, are isolated from the reactor core walls by
means of a gaseous blanket formed by flowing nitrogen radially inward
through the porous core walls. Carbon electrodes are heated and, in
turn, heat the reactor core to incandescence so that the heat transfer is accomplished by thermal radiative coupling from the core to

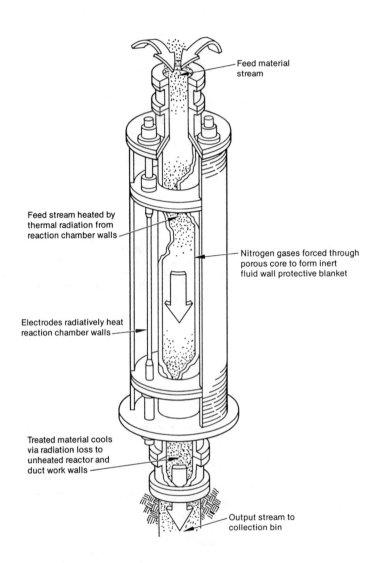

Figure 1. Advanced Electric Reactor.

the feed materials. The only feed streams to the reactor are the solid, liquid, or gaseous wastes and the nitrogen blanket gas.

Destruction is accomplished by pyrolysis rather than oxidation; therefore, typical products and by-products produced by incineration such as carbon monoxide, carbon dioxide, and oxides of nitrogen are not formed in significant concentrations. The principal products from soil-affixed TCDD using the Huber process are hydrogen, chlorine, hydrochloric acid, elemental carbon, and granular free-flowing soil material.

Figure 2 is a simplified process diagram of the AER process for solid hazardous waste destruction. The solid feed steam is introduced at the top of the reactor by means of a metered screw feeder connecting the airtight feed hopper to the reactor. Nitrogen is introduced primarily at two points in the reactor annulus. The solid feed passes through the reactor where pyrolysis occurs at temperatures between 1900 and 2500°C. After leaving the reactor, the product gas and waste solids pass through a postreactor treatment zone (PRTZ). The PRTZ provides for additional residence time but primarily cools the gas to less than 550°C before downstream particulate cleanup.

Solids exiting the PRTZ are collected in a solids collection bin that is sealed to the atmosphere. Any entrained solids in the product gas are removed as the gases enter a baghouse. Any residual organics and chlorine are removed by passing the product gas through activated carbon beds (or a caustic scrubber, if necessary) just upstream of the process stack. The clean product gas, composed almost entirely of nitrogen (some moisture), is then emitted to the atmosphere through the process stack.

An integral part of the AER design is to ensure safety of personnel and the environment when processing hazardous wastes. For example, if electrical power to the process is interrupted, the motor-driven screw feeder stops feeding solids, and within one to two seconds, all solids are purged from the reactor by gravity flow. The large amount of thermal inertia, in proportion to the feed rate, ensures continued waste destruction and safe clearing of feed from the reactor. To protect the electrodes and maintain a noncombustible environment, nitrogen purge to the reactor remains until the reactor temperature is approximately 100°C. The AER is also equipped with an automatic trip to cut electrical power in the event of electrode failure.

Huber maintains two fully equipped AERs (AER3 and AER12). The AER3, which was used for the NCBC test and is the smaller reactor, has an inside core diameter of 7.6 cm, with a heated length of 91.4 cm. The unit, installed in a trailer for mobility, is used for proof-of-concept experiments and onsite demonstrations. The AER12, which is of pilot/commercial scale (a 30.5-cm core diameter with a heated length of 365.8 cm), is used for research such as scale-up design, process engineering, economic studies, and technology demonstrations.

<u>Site Conditions</u>. The indigenous soil at NCBC is sand to sandy loam, intermixed with some clay. The HO storage site was stabilized with Portland cement approximately 30 years ago. Since that time, additional fill materials, including shell, rock, asphalt, and tar, were

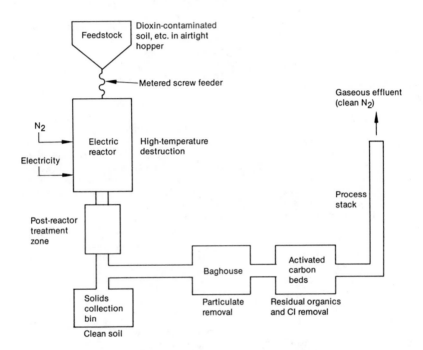

Figure 2. Simplified AER Process Diagram.

added to the storage area, providing a cover ranging up to 10 cm over the cement-stabilized soil.

Before the demonstration testing, a surface and subsurface soil sampling program was conducted to characterize the storage area conditions. At the soil surface, a maximum indicated hot spot concentration of 2,3,7,8-TCDD was found to be 646 ppb. However, the maximum indicated 2,3,7,8-TCDD concentration was 998 ppb, found in the subsurface in the 15-cm-thick cement-stabilized soil. The 2,3,7,8-TCDD concentration in the soil beneath the cement-stabilized soil decreased to a value <1 ppb within a 1-m depth.

Procedure. Testing was performed during June 1985 and included site setup, soil preparation, checkout, treatment of contaminated soil, decontamination, and equipment removal. Soil feedstock was chosen from a plot of known high concentration of 2,3,7,8-TCDD. The material was excavated by use of a shovel, ground to 35 mesh, and loaded into the feed hopper. Analysis of a sample taken from the feedstock showed a 2,3,7,8-TCDD concentration of 111 ppb.

Composition of the feedstock was approximately 50% sand and gravel, 30% shell, 20% cement-stabilized soil, and trace amounts of asphalt and tar. For proper operation of the AER3, it was necessary to pretreat the feedstock soil by reducing the moisture content to less than 1% and crushing the material to pass a 35-mesh sieve with jaw crusher and pulverizer. The feedstock moisture was reduced by placing the material in drums with controlled drum heaters. Comparing sample data before and after this drying process showed some of the TCDD was driven off from the dried soil; however, the effluent was exhausted through a carbon filter to retain released organics.

The NCBC demonstration test, which lasted approximately 58 h, treated 436 kg of soil. The average operating parameters for the run are summarized in Table I. The feed rate normally started from 0.18 kg/min to a constant rate of 0.27 kg/min. For a 2.5-h test, a feed rate of 0.32 kg/min was maintained.

Personnel Protection Equipment. Stringent personnel protection (Class C1) was required whenever soil was being prepared (e.g., grinding and pulverizing) or the AER system was open (e.g., filling feed bins, changing treated soil collection bin, and inspecting the reactor internals). Polyethylene-coated tyvek environmental suits were worn to preclude skin exposure. Soil preparation activities required air-supplied respirators because of dust levels. Full-face respirators were worn for the AER open-system activities. During actual AER operation when the system was closed, less stringent

Table I.  AER3 Process Parameters

| Parameter | Value |
|---|---|
| Feed rate | 0.25 kg/min |
| Reactor core temperature | 2010°C |
| Nitrogen flow rate | 0.25-0.28 Nm$^3$/min |
| Stack gas flow rate | 0.377 Nm$^3$/min |
| Power requirement | 37-40 kW |

personnel protection (Class C2) was used to reduce the chance of
heat stress from high ambient temperatures while providing adequate
personnel protection.

Process Sampling and Analysis.    An independent sampling and analysis
program was conducted to verify the detoxification capability of the
AER3 operation.    Samples of the feedstock, treated soil, baghouse
material, and activated carbon filter samples were collected in
470-mL wide-mouth bottles and shipped to an analytical laboratory,
which is a certified participant in the EPA Contract Laboratory Program (CLP).    A treated soil sample was sent to a second analytical
laboratory for comparison of results.    Although not a participant in
the CLP, this laboratory has performed a variety of special analytical services for EPA, including analysis for dioxins and furans.
Analytical methods are given in Table II.

Ambient Air Monitoring.    Four high-volume air particulate samplers
were operated during field operations for the Huber testing and for
another Air Force small-scale technology demonstration being performed at NCBC by the IT Corporation.    Sampler 1 was placed upwind
for control data.    Samplers 2 and 3 were located onsite, just downwind of the operations.    Sampler 4 was placed downwind at the perimeter of the storage area to provide exposure data representing the
general NCBC workforce and the public.    Samplers 1, 3, and 4 were
operational whenever there was field activity.    Sampler 2 was operated an equivalent amount of time but when there was no field activity to represent an onsite control.    The full operation for the two
technology demonstrations covered three sampling periods.

Personnel Monitoring.    Personnel samples and an area sample were
obtained for 2,3,7,8-TCDD analysis.    The personnel sampling equipment
(mini-ram) was placed on individuals working in the soils preparation
room, near the feedstock bin area atop the reactor and the reactor
discharge area near the solids collection bin.    The area sample was
taken inside the trailer near the solids collection bin.

Table II.    Analytical Methods

| Type | EPA Method |
|---|---|
| Isomer class dioxins and furans | Method 8280* |
| 2,3,7,8-TCDD | CLP-IFB |
| Semivolatile organics | CLP-IFB, based on Method 625 (13) |
| Pesticides and PCB | CLP-IFB, based on Method 608 (13) |
| Herbicides | Method 8150 (14) |
| Inorganics | CLP-IFB, based on methods in (15) |

* As modified by EPA's Environmental Monitoring and Science
  Laboratory, Las Vegas.    At time of analysis, method was in the
  review process.

## Results and Discussion

The ability of the process to destroy dioxins and furans in the soil is readily seen in Table III, which compares results for the treated soil from the two laboratories with the concentrations in the feedstock. Except for the very low concentration of tetrachlorodibenzofuran (TCDF) (0.028 ppb) found by one laboratory, dioxin and furan isomers were not detectable in the treated soil. The sum of the detection levels for the six isomer classes shows an overall level less than 0.12 ppb and 0.35 ppb for the two laboratories, respectively, which are well within the 1-ppb criteria set for the technology.

The herbicide compounds 2,4-D and 2,4,5-T, found to be 280 and 610 ppm in the feedstock, respectively, were also destroyed during the process to levels less than detectable, which were 0.01 ppm. 2,4,5/2,4,6-trichlorophenol and 2,4-dichlorophenol, found at 55 ppm and 10 ppm in the feedstock, were destroyed to levels less than detectable, which were 1 ppm. Chlorinated organic pesticides and PCBs were not detected in the feedstock; hence, destruction could not be evaluated. Earlier AER tests conducted by Huber on the destruction of PCBs and carbon tetrachloride in soil for Toxic Substance Control Act (TOSCA) and Resource Conservation and Recovery Act (RCRA) permits have shown the process to be highly effective.

Table IV compares the concentrations of analyzed inorganics in the feedstock and treated soil. Zinc and lead were the major elements in the feedstock at 70 and 15 ppm, respectively. Both elements showed significantly reduced concentrations in the treated soil. Lead was reduced the most by 49%. Zinc reduction was 11%. Other detectable elements in the feedstock at low concentrations showed minor gains or losses. Analytical results for the baghouse filtered material show substantial enrichment of zinc and lead (Table IV).

Table III.  Dioxin and Furan Concentrations in Feedstock and Treated Soil

|                  |            | Concentration (ppb) | |
| | | Treated Soil | |
| Dioxin/Furan | Feedstock | Set A[a] | Set B[b] |
|------------------|------------|---------|---------|
| Total TCDD    | 113[c]  | <0.036[d] | <0.04 |
| 2,3,7,8-TCDD  | 111     | <0.036[d] | <0.04 |
| Total PCDD    | 3.2     | <0.018[d] | <0.03 |
| Total HCDD    | 1.1     | <0.07[d]  | <0.02 |
| Total TCDF    | 12.7    | 0.028     | <0.01 |
| 2,3,7,8-TCDF  | 2.7     | 0.028     | <0.01 |
| Total PCDF    | 18.8    | <0.19[d]  | <0.01 |
| Total HCDF    | 0.65    | <0.20[d]  | <0.01 |

a.  Analysis by CLP analytical laboratory.
b.  Analysis by comparison laboratory.
c.  Data taken from 2,3,7,8-TCDD specific analysis.
d.  Not detected. Detection limit value shown.

Table IV.   Inorganic Concentrations in Feedstock, Treated Soil, and Baghouse Filtered Material

| Element | Concentration (ppm) | | |
|---------|-----------|--------------|----------|
| | Feedstock | Treated soil | Baghouse |
| Antimony | <3.[a,b] | <3.[a,b] | <3.[a,b] |
| Arsenic | 5.5 | 6.4 | 1.3 |
| Beryllium | <0.3[a] | <0.3[a] | <0.3[a] |
| Cadmium | <0.3[a] | 0.34 | 3.8 |
| Chromium | 6.1 | 8.2[c] | 21. |
| Copper | 6.2 | 5.8 | 39. |
| Lead | 15.[b] | 7.6 | 512. |
| Mercury | <0.1[a] | <0.1[a] | 0.4 |
| Nickel | 1.6 | 3.0 | 9.9 |
| Selenium | <0.5[a,b] | 0.58[b] | 2.2[b] |
| Silver | <0.3[a,b] | <0.3[a,b] | <0.3[a,b] |
| Thallium | <0.5[a,b] | <0.5[a,b] | <0.5[a,b] |
| Zinc | 70. | 62. | 1260. |
| Total cyanide | <0.5[a] | <0.5[a] | <0.5[a] |

a.   Not detected.  Detection limit value shown.
b.   Spike sample recovery was not within control limits.
c.   Anomaly attributed to analysis.


The material enrichment is due to the volatility of these elements within the temperature range of the process. The boiling points for both elements are less than the 2010°C operating temperature. The transport mechanism is likely due to condensation onto an aerosol-sized particulate that was swept to the baghouse filter by the exhaust gas stream. This is analogous to the vapor-condensation phenomenon widely observed on microparticle-sized coal-fired fly ash. Some enrichment is also shown for copper, chromium, and nickel; however, data are insufficient to establish the mechanism. This process shows promise in reducing volatile-type metal contamination in the treated soil and in providing a method of metal recovery from soils heavily contaminated with inorganics.

The treated soil was examined according to EPA's four hazardous characteristics (ignitability, corrosivity, reactivity, and toxicity) to show that the technology produced a residual material that can satisfy the regulation requirements (16) for restoration use. This would permit returning the soil to its original location without further restrictions. The high temperature of the AER process produces glassy spherical particles composed largely of common soil elements. These characteristics ruled out concerns about three of the EPA characteristics: ignitability, corrosivity, and reactivity. The fourth characteristic, extraction procedure (EP) toxicity, was satisfied by showing that the EP extract would never contain amounts of the eight elements, four pesticides, and two herbicides equal to or above the threshold limitations set forth in the regulation (16), even if all the amounts could leach from the treated soil. In all cases, there was a factor 10 or more margin between the limits and the individual concentrations.

Ten semivolatile organic compounds were detected in the baghouse material sample at concentrations above 1 ppm, none of which were detected in the feedstock and treated soil samples. The significant compounds and their concentrations were pyrene (47 ppm), acenaphthylene (36 ppm), fluoranthene (33 ppm), naphthalene (18 ppm), and phenanthrene (13 ppm). Their existence is thought to be the result of recombination from destructed components during the pyrolysis process. It is possible during pyrolysis at oxygen deficient conditions, such as in the AER process, to build higher order organic components. The recombination would be occurring near the end of the high temperature process where there is insufficient time for the new organic component to be destroyed. Because these compounds were not detected in the treated soil, the organics must volatize at the high temperature, transport in the exhaust, and later condense on aerosol particles as the exhaust temperature reduces. These results emphasize the need for mitigating features being installed in the exhaust line from the reactor (e.g., baghouse, carbon filters). Because the organic compounds are listed as priority pollutants, the baghouse material can be recycled as feedstock to the reactor to eliminate the hazardous waste.

Problems encountered in the NCBC field demonstration were attributable to pilot-scale operation. Small pieces of metal in the raw feedstock soil caused breakdown of the pulverizer during soil preparation; however, operation of a jaw crusher and screener was within normally expected wear and tear experience. Alignment of the feedstream as it passed through the reactor was a sensitive parameter. At times, melted soil accumulated at the exit of the reactor. The alignment problem has not been experienced in operation of the larger AER12 reactor.

For full-scale operation, Huber has scaled up an AER configuration based on its AER12 experience. Core dimensions are 46 cm in diameter, with a heated length of about 548 cm. A supporting soil pretreatment facility has been designed to blend, dry, pulverize, and size a variety of composite soils of sizes up to 10 in., with an input moisture content up to 30% in the feedstock and an output of 1% moisture content and 35-mesh size. The pretreatment plant and the scaled-up AER are both designed to perform at a soil processing rate of 42 kg/min, with continuous operation seven days a week. The approach is to return the treated soil, as delisted material, to the original excavation area.

<u>Conclusions</u>

The NCBC field test demonstrated that the AER pyrolysis process can meet performance requirements in a reliable manner. Problems encountered were resolved at the HO site and are considered to have no impact on full-scale operation. The six dioxin/furan isomer classes were destroyed in soil to a level of less than 0.12 ppb, which is well within the program objective of 1 ppb. Analytical results show that the treated soil can satisfy EPA requirements for restoration use.

The AER process shows promise in reducing metal contamination in the feedstock. Significant enrichment of lead and zinc in the baghouse filter suggests that the AER process may also be useful in the recovery of inorganics in wastes that can volatilize at AER operating conditions.

## Acknowledgments

This activity was conducted by EG&G Idaho, Inc., under a Military Interdependent Purchase Request (FT-8952-85-10009) from the Air Force Engineering and Services Center, Engineering and Services Laboratory, Tyndall Air Force Base, FL, for the U.S. Department of Energy, Idaho Operations Office. The authors wish to thank Mr. D. B. Derrington, Jr., now of Versar Inc., who was the field engineer in charge at the time for the J. M. Huber Corp., and EG&G Idaho chemists W. A. Propp, A. E. Grey, and D. L. Miller for their careful review of the analytical data.

## Literature Cited

1. Rappe, C. Environ. Sci. Technol. 1984, 18, 78A-90A.
2. Young, A. L. In "Human and Environmental Risks of Chlorinated Dioxins and Related Compounds"; Tucker, R. E., Young, A. L., Gray, A. P., Eds; Plenum Press: New York, 1981; pp. 173-190.
3. Courtney, K. D.; Gaylor, D. W.; Hogan, M. D.; Falk, H. L.; Bates, R. R.; Mitchell, I. Science 1970, 168, 864-866.
4. Courtney, K. D.; Moore, J. A. Toxicology and Applied Pharmacology 1971, 20, 396-403.
5. Kimbrough, R. D.; Falk, H.; Stehr, P.; Fries, G. J. Toxicol. and Environ. Health, 1984, 14, 47-93.
6. diDomenico, A.; Viviano, G.; Zapponi, G. In "Chlorinated Dioxins and Related Compounds"; Hutzinger, O.; Frei, R. W.; Merian, E.; Pocchiari, F. Eds, Pergamon Press: Oxford, 1982; 105-114.
7. Ahling, B.; Lindskog, A. In "Chlorinated Dioxins and Related Compounds"; Hutzinger, O.; Frei, R. W.; Merian, E.; Pocchiari, F. Eds; Pergamon Press: Oxford, 1982; 215-225.
8. Olie, K.; Lustenhouwer, W. A.; Hutzinger, O. In "Chlorinated Dioxins and Related Compounds"; Hutzinger, O.; Frei, R. W.; Merian, E.; Pocchiari, F. Eds; Pergamon Press: Oxford, 1982; 227-224.
9. Liberti, A.; Brocco, D.; In "Chlorinated Dioxins and Related Compounds"; Hutzinger, O.; Frei, R. W.; Merian, E.; Pocchiari, F. Eds; Pergamon press: Oxford, 1982; 245-251.
10. Choudhry, G. G.; Olie, K.; Hutzinger, O. In "Chlorinated Dioxins and Related Compounds"; Hutzinger, O.; Frei, R. W.; Merian, E.; Pocchiari, F. Eds; Pergamon Press: Oxford, 1982; 275-301.
11. Czuczwa, J. M.; Hites, R. A. Environ. Sci. Technol. 1984, 18, 444-450.
12. Shaub, W. M.; Tsang, W. Environ. Sci. Technol. 1983, 17, 721-730.
13. "Methods of Organic Chemical Analysis of Municipal and Industrial Wastewater", U.S. Environmental Protection Agency, 1982, EPA-600/4-82-057.

14.  "Test Methods for Evaluating Solid Waste", U.S. Environmental
     Protection Agency, 1982, SW-846, Second Edition.
15.  "Methods of Chemical Analysis of Water and Wastes", U.S. Envir-
     onmental Protection Agency, 1979, EPA-600/4-79-020.
16.  Title 40, <u>Code of Federal Regulations</u>, Part 261, Identification
     and Listing of Hazardous Waste, Subpart C, Characteristics of
     Hazardous Waste.

RECEIVED January 13, 1987

# Chapter 25

# Performance Assessment of a Portable Infrared Incinerator: Thermal Destruction Testing of Dioxin

Philip L. Daily

Shirco Infrared Systems, Inc., 1195 Empire Central, Dallas, TX 75247-4301

The Shirco Portable Unit was built in response
to the increasing interest in on-site thermal
treatment of waste and successfully demonstrated thermal destruction of dioxin in soil
at Times Beach, Mo. The Portable Unit consists of a feed system, a primary chamber
fired with electric infrared heating elements,
a gas-fired secondary chamber, a wet gas
scrubber, monitoring and control systems, and
heating element power centers. All equipment
is enclosed in a 45 foot trailer. Material is
conveyed through the incinerator in a thin
sheet on a wire mesh belt, giving all material
the same residence time under controlled process conditions. One of the on-site tests
performed by the Unit was the thermal destruction of dioxin at Times Beach, Mo. No dioxin
was detected in the treated soil, flue gases,
or scrubber effluent. The resulting Destruction and Removal Efficiencies (DRE) were
greater than 99.9999 % and the particulate
emissions were well below 0.08 gr/dscf
required by RCRA.

The difficulty of transporting hazardous material to Shirco's
Test Facilities in Dallas, Texas, was increased significantly
by the implementation of RCRA Regulations. A substantial need
existed for a trailer-mounted system which could be moved to
waste producing and waste storage sites for thermal treatment
testing. Past experience indicated that the ceramic fiber
insulated, infrared incinerator was much easier to transport
than other similar equipment and was uniquely suited for this
type of portable application. In response to this need, Shirco
designed and built the Portable Unit to demonstrate the capabilities of a portable infrared incinerator at waste sites. The
construction details of the Portable Unit and the results from

0097-6156/87/0338-0311$06.00/0

the thermal destruction testing of dioxin contaminated soil
will be reviewed herein.

## Portable Unit Construction

The Portable Unit was designed to demonstrate the performance
of the Shirco Infrared Incinerator in many thermal treatment
applications.  The construction details and process functions
of the trailer-mounted incinerator are identical to a full-
scale infrared incinerator.  The system consists of a feed
preparation system, an infrared primary chamber, a gas-fired
secondary chamber, a wet gas scrubber, an exhaust system,
heating element power centers (HEPC), and data acquisition and
control systems.  All equipment is enclosed within a 45-foot
trailer.  A schematic representation of the Portable Unit is
shown in Figure 1.

Feed Preparation System.  Material for thermal treatment is fed
by a pail or inclined conveyor onto a short conveyor located
above the primary chamber at the feed end.  The feed end is
located at the rear door of the trailer to facilitate access.
The belt is synchronized with the primary chamber conveyor to
control the material feed rate.  The drive system includes a
clutch for automatic feed shut off should process conditions
necessitate.  The preparation section includes a hopper mounted
over a conveyor belt.  The conveyor is shrouded and has rubber
skirts to minimize air leaking in or furnace gases escaping
out of the incinerator.  An adjustable knife gate at the conveyor discharge distributes the material across the width of
the belt.  Final sealing in the feed area is provided by an
additional adjustable knife gate in the feed chute at the
entrance to the primary chamber.

Primary Chamber.  The primary chamber has a rectangular cross-
section and has an external shell of carbon steel with nominal
dimensions of 2.5 ft wide X 9 ft long X 3 ft high.  The
installed weight of the chamber is 3000 pounds.  The inner
chamber is lined with multiple layers of ceramic fiber blanket
insulation.  The insulation is mounted on stainless steel studs
and retained by ceramic fasteners.  The feed material is conveyed through the incinerator on a wire mesh belt which rides
upon high-temperature alloy shafts supported by externally
mounted bearings.  The belt is woven with alloy steel wire.  A
friction drive system pulls the belt through the primary
chamber.  When the material reaches the discharge end, it drops
from the belt into an enclosed hopper.  The hopper contains a
sampling drawer for collection of ash samples during operation.
A discharge screw conveyor is located at the bottom of the
tapered hopper and transports the treated material out of the
trailer into a sealed collection drum.  The primary chamber top
is constructed such that the gas flow within the chamber can be
either counter-current or co-current.  Infrared energy is
supplied by heating elements which are transversely mounted
across, and equally spaced along, the length of the chamber.  The
elements are silicon carbide rods and are connected in wireways
external to the chamber.  The connections are accessed by

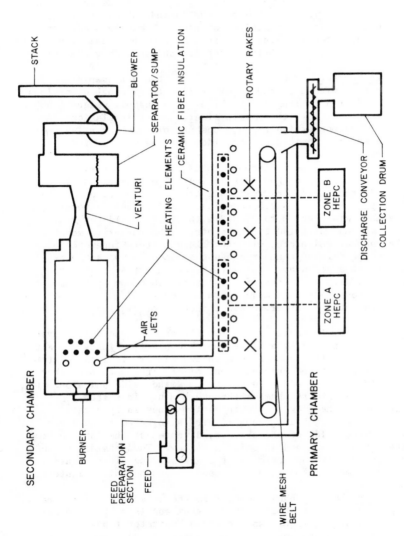

Figure 1. Shirco portable unit schematic.

removing wireway covers.  The heating elements are grouped into
two control zones.  Each zone is powered by a 12 KVA heating
element power center (HEPC).  The processing capabilities
include up to an 1850°F temperature, with the residence time of
solid phase material variable between 10 and 180 minutes.  Any
atmosphere, oxidizing, reducing, or neutral, can be used.  An
exhaust duct which is internally insulated with ceramic fiber
insulation connects the primary chamber and secondary chamber.

Secondary Chamber.  The secondary chamber has a rectangular
cross-section with a carbon steel shell with external dimensions
of 3 ft wide X 9 ft long X 3 ft high.  The chamber weighs 1,500
pounds and is lined with ceramic fiber blanket insulation.  A
propane-fired burner ignites any combustible gases carried over
from the primary chamber and provides the energy to maintain
the primary chamber exhaust gases at a predetermined temperature.  An array of silicon carbide bars are installed to
provide turbulence for good gas mixing.  The chamber is sized
to provide sufficient gas residence time for combustion of the
gases (typically 1.5 to 2.5 seconds).  The process temperature
can be maintained at up to 2300°F with a 2.2 second gas residence time and up to 100 % excess air.  The burner is mounted
in the chamber end plate, with the flame pattern intersecting
the incoming primary chamber exhaust gases at a 90° angle as
they enter the secondary chamber.  Electronic flame monitoring
is included with the burner for automatic shutdown upon loss of
flame.  Provisions were made in the chamber end plate on
either side of the burner to add injection of liquids.

Combustion Air.  Combustion air for the primary and secondary
chambers is supplied by a blower which manually adjusts the air
flowrate.  A splitter manifold with two dampers is located at
the blower outlet and provides control of airflow to both chambers.  Air is injected at 10 points on either side and along the
length of the primary chamber through a manifold system.
Adjustment of the flow to the injection tubes is by a gate
valve.  In the secondary chamber, air is injected through two
jets on either side of the chamber, directed at the intersection
of the burner flame and incoming gas flow.  The jets are offset
to produce a swirling action of the gases.  The air flowrate is
adjusted by means of a gate valve and the burner air registers.

Wet Gas Scrubber.  Exhaust gases from the secondary chamber pass
through a wet gas scrubber.  This system consists of a venturi
section containing liquid sprays and a separator tower with
additional liquid sprays and a sump tank.  A cone-type damper is
located in the venturi section and is used to control scrubber
pressure drop.  The sprays in the venturi inject a fine liquid
mist into the exhaust stream to agglomerate particulate grains.
The larger and heavier particulate grains are then removed in
the separator tower by gravity, centrifugal force, and the additional liquid sprays.  The scrubber also cools the gases from
their incoming temperature (1000°F to 2300°F depending on processing conditions) to saturation temperature, usually about
180°F.  Subcooling can be performed, but consumes substantially

more liquid.  A recirculation pump is used to transport the
liquid from the sump tank to the scrubber sprays.  Reactive
material, such as lime or caustic soda, can be added to the
scrubber sump tank for acid removal.

Exhaust System.  An induced draft exhaust blower is located on
the discharge side of the scrubber.  The blower is capable of
exhausting the primary and secondary chambers, producing a
slight draft on the system, while overcoming the pressure drop
of the scrubber.  A butterfly damper is located on the outlet
side of the blower to provide a means of adjusting the exhaust
gas flow.  A removable exhaust stack is installed through the
trailer roof.  The stack extends 10 feet above the trailer roof
and is equipped with two standard EPA sampling ports.  Access
to the sampling ports is provided by scaffolding installed
beside the trailer.

Data Acquisition and Control.  The system includes a master
control cabinet which contains process controllers, alarm and
status lights, and data recording and monitoring equipment.  The
cabinet has a temperature controller for each of the two primary
chamber heated zones.  A six point temperature recorder and a
twelve point thermocouple switch with digital indicator are used
for temperature monitoring and recording.  Table I lists the
process instrumentation included for monitoring and control of
the Unit.  The main electrical components use lights to annunciate their status.  Alarm lights are also installed in the
cabinet to annunciate high primary chamber temperature, an open
wireway cover, both low and high secondary chamber temperature,
and high stack temperature.

Table I.  Portable Unit Process Instrumentation

| Measured Variable | Identification |
|---|---|
| Temperature | Primary Chamber (5 points) |
| | Primary Chamber Exhaust |
| | Secondary Chamber |
| | Secondary Chamber Exhaust |
| | Stack |
| | Discharge Chute |
| Pressure | Primary Chamber |
| | Secondary Chamber |
| | Burner Gas |
| | Combustion Air |
| | Venturi Water |
| | Separator Tower |
| Level | Scrubber Water |
| Flowrate | Venturi Sprays |
| | Separator Tower Sprays |
| Time | Primary Chamber Run Time |
| Voltage | all 3 phases, each HEPC |
| Current | all 3 phases, each HEPC |
| Power | each HEPC |

Heating Element Power Center (HEPC). The heating elements in
the two primary chamber zones are powered by two heating element power centers. The primary power connection is to a 3-
phase, 480-volt source. Each HEPC has a transformer and a
power control unit. The power control unit (PCU) regulates the
power by the phase-angle firing method. A bank of silicon
control rectifiers (SCR) adjusts the current waveform, allowing
only a percentage of the incoming power to reach the transformer section. The transformer receives power from the PCU
and lowers the voltage, increasing the current, of the heating
element circuit. The transformer and PCU are mounted in a ven-
tilated enclosure.

## Thermal Destruction Testing

Times Beach, Missouri, had a population of over 2000 when the
roads were sprayed with waste oil for dust control. The roads
were later found to be contaminated with dioxin. The property
in the town was eventually purchased by the U.S. Government and
is now deserted and under guard with restricted entry.

Shirco talked with the Missouri Department of Natural
Resources in early 1985 about the Times Beach site and convinced
them of the Unit's capability based on these discussions and
their observation of another test. Subsequently, the decision
was made to take the Unit to the Times Beach site to demonstrate
its capability with dioxin decontamination.

The Portable Unit arrived at the Times Beach Dioxin
Research Facility on July 8, 1985, to demonstrate decontamination of the dioxin laden soil. The Unit was set up and
made ready for operation within a few hours after arrival to the
site. This rapid setup demonstrated its unique capability for
mobility. The testing personnel followed a safety plan developed by the Missouri DNR which included pretest physical examinations, use of Class C safety clothing, and vital sign
monitoring and rest periods for personnel. The weather was hot
and humid which required the work in the trailer to be limited
to 20 minutes at a time.

The soil used for testing was contaminated with 2,3,7,8-
tetrachlorodibenzo-p-dioxin (TCDD) at a concentration of about
200 ppb. Two tests were run at a 48 lb/hr feed rate and solid
phase residence times of 30 minutes and 15 minutes. The primary
chamber temperature was 1490°F to 1560°F. The secondary chamber
temperature was maintained above 2200°F. The thermal treatment
conditions for both tests are listed in Table II. The testing
was performed over two days followed by decontamination of the
incinerator and trailer. The incinerator was decontaminated by
an extended, high temperature bake out.

Flue gas samples were taken over a 7 hour period for the
30 minutes residence time case and over a 2.5 hour period for
the 15 minute case. These sampling times were chosen so that
sufficient gas sample could be collected to demonstrate the
required destruction efficiency. The flue gas sampling was
conducted in accordance with a modified EPA Method 5 procedure
and the ASME dioxin protocol (1). The samples were collected
isokinetically at a single stack sampling point. At the conclu-

sion of each test run, the sampling train was taken to a
designated clean area for sample recovery.  Orsat analyses of
the flue gases were also performed using EPA Method 3.  Several
grab samples were collected of the thermally treated soil for
each run condition.  Samples from the scrubber recirculation
system were collected to provide a composite, 1000 ml sample for
each run.  All samples were placed in a precleaned, 1000 ml
amber glass container for subsequent analysis.  Laboratory analyses for the TCDD isomer were performed using a gas chromatograph coupled with tandem mass spectrometry (GC/MS/MS).

Table II.  Incinerator Operating Conditions

|  | Solid Phase Residence Time (minutes) | Feed Rate (lb/hr) | Primary Chamber Zone A Temp. ($^\circ$F) | Zone B Temp. ($^\circ$F) | Secondary Chamber Temp. ($^\circ$F) |
|---|---|---|---|---|---|
| Test #1 | 30 | 47.68 | 1560 | 1550 | 2250 |
| Test #2 | 15 | 48.12 | 1490 | 1490 | 2235 |

The sampling results are presented in Table III and indicate that the flue gas, the treated soil, and the scrubber
effluent were free of dioxin at the detection limits listed.
The particulate sampling results indicate that the particulate
was a small percentage of the 0.08 gr/dscf RCRA Regulation
requirement.
The flue gas and feed material sampling data were combined
for the calculation of the destruction and removal efficiencies.  Table IV tabulates the calculation of the DREs for both

Table III.  Results of Dioxin Destruction Testing

| Sample Stream | Units | Test #1 | Test #2 |
|---|---|---|---|
| Analyses for 2,3,7,8-TCDD: | | | |
|   Waste Feed | ng/g | 227 | 156 |
|   Treated Soil* | ppt | <38 | <33 |
|   Scrubber Effluent* | ug/l | – | <1 |
|   Flue Gas* | pg | <14 | <8.4 |
| Analyses for Particulate: | | | |
|   Filter Catch at 7 % $O_2$ | gr/dscf | 0.0010 | 0.0002 |
| Orsat Analyses of Flue Gas: | | | |
|   $CO_2$ | % | 3.8 | 3.0 |
|   $O_2$ | % | 14.4 | 10.0 |
|   CO | % | 0.0 | 0.0 |
|   $N_2$ | % | 81.8 | 87.0 |

* TCDD was non-detectable and shown at detection limit

test runs. These calculations show that the DREs for
2,3,7,8-TCDD were in excess of the EPA criteria of 99.9999 %.
These results indicate that the infrared incinerator can very
effectively decontaminate dioxin contaminated soil while main-
taining compliance with all state and federal emissions
requirements.

Table IV. Calculation of Destruction and Removal
Efficiency for 2,3,7,8-TCDD

|  | Units | Test #1 | Test #2 |
|---|---|---|---|
| Waste Feed Inlet: |  |  |  |
| Waste Feed Rate | kg/hr | 21.68 | 21.83 |
| TCDD Concentration | ug/kg | 227 | 156 |
| TCDD Mass Rate | ug/hr | 4921 | 3405 |
|  |  |  |  |
| Exhaust Gas Outlet: |  |  |  |
| Sample Volume | $dsm^3$ | 7.066 | 3.044 |
| Stack Gas Flowrate | $dsm^3/hr$ | 97.19 | 129.99 |
| TCDD in Sample | pg | <14 | <8.4 |
| TCDD Concentration | $pg/m^3$ | <1.981 | <2.760 |
| TCDD Mass Rate | pg/hr | <192.6 | <358.7 |
|  |  |  |  |
| Destruction and Removal Efficiency (DRE) | % | >99.999996 | >99.999989 |

## Conclusion

The Portable Unit has successfully demonstrated its capability
for thermal treatment of hazardous wastes at the source of the
material. This type of on-site treatment would eliminate the
need of transportation of hazardous materials to a distant site
of stationary treatment equipment. The Portable Unit also has
demonstrated that it can be moved to a site and be ready to
treat material very quickly, a capability which will be very
important in operation of full scale equipment. The on-site
treatment of the Times Beach dioxin contaminated soil resulted
in no dioxin detected in any of the incinerator effluent
streams. The product of the testing activity was soil with no
detectable level of dioxin. Dioxin contaminated soil thermally
treated in this manner will yield soil which can be disposed as
non-hazardous material. The decontamination was performed
without exceeding RCRA requirements for particulate emissions
and with dioxin destruction efficiencies surpassing the required
percentage. The overall conclusion was that the infrared incinerator can very effectively remove dioxin from contaminated
soil at the source of the contaminated soil.

## Literature Cited

1. "Sampling For the Determination of Chlorinated Organic
   Compounds in Stack Emissions," ASME Draft, October, 1984.

RECEIVED December 15, 1986

# Chapter 26

# Technology Demonstration of a Thermal Desorption–UV Photolysis Process for Decontaminating Soils Containing Herbicide Orange

R. Helsel[1], E. Alperin[1], T. Geisler[1], A. Groen[1], R. Fox[1], T. L. Stoddart[2], and H. D. Williams[3]

[1]International Technology Corporation, 312 Directors Drive, Knoxville, TN 37923
[2]Headquarters, Air Force Engineering Services Center, Research & Development Directorate, Environics Division, Environmental Engineering Branch, Tyndall Air Force Base, FL 32403
[3]Waste Technology Programs, EG&G Idaho, Idaho Falls, ID 83415

Laboratory and field testing determined the effectiveness of a new decontamination process for soils containing 2,4-D/2,4,5-T and traces of dioxin. The process employs three primary operations - thermal desorption to volatilize the contaminants, condensation and absorption of the contaminants in a solvent, and photochemical decomposition of the contaminants. Bench-scale experiments established the relationship between desorption conditions (time and temperature) and treatment efficiency. Laboratory tests using a batch photochemical reactor defined the kinetics of 2,3,7,8-TCDD disappearance. A pilot-scale system was assembled to process up to 100 pounds per hour of soil. Tests were conducted at two sites to evaluate treatment performance and develop scale-up information. Soil was successfully decontaminated to less than 1 ng/g 2,3,7,8-TCDD at temperatures above 460°C.

As part of a major program being conducted by the U.S. Air Force to restore to normal use several Department of Defense sites where soils have been contaminated with low levels of Herbicide Orange (HO), International Technology Corporation (IT), under subcontract to EG&G Idaho, has been conducting a project involving laboratory bench-scale and field pilot-scale tests to demonstrate a new soil treatment process - thermal desorption/UV photolysis (TD/UV). The intent of the demonstration was to reduce the combined tetra-, penta-, and hexa-chlorinated dibenzodioxin (CDD) and furan (CDF) congeners, which originated from the HO, to less than 1 ng/g, which represented the anticipated soil clean-up criteria. Treatment should also effectively remove the primary HO constituents, 2,4-D

0097-6156/87/0338-0319$06.00/0
© 1987 American Chemical Society

and 2,4,5-T. Two sites were included in the field demonstration project for the TD/UV process, each having substantially different types of soil but reasonably similar concentrations of the HO constituents. Testing at the Naval Construction Battallion Center (NCBC) at Gulfport, Mississippi was conducted by IT during May 1985; testing at Johnston Island (JI) in the Pacific Ocean occurred in July 1986. Based on the results of these field pilot demonstrations, an engineering and cost evaluation is being performed for applying TD/UV technology using large, mobile systems for these two sites or other sites having similar contaminated soil problems. This paper describes the technology, highlights the results of the initial laboratory test phase, and summarizes the field demonstration results.

## Process Description

The thermal desorption/UV photolysis process developed by IT accomplishes substantial volume reduction and toxicity reduction by concentrating the hazardous constituents contained in the soil into a small volume which is easier to treat than large quantities of soil. The process incorporates three steps:

Desorption - heating the soil to volatilize the organic
              contaminants
Scrubbing  - collecting the volatilized organics in a
              suitable solvent
Photolysis - converting the contaminants to relatively
              non-hazardous residues through photochemical
              reactions.

A schematic block-flow diagram is presented as Figure 1. Contaminated soil is passed continuously through an indirectly heated desorber which can be one of many types of conventional equipment applicable for thermal processing of solids. The treatment performance of the desorber is controlled by the residence time and temperature of the soil. Treatment requirements (i.e., operating conditions) are determined by the volatility of the soil contaminants and the required contaminant removal efficiency (final versus initial concentration).

The off-gas leaving the desorber contains organic vapors, water vapor originating as initial soil moisture, and small quantities of air which enter with the soil. Scrubbing using a high boiling hydrocarbon solvent is used to treat the off-gas to remove the organic contaminants and water vapor by cooling, condensation, and absorption. Particulates (e.g., fine soil) which may be entrained by the off-gas are also collected by the scrubbing solvent. Scrubbed off-gas is passed through a conventional emission control system, such as carbon adsorption, to ensure that no organic contaminants or solvent vapors are released. Scrubber solvent is recirculated to the scrubber after being processed through a system of phase separation, filtration, and cooling. Condensed water, which is immiscible with the solvent, is separated and either directly treated using conventional techniques, such as filtration and carbon adsorption, or discharged to an existing

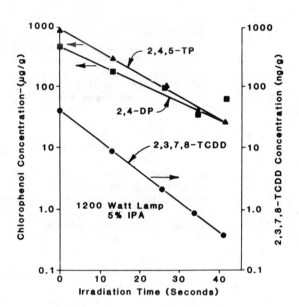

Figure 1. Thermal desorption/UV photolysis process concept.

wastewater treatment facility. Filtered solids are recycled to the
desorber or packaged as process waste for off-site disposal,
depending on the relative quantity and composition.

A small portion of the recirculated solvent stream is
diverted to a UV photolysis system to treat (detoxify) and remove
the organic contaminants, with the treated solvent purge recycled
to the scrubbing system. The equilibrium concentration of the
contaminants in the scrubber solvent is maintained as high as
practical to minimize the purge stream and afford higher photolysis
reaction rates, thereby decreasing the size of the photolysis
treatment system. The concentration limitation is dependent on the
solubility properties and partial pressure of the contaminants in
the solvent, and the resultant effect on scrubber efficiency and
emission potential. The photolysis system contains a specially
designed flow reactor which subjects the contaminant-laden solvent
to UV radiation to induce molecular decomposition. High intensity
mercury vapor lamps produce a band of wavelengths, some of which
match the absorption energy of the specific organic molecules being
treated. Cooling is provided to the reactor to remove the thermal
output of the lamp. The photolyzed solvent is treated by using
selected conventional physical or thermal separation processes,
such as distillation, to remove the reaction product residue.
Alternatively, a purge of the photolyzed solvent can be discarded
as waste to control the levels of reaction products in the
recirculated solvent system.

Other configurations of treatment processes using thermal
desorption as the primary separation technique can be applied to
organically contaminated soils. Alternative physical/chemical
processes can be used to treat the desorber off-gas and the
contaminants. To achieve complete contaminant destruction, the
off-gas can be treated by using conventional fume incineration or
other thermal treatment technology. The choice of the type of
desorber and off-gas treatment system depends on the concentration
and properties of the chemical contaminants, soil characteristics,
quantity of contaminated material, site characteristics, availability of off-site disposal, and regulatory and related requirements.

## Laboratory Testing and Results - Thermal Desorption

Thermal desorption is a physical separation process, although
chemical transformation of the organic contaminants may occur
depending on the thermal stability and the operating temperatures
required to achieve adequate decontamination efficiency. Thermal
desorption has been used only in a limited number of cases ([1-4])
for treating contaminated soil, and these applications have
involved relatively volatile organic compounds, such as solvents.
Because of the extremely low volatility of CCD and CDFs, the
development of basic treatability data was essential to confirm
that 1 ng/g levels in soil could be achieved and that the required
desorption conditions were practical, considering the design
features and operating rates of equipment available for performing
such treatment.

Desorption treatability testing was conducted on samples of
contaminated soil from three HO contaminated sites - NCBC, JI, and

Eglin Air Force Base.    The goals of the test effort were to
evaluate the effect of time and temperature on 2,3,7,8-TCDD removal
efficiency and to establish the importance of soil type.    The
samples were selected by the Air Force based on results of site
surveys to yield high contamination levels in order to investigate
a broad range of treatability.    This testing was an extension of
earlier testing performed for the EPA on two dioxin-contaminated
soil samples from Missouri to support EPA's mobile incinerator
trial burn in 1985 (5).

   After each soil sample was blended, air dried, and screened
(2 mm sieve opening) triplicate aliquots were taken and analyzed
for 2,3,7,8-TCDD, CDD and CDF congeners, and 2,4-D and 2,4,5-T.
The three prepared soils had 2,3,7,8-TCDD levels greater than
100 ng/g and 2,4-D/2,4,5-T levels of about 1000 µg/g.    The JI soil
had significant concentrations of hepta and octa CDD compared with
the other two samples.    In addition, selected physical and chemical
properties presented in Table I, were measured (6).    The EPA test
program (5) had indicated that soil properties had only a minor
influence on removal efficiencies for 2,3,7,8-TCDD.

Table I.   Physical-Chemical Analysis of Prepared Soil Samples
Used for Laboratory Thermal Desorption Tests

| Parameter | JI | Eglin | NCBC |
|---|---|---|---|
| pH | 8.4 | 3.8 | 8.6 |
| Conductivity (millimhos/cm) | 5.0 | 0.15 | 0.21 |
| Organic matter (percent) | 4.2 | 1.2 | 2.3 |
| Cation exchange capacity milliequivalents/100g) | 0.73 | 0.77 | 2.4 |
| Oil and grease content (grams/100g) | 0.19 | 0.41 | 0.34 |
| Surface area (m$^2$/g) | 6.7 | 2.5 | 12.3 |
| Particle size distribution (percent) | | | |
| Medium sand | 41 | 41 | 26 |
| Fine sand | 37 | 52 | 59 |
| Silt | 19 | 5 | 12 |
| Clay (<5 microns) | 3 | 2 | 3 |
| Moisture | 2.3 | 0.79 | 1.1 |

   A series of 10 individual tests was performed using
temperatures between 430 and 560°C and treatment times of 8 to 30
minutes.    Table II presents the test results, which are comparable
to the earlier results for Missouri soils.    The objective of 1 ng/g
2,3,7,8-TCDD residual in soil was achieved for all three soils
subjected to the highest temperature.    There was some difference in
treatability observed between the three soils at the lower temperatures.    Also, longer treatment times were required for the NCBC
soil because of the higher initial 2,3,7,8-TCDD level (500 ng/g vs.
100 ng/g).    One set of treated test samples which contained less
than 1 ng/g 2,3,7,8-TCDD was also analyzed for the other CDD and
CDF congeners and 2,4-D/2,4,5-T.    These results, shown in Table
III, indicate greater than 99.999 percent removal of the initial

2,4-D/2,4,5-T and the effective removal of higher chlorinated CDDs and CDFs.

Table II.  Effect of Treatment Conditions on Residual 2,3,7,8-TCDD in Soil During Laboratory Thermal Desorption Tests

| Nominal Test Temperature (°C) | Soil Identification | Time at Test Temperature (min) | 2,3,7,8-TCDD Concentration (ng/g) Initial | Final |
|---|---|---|---|---|
| 430 | JI | 20 | 106 | 38.5 |
|  | Eglin | 20 | 101 | 4.4 |
|  | NCBC | 30 | 494 | 26.6[a] |
| 481 | JI | 15 | 106 | 4.5 |
|  | JI | 30 | 106 | 1.6 |
|  | Eglin | 15 | 101 | 1.1[a] |
|  | Eglin | 30 | 101 | 0.45 |
|  | NCBC | 15 | 494 | 10.1 |
|  | NCBC | 30 | 494 | 4.6 |
| 558 | JI | 8 | 106 | 0.56[a] |
|  | Eglin | 8 | 101 | 0.71 |
|  | NCBC | 15 | 494 | 0.76[a] |

[a]Average of duplicate tests or duplicate analyses.

Table III.  Residual 2,4-D, 2,4,5-T, and CDD/CDF in Soil Samples Treated at 558°C in Laboratory Thermal Desorption Tests

| Compound | Concentration (ng/g) JI | Eglin | NCBC |
|---|---|---|---|
| 2,4-D | ND[a] | ND | ND |
| 2,4,5-T | 16 | 0.8 | 3 |
| TCDF | 0.6 | 0.4 | ND |
| OCDF[b] | 0.3 | ND | ND |

[a]ND = Not detected.
[b]No other CDD and CDF congeners were detected.

## Laboratory Testing and Results - Photolysis

Photolysis has had limited application for treatment of hazardous waste or detoxification of chemically contaminated materials.  The susceptibility of chlorinated aromatics, including herbicides such as 2,4-D and 2,4,5-T, to UV-induced decomposition is well established ([7,8]).  Photodecomposition of such compounds leads to successive dechlorination followed by condensation reactions to form phenolic polymers ([7,8]).  Other research has demonstrated that CDD and CDF decompose in the presence of UV light ([8,9,10]).  Development of a photochemical process for destroying 2,3,7,8-TCDD in a waste tar indicated similar dechlorination and condensation reactions and products ([8]). The high-molecular weight end products, which are similar in structure to humic acids, would be expected to have low toxicity and mobility.  Therefore, essentially complete conversion of toxic constituents could produce a potentially non-hazardous (according to RCRA), easily disposable residue.

Laboratory photolysis experiments were designed to confirm that 2,3,7,8-TCDD contained in the selected scrubber solvent could be reduced to 1 ng/g and to determine the reaction rates of the primary HO constituents and 2,3,7,8-TCDD in that solvent matrix. A previous photolysis process for 2,3,7,8-TCDD used hexane as a solvent (8). The solvent selected for use in the TD/UV process was different - a high boiling (kerosene-like) mixture of isoparaffins. This hydrocarbon solvent was selected because of its very low vapor pressure and water solubility, nontoxic and nonflammable characteristics, relatively low cost, chemical stability, and good solvent properties for HO constituents. A second major difference from earlier IT photolysis studies was the presence in the scrubber solution of significant concentrations of other chlorinated organic reactants (2,4-D and 2,4,5-T) which were also subject to photolysis. In fact, the typical concentration ratio between 2,4-D or 2,4,5-T and 2,3,7,8-TCDD in the soil samples used in the desorption treatability testing was 2000:1.

The three steps of the laboratory program included generation of scrubber solution, bench-scale batch photolysis reactions, and a pilot system trial. In order to generate a representative sample of scrubber solution for photolysis tests, a small desorption and scrubbing system was assembled. A portion of the prepared samples of both NCBC and JI soil used for the thermal desorption tests was used to generate scrubber solution. Contaminated soil (~100 g) was placed in a standard tube furnace apparatus which was heated to about 500°C for 15 to 30 minutes. A nitrogen purge swept the vapors into the scrubbing system, which consisted of several solvent-filled impingers. Analysis of the prepared scrubber solutions indicated thermochemical conversion of the 2,4-D and 2,4,5-T in the contaminated soil to the corresponding chlorophenols at molar equivalents. In addition to using prepared scrubber solutions, solvent spiked with 2,4-D and 2,4,5-T, the corresponding chlorophenols, or 2,3,7,8-TCDD was used for baseline photolysis tests.

Most photolysis experiments were conducted in a 0.5 liter capacity standard quartz photochemical reactor using either recirculation or bottom agitation for heat and mass transfer. Both 100- and 450-watt high pressure quartz mercury vapor lamps (Canrad-Hanovia, Inc., Catalog Nos. 608A and 679A) were used, depending on the initial reactant concentration in the particular solvent solution being tested. The wavelengths of interest based on spectrophotometric absorbance measurements of 2,3,7,8-TCDD, 2,4-D and 2,4,5-T were in the 280 to 320 nm region. Isopropyl alcohol (~0.05 g/g solvent solution) was used as a proton donor to minimize formation of polymeric reaction by-products which tend to foul the light transmission surfaces (8). The bench-scale photolysis tests gave the following results:

1. All compounds disappeared to below the analytical detection limits.
2. The concentration of 2,3,7,8-TCDD was reduced to less than 1 ng/g from initial concentrations as high as 200 ng/g.

3.  For a given reactor configuration and lamp wattage, the reaction rates of 2,3,7,8-TCDD and 2,4,5-trichlorophenol were proportional to the concentration, indicating pseudo-first order kinetics in agreement with previous work (8).

4.  Absorbence of UV energy by the solvent, which increased during irradiation, resulted in low quantum yields and low rate constants.

5.  Insoluble brown reaction products (presumably phenolic tars) were deposited on the surfaces of the reactor vessel and lamp well. This expected phenomenon plus the high solvent absorbence demanded a careful reactor selection and photolysis system design.

Trials using a pilot reactor system described in the following section were performed in the laboratory to establish reactor efficiencies and operating characteristics prior to transport to the field. A synthetic scrubber solution was prepared containing 2,4,5-trichlorophenol at a concentration (~2,000 μg/g) projected to be representative of the planned field tests. Kinetics were determined to be first-order with a rate constant of 0.07 sec$^{-1}$

## On-site Pilot Testing and Results

Based on the information developed from the laboratory test program, a pilot-scale TD/UV system was designed and assembled. Three skids were used to mount the desorber, scrubber, and photolysis systems; the largest skid was 1.5 meters by 4.3 meters. A conventional pilot-scale, rotary, indirect-fired calciner was used as the desorber. The calciner consisted of a 3.3 meter long by 16 cm internal diameter rotating tube through which the soil was transferred, and a gas-fired furnace which surrounded the middle 2.0 meters of the tube length. The initial and final tube sections were used for soil feeding and cooling. The flow rate and residence time of soils traveling through the desorber were controlled by varying the tube inclination and rotational speed. Temperature of the soil was measured at different locations by a thermowell probe extending inside the tube. Soil was fed to the desorber from a small hopper using a variable speed screw conveyor. Soil leaving the tube was collected in a sealed metal can.

The off-gas transfer and scrubbing system was designed to enable recirculation of scrubbed off-gas through the desorber. The entire off-gas treatment and recirculation system, including the desorber and scrubber, was operated at a slightly negative pressure to prevent potential fugitive emissions. A small amount of air entered the system with the soil feed or through seal leakage. Nitrogen was added to the recirculated gas stream to maintain the oxygen concentration below the level necessary to support combustion. This was an extra safety feature since the vapor pressure of the solvent at normal scrubber operating conditions is very low. A portion of the scrubbed off-gas was vented from the recirculation system to maintain proper pressure in the system. This purge stream was passed through a small HEPA filter and carbon adsorber before being discharged to the atmosphere. The solvent system consisted of a scrubber, receiving and separation tank, storage tank, recirculation pump, filters for removing suspended solids, and solvent cooler.

The photolysis system was independent of the desorber and scrubber systems; its design capacity was lower than necessary to match the desorber's soil-processing rate. A portion (about 40 kg) of contaminant-laden solvent was taken from the scrubber system after completion of one or more desorption tests and transferred to the photolysis system. This system consisted of an agitated storage tank, solvent recirculation pump, and photochemical reactor with associated cooling, DC power supply, and controls. The selected type reactor was a standard quartz falling-film unit, approximately 10 cm in diameter and 50 cm long (Ace Glass, Inc., Part No. 7898). A 1200 watt high intensity mercury vapor lamp was inserted through a central quartz tube within the reactor to irradiate the solvent as it flowed by gravity down the circumference of the reactor body. The solvent was recirculated through the reactor for many cycles to achieve sufficient irradiation (e.g., reaction) time.

Five desorption tests were carried out at NCBC at various treatment conditions. A total of 800 kg of soil was processed; soil was prepared by drying and crushing to less than 1/2 inch to allow proper flow in the desorber feed mechanism, and blending for uniformity. Each test lasted 5 to 10 hours, including the heat-up and cool-down cycle. Samples of feed soil and treated soil were taken during steady-state operation, and samples of the scrubber solvent and vent carbon were taken at the conclusion of each run. Samples were analyzed for 2,4-D, 2,4,5-T, other HO indigenous compounds, priority pollutant organics and metals, and tetra-hexa congeners of CDD and CDF. In addition, 2,3,7,8-TCDD concentrations of treated soil and photolyzed solvent samples were determined on a quick-response basis to enable adjustment of the operating conditions in subsequent tests. Fresh solvent and carbon were used for each test, and the entire desorber and scrubber network was cleaned out between tests. This cleaning enabled thorough inspection of the condition of the equipment and provided several different compositions of contaminated solvent to use in the photolysis tests.

Table IV shows the effect of different soil temperatures and residence times on residual 2,3,7,8-TCDD for NCBC pilot tests. Table V presents the analytical results for 2,4-D, 2,4,5-T, and total CDD and CDF. Analytical detection levels for 2,3,7,8-TCDD and the various congeners were generally less than 0.1 ng/g but varied from sample to sample, ranging from 0.018 ng/g to 0.51 ng/g.

All test conditions produced soil containing less than 1 ng/g 2,3,7,8-TCDD. The total quantified tetra-hexa congeners were less than the treatment goal of 1 ng/g for the first three tests, which were performed at the lower feed rates. Test 4, made at the highest feed rate, nearly met this value, whereas the much lower soil temperature used for the final test resulted in almost 3 ng/g combined residual CDD and CDF. A longer residence time could have improved this performance. Residual 2,4-D and 2,4,5-T concentrations were less than 1 µg/g for all but the final test. This reduction represents greater than 99.97 percent removal efficiency for these primary HO constituents.

Table IV.  Effect of Treatment Conditions on Residual 2,3,7,8-TCDD
During NCBC Pilot Thermal Desorption Tests

| Test No. | Soil Feed Rate (kg/hr) | Residence Time[a] (min) | Soil Temperature (°C) | 2,3,7,8-TCDD (ng/g) | |
|---|---|---|---|---|---|
| | | | | Initial | Residual |
| 1 | 13.6 | 40 | 560 | 260 | ND |
| 2 | 13.6 | 40 | 560 | 272 | ND |
| 3 | 25 | 19 | 560 | 236 | ND |
| 4 | 44 | 10.5 | 560 | 266 | ND |
| 5 | 20 | 24 | 460 | 233 | 0.5 |

[a]Soil residence time in heated zone.

Table V.  Residual 2,4-D, 2,4,5-T, and CDD/CDF in
NCBC Pilot Thermal Desorption Test

| Compound | Concentration (ng/g) | | | | |
|---|---|---|---|---|---|
| | Test 1 | Test 2 | Test 3 | Test 4 | Test 5 |
| 2,4-D | 180 | 150 | 20 | - | 170 |
| 2,4,5-T | 500 | 270 | 60 | - | 1240 |
| TCDD | ND[a] | 0.23 | 0.11 | 0.61 | 0.75 |
| PCDD | ND | ND | ND | ND | ND |
| HCDD | ND | ND | ND | ND | ND |
| TCDF | ND | ND | ND | 0.13 | 0.95 |
| PCDF | ND | 0.14 | ND | 0.54 | 1.0 |
| HCDF | ND | ND | ND | ND | ND |
| CDD and CDF[b] | ND | 0.37 | 0.11 | 1.28 | 2.70 |

[a]ND = not detected.
[b]Total of quantified values for detected cogeners.

    Because of the very low moisture content of the prepared soil
feed, an insufficient volume of aqueous condensate was collected
from the tests to perform analysis or treatability tests.  A vent
gas sample was taken, but no valid analytical results were generated because of delays in sample processing.  However, analysis of
the carbon used in the emission control adsorbers enabled some
evaluation of scrubber performance and process emission potential.  Only the front (upstream) portion of carbon from one of the
tests showed detectable levels of any CDD or CDF.  No HO constituents were detected in the downstream portion of carbon.  Calculated scrubber removal efficiencies exceeded 99.9 percent for CDD,
CDF, 2,4-D, and 2,4,5-T.  Vent gas volume was about 0.05 m$^3$/minute
for all tests.
    Results of the photolysis tests are presented in Table VI.
The total solvent volume (~10.5 l) was recirculated through the
reactor at 0.75 l/min for 6.5 hr, resulting in 28 cycles with an
irradiation time of about 1.5 sec/cycle.  The photolysis system
operating time was selected based on the laboratory trials to
achieve less than 1 ng/g 2,3,7,8-TCDD; the actual residual level of

0.36 ng/g represented greater than 99 percent conversion.   The reaction conversion of the other CDD and CDF congeners varied from 85 to 99 percent.   Photolysis reduced the concentrations of 2,4-dichlorophenol (2,4-DP) and 2,4,5-trichlorophenol (2,4,5-DP), (corresponding to the 2,4-D and 2,4,5-T present in the initial soil) by 85 and 97 percent respectively.   Figure 2 shows the rate of disappearance of 2,3,7,8-TCDD, 2,4-DP, and 2,4,5-TP.   As demonstrated during the laboratory tests, the reaction kinetics were pseudo-first order over the given range of concentrations. The reaction rate constants were similar for the three species (0.11 sec$^{-1}$, 0.04 sec$^{-1}$, and 0.08 sec$^{-1}$, respectively); the rate constant for 2,4,5-TP was comparable to that determined in the laboratory trials of the pilot system.

Table VI.   Initial vs Final Concentration of Selected Compounds in Scrubber Solution from NCBC Pilot Photolysis Tests

| Compound | Concentration (ng/g) | |
|---|---|---|
| | Initial | Final |
| 2,4-Dichlorophenol | 490,000 | 82,000 |
| 2,4,5-Trichlorolorophenol | 977,000 | 31,000 |
| 2,3,7,8-TCDD | 43.3 | 0.36 |
| Total TCDD | 46.3 | 0.92 |
| Total PCDD | 15.7 | 2.3 |
| Total HCDD | 0.84 | 0.037 |
| Total TCDF | 31.0 | 3.8 |
| Total PCDF | 3.7 | 1.1 |
| Total HCDF | 1.7 | 0.0031 |

Three desorption tests and one photolysis test were conducted at JI to compare the effects of different soil characteristics and investigate higher processing rates.   The coral-like soil used for the tests contained lower levels of HO contamination than NCBC (about 50 ng/g versus 250 ng/g).   As much as 95 kg/hr of soil was successfully decontaminated to less than 1 ng/g 2,3,7,8-TCDD using desorption temperatures of 550°C.   Treated soil from all three desorption tests had nondetectable residual tetra-hexa CDD and CDF cogeners, 2,4-D and 2,4,5-T, and corresponding chlorophenols. Analysis of carbon removed from the desorber-scrubber system vent showed no detectable concentration of CDD or CDF.   Gas samples taken downstream of the carbon adsorber showed nondetectable concentrations of CDD and CDF, 2,4-D and 2,4,5-T, and chloro-phenols.   Photolysis test results were comparable with NCBC tests.   Initial concentrations of HO contaminants were much higher in the scrubber solvent due to processing of considerably more soil and use of less solvent.   The concentration of 2,3,7,8-TCDD was reduced from 780 ng/g to less than 0.7 ng/g during 12 hours of system operation (representing about 80 sec reaction or irradiation time).   Total chlorophenols were reduced from 430 µg/g to less than 6 µg/g, and tetra-hexa CDD and CDF cogeners were effectively treated.   Reaction rate constants for specific compounds were essentially the same between the NCBC and JI photolysis tests.   At JI as at NCBC, brown residues were deposited on the reactor surfaces, and solvent discoloration was obvious, but there was no evidence of rate retardation.

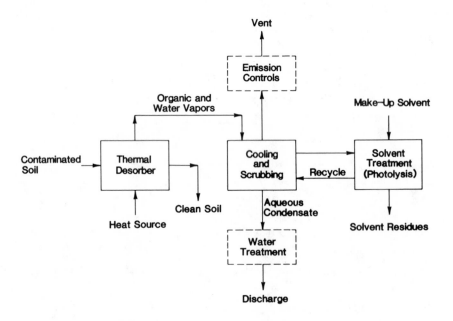

Figure 2.   Photolysis reaction kinetics for pilot test at NCBC.

## Conclusions

The effectiveness of thermal desorption to decontaminate soil containing HO and of UV photolysis to destroy HO toxic constituents has been demonstrated in bench- and pilot-scale tests. Some additional technical information is needed for a complete evaluation of the process and to provide the basis for design of a full-scale system for on-site remedial action. This project illustrates the requirements for developing and implementing new process technology for solving contaminated-soil environmental problems. Only through such demonstration efforts can more cost-effective and environmentally sound remedial action alternatives be made available.

## Literature Cited

1.  Noland, J. W.; McDevitt, N. P.; Koltuniak, D. L. Proc. of the National Conference on Hazardous Wastes and Hazardous Materials, Atlanta, GA, March 4-6, 1986, pp. 229-232.
2.  Hazaga, D; Fields, S; Clemmons, G. P. The 5th National Conference on Management of Uncontrolled Hazardous Waste Sites, Washington, DC, November 7-9, 1984, pp 404-406.
3.  Webster, David M. J. Air Pollution Control Association, 1986, 36, pp 1156-1164.
4.  Hoogendoorn, D. Proc. of the 5th National Conference on Management of Uncontrolled Hazardous Waste Sites, Washington, DC, November 7-9, 1984, pp 569-575.
5.  Helsel, R.; Alperin, E.; Groen, A.; and Catalano, D. "Laboratory Investigation of Thermal Treatment of Soil Contaminated With 2,3,7,8-TCDD," draft report to U.S. EPA, Cincinnati, OH on Work Order BAD001, D.U.D-109, IT Corporation, Knoxville, TN, Dec. 1984.
6.  Arthur, M. F.; Zwick, T. C. "Physical-Chemical Characterization of Soils," Battelle Columbus Laboratories, Columbus, OH, 1984.
7.  "Report on 2,4,5-T, A Report on the Panel on Herbicides of the President's Science Advisory Committee," Executive Office of the President, Office of Sciences and Technology, March 1971.
8.  Exner, J. H.; Johnson, J. D.; Ivins, O. D.; Wass, M.N.; and Miller, R. A. "Detoxication of Hazardous Waste," Ann Arbor Science Publishers, Ann Arbor, MI, 1982, p 269.
9.  Exner, J. H.; Alperin, E. S.; Groen, A.; Morren, C. E.; Kalcevic, V.; Cudahy, J. J.; and Pitts, D. M. "Chlorinated Dioxins and Dibenzofurans in the Total Environment," Keith, L. H.; Rappe, C.; Choudhary, G.; Eds., Butterworth Publishers, Stoneham, MA, 1985, p 47.
10. Exner, J. H., Alperin, E. S.; Groen, A; Morren, C. E. Hazardous Waste, 1, 1984, pp 217-223.

RECEIVED December 29, 1986

Chapter 27

# In Situ Radio Frequency Heating Process for Decontamination of Soil

H. Dev[1], P. Condorelli[1], J. Bridges[1], C. Rogers[2], and D. Downey[3]

[1]IIT Research Institute, Chicago, IL 60616
[2]U.S. Environmental Protection Agency, Cincinnati, OH 45268
[3]Headquarters, Air Force Engineering Services Center,
Tyndall Air Force Base, FL 32403

In-situ radio frequency (RF) heating is accomplished
by inserting tubular electrodes into boreholes, or by
laying horizontal electrodes over the surface of the
soil, and connecting them to a source of electromagnetic (EM) energy in the frequency range of 6 to
13 MHz. An overview of the RF heating techniques is
presented. Experiments were performed on 75 g batches
of sandy soil to determine the feasibility of removing
chlorinated hydrocarbons. Tetrachloroethylene was
selected as a simulant. Soil containing 9.28 and
957 ppm tetrachloroethylene was heated for four hours
in a temperature range of 90° and 130°C. It was
demonstrated that under these conditions 95% of the
contaminant can be removed from soil.

Radio Frequency (RF) in-situ heating is an electromagnetic (EM)
technique originally developed and demonstrated by Krstansky et al.
(1) for in-situ thermal processing of hydrocarbonaceous earth
formations for resource recovery. This technique uses EM energy in
the radio frequency band for rapid in-situ heating of earth and
mineral formations. The mechanism of absorption and conversion of
EM energy to heat is similar to that of a microwave oven, except
that the frequency is lower and the scale of operation is much
larger. In-situ RF heating to 200°-400°C of large blocks of earth
from 35 cu ft (1.0 cu m) to 660 cu ft (25 cu m) in size has been
demonstrated in field tests (1). A sustained average heating rate
of 0.8°-1.0°C/hr was achieved in these tests.
 The purpose of this paper is to present the results of
laboratory studies performed to determine the feasibility of using
RF heating techniques to decontaminate soils containing hazardous
chemicals such as chlorinated hydrocarbons, benzene, and toluene.
The occurrence of numerous large uncontrolled sites of contaminated
soil containing the above-mentioned chemicals is well documented and
previously reported in the literature (2-6).
 In-situ RF heating offers two alternatives for decontaminating
soil. These alternatives are: (1) thermal decontamination of soil

by vaporization and recovery of contaminants, and (2) in-situ RF
heat treatment in conjunction with the application of a chemical
dechlorinating agent for contaminants such as PCB.  In alternative
(1) the contaminants will be vaporized, distilled, or steam-stripped
from the soil and recovered at the surface.  In alternative (2) RF
heating of the soil will be used to improve the rate of reaction
between the contaminant and the applied reagent.  In addition, the
heating can be used to condition the soil by removing the moisture
either before or after reagent application.

## Thermal Decontamination of Soil

Chlorinated organic contaminants are found at various sites of
interest to the U.S. Air Force.  Among these contaminants are
compounds such as tetrachloroethylene, dichloroethane, trichloro-
ethylene, chlorobenzene, benzene, toluene, and components of JP-4
jet fuel.  These materials have a boiling range of 80° to 232°C,
have substantial vapor-pressure at 100°C, and can be steam distilled
if present in excess of their solubility limit.  To establish the
feasibility of thermal recovery of such chemical contaminants,
tetrachloroethylene (120.8°C, nbp) was selected as a representative
contaminant.  Uncontaminated (clean) sandy soil from the vicinity of
a waste site was spiked with tetrachloroethylene and used in
recovery experiments.

## Experimental

**Procedure.**  A large amount of sandy soil was obtained from the
field.  Approximately 1000 g of this soil was placed in a large
glass jar and tumbled overnight.  A soil sample was analyzed for
chlorinated solvents by extraction in a Nielson-Kryger (7) steam
distillation apparatus followed by analysis of the extract on a gas
chromatograph (GC) equipped with an electron capture (EC) detector.
When it was verified that the soil did not contain any chlorinated
solvents, the moisture content of the soil was adjusted to 5 or 10%.
     The clean moist soil was prepared for experiments by placing it
in the 500 ml round bottom flask and spiking it with a solution of
tetrachloroethylene to a concentration of either 9.28 or 957.3 ppm.
The flask was sealed and rotated in an ice bath for 3 hr to
homogenize the soil and the spike by tumbling.  At the end of this
tumbling period, the flask was attached to a water-cooled solvent-
recovery condenser.  The side leg of the condenser was placed in a
chilled receiver containing approximately 10 ml of pesticide grade
hexane.  A Tenax trap was placed on the gas outlet port of the
condenser to trap uncondensed vapors.
     The soil was heated with a heating mantle to the desired final
temperature and maintained at that temperature for 4 hr.  At the end
of this time, the heating mantle was removed and the flask was
cooled to room temperature.  The condenser was washed with
hydrocarbon-free water and hexane.  These washings were combined
with the distillate.  The Tenax trap was also washed with pesticide
grade hexane and the washings were combined with the distillate.
The distillate and washings were dried by passing through a bed of
anhydrous sodium sulfate.  The dried distillate and washings were

brought up to volume with hexane in a 100 ml volumetric flask and analyzed for tetrachloroethylene on a Hewlett Packard 5840 GC equipped with a Ni[63] EC detector.

The glass flask containing the treated soil was attached to the Nielson-Kryger distillation head to determine the residual tetrachloroethylene. The amount of tetrachloroethylene extracted by this procedure was corrected for the extraction efficiency. The extraction efficiency of tetrachloroethylene from sandy soil was determined by extraction of soil spiked at nine levels in the concentration range of 0.1 to 1190 ppm. The average extraction efficiency based on all nine samples was 97.1% with a standard deviation of ±4.3.

**Results.** The results of decontamination experiments are summarized in Tables I and II. The results of all high concentration experiments (Table I) show that the average recovery was 96.6% with a standard deviation of ±2.0. The results were not affected significantly by varying the temperature in the range of 90° to 130°C. Similarly, recovery was not affected by varying soil moisture in the range of 5.7 to 9.85 wt%. Similar results were obtained when soil containing 9.28 ppm tetrachloroethylene and approximately 5.7% moisture was treated at 90° and 100°C (Table II). The average recovery of tetrachloroethylene in five experiments using 9.28 ppm tetrachloroethylene and approximately 5.7% moisture at 90° and 100°C was 95% with a standard deviation of ±1.5.

The results show that substantial recovery of tetrachloroethylene from soil is feasible in the temperature range of 90° to 130°C. Considering the data shown in Tables I and II, and extrapolating the result obtained at a concentration of 957.3 ppm heated to 130°C, it may also be stated that there is no significant difference between the amount of tetrachloroethylene recovered when the soil is heated to 90° and when it is heated to 130°C.

Table I.   Thermal Recovery of Tetrachloroethylene
from Soil (containing 957.3 ppm)

| Initial Moisture, % | Temp., °C | Time, hr | Residual Concentration, ppm | Recovery, % |
|---|---|---|---|---|
| 5.9 | 21 | 4.00 | 1089[‡] | 0.4 |
| 5.7 | 90 | 4.00 | 58.4 | 94.2 |
| 5.7 | 90 | 4.10 | 52.0 | 94.9 |
| 5.7 | 101 | 3.55 | 29.1 | 97.1 |
| 5.7 | 101 | 3.62 | 18.4 | 98.2 |
| 5.7 | 101 | 4.02 | 56.3 | 94.5 |
| 5.7 | 131 | 3.75 | 20.6 | 98.0 |
| 9.85 | 89 | 4.00 | 1.6 | 99.8 |
| 9.85 | 102 | 3.50 | 25.0 | 97.6 |

[‡]Initial concentration:  992 ppm.  Difference is within the bounds of experimental error.

Table II.  Thermal Recovery of Tetrachloroethylene
from Soil (containing 9.28 ppm)

| Initial Moisture, % | Temp., °C | Time, hr | Residual Concentration, ppb | Recovery, % |
|---|---|---|---|---|
| 5.9 | 21 | 4.0 | 9690[‡] | 0.3 |
| 5.7 | 89 | 4.07 | 242 | 97.5 |
| 5.7 | 90 | 3.73 | 499 | 94.9 |
| 5.7 | 99 | 3.58 | 461 | 95.3 |
| 5.7 | 100 | 3.72 | 635 | 93.5 |
| 5.7 | 101 | 3.45 | 525 | 94.7 |

[‡]Initial concentration:  9.92 ppm.  Difference is within the bounds
of experimental error.

## Principles of Radio Frequency Heating

The term radio frequency (RF) generally refers to the frequencies
used in wireless communications.  These frequencies can be as low as
45 Hz or extend well above 10 GHz.  The frequencies primarily used
for radio frequency, dielectric, or microwave heating range from
6.78 MHz to 2.45 GHz.

The principles of RF heating are similar to those of a microwave oven, except that the frequency of operation is different and
the size of the application is much larger.  In these systems, the
temperature rise occurs as a result of ohmic or dielectric heating
mechanisms. Ohmic heating arises from an ionic current or conduction
current that flows in the material in response to the applied electric field.  Dielectric heating results from the physical distortion
of the atomic or molecular structure of polar materials in response
to an applied electric field.  Since the applied AC electric field
changes rapidly, the alternating physical distortion dissipates
mechanical energy that is translated into thermal energy in the
material.

The dielectric properties of soil determine the amount of RF
power that can be dissipated in the soil.  These properties are the
relative dielectric constant ($\varepsilon_r$) and the loss-tangent. The loss-
tangent, tan $\delta$, is defined as $\sigma/\omega\varepsilon_0\varepsilon_r$ where $\sigma$ is the apparent
conductivity, $\omega$ is the frequency of the applied electric field,
radians/sec, and $\varepsilon_0$ is the permittivity of free space which equals
$8.85 \times 10^{-12}$ Farads/meter.  All the dielectric properties are a
function of soil temperature, the frequency of the applied field,
and the composition of the soil.

The amount of RF power dissipated in the soil is directly
related to the frequency of the applied electric field, to the
square of the amplitude, to the relative dielectric constant, and to
the loss-tangent (8).

The depth of penetration of the electromagnetic energy is
measured by its skin depth.  Skin depth is defined as the distance
from the power source at which the amplitude of the EM wave falls to

37% of its initial amplitude (8). Skin depth is inversely related to the square root of frequency, apparent AC conductivity, or the loss-tangent.

The dielectric parameters determine the depth of penetration of EM fields into the soil for a given operating frequency. If the depth of penetration is small compared to that needed, only the volume nearest the energy source would be heated initially. This suggests that for any reasonable volume, as low a frequency as possible should be chosen. On the other hand, if too low a frequency is chosen, very little energy absorption will occur for an acceptable level of electric field. While the electric field can be increased, electrical breakdown, corona discharge, or other undesirable effects can result. Thus, there is an optimum range wherein a suitable frequency can be chosen for a given volume of material and a given set of dielectric parameters.

## In-Situ RF Heating Systems

A fully operational in-situ RF heating system for decontamination requires the development and testing of at least four major sub-systems. These are: (1) RF energy deposition electrode array; (2) RF power generation, transmission, monitoring and control system; (3) vapor barrier and containment system; and (4) gas and liquid condensate handling and treatment system.

Among the sub-systems mentioned above, the design of the electrode array (also called the exciter array) is the critical factor that will determine the design requirements and constraints for the other three sub-systems.

Previous attempts (9-12) to use electrical energy for heating earth formations were aimed at resource recovery from hydrocarbonaceous deposits. Simple techniques such as burying electrical heating elements or a pair of electrodes to which 60 cycles AC power is applied were not successful for two main reasons: (1) nonuniform heating led to unacceptable levels of energy inefficiency; and (2) heating beyond the boiling point of free water was not possible. To overcome the temperature limitation imposed by 60 Hz heating, antennas radiating very high frequency or microwaves have been considered (9). Though these methods provide rapid volumetric heating even above the boiling point of free moisture, they suffer from inefficient use of the applied energy.

To overcome these limitations, it is necessary to use bound-wave exciters as opposed to the radiated wave horns or antennas previously used. The bound-wave exciters are designed to fully contain the EM radiation within a defined volume of soil. There are two basic types of bound-wave exciter arrays. These are the tri-plate line and the fringing-field transmission line.

**Triplate Line.** The triplate transmission line is the rectangular analogue of the more familiar cylindrical coaxial cables. The triplate line is formed by a fully enclosed rectangular cavity in which a central planar conductor has been inserted parallel to the large sides of the cavity. Clearly emplacement of solid metal plates that enclose a rectangular cavity below the soil surface is impractical. This problem has been resolved (1, 13) by simulating the fully contained rectangular cavity by inserting an array of electrodes into bore-holes drilled through the soil.  The electrodes are inserted in three parallel rows that represent the two outer walls and the central conductor of the fully contained rectangular triplate.  It has been demonstrated (1, 13) that through appropriate selection of the row-spacing and the spacing of the electrodes within each row, it is possible to fully contain the applied electromagnetic field within the two outer rows of electrodes.

The triplate line is suitable for those soil decontamination applications where the contaminants have penetrated more than three feet below the surface and for contaminants that require treatment temperatures in excess of 130° to 150°C.

Figure 1 illustrates a conceptual design of such an array that is covered by a vapor barrier to contain and collect gases and vapors as they rise from the surface of the soil.  A triplate line was tested by Krstansky et al. (1) by heating 660 cu ft of a tar sand formation to 200°C to an average depth of 14.7 ft.

**Fringing-Field Line.**  This concept makes use of the fringing fields or leakage fields that exist near a transmission line. Figure 2 illustrates a schematic diagram showing rows of horizontal electrodes placed over the surface of the soil.  Fringing fields are formed around the electrodes when they are energized.  Thus EM energy is first absorbed by the moist layers of soil nearest the electrodes.  As the moisture is driven out of the soil, the energy is selectively absorbed at greater depths.  The heating zone is eventually restricted because of the exponential fall-off of the fields into the soil.

A 1:3 scale model of a single electrode from the fringing-field line shown in Figure 2 was made and tested (14).  The results of this test show that the fringing field line is suitable for the treatment of soils in which the depth of contaminant penetration is less than three feet and where the required treatment temperatures do not exceed 130°C.  Additional development and testing is, however, necessary to fully explore the limitations of the fringing field lines, and in particular, to determine ways to improve the penetration depth.

## Cost Estimate

Preliminary cost estimates for treating contaminated soil using the tri-plate exciter have been reported (14).  It was estimated that the cost of treating soil containing 12.1% moisture to a temperature of 170°C was $42/ton.  This estimate was based on the treatment of a 3-acre site to a depth of 8 ft by the progressive heating of a 96 x 96 x 8 ft module.  It was estimated that the 3-acre site can be treated in one year.  Appropriate pilot and field tests currently in the planning phase will validate operating and economic parameters.

## Conclusions

Laboratory-scale studies have shown that 95% of the tetrachloro-ethylene present in soil can be recovered by heating to a temperature range of 90° to 130°C for 4-hr.  Additional experiments are necessary to determine whether similar recovery efficiencies can be sustained over deep soil beds.  The RF heating techniques have

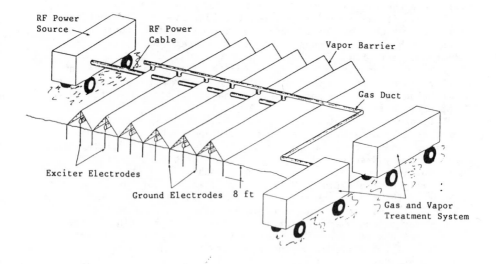

Figure 1.   In situ treatment module for area 10,000 ft$^2$, depth 8 ft.

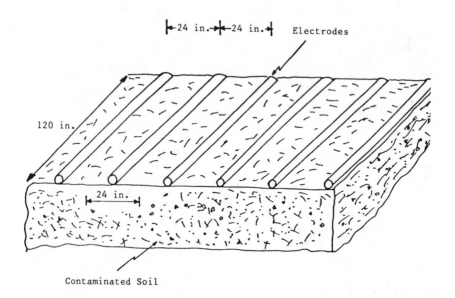

Figure 2.   Schematic representation of a fringing field line (size 10 x 10 ft).

been tested on hydrocarbonaceous earth formations in the temperature range of 200 °C to 400 °C. Appropriate field and pilot tests are necessary to validate the technical feasibility and the cost parameters of using the in situ RF heating methods for soil decontamination.

## Acknowledgment

This work was supported by the U.S. EPA, USAF, and IIT Research Institute through a U.S. EPA co-operative agreement CR-811529-01-0.

## Literature Cited

1. Krstansky, J., et al. "RF Heating of Utah Tar Sands"; IIT Research Institute: Chicago, 1982; Final Report, IITRI E06482.
2. Barnhart, Benjamin J. Environmental Science Technology 1979, 12, 1132-6.
3. Murray, C. Chemical & Engineering News 1979, 57, 12-16.
4. Rogers, C. J. Proc. 8th Annual EPA Symposium on the Treatment of Hazardous Waste, 1983, p. 197.
5. "Solid Waste Facts - A Statistical Handbook," U.S. Environmental Protection Agency, Office of Public Awareness, 1978.
6. "Everybody's Problem: Hazardous Waste," U.S. Environmental Protection Agency, Office of Water and Waste Management, 1980.
7. Onuska, F. I; Terry, K. A. Analytical Chemistry 1985, 57, 801-5.
8. Dev, H., J. Bridges, and Clark, D. "Radio Frequency Enhanced Decontamination of Soils Contaminated with Halogenated Hydrocarbons, Interim Report"; IIT Research Institute; Chicago, 1985; IITRI C06600.
9. Abernathy, E. R. 1974 Annual Technical Meeting of the Petroleum Society of CIM, Calgary, Alberta, 1974, paper 374007.
10. Flock, D. L; Tharin, A. J. Journal of Canadian Petroleum Technology 1975, 14, 17.
11. Ljungstrom, F. Teknisk Tidskrift 1951, 81, 33.
12. Salomonsson, G. Tidskrift För Tekniski-Vetenskaplig För Skning 1953, 24, 118.
13. Sresty, G. C.; Dev, H.; Snow, R. H.; Bridges, J. E. SPE Reservoir Engineering 1986, I, 85.
14. Dev, H. Proc. 12th Annual Research Symposium, 1986, p. 402. EPA/600/9-86/022.

RECEIVED December 5, 1986

# Chapter 28

# Biodegradation of Chlorinated Organic Compounds by *Phanerochaete chrysosporium*, a Wood-Rotting Fungus

John A. Bumpus and Steven D. Aust

Department of Biochemistry, Michigan State University, East Lansing, MI 48824

The white rot fungus, Phanerochaete chrysosporium, is able to mineralize a number of environmentally persistent organochlorides such as 1,1-Bis(4-chlorophenyl)2,2,2-trichloroethane (DDT), polychlorinated biphenyls (PCBs), 2,3,7,8-tetrachlorodibenzo[p]dioxin (2,3,7,8-TCDD), Lindane (1,2,3,4,5,6-hexachlorocyclohexane), and pentachlorophenol (PCP). Studies suggest that the ability to degrade these compounds is dependent upon the lignin degrading system of this fungus. For example, we have shown that, like $^{14}$C-lignin mineralization, mineralization of $^{14}$C-pentachlorophenol ($^{14}$C-PCP) and $^{14}$C-DDT is promoted in nutrient nitrogen deficient cultures of P. chrysosporium whereas their mineralization is suppressed in nutrient nitrogen sufficient cultures. Also, the temporal onset and disappearance of both $^{14}$C-PCP and $^{14}$C-DDT mineralization appeared similar to that observed for $^{14}$C-lignin, thus suggesting that the same general degradative system may be responsible. It is suggested that the ability of P. chrysosporium to mineralize such a wide variety of organochlorides may make this fungus a useful microorganism for use in the biological treatment of contaminated soils, sediments and aqueous wastes when used in appropriate aerated waste treatment systems.

During the past 40 years large quantities of chlorinated organic compounds have been manufactured for use worldwide. Some of these compounds, such as the pesticides DDT, Lindane and pentachlorophenol, were purposely introduced into the environment to control various noxious or harmful plant and animal pests ([1]). Others, such as polychlorinated biphenyls, contaminated the environment through use or as waste from manufacturing processes ([1]). Some, such as 2,3,7,8-TCDD, were unknowingly introduced as contaminants of other compounds or preparations ([1]).

0097-6156/87/0338-0340$06.00/0

Regardless of the manner by which they were introduced into the environment, organohalides as a group represent an environmentally persistent class of chemicals, many of which accumulate in the food chain in the body fat of animals occupying higher trophic levels (1). Many of these compounds are toxic, mutagenic and/or carcinogenic. Furthermore, many sites exist worldwide that are contaminated with these compounds. Often these sites are old production or use facilities which contain high concentrations of the pollutant in question and represent potential health hazards. Of great concern in many cases is the threat of ground water contamination. Thus these sites are candidates for decontamination and reclamation.

Recent attention has focused on the possible usefulness of the white rot fungus Phanerochaete chrysosporium for the biodegradation of hazardous and environmentally persistent organohalides (2-7). This paper summarizes our present knowledge concerning the ability of this fungus to degrade halogenated organic compounds.

Phanerochaete chrysosporium and the Biodegradation of Lignin. Lignin is an abundant, naturally occurring polymer whose function in nature is to provide structural support to woody plants (8). Its formation in vivo is catalyzed by the free radical oxidative polymerization of cinnamyl alcohols (8). Because the type and quantity of cinnamyl alcohols may vary and because its biosynthesis occurs via a non-stereospecific free radical mechanism, the lignin polymer is a racemic heteropolymer whose structure varies from species to species (8). The lack of an ordered and repeating structure coupled with the racemic nature of the polymer (8) combine to make lignin resistant to attack by most enzyme systems.

Initial studies in our laboratory (9) and by others (10-15) suggested that, like lignin biosynthesis, lignin biodegradation by the white rot fungus P. chrysosporium also proceeded via a free radical process. It had been known for some time that hydrogen peroxide ($H_2O_2$) is secreted by many wood rotting fungi (16,17) and it was suspected that $H_2O_2$ was required for lignin biodegradation (17). Forney et al. (9) subsequently presented evidence which showed that, in cultures of P. chrysosporium, $H_2O_2$ gave rise to the formation of hydroxyl free radicals (Figure 1), a very reactive oxygen species that is able to cause depolymerization of the lignin polymer (13). Furthermore, it was shown that $H_2O_2$ formation coincided with the onset of lignin mineralization in P. chrysosporium (Figure 2) (9). Subsequent work in a number of laboratories (18-25) has confirmed the requirement for $H_2O_2$ and that an active oxygen species is indeed required for lignin depolymerization and/or degradation. However, these detailed studies of lignin degradation in P. chrysosporium have shown that the most important oxygen activation step is enzyme-mediated by a family of $H_2O_2$-requiring hemeproteins, collectively referred to as ligninases, that are secreted by this fungus during idiophasic metabolism in response to nutrient starvation (18-25). By catalyzing various oxidations of the lignin molecule these enzymes mediate cleavage of many C-C and C-O bonds, thus achieving depolymerization. Furthermore, Schoemaker et al. suggest that carbon centered free radicals of lignin-derived metabolites may be able to diffuse away from the

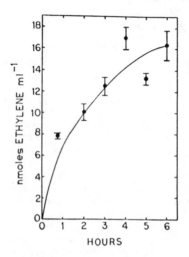

Figure 1.  The production of hydroxyl radical (·OH) in lignino-
lytic cultures of P. chrysosporium as detected by ethylene formation.  The ·OH was detected by the ·OH-dependent formation of
ethylene following the addition of α-keto-γ-methiolbutyric acid
(KTBA) (3.3 mM final concentration) to cultures grown for 14
days in nutrient nitrogen deficient media.  The ethylene produced was detected using gas chromatography and is expressed as
nanomoles of ethylene/ml of headspace.  Reproduced with permission from Ref. 9.

ligninases and catalyze further oxidation of lignin at sites that
are remote from the active site of the enzyme (26).  Once the initial oxidative depolymerization of lignin occurs, the smaller and
more soluble lignin derived metabolites then undergo further modification and, ultimately, metabolism to carbon dioxide.

Although the most important factor in the initial oxidative
depolymerization of lignin is undoubtedly the catalytic action
attributed to the ligninases, the hydroxyl radical may still play a
role in lignin degradation (26).  Additionally, a manganese dependent peroxidase, which is also secreted by this fungus may have an
important function in lignin degradation (24,27-29).  Regardless of
the precise mechanism of lignin degradation, it is apparent that
this system is a very non-specific and non-stereoselective biodegradation system.  It is this lack of specificity that makes this fungus a potentially useful microorganism for the treatment of hazard-

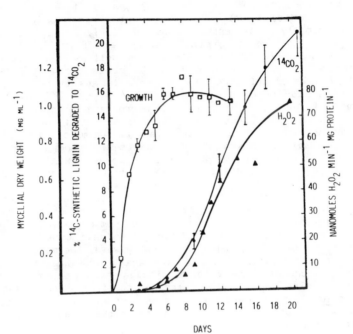

Figure 2. Relationship between the specific activity for $H_2O_2$ production in cell extracts (Δ), the metabolism of 2' $^{14}$C-labeled synthetic lignin to $^{14}CO_2$ (O), and mycelial dry weight (□). P. chrysosporium was grown in low nitrogen medium. Reproduced with permission from Ref. 9.

ous chlorinated organics. Furthermore, a free radical mechanism would allow cleavage of C-Cl bonds.

Degradation of Chlorinated Compounds by P. chrysosporium: An Overview. The first use of P. chrysosporium in the treatment of chlorinated organic compounds focused on the treatment of chlorinated lignin (30) and chlorinated lignin-derived low molecular weight compounds that are by-products of the bleaching procedure that is often used with the Kraft pulping process (6,7). In these studies, it was demonstrated that even highly chlorinated compounds like tetrachloroguiacol could be degraded by the lignin degrading system of this organism (6,7). Other studies showed that chlorinated lignins, like their nonchlorinated precursors, could be degraded to carbon dioxide (30). A somewhat surprising finding was that the chlorinated lignin was mineralized faster than unmodified lignin (30).

The fact that P. chrysosporium degraded chlorinated lignin and lignin by-products, coupled with the finding that lignin degradation proceeded via a non-specificfree radical process, suggested to us that even more recalcitrant organohalides might be degraded by this microorganism (2-4). We subsequently demonstrated that a number of normally persistent organohalides (DDT, Lindane, 2,3,7,8-TCDD, 3,4,3'4'-tetrachlorobiphenyl (3,4,3',4'-TCB), 2,4,5,2',4',5'-hexachlorobiphenyl (2,4,5,2',4',5'-HCB)) as well as the polyaromatic hydrocarbon benzo[a]pyrene,can be mineralized by nitrogen starved cultures of this fungus (Table Ia). Nearly coincidental degradation studies of a polychlorinated biphenyl (PCB) mixture (Aroclor 1254) by Eaton (5) using this microorganism produced similar results and conclusions. It is interesting to note that lignin, chlorinated lignin, and the overwhelming majority of lignin-derived low molecular weight by-products are already partially oxidized. In contrast, most of the compounds examined in our studies (3,4) and Eaton's (5) were highly reduced, having only an aromatic pi electron cloud, a hydrogen or a typically unreactive chlorine substituent available for attack. This demonstrates that P. chrysosporium is able to catalyze the initial oxidative step in the biodegradation of many highly reduced compounds. This step is important because the initial oxidation of an environmentally persistent xenobiotic is often (though not always) the most difficult step and a rate limiting step in its overall biodegradation. Thus, unlike many microorganisms which typically catalyze one or a few reactions during the microbial degradation of organopollutants, P. chrysosporium is able to initiate degradation of many organopollutants and to catalyze all of the steps in their complete degradation pathways to carbon dioxide.

Potential Advantages to the use of White Rot Fungi in Waste Treatment Systems. The potential usefulness of the white rot fungus P. chrysosporium in waste treatment systems has been discussed in greater detail elsewhere (3). Briefly the potential advantages to using this microorganism are: (1) The system normally attacks an insoluble substrate. (2) The lignin degrading system is relatively non-specific, thus it may be useful in the treatment of mixtures of organopollutants. (3) P. chrysosporium is a successful competitor, especially when wood based products are a major carbon source. (4) Biodegradation is not dependent on prior exposure to lignin or to a specific organopollutant. (5) Biodegradation of lignin proceeds to zero levels and the end product is carbon dioxide. This is precisely the type of degradation one would try to achieve for unwanted xenobiotics.

Perhaps the most interesting aspect concerning the use of this microorganism in the biological destruction of organopollutants, is the fact that it is able to dechlorinate chlorinated organic compounds. Unfortunately, dechlorination of organochlorides per se by P. chrysosporium has not been well studied. Our information concerning this process comes from the following: (1) In studies of the decolorization of the alkaline extract ($E_1$) obtained from a Kraft bleach plant, it was demonstrated that many of the organochlorides originally present were removed by treatment with P. chrysosporium in a rotating biological contactor (6,7). Furthermore, most

Table Ia. Mineralization of Selected [14]C-labeled Compounds by
Phanerochaete chrysosporium.[a]

| | Mineralization[b] (pmoles) | % Mineralization |
|---|---|---|
| Lindane | 267.6 | 21.4 |
| Benzo(a)pyrene | 171.9 | 13.8 |
| DDT | 116.4 | 9.3 |
| 2,3,7,8,-TCDD | 49.5 | 4.0 |
| 3,4,4',4'-TCB | 25.1 | 2.0 |
| 2,4,5,2',4',5'-HCB[c] | 86.0 | 1.7 |

Table Ib. Mineralization of [14]C-Labeled Biphenyl and Two
Polychlorinated Biphenyl Mixtures.

| | Mineralization (pmoles) | % Mineralization |
|---|---|---|
| Biphenyl | 455.8 | 36.5 |
| Aroclor 1242 | 256.3 | 20.5 |
| Aroclor 1254 | 224.4 | 18.0 |

Table Ic. Mineralization of [14]C-Labeled Hexachlorobenzene and
Pentachlorophenol.

| | Mineralization (pmoles) | % Mineralization |
|---|---|---|
| Pentachlorophenol | 570.4 | 45.6 |
| Hexachlorobenzene | --- | <1.0 |

Table Id. Mineralization of Chlordane and Mirex.

| | Mineralization (pmoles) | % Mineralization |
|---|---|---|
| Chlordane[c] | 607.7 | 12.2 |
| Mirex | 30.2 | 2.4 |

[a]Culture conditions were the same as those described in ref. 2,
except that supplemental glucose (56 mM) was added to each culture
after 30 days of incubation and incubations were continued for a
total of 60 days. The [14]CO$_2$ evolution assay was performed as
described in ref. 2. DDT, 2,3,7,8-TCDD, 3,4,3',4'-TCB, 2,4,5,2',4'-
5'-HCB, biphenyl, Aroclor 1242, Aroclor 1254, pentachlorophenol and
hexachlorobenzene were uniformly labeled ([14]C) in aromatic ring
carbons atoms. Lindane, Chlordane and Mirex were uniformly labeled
([14]C). Benzo[a]pyrene was labeled ([14]C) in the 7 and 10 position.
Except for hexachlorobenzene (purity = 96%), the radiochemical
purity of the compounds used in this study was 97% or better.

[b]pmoles of [14]C-labeled substrate evolved as [14]CO$_2$.

[c]The initial concentration of 2,4,5,2',4',5'-HCB and Chlordane was
5 nanomoles per culture. The initial concentration of all other
compounds under study was 1.25 nanomoles/culture.

available evidence to support this position. Furthermore, reductive dechlorination of otherwise unsubstituted halogenated aromatic compounds under aerobic conditions would be predicted to be an unlikely event. An alternative method by which dechlorination could reasonably take place could entail direct substitution of chlorine by a hydroxyl group (31-33). This is an attractive hypothesis as the product can be considered to be a substituted phenol. This is important because chlorinated phenols are known to undergo dehalogenation in some systems (34,35). A similar pathway for dehalogenation might involve hydroxylation of one of the non-chlorinated carbon atoms (in a PCB, for example) followed, again, by dehalogenation of the phenol product. Still another mechanism of dechlorination requires that aromatic ring cleavage occur followed by dechlorination of the alkyl halide formed as a ring cleavage product. This appears to be the most common method of dehalogenation in nature (36-39). The mechanism(s) by which dechlorination is accomplished by P. chrysosporium and the role of the $H_2O_2$ dependent extracellular oxidases secreted by this fungus is at present unknown, but is the subject of current investigation.

In addition to studies demonstrating mineralization of the compounds presented in Table Ia, we have studied mineralization of other organic compounds in nutrient nitrogen deficient cultures of P. chrysosporium, in order to gain information concerning structural effects on biodegradation. From these studies the following generalization can be made: (1) Chlorination of an organic compound inhibits, but does not prevent, mineralization. This is seen most graphically when one compares the mineralization of biphenyl with the PCB mixtures Aroclor 1242 and Aroclor 1254 (Table Ib). Both Aroclor mixtures were mineralized but at a slower rate than biphenyl. However, comparison of our data regarding mineralization of the chlorinated compounds present following treatment were found in significantly reduced concentrations and some appeared to be metabolites of compounds present before treatment. In general, these metabolites appeared to contain fewer chlorine substituents than their presumptive precursors (6,7). (2) Studies in our laboratory (2,3) demonstrated that Lindane, an aliphatic compound that is chlorinated at every carbon atom, is degraded to $CO_2$ by this fungus, thus, demonstrating, albeit indirectly, that aliphatic dechlorination occurs. In another experiment we presented direct evidence for aliphatic dechlorination by showing that DDT undergoes reductive dechlorination to form DDD (2,4). (3) Eaton's work also provides evidence that supports the hypothesis that P. chrysosporium has the ability to dechlorinate organic compounds (5). In his study of the degradation and mineralization of [14]C-labeled Aroclor 1254, a PCB mixture, it was shown that after 19 days of incubation with nutrient nitrogen deficient cultures of P. chrysosporium, considerable non-polar radiolabeled material could be extracted which did not contain chlorine as measured by GLC using a Hall detector (5).

Because compounds like PCB are mineralized by P. chrysosporium, it is reasonable to suggest that these otherwise unsubstituted chlorinated aromatic compounds might undergo reductive dechlorination (substitution of Cl by H). There is, however, no currently of individual PCB congeners (3,4,3',4'-TCB and 2,4,5,2',4',5'-HCB) with that of the Aroclor mixtures indicated that these individual congeners were mineralized much more slowly than the mixtures. The reason for this apparent anomalous finding is unknown. However, it may be due to the inherent stability of the two congeners selected for study. (2) The presence of at least one substituent other than chlorine appears to be required for the mineralization of chlorinated aromatic compounds as demonstrated by the comparison of hexachlorobenzene (HCB) mineralization and pentachlorophenol mineralization (Table Ic). HCB did not appear to be mineralized by P. chrysosporium whereas pentachlorophenol, a compound that differs from HCB only by the presence of a hydroxyl group in the place of one of the chlorine atoms, was extensively mineralized by this fungus. The fact that PCBs are mineralized demonstrates that hydrogen atom substituents are sufficient to allow the initial oxidation of the molecule. The recalcitrance of HCB is likely related to the stable nature of aromatic carbon-chlorine bonds and the probability that the highly electronegative chlorines coupled with their uniform symmetry in the HCB molecule prevents oxidation of the aromatic ring. (3) Chlorinated aliphatic compounds were also mineralized by P. chrysosporium. Interestingly, no generalizations can yet be made comparing the rate and extent of mineralization of chlorinated aliphatics with those of chlorinated aromatic compounds. For example, mineralization of Lindane (Table Ia) was slightly more rapid and extensive than Aroclor 1254 or Aroclor 1242 (Table Ib). However, mineralization of pentachlorophenol (Table Ic) was much more rapid and extensive than Lindane. In addition to Lindane (Table Ia), we have studied mineralization of two other polychlorinated aliphatic insecticides, Chlordane and Mirex (Table Id). Of all the non-aromatic organochlorines studied, Mirex was the most poorly mineralized. This lack of reactivity probably is due to the fact that this compound contains no hydrogen atoms and consists solely of C-C and C-Cl bonds. (4) In addition to hexachlorobenzene, the heterocyclic herbicide Atrazine was the only other compound in our study which was refractory to ring cleavage as assayed by mineralization of $^{14}$C-ring labeled carbon atoms (data not presented). Apparently, ring nitrogen atoms in this heterocyclic compound prevent attack by the aromatic ring cleavage system(s) of this fungus.

Conclusions

The white rot fungus, Phanerochaete chrysosporium has the ability to degrade and mineralize many structurally diverse chlorinated organic compounds (2-7). Studies in our laboratory and by others demonstrate that degradation and mineralization is dependent, at least in part, on the lignin degrading system of this fungus that is expressed in response to nutrient starvation (2-7).

The ability to degrade a wide variety of chlorinated organic compounds coupled with the fact that the initial oxidation of these compounds is likely to be extracellular suggests that this system may be of value in the microbial treatment of materials contaminated with these compounds.

## Acknowledgments

This work was supported by Cooperative Agreement #CR811464, U.S. Environmental Protection Agency, Office of Research and Development, Hazardous Waste Engineering Research Laboratory, Cincinnati, OH, P.R. Sferra, Project Officer. The authors thank Teresa Vollmer for secretarial assistance in the preparation of this manuscript.

## Literature Cited

1.  Murphy, S. D.  In "Casarett and Doull's Toxicology: The Basic Science of Poisons"; Doull, J.; Klaassen, C. D.; Amdur, M. O., Eds.; MacMillan: New York, 1980; pp. 357-408.
2.  Bumpus, J. A.; Tien, M.; Wright, D; Aust, S. D.  Science 1985, 228, 1434-6.
3.  Bumpus, J. A.; Tien, M.; Wright, D. S.; Aust, S. D.  Proc. 11th Ann. Res. Symp., 1985, USEPA, EPA/600/9-85/028, pp. 120-6.
4.  Bumpus, J. A.; Aust, S. D.  Proc. International Conference New Frontiers for Hazardous Waste Management, 1985, USEPA, EPA/600/9-85/025, pp. 404-10.
5.  Eaton, D. C.  Enzyme Microb. Technol. 1985, 7, 194-6.
6.  Chang, H.-M.; Joyce, T. W.; Campbell, A. G.; Gerrard, E. D.; Huynh, V. B., Kirk, T. K.  In "Recent Advances in Lignin Biodegradation"; Uni Publishers: Tokyo, 1983; pp. 257-68.
7.  Huynh, V. B.; Chang, H.-M.; Joyce, T. W.; Kirk, T. K. T.A.P.P.I. J. 1985, 68, 98-102, 7.
8.  Crawford, R.  In "Lignin Biodegradation and Transformation"; John Wiley and Sons: New York, 1981; p. 154.
9.  Forney, L. J.; Reddy, C. A.; Tien, M.; Aust, S. D.  J. Biol. Chem. 1982, 257, 11455-62.
10. Hall, P.  Enzyme Microb. Technol. 1980, 2, 170-6.
11. Amer, G. I.; Drew, S. W.  Dev. Ind. Microbiol. 1980, 22, 479-84.
12. Nakatsubo, F.; Reid, I. D.; Kirk, T. K.  Biochem. Biophys. Res. Commun. 1981, 102, 484-91.
13. Gold, M. H.; Kutsuki, H.; Morgan, M. A.  Photochem. Photobiol. 1983, 38, 647-51.
14. Kutsuki, H.; Enoki, A.; Gold, M. H.  Photochem. Photobiol. 1983, 37, 1-7.
15. Kutsuki, H.; Gold, M. H.  Biochem. Biophys. Res. Commun. 1982, 109, 320-7.
16. Koenigs, J. W.  Arch. Microbiol. 1974, 99, 129-45.
17. Koenigs, J. W.  Phytopath. 1972, 62, 100-10.
18. Tien, M.; Kirk, T. K.  Science 1983, 221, 661-3.
19. Tien, M.; Kirk, T. K.  Proc. Natl. Acad. Sci. USA 1984, 81, 2280-4.
20. Andersson, L. A.; Renganathan, V.; Chiu, A. A.; Loehr, T. M.; Gold, M. H.  J. Biol. Chem. 1985, 260, 6080-7.
21. Gold, M. H.; Kuwahara, M.; Chiu, A. A.; Glenn, J. K.  Arch. Biochem. Biophys. 1984, 234, 353-62.
22. Huynh, V. B.; Crawford, R. L.  FEMS Microbiol. Lett. 1985, 28, 119-23.

23. Kirk, T. K.; Mozuch, D.; Tien, M. Biochem. J. 1985, 226, 455-60.
24. Paszczynski, A.; Huynh, V. B.; Crawford, R. L. Arch. Biochem. Biophys. 1986, 244, 750-65.
25. Harvey, P.J.; Schoemaker, H. E.; Bowen, R. M.; Palmer, J. M. FEBS Lett. 1985, 183, 13-16.
26. Schoemaker, H. E.; Harvey, P. J.; Bowen, R. M.; Palmer, J. M. FEBS Lett. 1985, 183, 7-12.
27. Kuwahara, M.; Glenn, J. K.; Morgan, M. A.; Gold, M. H. FEBS Lett. 1984, 169, 247-50.
28. Glenn, J. K.; Gold, M. H. Arch. Biochem. Biophys. 1985, 242, 329-41.
29. Paszczynski, A.; Huynh, V. B.; Crawford, R. L. FEMS Microbiol. Lett. 1985, 29, 37-41.
30. Lundquist, K.; Kirk, T. K.; Connors, W. J. Arch. Microbiol. 1977, 112, 291-6.
31. Johnston, H. W.; Briggs, G. G.; Alexander, M. Soil Biol. Biochem. 1972, 4, 187-90.
32. Klages, U.; Ligens, F. FEMS Microbiol. Lett. 1979, 6, 201-3.
33. Marinucci, A. C.; Bartha, R. Appl. Environ. Microbiol. 1979, 38, 811-17.
34. Chu, J.; Kirsch, E. J. Appl. Microbiol. 1972, 23, 1033-35.
35. Chu, J.; Kirsch, E. J. Dev. Ind. Microbiol. 1973, 14, 264-73.
36. Goldman, P.; Milne, G. W. A.; Pignataro, M. T. Arch. Biochem. Biophys. 1967, 118, 178-84.
37. Hartman, J.; Reineke, W.; Knackmuss, H.-J. Appl. Environ. Microbiol. 1979, 37, 421-8.
38. Reineke, W.; Knackmuss, H.-J. J. Bacteriol. 1980, 142, 467-73.
39. Reineke, W. In "Microbial Degradation of Organic Compounds"; Marcel Dekker, Inc.: New York, 1984; pp. 319-60.

RECEIVED November 25, 1986

# Chapter 29

# Photochemical Surface Decontamination: Application to a Polychlorinated Biphenyl Spill Site

William M. Draper[1,4], Robert D. Stephens[2], and Luis O. Ruzo[3]

[1]Environmental Health Division, School of Public Health, University of Minnesota,
Minneapolis, MN 55455
[2]Hazardous Materials Laboratory, California Department of Health Services,
2151 Berkeley Way, Berkeley, CA 94704
[3]Pesticide Chemistry and Toxicology Laboratory, Department of Entomological Sciences,
University of California—Berkeley, Berkeley, CA 94720

A photochemical treatment process is evaluated for decontamination of PCB-tainted surfaces. In the laboratory commercial PCB mixtures were photochemically reactive under fluorescent "sunlight" (maximal output 300 nm) but not "blacklight" lamps (maximal output 360 nm). PCB were photolabile in either organic solvents or neat thin films indicating that supplemental H-donors were not required for reactivity. A prototype surface photoreactor constructed of a Flexiform aluminum frame, lamp fixtures and Westinghouse FS40 fluorescent lamps irradiated a 1.5 $m^2$ surface with a light intensity of 4,600 uW/$cm^2$. In a field test on concrete contaminated with Aroclor 1260 about 10 years ago, the prototype reactor destroyed 47% of the PCB residue after 21 hr of treatment. Means for improving the destruction efficiency are discussed.

Polychlorinated biphenyls (PCB) are noted for their stability. They are resistant to heat, oxidation and attack by strong acids and bases. As a result of these extraordinary properties PCB have been used widely and successfully as dielectric fluids, fire retardants, heat transfer agents, hydraulic fluids, plasticizers and in other applications (1).

[4]Current address: California Public Health Foundation, 2151 Berkeley Way, Berkeley, CA 94704

We now know that PCB are hepatotoxic and that they
impair reproductive function and produce cancer in
experimental animals (2,3).   PCB undergo food chain
"biomagnification" and accumulate in human and animal
tissues, sometimes exceeding acceptable levels.   As a
result of the once valued stability and potential for
chronic or delayed toxicity, widespread environmental
contamination by PCB is now viewed as a threat to both
environmental quality and public health (4).

The 1977 U. S. Environmental Protection Agency (EPA)
ban on PCB manufacture greatly curtailed occupational
PCB exposure.   Potentially hazardous exposures
continue, however, for workers in spill clean-up,
servicing and dismantling of transformers and
capacitors, electrical utility work, and firefighting.
A tremendous volume of PCB is still in use and numerous
sites in this country and abroad remain contaminated
with PCB oil.

In contrast to their chemical stability, PCB are
remarkably reactive when exposed to ultraviolet (UV)
light.   Over the past several decades the
photoreductive dehalogenation reactions of PCB have
been examined in organic solvents (5,6), neat thin
films and solid phase (7,8) and as surface deposits on
silica (9).

The "classical" photoreduction mechanism involves
the formation of free radicals by homolytic cleavage.
Absorbed light energy (hv) is transformed to electronic
energy in a π to π* transition.   In the
electronically-excited state (indicated by an asterisk)
the carbon-chlorine bonds undergo fission yielding
aromatic radicals and chlorine atoms, both of which
abstract hydrogen atoms from the solvent yielding
intermediate photoproducts (Figure 1).   The
photochemical sequence is repeated ultimately yielding
the chlorine free biphenyl nucleus.   Alternate
photoreductive dechlorination mechanisms involving
heterolytic cleavage of C-Cl bonds (10) and electron
transfer (11) have been proposed.

The principal direction   of the published
photochemical research to date has been to elucidate
pathways which might be responsible for the degradation
of these refractory substances in nature.   This basic
research has not been extensively applied either to on-
or off site treatment of hazardous substances.   In this
chapter we extend the existing PCB photochemistry
literature by considering this potential.   The
development and fabrication of a prototype surface
photoreactor, and its preliminary evaluation at a PCB-
contaminated site are described.   Photochemical
treatments may be applicable to many other classes of
hazardous chemicals as well including the
polychlorinated dibenzodioxins (PCDD) and dibenzofurans
(PCDF) about which this monograph is chiefly concerned.

## Methods and Materials

Chemicals. Analytical reference standards for Aroclor
1254 and 1260 were provided by the U. S. EPA (Research
Triangle Park, NC). Solvents were commercially
available, pesticide grade and were used as received.

Irradiation. Solutions were irradiated in sealed
borosilicate or quartz test tubes held in a merry-go-
round apparatus ensuring uniform illumination. A
Rayonet Model RPR-100 photoreactor (Southern New
England Ultraviolet Co., Hamden, CT) equipped with 16
RPR-3500 "blacklight" lamps or 16 RPR-3000 "sunlight"
lamps was used in preliminary laboratory studies of PCB
photolability. For solution phase experiments a 1.0
mg/L petroleum ether solution of Aroclor 1254 was
studied. Periodically, irradiated samples were
subjected to direct analysis by capillary electron
capture gas liquid chromatography (EC-GLC). The
photolability of PCB on surfaces was determined by
irradiation of neat Aroclor 1254 thin films (18 ug/cm$^2$)
on glass Petri plates fitted with borosilicate glass
covers. After irradiation plates were withdrawn from
the photoreactor and the PCB residue dissolved in 2 X 5
mL of hexane for EC-GLC analysis.

Actinometry. The trifluralin actinometer was used to
measure light intensity from polychromatic sources
(12,13). Table I. provides Westinghouse FS40 spectral
energy distribution and irradiance data and trifluralin
extinction coefficients needed for actinometry. For
the sunlight phosphor lamps the actinometry procedure
was modified by using isooctane as the solvent and
quartz cells, both transparent to wavelengths emitted
by these lamps. Calculations were adjusted for the
higher reaction quantum yield of trifluralin in
isooctane ( $\Phi$ = 0.018) relative to toluene ( $\Phi$ =
0.0091) (12).

Sampling PCB on Concrete. A template was used to
demarcate 10 X 10 cm squares on contaminated concrete
surfaces. Isooctane (1.5 mL) was applied and after
about 45 seconds the solvent was imbibed on two filter
paper disks. The filter paper disks were held in
stoppered, prerinsed test tubes for shipment to the
laboratory. Filter paper disks were extracted by
immersion in 40 mL of petroleum ether for one hr and
the extracts dried (NaCl) and diluted with isooctane
prior to analysis.

Chemical Analysis. All chemical measurements were made
by EC-GLC using a 15 m X 0.53 mm (ID) fused silica
capillary (DB-5, J & W Scientific) mounted in a packed
injection port with the following conditions: inlet
temperature, 250°C; detector temperature, 300°C; He

**Table I.** Emission Characteristics and Spectral Irradiance Values for Westinghouse FS40 Lamp and Trifluralin Absorption Coefficients[a]

| Wavelength (nm) | Spectral Energy Distribution, % | Spectral Irradiance Joules/s/cm² | Spectral Irradiance Photons/s/cm² | Trifluralin Extinction Coefficients, ε |
|---|---|---|---|---|
| 265 | 0.24 | 1.1E-5 | 1.5E13 | 6,420 |
| 275 | 1.3 | 5.8E-5 | 8.0E13 | 7,425 |
| 285 | 5.0 | 2.3E-4 | 3.3E14 | 6,260 |
| 295 | 16 | 7.2E-4 | 1.1E15 | 3,750 |
| 305 | 21 | 1.0E-3 | 1.5E15 | 2,210 |
| 315 | 19 | 8.9E-4 | 1.4E15 | 1,500 |
| 325 | 14 | 6.3E-4 | 1.0E15 | 1,460 |
| 335 | 7.8 | 3.6E-4 | 6.1E14 | 1,500 |
| 345 | 4.2 | 1.9E-4 | 3.3E14 | 1,670 |
| 355 | 1.8 | 8.3E-5 | 1.5E14 | 1,840 |
| 365 | 2.1 | 9.2E-5 | 1.7E14 | 2,060 |
| 375 | 0.64 | 2.9E-5 | 5.5E13 | 2,230 |
| 385 | 0.40 | 1.8E-5 | 3.5E13 | 2,320 |
| 395 | 0.32 | 1.5E-5 | 3.0E13 | 2,320 |
| 405 | 1.9 | 8.7E-5 | 1.8E14 | 2,320 |
| 415 | 0.32 | 1.5E-5 | 3.1E13 | 2,260 |
| 425 | 0.32 | 1.5E-5 | 3.2E13 | 2,160 |
| 435 | 3.7 | 1.7E-4 | 3.7E14 | 1,960 |
| 445 | 0.16 | 7.3E-6 | 1.6E13 | 1,660 |
| 455 | 0.16 | 7.3E-6 | 1.7E13 | 1,290 |

a  Spectral irradiance values are based on a total radiant intensity (250-460 nm) of 4,600 uW/cm², a typical light flux for the operating reactor as determined by the trifluralin actinometer.  The FS 40 lamp has negligable output at 253.7 nm and several minor emission bands above 500 nm in a region trifluralin does not absorb.

carrier gas flow rate, 7 mL/min; detector purge gas flow rate, 60 mL/min Ar-methane (95:5, v/v). Trifluralin eluted in 2.7 min with an oven temperature of 195°C. At 220°C the following peaks were used to quantitate Aroclor 1260: 1.21; 1.40; 1.65; 1.84; 2.52; and 3.03 (retention times relative to p,p'-DDE which eluted in 8.2 min). Determinations of Aroclor 1254 were based on the following peaks: 0.75; 0.85; 1.05; 1.22; 1.43; and 1.65. Quantitation was achieved by suming peak areas with absolute calibration relative to external Aroclor standards.

**Fabrication of Surface Photoreactor.** A prototype surface photoreactor was constructed using commercially-available, 1.2-meter fluorescent lamp fixtures mounted on an aluminum Flexiform frame. The configuration consisted of two fixtures holding four 40-watt, Westinghouse FS40 lamps mounted in parallel. The enamel surfaces of the canopy were covered with aluminum foil to increase the reflectance of UV and near UV radiation. With the lamps suspended 10 cm from the contaminated concrete a 1.5 m$^2$ surface was exposed to intense light.

**Field Test.** The University of Minnesota Rosemount Research Center (RRC) is listed on the U. S. EPA Superfund National Priorities List for hazardous waste disposal site cleanup and is one of two university-owned sites so designated (14). The RRC, briefly operated as the federal government's Gopher Ordinance Plant in the second world war, was converted by the university to an agricultural research facility. Areas were designated for disposal of university-generated solvents and chemicals, and some facilities were leased to private companies. Several areas at the RRC are contaminated with PCB; in particular, Aroclor 1260 has been detected in samples taken from the site. Between August, 1973 and January, 1978 buildings and grounds now contaminated with PCB were leased to a private firm engaged in servicing and dismantling transformers and other electrical equipment. Other commercial concerns dealing in used equipment, also spread PCB oil at RRC, and some waste transformer oils were incinerated.

The extent and distribution of PCB contamination at RRC was investigated by the Minnesota Pollution Control Agency in 1978, and again in 1984 by a contract laboratory as part of a site remedial investigation (15). The facility features highly contaminated gravel-covered areas and debris pits. Soil profiles in discolored areas indicated Aroclor 1260 levels of 0.14-0.41% (w/w). A concrete building floor also was contaminated with Aroclor 1260, but at comparatively low levels. The measured PCB contamination of these concrete surfaces exceeded levels deemed safe by the Minnesota Department of Health. The applicable state standard at work sites is 50 ug PCB/100 cm2 as determined by a wipe test of the type used here.

The field test consisted of decontaminating the PCB-tainted concrete surface. Before and after 21 hr of photochemical treatment a 1.2 m$^2$ area was sampled extensively (n = 8) to quantify PCB residues. Treated and control samples were located on alternate positions of a grid to minimize sampling error.

## Results

Energy Requirements for PCB Photodecomposition. PCB photodegrade very slowly on irradiation with fluorescent blacklight lamps. After 48 hr of irradiation (8,600 uW/cm$^2$) 87% of the Aroclor 1254 was recovered from petroleum ether solutions. In contrast, PCB are highly reactive on exposure to fluorescent sunlamps (Figure 2). Aroclor 1254 irradiated in Pyrex tubes that are opaque to the RPR-3000's 253.7 nm emission line had a half-life of one hr. The photolysate mixtures exhibit a pungent, noxious odor indicating the formation of volatile photoproducts, possibly chlorine or low molecular weight chlorinated hydrocarbons derived from free-radical chlorination of the solvent. Similar photochemical chlorination of the solvent was observed by Crosby and Hamadmad (16) on irradiation of pentachloronitrobenzene in hexane.

Differences in PCB photolability are attributed to the emission spectra of the lamps tested (Figure 3). The blacklight lamp has a UV cutoff of about 310 nm whereas the sunlamp has considerable output in the 270-300 nm range and as much as 15% of the radiant energy at the 253.7 nm mercury line. Because the borosilicate cells are opaque below about 285 nm we conclude that the observed photoreactivity is due to near UV light in the 285-300 nm wavelength range. When quartz cells were used in the laboratory photoreactor the Aroclor 1254 half-life dropped to 12 min. In general then, the efficacy of light for PCB treatment is ranked as follows:  UV (253.7 nm) > near UV (285-300 nm) >>> near UV (>300 nm). Light absorption alone may account for these differences as the 253.7 nm Hg line corresponds roughly to PCB absorption maxima.

The presence of a hydrogen-donating solvent is not essential for PCB photoreactivity. Neat Aroclor 1254 thin films on glass (18 ug/100 cm$^2$) were photolabile with surface deposits exhibiting half-lives of ~50 min.

Prototype Photoreactor. The Westinghouse FS40 sunlight lamp envelope does not transmit the 253.7 nm Hg line and has its major emission band shifted about 10 nm toward higher wavelengths relative to the RPR-3000 lamp (Figure 3). Light output from the prototype reactor was increased 38% on covering the white enamel fixtures with metal foil. The light intensity under the

$$ArCl \xrightarrow{hv} {}^{1}ArCl^{*} \xrightarrow{ISC} {}^{3}ArCl^{*} \longrightarrow Ar\bullet + \bullet Cl$$

$$Ar\bullet + RH \longrightarrow ArH$$

$$Cl\bullet + RH \longrightarrow HCl$$

**Figure 1.** Generalized photoreduction scheme for haloarenes.

$$ArCl^{*} + ArH \longrightarrow Ar\bullet + Cl^{-} + ArH^{+}\bullet$$

$$Ar\bullet + RH \longrightarrow ArH + R\bullet$$

$$ArCl^{*} + Q \longrightarrow Ar\bullet + Cl^{-} + Q^{+}\bullet$$

$$Ar\bullet + ArH \longrightarrow \longrightarrow Ar\text{-}Ar$$

$$Ar^{+}\bullet + CH_{3}OH \longrightarrow Ar\text{-}OCH_{3}$$

**Figure 2.** Photodecomposition of Aroclor 1254 in petroleum ether solutions irradiated with fluorescent sunlight lamps (borosilicate cells).

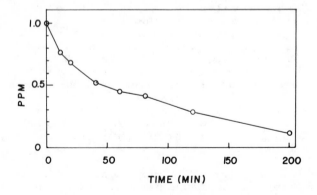

**Figure 3.** Normalized emission spectra for sunlight and blacklight, mercury-excited phosphor lamps.

photoreactor canopy at the irradiated surface was 4,600 uW/cm$^2$, well below values measured in the laboratory photoreactor which were typically 11,800 and 24,500 uW/cm$^2$ with blacklight and sunlight lamps, respectively.  The fluorescent lamps studied emit very little heat and under operating conditions the irradiated surface was not appreciably elevated in temperature.  The shift in emission spectrum in combination with reduced light output indicated that reactions would proceed much more slowly under the surface reactor when compared to the laboratory system.

Field Test.  Before treatment the concrete floor was contaminated with 81 $\pm$ 31 ug Aroclor 1260/100 cm$^2$ (n = 8).  The high relative standard deviation has contributions from surface PCB distribution (sampling error), PCB recovery during sampling and precision in quantitation.  Because the analytical method had few steps, sample concentrations were similar, and the EC detector was operated in a linear region, analytical error was probably a minor contributing factor.  A fine layer of dust and soil was present on the concrete, but no surface preparation was undertaken prior to the test.

After 21 hours of irradiation the concrete was again sampled in close proximity to pretreatment samples (Figure 4).  Post-treatment Aroclor 1260 levels were 43 $\pm$ 13 ug/100 cm$^2$ (n = 8).  The 47% reduction in PCB concentration is statistically significant at the 99% confidence level.

The field test of this photochemical reactor to our knowledge represents the first demonstration of a photochemical treatment process for in-situ remedial cleanup of PCB contaminated surfaces.  At this site PCB oils were deposited 7 to 13 years prior to treatment and represent residues weathered by volatilization and allowed to thoroughly migrate in the concrete surface layers.  It is expected that overlying dust and soil may have provided shade, possibly reducing the PCB destruction efficiency.  PCB sorbed on particulate matter would react more slowly due to reduced light penetration.

## Discussion

The Photochemistry of PCB.  The light-mediated reactions of PCB and their analogs have received considerable attention and several reviews of PCB photochemistry are available (1,17,18).  Rappe (19) has reviewed the photochemistry of halogenated aromatics in general.

PCB absorb UV light efficiently, but absorption of near UV light is relatively weak.  The long wavelength UV absorption band of biphenyl and its meta- and para-substituted derivatives appears at ~250 nm ( $\varepsilon$ =

20,000). The absorption of light by PCB is determined by their geometry (20,21). Ortho-chlorines lower ε drastically while para-chlorines have the opposite effect. When the biphenyl conformation is twisted by substituents there is reduced overlap in molecular orbitals increasing the energy of the excited state and shifting absorption maxima to lower wavelengths. UV absorbance also increases with the degree of chlorination. Decachlorobiphenyl, for example, absorbs strongly at ~300 nm (22).

Photochemical reactivity is affected both by the rate of light absorption and reaction quantum yield (Φ), that fraction of molecules reacting per photon absorbed. Quantum yields for individual PCB isomers vary tremendously (21,23) although, in general, they are quite high in comparison to other pollutants. PCB with para- and particularly ortho- chlorines react most rapidly (see 2,2',4,4'-tetrachlorobiphenyl, Table II.). As a general rule halogenated aromatic molecules including PCB react far more rapidly in hydrocarbon solvents than in water, i.e., Φ for TCDD is 20 times higher in hexane than water (24). There are exceptions to this generality, however. 3,4-Dichloroaniline and monochloro aromatics react as fast or faster in water because cationic and not radical intermediates are involved (24, 25). In cyclohexane Φ range from 0.002 to 0.1 and in aqueous acetonitrile PCB quantum yields as high as 0.25 have been reported (Table II.). Reaction rates in methanol are greater than in cyclohexane (21).

The majority of PCB photodegradation studies have been carried out in solution with organic or combined solvents preferred due to their low water solubility. Reductive dechlorination is the predominant photodegradation pathway in hydrocarbon solvents as well as alcohols. In aqueous media and alcohols photonucleophilic displacement reactions yielding phenols or alkoxy derivatives, respectively, also are detected. In the gas phase PCB are photochemically converted to hydroxylated derivatives (26). Photochemical reduction also is the major reaction pathway in thin films (7), solid phase (8) and on silica gel surfaces (9).

Not all chlorines in PCB structures are equally reactive. Ortho-chlorines are removed preferentially to those in meta- and para-positions (21,23). Thus, 2,2',4,4'-tetrachlorobiphenyl yields sequentially 2,4,4'-trichloro- and then 4,4'-dichlorobiphenyl. Deuterium also is incorporated preferentially in the ortho-positions when deuterated solvents are employed (27) demonstrating H abstraction from the solvent.

As noted earlier there are various photoreductive dechlorination mechanisms. The triplet excited state is believed to undergo homolytic cleavage in the case of ortho-chlorinated PCB, a hypothesis supported by

Table II. Extinction Coefficients and Reaction
Quantum Yields for PCB[a]

| PCB Isomer/Mixture | Extinction[b] Coefficient | Quantum[c] Yield |
|---|---|---|
| $2,2',4,4'-Cl_4$ | 140 | 0.10 |
| $2,2',3,3'-Cl_4$ | 116 | 0.007 |
| $2,2',5,5'-Cl_4$ | 120 | 0.010 |
| $2,2',6,6'-Cl_4$ | 30 | 0.006 |
| $3,3',5,5'-Cl_4$ | 1410 | 0.002 |
| $3,3',4,4'-Cl_4$ | 6740 | 0.005 |
| $4-Cl$ | 120 | 0.004 |
| $2,4-Cl_2$ | 25 | 0.22 |
| $2,4,6-Cl_3$ | 7 | 0.25 |
| $2,2',5,5'-Cl_4$ | 30 | 0.017 |
| $Cl_{10}$ | 1200 | >0.21 |
| Aroclor 1232 | 60 | 0.036 |
| Aroclor 1268 | 770 | 0.16 |

a   According to references 21 and 22.
b   Extinction coefficients for the tetrachloro series
    were measured at 290 nm. Extinction coefficients
    for the remaining isomers and mixtures were
    determined at 300 nm.
c   Quantum yields for the tetrachloro series were
    determined in cyclohexane irradiated at 300 nm. The
    second series of isomers and mixtures were
    irradiated in acetonitrile-water (4:1, v/v) with 254
    nm light.

heavy atom effects (28,29) and phosphorescence studies
(23). PCB generally exhibit low fluorescence quantum
yields (22), but phosphoresce efficiently (21) due to
high intersystem crossing yields from the singlet to
the triplet excited states. Dechlorination of the
meta- and para- isomers may involve excimer formation
(29). In condensed PCB films the major photoprocesses
probably include e⁻ transfer reactions leading to both
dechlorination and polymerization.

Photolysis of Related Haloaromatics. Many other
classes of hazardous materials may be susceptible to in
situ photochemical treatment. Polybromobiphenyls (PBB)
photodecompose more readily than PCB due to the weaker
C-Br bonds. The major reaction is reductive
debromination but quaterphenyls also are formed in low
yield (30). Ortho-bromines are cleaved preferentially
for pure isomers but apparently not in commercial PBB
mixtures (29).

Chlorinated terphenyls are reductively
dechlorinated, but also undergo substantial
photosubstitution in alcohol solvents (31) in contrast
to the low yield of substitution products from PCB. In
the terphenyl series photosubstitution is believed to
take place by attack of the nucleophile directly on the
excited state with concomitant chloride ejection.
Alkylated PCB molecules (chloroalkylenes), candidate
PCB replacement compounds, exhibit UV electronic
spectra nearly identical to those of PCB yet
photodegrade more rapidly (28). Another possible PCB
substitute consists of a mixture of bis-
(chlorophenyl)ethanes (Iralec) that also undergoes
dechlorination and substitution reactions on
irradiation (32).

Support for electron transfer processes leading to
dehalogenation is provided in studies of
chloronaphthalenes (33). Reductive dechlorination,
binaphthyl formation and photonucleophilic reactions
can be rationalized with the scheme depicted in Figure
5. Analogous electron transfer processes have been
proposed for the cyclization/dehalogenation of
polyhalogenated-2-phenoxyphenols (so-called "predioxins") yielding PCDF and PCDD (34). The
photocyclization of predioxins increases with solvent
dielectric constant and, based on the dependence of Φ
on concentration, intramolecular rather than
intermolecular electron transfer appears to predominate
(35).

Accelerated PCB Photodegradation. Sensitized or
accelerated PCB photodegradation has been observed in
many published reports suggesting possible applications
in treatment of hazardous substances. Substantial rate
enhancements have been obtained in photochemical
reaction mixtures containing added amines as electron

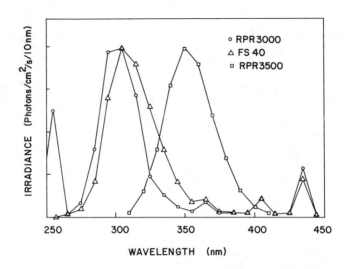

Figure 4. Photochemical decomposition of Aroclor 1260 on concrete. The rectangle denotes the photoreactor canopy. Pretreatment levels ($ug/cm^2$) are indicated with filled symbols, open symbols indicate PCB levels measured after 21 hr of light treatment.

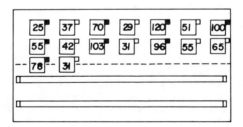

Figure 5. Electron transfer induced photochemical dehalogenation, dimerization and displacement. "Q" indicates a triplet quencher like cyclohexadiene.

transfer agents. The radical anion formed on initial electron transfer (ArCl$\cdot^-$) is believed to expel chloride directly, or undergo protonation prior to release of chlorine atoms (17). Triethylamine increases photocyclization of chlorinated phenoxyphenols (34,36), debromination of PBB (30), photoreduction of chloronaphthalenes (37), and dechlorination of PCB (22) and polychlorinated terphenyls (31). Triethylamine also sensitizes the photodechlorination of PCB on silica gel and clay minerals (38). Generally, these reactions are less effective for ortho chloro isomers and when these additives are used the isomeric photoproduct distribution changes (11). Other electron-rich molecules including aromatic amines, indoles and phenols are effective sensitizers for photodechlorination of chloroacetic acid (39).

Enhancement of PCB photodegradation also is observed in the presence of trifluoroacetic acid (40), presumably via the protonated intermediates (ArClH$^{+\cdot}$). Dienes, such as 1,3-cyclohexadiene, accelerate haloaromatic photoreactions (41) and modify chloronaphthalene photochemistry by enhancing reductive dechlorination and suppressing dimerization (42). The mechanism is believed to involve exciplex formation with the diene or protonation by the olefin (43).

Other compounds enhance PCB photodegradation including sodium borohydride (44), alkaline alcoholic solutions (45) and aqueous suspensions of titanium dioxide (46), a system also effective in treating pentachlorophenol (47).

**Does Photochemical Treatment of PCB Reduce Health Hazard?** As with any new technological process, and particularly in the decontamination of hazardous materials, potential health consequences need to be considered. Photochemical or other treatment processes for PCB may reduce or increase potential hazard because the composition and isomer distribution is altered. In the case of PCB three situations require special attention: 1) the potential for photochemical formation of PCDF and PCDD or other extremely toxic products; 2) the selective photochemical destruction of these substances in PCB mixtures; and 3) shifts in PCB congener distribution to structures with exceptional toxicity.

There are several examples of the first situation in the literature. Predioxin contaminants in PCB mixtures (48) undergo photochemical ring closure to PCDD on irradiation (34,49). Chlorinated diphenyl ethers, also trace PCB contaminants, are cyclized to PCDF on irradiation in hexane solution although photodechlorination predominates (50). Acetone sensitizes this photocyclization as well as that of polychlorophenols (35) suggesting that triplet excited states are involved. Under alkaline conditions pentachlorophenol and other acidic ortho-chlorophenols have been reported to condense by way of photonucleophilic displacement reactions to PCDD (51).

The degree to which PCDF and PCDD accumulate in irradiated PCB mixtures will depend on many factors including the concentration of precursor molecules and, in turn, the photolability of the dibenzo products. In any event, the photochemical removal of PCDD and PCDF is likely to be far more efficient than PCB photodegradation itself. PCDD and PCDF are more photolabile than PCB because of their large absorption cross sections and high reaction quantum efficiencies. Chlorinated dibenzodioxins are extremely unstable in UV light in methanol, diesel oil, liquid phenoxy ester formulations and other organic media (52,53). Fortunately, chlorines in the lateral positions (i.e., 2-, 3-, 7-, 8-) of PCDD are preferentially cleaved on photoreduction (54) leading to the least toxic products. PCDF, like PCDD, appear to be quite photoreactive (55) and in these structures the chlorines para- to biphenyl linkage are most reactive (56). The high photochemical reactivity of PCDD and PCDF relative to PCB supports the view that, if formed, these toxic molecules will occur only in very low steady-state levels. This consideration, however, warrants further study.

The toxicity of PCB mixtures in vivo and in vitro is largely attributable to tetra-, penta- and hexachloro congeners that are capable of assuming a planar conformation (57,58,59). Mono ortho-chloro, coplanar congeners mimic the toxicological effects of 2,3,7,8-TCDD (57). Any photochemical or chemical treatment process which would substantially enrich a PCB deposit in these structures, regardless of its destruction efficiency, would be undesirable. PBB photoproduct mixtures are of increased toxicity due to this sort of isomer redistribution (60). In the case of PCB the preferential photochemical reaction of ortho-halogens may lead to intermediate mixtures of enhanced toxicity and this aspect of PCB reactivity warrants further study. As noted above the product distribution ratio changes markedly on going from direct to sensitized photolysis (11) and thus it may be possible to control the nature of the photolysate residue.

## Conclusion

Photochemical treatments hold promise for on-site decontamination of hazardous substances on various surfaces including building walls and floors, machinery and electrical equipment (e.g., transformer cases). Further applications include cleaning equipment used in remedial activities at contaminated sites and in routine small scale decontamination in chemical laboratories. The destruction efficiency on concrete may be improved by: 1) increasing the interception of light (i.e., by use of a solvent to desorb the pollutant, or prior removal of surface dust); 2) use of a photoreactor with increased light output, particularly UV output; and 3) possible use of hydrogen- or electron donating solvents or photochemical sensitizers. The present study demonstrates qualitatively that photochemical treatments are effective under field conditions. Further basic studies and engineering development will be needed to define the the ultimate destruction efficiency achievable, the applicability to other contaminants and surfaces, and the nature of the photolysate residue and its modification.

## Acknowledgment

John Lulewicz assisted in the analysis of PCB and Danny Mar assisted in manuscript preparation. Fay Thompson (University of Minnesota) provided valuable discussions and arranged the field experiment at RRC. The authors gratefully acknowledge the support of the National Institute of Environmental Health Sciences (Grant Nos. R23 ES03524, WMD; P01 ES00049, LOR) and the National Institute for Occupational Safety and Health of the Centers for Disease Control (Grant No. R01 OH02119, WMD).

## Literature Cited

1.   Hutzinger, O.; Safe, S.; Zitko, V. The Chemistry of PCB's, CRC Press: Cleveland, 1974.
2.   DHEW: Subcommittee on health effects of PCB's and PBB's.Environ. Health Perspect. 1978, 24, 146.
3.   IARC: Working group on the evaluation of the carcinogenic risk of chemicals to humans - Polychlorinated biphenyls. 1978, 18.
4.   "The Toxicology of PCBs: An Overview with Emphasis on Human Health Effects and Occupational Exposures"; State of California Department of Health Services/Department of Industrial Relations: Berkeley, CA, 1981.
5.   Safe, S.; Hutzinger, O. Nature (London) 1971, 232, 641.
6.   Ruzo, L.O.; Zabik, M.J.; Schuetz, R. D. Bull. Environ. Contam. Toxicol. 1972, 8, 217.
7.   Hustert, K.; Korte, F. Chemosphere 1972, 1, 7.
8.   Hutzinger, O.; Safe, S.; Zitko, V. Environ. Health Perspect. 1972, 1, 15.
9.   Gab, S.; Nitz, S.; Parlar, H.; Korte, F. Chemosphere, 1975, 4, 251.
10.  Mamantov, A. Chemosphere 1985, 14, 901.

11.  Soumillion, J. P.; DeWolf, B. J. Chem. Soc. Chem. Comm. 1981, 436.
12.  Draper, W. M. Chemosphere 1985, 14, 1195.
13.  Draper, W. M. In Photochemistry of Environmental Aquatic Systems; W. Cooper and R. Zika, Eds.; ACS Symposium Series 327; American Chemical Society: Washington, DC, 1986; 268-280.
14.  Sanders, H. J. Chem. Eng. News 1986, 64, 21.
15.  "Phase I Report - University of Minnesota Rosemount Research Center Remedial Investigation"; Soil Exploration, February, 1985.
16.  Crosby, D. G.; Hamadmad, N. J. Agric. Food Chem. 1971, 19, 1171.
17.  Bunce, N. J. Chemosphere 1982, 11, 701.
18.  Zabik, M. J.; Leavitt, R. A.; Su, G. C. C. Ann. Rev. Entomol. 1976, 21, 61.
19.  Rappe, C. In Halogenated Biphenyls, Terphenyls, Naphthalenes, Dibenzofurans and Related Products; R. D. Kimbrough, Ed; Elsevier: New York, 1980.
20.  Wagner, P.J. J. Amer. Chem. Soc. 1967, 89, 2820.
21.  Ruzo, L.O., Zabik, M. J.; Schuetz, R. D. J. Agric. Food Chem. 1974, 22, 199.
22.  Bunce, N. J.; Kumar, Y.; Brownlee, B. G. Chemosphere, 1978, 7, 155.
23.  Ruzo, L.O.; Zabik, M. J.; Schuetz, R.D. J. Amer. Chem. Soc. 1974, 96, 3809.
24.  Dulin, D.; Drossman, H.; Mill, T. Environ. Sci. Technol. 1986, 20, 72.
25.  Miller, G. C.; Miille, M. J.; Crosby, D. G.; Sontum, S.; Zepp, R. G. Tetrahedron, 1979, 35, 1797.
26.  Hustert, K,; Korte, F. Chemosphere 1974,3, 153.
27.  Mansour, M.; Parlar, H.; Korte, F. Chemosphere 1980, 9, 59-60.
28.  Ruzo,, L. O.; Sundstrom, G.; Hutzinger, O.; Safe, S. J. Royal Netherland Chem. Soc. 1977, 96, 249.
29.  Bunce, N. J.; Bergsma, J.P.; Bergsma, M.D.; De Graaf, W.; Kumar, Y.; Ravanal, L. J. Org. Chem. 1980, 45, 3708.
30.  Bunce, N. J.; Safe, S.; Ruzo, L. O. J. Chem. Soc. Perkin I 1975, 1607.
31.  Chittim, B.; Safe, S.; Bunce, N. J.; Ruzo, L. O.; Olie, K.; Hutzinger, O. Can. J. Chem. 1978, 56, 1253.
32.  Sundstrom, G.; Olie, K.; Hutzinger, O.; Safe, S.; Chittim, B. Chemosphere, 1977, 6, 103.
33.  Ruzo, L.O.; Safe, S., Zabik, M. J. J. Agric. Food Chem. 1975, 23, 594.
34.  Freeman, P. K.; Srinivasa, R. J. Agric. Food Chem. 1983, 31, 775.
35.  Freeman, P. K.; Srinivasa, R. J. Agric. Food Chem. 1984, 32, 1313.
36.  Freeman, P. K.; Jonas, V. J. Agric. Food Chem. 1984, 32, 1307.

37.  Bunce, N. J.; Pilon, P.; Ruzo, L. O.; Sturch, D.
     J. J. Org. Chem. 1976, 41, 3023.
38.  Occhiucci, G.; Patacchiola, A. Chemosphere 1982,
     11, 255.
39.  Draper, W. M.; Crosby, D. G. J. Agric. Food Chem.
     1983, 31, 734.
40.  Bunce, N. J.; Kumar, Y.; Ravanal, L. J. Org. Chem.
     1979, 44, 2612.
41.  Ruzo, L. O.; Bunce, N. J. Tet. Lett. 1975, 511.
42.  Ruzo, L. O.; Bunce, N. J.; Safe, S. Can. J. Chem.
     1975, 53, 688.
43.  Smothers, W. K.; Schanze, K. S.; Saltiel, J. J.
     Amer. Chem. Soc. 1979, 101, 1895.
44.  Tsujimoto, K.; Tasaka, S.; Ohashi, M. J. Chem.
     Soc. Chem. Comm. 1975, 758.
45.  Nishiwaki, T.; Usui, M.; Anda, K.; Hida, M. Bull.
     Chem. Soc. Jap. 1979, 52, 821.
46.  Carey, J. H.; Lawrence, J.; Tosine, H. M. Bull.
     Environ. Contam. Toxicol. 1976, 16, 697.
47.  Barbeni, M.; Pramauro, E.; Pelizzetti, E.;
     Borgarello, E.; Serpone, N. Chemosphere, 1985, 14,
     195.
48.  Rappe, C.; Nilsson, C. J. Chromatogr. 1972, 67,
     247.
49.  Nilsson, C.; Andersson, K.; Rappe, C.; Westermark,
     S. J. Chromatogr. 1974, 96, 137.
50.  Choudhry, G. G.; Sundstrom, G.; Ruzo, L. O.;
     Hutzinger, O. J. Agric. Food Chem. 1977, 25, 1371.
51.  Crosby, D. G.; Wong, A. S. Chemosphere 1976, 5,
     327.
52.  Crosby, D. G.; Wong, A. S.; Plimmer, J. R.;
     Klingebiel, U. I. Science (Washington, DC) 1971,
     173, 748.
53.  Crosby, D. G.; Wong, A. S. Science (Washington,
     DC) 1977, 195, 1337.
54.  Hutzinger, O.; Blumich, M. J.; v. d. Berg, M.;
     Olie, K. Chemosphere 1985, 14, 581 and references
     cited therein.
55.  Hutzinger, O.; Safe, S.; Wentzell, B. R.; Zitko,
     V. Environ. Health Perspect. 1973, 5, 267.
56.  Mazer, T.; Hileman, F. D. Chemosphere 1982, 11,
     651.
57.  Safe, S.; Safe, L.; Mullin, M. J. Agric. Food
     Chem. 1985, 33, 24.
58.  Safe, S.; Bandiera, S.; Sawyer, T.; Zmudzka, B.;
     Mason, G.; Romkes, M.; Denomme, M.; Sparling, J.;
     Okey, A.; Fujita, T. Environ. Health Perspect.
     1985, 61, 21.
59.  Leece, B.; Denomme, M. A.; Towner, R.; Li, S. M.
     A.; Safe, S. J. Toxicol. Environ. Health 1985, 16,
     379.
60.  Robertson, L. W.; Chittim, B.; Safe, S.; Mullin,
     M.; Pochini, C. M. J. Agric. Food Chem. 1983, 31,
     454.

RECEIVED December 5, 1986

# Chapter 30

# Sampling and Decontamination Methods for Buildings Contaminated with Polychlorinated Dibenzodioxins

Richard L. Wade[1] and John P. Woodyard[2]

[1]International Technology Corporation, 4585 Pacheco Boulevard, Martinez, CA 94553
[2]International Technology Corporation, 23456 Hawthorne Boulevard, Torrance, CA 90505

The advent of state real estate transfer laws such as New Jersey's Environmental Cleanup Responsibility Act (ECRA), as well as Comprehensive Environmental Response, Compensation and Liability Act (CERCLA) and Resource Conservation and Recovery Act (RCRA) project evolution toward inclusion of buildings and equipment, has brought a new focus to technology for building and equipment decontamination. This paper reviews sampling and decontamination technology specifically for buildings and equipment contaminated with polychlorinated dibenzodioxins (PCDD). Several large-scale decontamination projects have been undertaken in which building structures, equipment, and machinery were decontaminated to remove PCDD and related compounds. The three basic types of building contamination are:

- Fugitive deposits of contamination from adjacent sites,
- Contamination from pyrolysis by-products generated during chemical fires, particularly PCB, and
- Incidental contact with contaminants during related product manufacture or storage (pentachlorophenol use, PCB electrical equipment, 2,4,5-T pesticide manufacture, etc.).

In any remediation effort, the selection of samples and implementation of sampling techniques is often considered as much an art as a science and depends heavily on the experience of the sampling team and knowledge of the former use of the building and/or transport mechanics for the contaminants. This paper focuses on the state of knowledge surrounding the decontamination of buildings and equipment and the associated sampling for project assessment and completion. The information contained here is derived primarily from project experience that is not documented in the literature.

0097-6156/87/0338-0367$06.00/0
© 1987 American Chemical Society

## Sources of Contamination

In cases involving building and equipment decontamination, the first problem is to design and execute a sampling plan that reliably represents the degree and distribution of contamination. While it is often simple to define the cause of contamination and conceptually trace its path of transport, the task of defining the contamination perimeter is often made difficult by the redistribution of contaminants from tracking or airborne deposition. In particular, the following sources are possible routes:

- Direct deposit of airborne dust, soot, and fumes
- Indirect airborne distribution of contaminants by air circulation systems
- Direct mechanical contact through tracking by people and equipment
- Spreading of firefighting water or other fire suppressants used in the case of emergencies
- Careless use of other routine janitorial or industrial cleaning operations.

A thorough assessment of possible contamination therefore looks first at the logical sources, and then tracks possible cross-contamination through the routes mentioned above.

## General Sampling Concepts

Sampling design must consider the physical nature of the contaminant source, its origin, and likely mechanisms for distribution. A thorough understanding of the mechanisms involved at each particular site is essential prior to initiating a full sampling protocol.

The first objective is to evaluate the contamination perimeter and its spread so as to effectively isolate contaminated areas from clean areas and prevent further spreading. This perimeter definition can be executed through a combination of a random sampling grid and a directed "pathway" analysis, the latter focusing on logical paths of mechanical tracking from the source. Until this perimeter is defined by the analytical results, all areas should be considered contaminated and isolated from the rest of the building.

Also, prior to finalizing a sampling plan, consideration should be given to the use of an analytical indicator, a compound that can be used to monitor the initial extent of contamination and the effectiveness of decontamination as the project proceeds. In the case of a PCB fire where PCDD and polychlorinated dibenzofurans (PCDF) are the contaminants of concern, PCB analysis costs approximately 10 percent of the cost of analysis for the other compounds. In most cases, a ratio between the two can be established and used to reduce the analytical cost and allow for a much broader sampling program.

Some representative ratios observed on PCB fire decontamination projects are shown in Table I. The ratio often changes due to selective removal in decontamination. Differences in vapor pressure and contaminant physical characteristics (soot, fume) can also affect the ratio.

Table I.  Typical Range of PCB/PCDF
Ratios During PCB Fire Decontamination

| Medium/Stage | PCB/PCDF Ratio* |
|---|---|
| Surfaces | |
| • Pre-Decon (gross) | 100 - 300 |
| • Post-Decon | 500 - 1,500 |
| Air | 5,000 - 10,000 |

\* Total Polychlorinated Dibenzofurans

Analytical costs can be reduced significantly through the use
of composites.  In situations where large samples are required
(1 m$^2$ for PCDD/PCDF), four 0.25 m$^2$ samples can be composited from
a surface or an individual room.  Composite sampling results of
this type are often accepted by regulatory agencies in determining
the effectiveness of cleanup.

Along with perimeter definition, additional data should be
collected to evaluate the nature of contamination spread and its
degree of penetration.  Bulk samples of liquids, soils, and other
dust should be collected and initially analyzed for PCDD/PCDF.
Air samples can also be taken to demonstrate the variation in the
ratios and determine the extent of contamination in air and
resulting deposition on surfaces.

The development of a directed sampling program is relatively
straightforward, involving selection of samples along routes where
contamination is expected to be tracked or deposited.  In
addition, consideration is often given to the development of a
grid system providing an overall contamination review for a
facility.  Such a grid system can be used for both random sampling
plans as well as the three dimensional identification of sampling
locations for the perimeter study.

The most commonly used grid systems are rectangular and
triangular.  The first critical decision in developing a grid
system is to decide upon the desired sample number.  As a guide,
the sample number n can be determined from the following equation:

$$n = \frac{\text{Total Area (ft}^2)}{S^2 (\text{ft}^2)},$$

where S is the distance between sampling locations or grid
centers, determined by the size of the building (greater "S" for
greater building size) and the perceived extent of contamination
based on the nature of the incident.

For triangular sampling grids, n is computed as follows:

$$n = \frac{0.66 \times \text{Total Area } (ft^2)}{T^2 (ft^2)}$$

where T is the distance between grid centers.

Once the grid is established, all samples can be obtained and analyzed, or a random selection scheme can be developed to sample only a subgroup, depending on budget. A common practice involves analyzing some randomly selected samples and archiving others for subsequent analysis if the results in a certain area prove positive. Another approach is to employ both the pathway and grid system, beginning with a pathway sampling design and employing the grid system once the pathway samples are demonstrated to be positive for PCDD or its indicators in a given area.

## Sampling Plan Design

Three basic types of sampling programs are typically executed during a PCDD decontamination effort, in the following sequence:

- Perimeter sampling before decontamination
- Confirmatory sampling during decontamination
- Closure sampling following decontamination

Perimeter sampling identifies the extent of contamination. This phase of sampling is often the most expensive, as many of the samples are used to confirm that contamination does not exist, and identification of contamination hot zones often triggers additional sampling and analysis.

The nature of the contamination incident determines the sample types. Air samples and wipe samples are taken when dust or fume deposition is the problem. Core samples or chips may be taken from porous surfaces when contaminant penetration is expected to have occurred. The cores in particular are often sliced into sections, with analysis beginning in the top section or two and proceeding downward if results continue to prove positive. The results of the core/chip analysis determine the extent to which porous surface removal is required.

Confirmatory sampling is used by the decontamination crews to determine the effectiveness of the cleaning technique being employed. If a cleaned surface tests clean, the surface should be isolated from further airborne deposition.

Closure sampling may be the least expensive part of sampling and analysis on a project, but it is the most important. Decontamination standards for large projects are often set on the basis of an exposure assessment, which assumes an average contact between workers and contaminated surfaces. A sampling plan for closure takes this into account by scientifically selecting sampling locations that together provide an average contact surface for the subject worker. Sampling locations are therefore well defined in most cases and are typically not biased toward areas where contamination was known to exist. The end product of closure sampling includes averaging of the sampling results and a final risk assessment to determine whether the contaminant level is adequate based on the standard set by EPA, NIOSH, or the cognizant state agency.

Table II describes some PCB fire incidents in recent years. The type of contamination varies between incidents based on the source of the problem (equipment overheating versus actual fire). Also, the levels of contamination, as computed as TCDD equivalents, vary significantly. Higher degrees of contamination often correspond with greater penetration into porous surfaces, and require different decontamination techniques and a more extensive three dimensional sampling program involving cores, chips, and bulk samples.

Quality control/quality assurance programs are critical to the success of decontamination efforts. For example, there are no concensus standard techniques for wipe sampling, although several variations on the same technique have been employed. The effectiveness of the sampling technique is not only a function of proper technique, but of the appropriateness of the chosen sampling method to detect contamination where it probably exists. In cases where fumes have deposited on painted surfaces, for example, repeated rewiping of the same location may continue to show contamination because the material has penetrated the paint and continues to diffuse to the surface. Knowledge of contaminant compatibility with surfaces combined with proper execution of the sampling technique is therefore important to the generation of useful data.

## Decontamination Execution

A variety of decontamination techniques are used. Key considerations in the selection of techniques include the appropriateness of wet or dry application, the nature of contaminant deposition, the depth of contamination, the sensitivity of the project to decontamination or surface damage, and the availability of ratios to monitor effectiveness.

Three basic types of decontamination techniques exist:

- Surface techniques for removing surface deposits
- Removal techniques for penetrated contaminants
- Airborne removal techniques for soot and fume

The conceptual selection of techniques is straightforward, depending initially on the thoroughness of the perimeter sampling program. A list of the most commonly used techniques and their range of effectiveness are provided in Table III.

The selection of a technique depends on many factors. One major factor is the sensitivity of the particular location to cross contamination. Techniques such as sand blasting and hydroblasting are difficult to control, and, in areas where ultra clean levels are required, do not provide sufficient assurance that cross contamination does not occur. Wet techniques in particular, although commonly used as cleaning techniques (hydroblasting and pressure washing), are notorious for spreading contamination if not properly controlled. The sequence of cleaning with wet techniques in particular is important, as water settles toward the floor and recontaminates previously clean surfaces if walls are cleaned.

Table II. Comparison of Noteworthy
PCB Fire Incidents

| Event | Date | Description | PCB/PCDF/PCDD Transport | | PCDF/PCB Ratio | Contamination Range 2,3,7,8-TCDD Equivalents (ng/m$^2$) | "Guidelines" 2,3,7,8-TCDD Equivalents (ng/m$^2$) |
|---|---|---|---|---|---|---|---|
| | | | Soot | Fume | | | |
| Reims, France | 1985 | Transformer Failure | No | Yes | 1/110 | > 124,000 (b) | – |
| Columbus, OH | 1984 | Capacitor Fire | Yes | Yes | 1/200 | > 20,000 (a) | 20 |
| Binghamton, NY | 1981 | Transformer Fire | Yes | Yes | 1/1200 | > 2,000 (b) | 3.3-28 |
| San Francisco, CA | 1983 | Transformer Fire | Yes | Yes | 1/1000 | > 1,300 (a) | 3 |
| Santa Fe, NM | 1985 | Transformer Fire | No | Yes | 1/1000 | > 20,000 (a) | 1 |
| Tulsa, OK | 1984 | Transformer Fire | No | Yes | 1/2000 | > 300 (a) | 3.3-28 |
| Montreal, Canada | 1984 | Capacitor Fire | Yes | Yes | 1/500 | > 20,000 (a) | 10 |

(a) Levels expressed in total PCDD/PCDF.
(b) Levels expressed in 2,3,7,8-TCDD equivalents using U.S. Environmental Protection Agency homologue method of calculation.

Table III. Gross and Final Decontamination Techniques and Their Effectiveness

| Contaminated Surface | Decon Technique | Removal Effectiveness % * |
|---|---|---|
| Concrete Floor + | • Scrubbing with detergent | 50 - 95 |
|  | • Acid etching | 80 - 98 |
|  | • Sandblasting/shotblasting | 25 - 95 |
| Unpainted Cinderblock Wall | • High pressure water spraying | 60 - 90 |
|  | • Steam cleaning | 90 - 99+ |
| Galvanized Painted Ceiling and Walls | • High pressure water spraying | 80 - 99+ |
| Painted Steel Walls, Ceiling, Floor and Cabinets | • High pressure water spraying | 70 - 95 |
|  | • Various methods | 10 - 50 |
| Electrical Equipment | • Solvent spraying | 98 - 99 |

* Single Cleaning Pass
+ Assuming short-term contact, no standing liquid

Dry techniques are used most commonly in commercial buildings. These techniques involve a light removal of surface deposits combined with vacuum attachments to minimize spreading of the cleaning media and the associated contaminants. Cleaning media include sand and grit, metal shot, granulated plastic, and less abrasive materials such as corn cobs and walnut shells. The potential for cross contamination from these media nevertheless exists; the choice is based primarily on the amount of damage that can be afforded on the clean surface. For some materials that are especially permeable or porous, decontamination is impractical. Disposal of materials such as fabric, wallpaper, wood, and other materials that are significantly contaminated is often the normal procedure.

Concrete presents a special problem. Because concrete is used as an integral structural component in many buildings, removal of concrete is not always appropriate or possible. Grinding and surface removal techniques are most often used for this application, and can be effective at up to two inches of depth. Few new developments in concrete decontamination have taken place. Most equipment suppliers and developers have focused either on increasing productivity or improving means of controlling fugitive dust emissions. In situ reagent-based techniques have been applied in Europe, but not in the United States. (1)

## Decontamination Closure

Since there are no national standards for decontamination, each site requires a specific exposure assessment to determine the appropriate "safe level" of PCDD contamination. The exposure assessment is normally developed as part of the remediation plan and is submitted with the closure sampling plan to the cognizant regulatory agency before beginning work.

Most closure sampling efforts therefore focus more on the overall level of contamination remaining. In accordance with the exposure assessment, average contamination levels need to be determined in order to qualify any long-term exposure risk. Proper closure sampling normally includes a good, statistically sound sample selection system that generates high and low contact contamination estimates by work zone. Use of such a statistical approach prevents disputes about cleanliness based on one or two positive samples.

The end result of closure sampling is a series of contamination statistics for different contact surfaces. These data and the exposure model determine the exposure risk to workers.

## Conclusion

Building decontamination technology continues to advance as each project is executed. New technologies are developed for specific applications, and participants gain a better understanding of the importance of exposure assessments, closure sampling, and perimeter sampling to successful completion of a project. A better understanding of decontamination techniques is needed, particularly for concrete and porous materials that may not be expendable as part of the decontamination program. Refinements in concrete removal technology and in situ treatment are expected to dramatically improve the state of the art within the next several years.

An improved understanding of closure sampling is an important part of the decontamination process, one which is unfortunately limited to only those state, NIOSH and EPA regional offices with extended experience in decontamination projects. The advent of national decontamination standards for PCDD, PCB, and other organic contaminants may not be the answer; each site is cleaned to a level that does not present an unreasonable risk to human health, and the considerations involved in that determination vary from site to site. It is therefore important that regulatory agencies gain a better understanding of proper closure sampling, and that a concensus be developed as to what constitutes a complete closure sampling plan.

## Literature Cited

1. Tumiatti, W.; Nobile, G.; Tundo, P.; Division of Environmental Chemistry Preprints, American Chemical Society 191st National Meeting, New York, 1986, p.259.

RECEIVED January 21, 1987

# Chapter 31

# Chemical Degradation of Selected Polychlorinated Compounds by Means of Polyethers, a Base, and an Oxidant

G. Nobile[1], W. Tumiatti[1], and P. Tundo[2]

[1]Sea Marconi Technologies, Strada Antica di Collegno, 196–10146 Torino, Italy
[2]Istituto di Chimica Organica dell'Università di Torino, Via G. Bidone, 36–10125 Torino, Italy

Mixtures of polyethyleneglycols (and ethylene oxide-propylene oxide copolymers), a base and a peroxide (or other radical initiators) allow the preparation of several reagents which, suitably formulated according to their different use, are able to degrade the chemically stable chlorinated aromatics. Such a method, called CDP-Process, is active on TCDD and can be applied in different ways; as an example, the reagent, when immobilized on a solid bed, allows the continuous-flow decontamination of mineral oils containing PCB; this is useful for the decontamination of an electrical transformer during operation. Another reported example is the decontamination of surfaces contaminated by PCB or PCB fires (where PCDF and PCDD are also present).

Since the ecological and environmental hazard related to stable polyhalogenated aromatic compounds has been recognized, many efforts have been done by chemists both for limiting their spreading in the environment and for their elimination. In order to reach this aim the contaminated material is put in landfills or incinerated, or the organic pollutants are chemically decomposed. Each method has its peculiarity and applicability. The advantages of chemical methods of decontamination are in the ultimate elimination of the problem, in the possibility of operating in situ, and in the use of inexpensive equipment. For these reasons new chemical methods able to destroy the stable molecules of chlorinated aromatics are being examined.

For polychorinated biphenyls (PCB), many methods have been reported. For example: the reaction of polyethyleneglycols (PEG) of low molecular weight (MW) in the presence of strong bases (i.e. KOH) and stirring (1, 2); the use of sodium polyethyleneglycolates (3); the utilization of alkali metal hydroxide/glycol mixture in the presence of dimethylsulfoxide (4) and u.v. irradiation (5). Several methods have also been described for the more toxic of such compounds, that is the 2,3,7,8- tetrachlorodibenzo-p-dioxin (TCDD); among them, remarkable are the u.v. irradiation (6), the

0097-6156/87/0338-0376$06.00/0

exhaustive chlorination ($\underline{7}$), the reaction with sodium glycolates ($\underline{8}$).

A new method of degradation, called CDP-Process (Chemical Degradation of Polyhalogenated compounds), is described together with its application in the field ($\underline{9}$). According to the CDP-Process polychlorinated compounds are easily degraded if the reaction is carried out in the presence of PEG of high MW, a base (even $K_2 CO_3$ or $NaHCO_3$ can be used), a peroxide or a radical initiator; moreover, the reagents mixture can be suitably formulated in order to obtain different applications.

## CDP-Process

Application of this method to TCDD, has been previously reported ($\underline{10}$). The related experiments were performed at the Establishment of the European Community (Ispra) and at the ICMESA plant (Seveso); these reactions, carried out on pure dioxin and on several contaminated materials of the reactor, gave good results ($\underline{11}$).

In Figure 1 is shown the elimination of pure TCDD from a n-decane solution. In both cases the two immiscible phases were stirred magnetically. Analyses were carried out on the hydrocarbon solution. The sole identifiable products in the reaction mixture were dibenzodioxins progressively dechlorinated (no cine substitution was observed); moreover, no trace of compounds containing - OH in place of - Cl was detected (GC/MS). Attention was not addressed in detection of eventual compounds having a polyethyleneglycol group bonded to the aromatic, since their chemical properties, very close to those of the reagent, make their separation very difficult. So, no quantitative results are at the moment available. It was also reported that the reaction mixture was not toxic on the guinea pigs ($\underline{10}$).

Such results indicate that, from a mechanistic point of view, it is not a matter of a simple aromatic nucleophilic substitution (in any case very difficult if not $\underline{via}$ benzyne), but more probably of a radical substitution on an activated complex of the TCDD (SRN1 mechanism) ($\underline{12}$); this mechanism is favoured by the fact that the radical anion of TCDD is particularly stabilized ($\underline{13}$). How this radical anion is generated from the initiator peroxide and how it reacts with the hydrogen donor (PEG or the solvent) is not at this moment clear; however, interesting to note, degradation of TCDD by u.v. irradiation leads to the same intermediate compounds.

The difference occurring in reactions carried out in the presence of peroxide or of strong bases ($\underline{1}$-$\underline{4}$) is explained by the following example which moreover illustrates a decontamination from PCB of mineral oils:

5.0 mL of mineral oil contaminated with 1300 ppm of PCB (Arochlor 1260) were magnetically stirred at 80 °C with 2.5 g of two different mixtures (A and B; % are in weight). A: 86% PEG 6000 (PEG of MW = 6000), 12% $K_2CO_3$, 2% $Na_2O_2$. B: 77.5% PEG 6000, 10% $K_2CO_3$, 12.5% $CH_3ONa$. Gas chromatographic analyses on the oil showed the following residual contaminations (ppm of PCB after 0.5, 1.0 and 1.5 h, respectively); A: 90, 26 and 13; B: 350, 211 and 142. From the respective concentration ratios it results that the reaction carried out with sodium peroxide is at least 15 times faster than the reaction carried out with methoxide, in spite of the stronger base character of the latter; accordingly, the reaction is not related to the strength of the base although its presence is needed (sodium bicarbonate is also effective if a peroxide is present). Other data indicate that the reaction does not depend on stirring; it is possible to operate with other peroxides ($BaO_2$ as an example) and even in the presence of water (till 30% is allowed).

Although the reaction mechanism is not at the moment fully clarified, some points seem to be well established: the radical character of the reaction and the contemporary need of an anion activator as PEG is (maybe the function of the anion activator is to increase the strength of the base as they do in Phase-Transfer Catalysis) (14). In place of PEG other anion activators may be used, as the condensation compounds between ethylene oxide and propylene oxide; such latter polymers, being viscous liquids, offer some advantage in particular applications such as the decontamination of surfaces.

## Applications

The CDP-Process works well on several stable, halogenated aromatic derivatives; mainly studied, also in connection with its industrial application has been the PCB and the degradation products that PCB forms as a consequence of fire; that is polychlorinated dibenzofurans and dioxins (PCDF and PCDD, respectively).

By suitably changing the type of polyether, the base and the peroxide, and in case by adding a solvent, different "reagents" can be prepared which are able to attack and decompose such supertoxic molecules even if they are present in different materials (mineral oils, surfaces, soil, etc.); in fact different procedures must be followed, in connection with the type of pollutant, the environmental requirements, and the involved materials.

A few applications of the method that illustrate its peculiarities are shown.

Decontamination of Mineral Oil Containing PCB in a Batch Process. Table I reports some results of CDP-Process in destroying PCB from its hydrocarbon solutions (for analytical convenience an n-decane solution was used). The reaction is effective even in the presence of actually catalytic quantities of peroxide; without peroxide, no reaction occurs at all.

At the end of the reactions no trace of PEG was detected in n-decane (experiments of Table 1) or in mineral oils treated in the same way (IR and NMR analysis). In the reactions of Table 1 as in the following ones here reported, the residual PCB were usually the low-chlorinated polychlorobiphenyls; these ones have been reported to be the less toxic.

The electrical properties of mineral oils after the CDP-Process render such dielectric fluids suitable for their use in electrical transformer without further treatment (usually the dielectrical characteristics of the oil are improved).

Table I. Chemical Degradation of PCB by CDP-Process.
Influence of % $Na_2O_2$

| % $Na_2O_2$ in the reagent mixture | Initial Contamination | Final Contamination (ppm) (ppm) |
|---|---|---|
| 8 | 16,000 | 23 |
| 2 | 16,000 | 32 |
| 0.78 | 16,000 | 190 |
| 0.21 | 16,000 | 5000 |
| 0.00 | 16,000 | no reaction |

Conditions: 3.0 mL of n-decane, 2.0 g of reagent mixture: 12% (by weight) $K_2CO_3$ and the difference at 100 of PEG 6000; T = 85°C; magnetic stirring for 3 hours.

Decontamination of Mineral Oils Containing PCB, in an Open and a Closed Continuous-Flow Process. The reagents in the CDP-Process can be immobilized by adsorption onto a soild bed; in such a way a solid reagent can be produced which can be used to decontaminate PCB mineral oils passing through it (15). This is made possible, from a chemical point of view, by two facts: i. the reagent is not soluble in the oil. ii. the PCB's decomposition products are completely retained on the solid bed (the PCB are not; it is not a matter of adsorbtion). Figure 2 illustrates the results obtained working with an immobilized reagent and by flowing through the contaminated oil; the oil containing 900 ppm PCB flowed continuously into the column containing a bed of 30 g solid reagent (2.6 g PEG 6000, 0.7 g potassium t-butoxide, 0.7 g $Na_2O_2$, 26 g $K_2CO_3$) and was collected at its outlet. As shown in Figure 2, the column is progressively exhausted; operating in appropriate conditions and changing the reactive bed when it becomes exhausted or operating in series with more than one column, one can obtain a decontaminated oil without the troubles of batch operation (stirring, charge of the reactor, drain, incidental filtration or centrifugation of the oil, etc.).

Another version of the CDP-Process utilizing immobilized reagents is a continuous and closed process; accordingly, the same contaminated oil is continuously recycled in the same column until the decontamination limits imposed by law are reached. The commercial version of such continuous processes involves the presence of the immobilized reagent in cartridges, easy to handle and to transport; such cartridges of standard dimensions are the core of a plant which continuously pumps the contaminated oil from a tank, heats it to the desired temperature, sends it to the cartridge and gives it back to the tank. In this way the volume of the oil to be treated is independent from the volume of the plant: it is enough to change the cartridge when it becomes exhuasted.

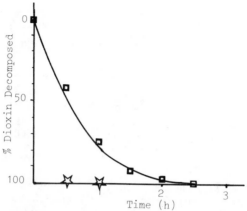

**Fig. 1. Degradation of TCDD.**
• T = 50°C; 2.0 mL of n-decane containing 5 g of TCDD, 0.9 g PEG 1500, 0.15 g $K_2CO_3$, 0.10 g diethyleneglycolmonobuthylether, 0.10 g $Na_2O_2$.
• T = 85°C; 2.0 mL of n-decane containing 5 g of TCDD, 2.06 g PEG 6000, 0.53 g $K_2CO_3$ and 0.37 g $Na_2O_2$.

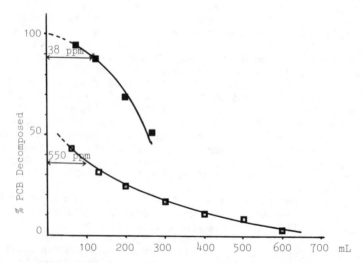

**Fig. 2. Decontamination from PCB of Mineral Oil in a Continuous and Open Process.**
• T = 90°C; flow 60 mL/h (the first 120 mL contained 38 ppm of PCB).
• T = 60°C; flow 120 mL/h (the first 100 mL contained 550 ppm of PCB).

Figure 3 shows how the PCB contamination of a large quantity of oil is progressively decreased to 42 ppm by changing five cartridges containing 16 Kg each of solid bed.   In this experiment, 440 kg of oil containing 4,000 ppm PCB was recycled continuously at 100 L/h at 80° C.

Some advantages of such a version of the method are that the plant, which can be closed in a container, works without the steady presence of manpower and that it can be directly connected to the apparatus containing the oil to be decontaminated.   Such characteristics allow this continuous-flow method, its reagents and conditions to be employed in the decontamination of electrical transformers.

Decontamination of Surfaces Contaminated by PCB, PCDF and PCDD.
This version of CDP-Process uses reagent mixtures in liquid phase and at room temperature; the reagent is spread on the surface to be decontaminated.   Usually the reagent is formulated by using copolymers between ethylene oxide and propylene oxide (these condensation polymers, manufactured by Montedison, are called 'Nixolen').

The efficacy of the reaction was peviously reported on TCDD (10).   Here is described an application in the field, for the clean-up of surfaces contaminated by PCDF and PCDD coming from a PCB accident.

In an electrical sub-station in Italy, because of a short-circuit, a rectifier with about 300 little capacitors containing PCB burned (50 g each capacitor and a total amount of PCB of about 10 Kg).   The fire lasted for about one hour before it was extinguished.   The thermal oxidation of PCB produced a large quantity of soot containing PCDF and PCDD.   The soot was spread inside the sub-station contaminating about 1500 m$^2$ of surfaces and items.

During the sampling operations for the mapping of the contamination and the data acquisition necessary for the design of the decontamination, a few tests were performed to characterize the best method of application of CDP-Process in order to reach the complete in situ destruction of PCDF and PCDD.

Different surfaces (floor, roof, walls) were selected to perform the assays.   On those surfaces the reagent, liquid at room temperature (95% of Nixolen and 5% of sodium alkoxide), was spread at room temperature to produce a liquid film; such a film at the same time avoided the transfer of the contaminant to the environment.   After about 90 hours of action at room temperature, the liquid film was then removed.   Samples were taken either on the surfaces (wipe tests, before and after the treatment were made) and on the removed reagent.

Table 2 shows the values of contamination on these representative surfaces before and the results after decontamination.   No contaminant was detected in the removed reagent.   All these data demonstrate the effective degradation of PCDF and PCDD by CDP-Process, either on the surfaces and in the reagent.

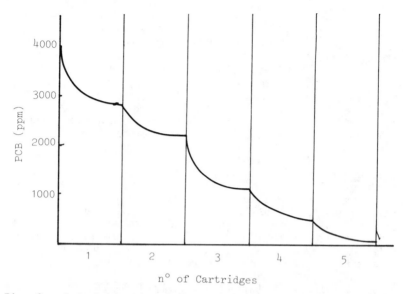

**Fig. 3.   Decontamination from PCB of Mineral Oil in a Continuous and Closed Process.**

**Table II. In Situ Decontamination of Surfaces Containing PCDF and PCDD, Coming from a PCB Fire**

| Contaminant (PCDF + PCDD) | Sample Taken on Floor | | Sample Taken on Roof | |
|---|---|---|---|---|
| | Before ($ng/m^2$) | After ($ng/m^2$) | Before ($ng/m^2$) | After ($ng/m^2$) |
| 2,3,7,8-TCDF | 256 | ND | 1060 | 174 |
| TCDF | 1169 | 27 | 4841 | 362 |
| PeCDF | 678 | 13 | 2809 | 92 |
| HxCDF | 426 | ND | 1762 | 22 |
| HpCDF | 336 | 11 | 1391 | ND |
| OCDF | 284 | 20 | 1029 | ND |
| 2,3,7,8-TCDD | ND | ND | 33 | ND |
| TCDD | 24 | ND | 100 | ND |
| PeCDD | 36 | ND | 148 | ND |
| HxCDD | 45 | ND | 187 | ND |
| HpCDD | 42 | ND | 174 | ND |
| OCDD | 35 | 114 | 143 | ND |

ND = Not Detectable (detection limit depends from the sample, varying from 2 to 8 $ng/m^2$).

## Acknowledgments

This work was partly a research program of the Consiglio Nazionale delle Ricerche, Progetto Finalizzato 'Chimica Fine e Secondaria'.

## Literature Cited

1. Brunelle, D. J.; Singleton, D.A. Chemosphere 1983, 12, 183.
2. Brunelle, D. J. U.S. Patent Appl. n° 314,163 (1981)
   (General Electric Company).
3. Pytlewsky, L. L.; Krevitz, K.; Smith, A. B. U.S. Patent Appl.
   n° 142,865 and 158,359 (1980) (Franklin Institute).
4. Peterson, R. L. U.S. Patent Appl. n° 501,620 (1983)
   (Galson Research Corporation).
5. Draper, W. M. Chemosphere, 1985, 14, 1195.
6. Kitchens, J. A. F. U.S. Patent Appl. n° 890,871
   (Atlantic Research Corporation).
7. Shannahan, C. E. et al. Report EPA-600/-78-146 (1978).
8. Howard, K. J.; Sidwell, A. E. Eur. Patent n° 0 021 294 A1
   (Vertac Chem. Corporation).
9. Tundo, P. U.S. Patent Appl. n° 771,404 (1985)
   (Sea Marconi Technologies).
10. Tundo, P.; Facchetti, S.; Tumiatti W.; Fortunati, U.
    Chemosphere, 1985, 14, 403.
11. Tundo, P.; Facchetti, S.; Tumiatti, W.; Fortunati, U.
    Report to the President of the Lombardia Region (1983).
12. March, J. "Advanced Organic Chemistry";
    Wiley: New York, 1985; 3rd Ed.; p. 582.
13. Miller, G.; Sontum, S.; Crosby, G.
    Bull, Environ. Contam. Toxicol. 1977, 18, 611.
14. Starks, C. M.; Liotta, C. "Phase Transfer Catalysis";
    Academic Press: New York, 1978.
15. Tundo, P. U.S. Patent Appl. n° 632,718 (1984)
    (Sea Marconi Technologies).

RECEIVED December 5, 1986

# Author Index

# Affiliation Index

384

Shirco Infrared Systems, Inc., 311
State University of New York, 162
Syntex (USA), Inc., 105,178,278,286
U.S. Air Force, 229,299,319,332
U.S. Department of Health and Human
  Services, 68,174
U.S. Environmental Protection
  Agency, 34,82,216,259,291,332
Universita di Torino, 376

University of California--
  Berkeley, 350
University of Medicine and Dentistry
  of New Jersey, 131
University of Minnesota, 350
University of Nevada--Reno, 82
University of Rochester Medical
  Center, 162
University of Umeå, 20

# Subject Index

## A

Abiotic transformation,
  2,3,7,8-TCDD, 86-90
Absorption spectra, 2,3,7,8-TCDD, 86
Acceptable daily intake
  safety factor approach, 196
  2,3,7,8-TCDD, 163
Acute lethality, comparative toxicity
  of dioxins, 55
Adipose tissue
  chemical residues, 100t
  PCDD and PCDF levels, 27-28
  2,3,7,8-TCDD levels, 76,164
Adults, uptake of contaminated
  soil, 184
Advanced electric reactor
  destruction of dioxin
      contamination, 299-309
  diagram, 301f
  full-scale operation, 308
  method, 300-306
  particle production, 307
  personnel protection equipment, 304
  postreactor treatment, 302
  process diagram, 303f
  process parameters, 304t
  site conditions, 302
Advanced electric reactor feedstock,
  inorganic concentrations, 307t
Agent Orange
  active ingredients, 230
  association with birth defects, 153
  composition, 299
  incineration at sea, 230
  photolysis on glass surfaces, 88
  soft tissue sarcomas, 151-152
  soil decontamination, 319-331
Air Force Engineering and Services
  Center, research and development
  program, 229
Air monitoring survey
  analytical methods, 270
  basic steps, 269
  data management, 273
  design, 268-269

Air monitoring survey--Continued
  information needed, 268
  objectives, 269
  parameters, 269
  quality control, 273
  sampling
    duration, 270
    method validation, 273
    site selection, 269-270
  See also Ambient air monitoring
Alewives, role in ecosystem, 99
Alum flocculation process, removal of
  dioxin-bearing particulates, 280
Aluminum, needed for flocculation, 287
Ambient air monitoring
  description, 267-276,305
  See also Air monitoring survey
American Society of Mechanical
  Engineers (ASME), 44
Ames test, mutagenicity studies, 196
Analytical methodology
  air monitoring survey, 270
  2,3,7,8-TCDD, 259-265
Analytical procedures, hazardous waste
  cleanup, 263-264
Analytical support, 2,3,7,8-TCDD-
  contaminated sites, 259-265
Animals
  ingestion of soil, 205-206
  PCDDs, 7
  species susceptibility to
      dioxin, 175
  toxicity data, deriving exposure
      control limit for humans, 62-65
Arkansas
  dioxin cleanup, 13-14
  2,3,7,8-TCDD contamination, 35
Aroclor 1254, photodecomposition, 356f
Aroclor 1260, photochemical
  decomposition on concrete, 361f
Aroclor mixtures
  mineralized by P. chrysosporium, 347
  See also Polychlorinated biphenyls
      (PCBs)

*Production by Paula M. Bérard*
*Indexing by Keith B. Belton*
*Jacket design by Carla L. Clemens*

*Elements typeset by Hot Type Ltd., Washington, DC*
*Printed and bound by Maple Press Co., York, PA*

# Recent ACS Books

Personal Computers for Scientists: A Byte at a Time
By Glenn I. Ouchi
288 pp; clothbound; ISBN 0-8412-1001-2

Writing the Laboratory Notebook
By Howard M. Kanare
145 pp; clothbound; ISBN 0-8412-0906-5

The ACS Style Guide: A Manual for Authors and Editors
Edited by Janet S. Dodd
264 pp; clothbound; ISBN 0-8412-0917-0

Chemical Demonstrations: A Sourcebook for Teachers
By Lee R. Summerlin and James L. Ealy, Jr.
192 pp; spiral bound; ISBN 0-8412-0923-5

Phosphorus Chemistry in Everyday Living, Second Edition
By Arthur D. F. Toy and Edward N. Walsh
342 pp; clothbound; ISBN 0-8412-1002-0

Pharmacokinetics: Processes and Mathematics
By Peter G. Welling
ACS Monograph 185; 290 pp; ISBN 0-8412-0967-7

High-Energy Processes in Organometallic Chemistry
Edited by Kenneth S. Suslick
ACS Symposium Series 333; 336 pp; ISBN 0-8412-1018-7

Particle Size Distribution: Assessment
and Characterization
Edited by Theodore Provder
ACS Symposium Series 332; 308 pp; ISBN 0-8412-1016-0

Radon and Its Decay Products:
Occurrence, Properties, and Health Effects
Edited by Philip K. Hopke
ACS Symposium Series 331; 609 pp; ISBN 0-8412-1015-2

Nucleophilicity
Edited by J. Milton Harris and Samuel P. McManus
Advances in Chemistry Series 215; 494 pp; ISBN 0-8412-0952-9

Organic Pollutants in Water
Edited by I. H. Suffet and Murugan Malaiyandi
Advances in Chemistry Series 214; 796 pp; ISBN 0-8412-0951-0

---

For further information and a free catalog of ACS books, contact:
American Chemical Society
Distribution Office, Department 225
1155 16th Street, NW, Washington, DC 20036
Telephone 800-227-5558